INTELLECTUAL PROPERTY

Philosophy and the Global Context
General Editor: Michael Krausz, Bryn Mawr College

This new series addresses a range of emerging global concerns. It situates philosophical efforts in their global and cultural contexts, and it offers works from thinkers whose cultures are challenged by globalizing movements. Comparative and intercultural studies address such social and political issues as the environment, poverty, consumerism, civil society, tolerance, colonialism, global ethics, and community in cyberspace. They also address related methodological issues of translation and cross-cultural understanding.

INTELLECTUAL PROPERTY

Moral, Legal, and International Dilemmas

Edited by
Adam D. Moore

ROWMAN & LITTLEFIELD PUBLISHERS, INC.
Lanham • Boulder • New York • Oxford

ROWMAN & LITTLEFIELD PUBLISHERS, INC.

Published in the United States of America
by Rowman & Littlefield Publishers, Inc.
4720 Boston Way, Lanham, Maryland 20706

12 Hid's Copse Road
Cummor Hill, Oxford OX2 9JJ, England

Copyright © 1997 by Rowman & Littlefield Publishers, Inc.

British Cataloging in Publication Information Available

Library of Congress Cataloging-in-Publication Data
Intellectual property : moral, legal, and international dilemmas /
    edited by Adam D. Moore.
        p.   cm.—(Philosophy and the global context)
    Includes bibliographical references and index.
    ISBN 0-8476-8426-1 (cloth : alk. paper).—ISBN 0-8476-8427-X
(pbk. : alk. paper)
        1. Intellectual property   2. Intellectual property—Moral and
ethical aspects.   3. Copyright—Computer programs.   I. Moore, Adam
D., 1965– . II. Series.
    K1401.I558   1997
    346.04'8—dc21   96-46626
                                                                 CIP

ISBN 0-8476-8426-1 (cloth: alk. paper)
ISBN 0-8476-8427-X (pbk.: alk. paper)

Printed in the United States of America

∞ ™ The paper used in this publication meets the minimum requirements of
American National Standard for Information Sciences—Permanence of Paper for
Printed Library Materials, ANSI Z39.48–1984.

To Kimberly

Contents

Acknowledgments   ix

1   Introduction   1
    Adam D. Moore

Part I
The Moral Foundations of Intellectual Property

2   Justifying Intellectual Property   17
    Edwin C. Hettinger

3   Trade Secrets and the Justification of Intellectual Property: A
    Comment on Hettinger   39
    Lynn Sharp Paine

4   The Moral Foundations of Intangible Property   57
    James W. Child

5   Toward a Lockean Theory of Intellectual Property   81
    Adam D. Moore

Part II
Intellectual Property Issues and the Law

6   The Philosophy of Intellectual Property   107
    Justin Hughes

7   Intellectual Property: A Non-Posnerian Law and Economics
    Approach   179
    Tom G. Palmer

8   Property, Monopoly, and Intellectual Rights   225
    Michael I. Krauss

9 The TRIPS Agreement: Imperialistic, Outdated, and
Overprotective 243
Marci A. Hamilton

10 International Copyright: An Unorthodox Analysis 265
Hugh C. Hansen

Part III
Information and Digital Technology

11 Why Software Should Be Free 283
Richard Stallman

12 The Virtues of Software Ownership 299
David H. Carey

13 Are Computer Hacker Break-ins Ethical? 307
Eugene H. Spafford

14 National and International Copyright Liability for Electronic
System Operators 321
Charles J. Meyer

15 The Economy of Ideas: Everything You Know about
Intellectual Property Is Wrong 349
John Perry Barlow

Selected Bibliography 373

Index 379

About the Contributors 385

Acknowledgments

Many people have contributed their ideas and time to this anthology. I would especially like to thank my advisors and friends at Ohio State University, Don Hubin, Peter King, Richard Garner, and Dan Farrell; David Mayer of Capital University, Scott Rothwell, James Summerford, Mark VanHook, Larry Sanger, Kimberly Moore, and Nancy Moore. I would also like to thank Jennifer Ruark and Julie Kuzneski of Rowman & Littlefield for all of their help in preparing and editing the manuscript.

A special thanks to the contributors: John P. Barlow, Electronic Frontier Foundation; David H. Carey, Whitman College; James W. Child, Bowling Green State University; Marci A. Hamilton, Benjamin N. Cardozo School of Law; Hugh C. Hansen, Fordham University School of Law; Edwin C. Hettinger, College of Charleston; Justin Hughes; Michael I. Krauss, George Mason University; Charles J. Meyer, Woodard, Emhardt, Naughton, Moriarty & McNett; Lynn Sharp Paine, Harvard Business School; Tom G. Palmer, The Cato Institute; Eugene H. Spafford, Purdue University; and Richard Stallman, The League for Programming Freedom.

The reprinted articles in this anthology appear in full, unless indicated.

"Justifying Intellectual Property," by Edwin C. Hettinger, originally appeared in *Philosophy & Public Affairs* 18 (winter 1989): 31–52. Copyright © 1989 by Princeton University Press. Reprinted by permission of Princeton University Press.

"Trade Secrets and the Justification of Intellectual Property: A Comment on Hettinger," by Lynn Sharp Paine, originally appeared in *Philosophy & Public Affairs* 20 (summer 1991): 247–63. Copyright © 1991 by Princeton University Press. Reprinted by permission of Princeton University Press.

"The Moral Foundations of Intangible Property," by James W. Child, originally appeared in *The Monist* 73 (October 1990): 578–600. Copyright © 1990 by The Hegeler Institute. Reprinted by permission of publisher.

"The Philosophy of Intellectual Property," by Justin Hughes, originally appeared in the *Georgetown Law Journal* 77 (1988): 287–366. Copyright © 1988 by the Georgetown Law Journal and Georgetown University. Reprinted by permission of publisher.

"Intellectual Property: A Non-Posnerian Law and Economics Approach," by Tom G. Palmer, originally appeared in the *Hamline Law Review* 12 (1989): 261–304. Copyright © 1989 by Hamline University School of Law. Reprinted by permission of publisher.

"Property, Monopoly, and Intellectual Rights," by Michael I. Krauss, originally appeared in the *Hamline Law Review* 12 (1989): 305–20. Copyright © 1989 by Hamline University School of Law. Reprinted by permission of publisher.

"The TRIPS Agreement: Imperialistic, Outdated, and Overprotective," by Marci A. Hamilton, originally appeared in the *Vanderbilt Journal of Transnational Law* 29 (1996): 613–34. Copyright © 1996 by Vanderbilt University. Reprinted by permission of publisher.

"International Copyright: An Unorthodox Analysis," by Hugh C. Hansen, originally appeared in the *Vanderbilt Journal of Transnational Law* 29 (1996): 579–93. Copyright © 1996 by Vanderbilt University. Reprinted by permission of publisher.

"Why Software Should Be Free," by Richard Stallman, originally appeared in *Computers, Ethics, & Social Values,* edited by Deborah Johnson and Helen Nissenbaum (Englewood Cliffs, N.J.: Prentice-Hall, 1995). Copyright © 1990 by the Free Software Foundation, Inc. Verbatim copying and redistribution is permitted without royalty.

"The Virtues of Software Ownership," by David H. Carey, originally appeared in *Software Ownership and Intellectual Property Rights,* edited by Walter Maner and John L. Fodor (New Haven: Research Center on Computing & Society, 1992). Copyright © 1992 by the Research Center on Computing & Society. Reprinted by permission of publisher.

"Are Computer Hacker Break-ins Ethical?" by Eugene H. Spafford, originally appeared in the *Journal of Systems Software* 17 (1992): 41–47. Copyright © 1992 by Eugene Spafford. Reprinted by permission of Eugene Spafford.

"National and International Copyright Liability for Electronic System Operators," by Charles J. Meyer, originally appeared in the *Indiana Journal of Global and Legal Studies* 2 (spring 1995). Copyright © 1995 by Indiana University School of Law. Reprinted by permission of publisher.

1

Introduction

Adam D. Moore

With the rise of the information age where digital recording, storage, and transmission are the norm, problems centering on the ownership of intellectual property have become acute. Computer programs costing thousands of research dollars are copied in an instant. Digital bootleg versions of almost any musical artist are available at rock-bottom prices. Moreover, there is a general asymmetry between the attitudes individuals have about physical property and intellectual property. Many who would never dream of stealing cars, computers, or VCRs regularly copy software or duplicate their favorite music from a friend's CD. The information superhighway, better known as the Internet or the World Wide Web, is poised to become the scene of information superhighway robbery. Finally, a salient feature of an on-line information age is that these concerns take on a global perspective.

Needless to say, developing answers to these problems is philosophically challenging. This anthology was put together so that a number of important articles centering on the ownership of intellectual property and digital information could be found in one work. My hope is that this volume will help education and research in this rapidly expanding area.

Before providing a summary of the articles included in this volume, I have given a brief overview of the subject matter or domain of intellectual property. Apart from cars, computers, land, or other tangible goods, intellectual property law enables individuals to obtain ownership rights to control works of literature, musical compositions, processes of manufacture, computer software, and the like. Setting aside concerns of justifying rights to intellectual property, which is the primary focus of this volume, a brief exposition of what counts as intellectual property would be helpful.

The Domain of Intellectual Property

At the most practical level the subject matter of intellectual property is largely codified in Anglo-American copyright, patent, and trade secret law, as well as in the moral rights granted to authors and inventors within the continental European doctrine.[1] Although these systems of property encompass much of what is thought to count as intellectual property, they do not map out the entire landscape.[2] Even so, Anglo-American systems of copyright, patent, and trade secret law, along with certain Continental doctrines, provide a rich starting point. We'll take them up in turn.

Copyright

The domain of copyright is expression. Section 102 of the 1976 Copyright Act determines the subject matter of copyright protection.

> § 102: (a) Copyright protection subsists, in accordance with this title, in original works of authorship fixed in any tangible medium of expression, now known or later developed, from which they can be perceived, reproduced, or otherwise communicated, either directly or with the aid of a machine or device.

Works of authorship include literary works; musical works, including any accompanying words; dramatic works, including any accompanying music; pantomimes and choreographic works; pictorial, graphic, and sculptural works; motion pictures and other audiovisual works; sound recordings; architectural works; and computer software.[3]

The scope or subject matter of copyright, as protected under federal law or the Copyright Act, is limited in three important respects. First, for something to be protected, it must be original. Thus the creative process by which an expression comes into being becomes relevant. Even so, the originality requirement has a low threshold. "Original" in reference to a copyrighted work means that the particular work "owes its origin" to the author and does not mean that the work must be novel, ingenious, or even interesting. Minimally, the work must be the author's own production; it cannot be the result of copying.[4] When deciding the issues of originality and copyright infringement, courts examine expressions and not the abstract ideas from which the expressions are derived.[5]

A second requirement that limits the domain of what can be copyrighted is that the expression must be "nonutilitarian" or "nonfunctional" in nature. Utilitarian products, or products that are useful for work, fall, if they fall anywhere, within the domain of patents. As with the originality requirement, the nonutilitarian requirement has a low threshold because the distinction itself is contentious. An example of an intellectual work that bumps against the nonfunctional requirement is copyright protection of computer software. While a computer program as a whole is functional and useful for producing things, its object code and source code have been deemed to be protectable expressions.

Finally, the subject matter of statutory copyright is concrete expression, meaning that only expressions as fixed in a tangible and permanent medium can be protected.[6] The crucial element is that there be a physical embodiment of the work. Moreover, within the system of copyright, the abstract idea, or *res*, of intellectual property is not protected.[7] Author's rights only extend over the actual concrete expression and the derivatives of the expression—not to the abstract ideas themselves. For example, Einstein's theory of relativity, as expressed in various articles and publications, is not protected under copyright law. Someone else may read these publications and express the theory in her own words and even receive a copyright in her particular expression. Some may find this troubling, but such rights are outside the domain of copyright law.[8] The individual who copies abstract theories and expresses them in her own words may be guilty of plagiarism, but she cannot be held liable for copyright infringement. The distinction between the protection of fixed expressions and abstract ideas has led to the "merger doctrine": If there is no way to separate idea from expression, then a copyright cannot be obtained. Suppose that I create a new recipe for spicy Chinese noodles and there is only one way, or a limited number of ways, to express the idea. If this were the case, then I could not obtain copyright protection, because the idea and the expression have been merged. Granting me a copyright to the recipe would amount to granting a right to control the abstract ideas that make up the recipe. According to many copyright theorists, this kind of expansion of copyright would have disastrous effects.[9]

There are five exclusive rights that copyright owners enjoy and three major restrictions on the bundle of rights.[10] The five rights are the right to reproduce the work, the right to adapt it or derive other works from it, the right to distribute copies of the work, the right to display the work publicly, and the right to perform it publicly.[11] Each of these rights may be parceled out and sold separately. The Copyright Act says, "The owner of any particular exclusive right is entitled, to the extent of that right, to all of the protection and remedies accorded to the copyright owner by this title."[12] Moreover, it is important to note the difference between the owner of a copyright and the owner of a copy (the physical object in which the copyrightable expression is embodied). Although the two persons may be the same, they typically are not. Owners of copies or particular expressions who do not own the copyright do not enjoy any of the five rights listed above. The purchaser of a copy of a book from a publisher may sell or transfer that book, but may not make copies of the book, prepare a screenplay based on the book, or read the book aloud in public.

The three major restrictions on the bundle of rights that surround copyright are fair use, the first sale doctrine, and limited duration. Although the notion of "fair use" is notoriously hard to spell out, it is a generally recognized principle of copyright law. Every author or publisher may make limited use of another's copyrighted work for such purposes as criticism, comment, news reporting, teaching, scholarship, and research. The enactment of fair use, then, restricts the control that copyright holders would otherwise enjoy. The first sale doctrine as codified in section 109(a) limits the rights of copyright holders in controlling the physical manifestations of their work after the first sale.[13] It says, "once a work is lawfully transferred the copyright owner's interest in the material object (the copy or the phonorecord) is extinguished so that the owner of that copy or phonorecord can dispose of it as he or she wishes."[14] The first sale rule prevents a copyright holder who has sold copies of the protected work from later interfering with the subsequent sale of those copies. In short, the owners of copies can do what they like with their property short of violating the copyrights mentioned above. Finally, the third major restriction on the bundle of rights conferred on copyright holders is that they have a built-in sunset, or limited term. All five rights lapse after the lifetime of the author plus fifty years—or in the case of works for hire, the term is set at seventy-five years from publication or one hundred years from creation, whichever comes first.[15]

Patents

Patent protection is the strongest form of protection, in that a twenty-year exclusive monopoly is granted over any expression or implementation of the protected work.[16] The domain or subject matter of patent law is the invention and discovery of new and useful processes, machines, articles of manufacture, or compositions of matter. There are three types of patents recognized by patent law: utility patents, design patents, and plant patents. Utility patents protect any new, useful, and nonobvious process, machine, article of manufacture, or composition of matter, as well as any new and useful improvement thereof. Design patents protect any new, original, and ornamental design for an article of manufacture. Finally, the subject matter of a plant patent is any new variety of plant.

As with copyright, there are restrictions on the domain of patent protection. The Patent Act requires usefulness, novelty, and nonobviousness of the subject matter. The usefulness requirement is typically deemed satisfied if the invention can accomplish at least one of its intended purposes. Needless to say, given the expense of obtaining a patent, most machines, articles of manufacture, and processes are useful in this minimal sense.

A more robust requirement on the subject matter of a patent is that the invention defined in the claim for patent protection must be new or novel. There are several categories or events, all defined by statute, that can anticipate and invalidate a claim of a patent.[17] In general, the novelty requirement invalidates patent claims if the invention was publicly known before the applicant for patent invented it.[18]

In addition to utility and novelty, the third restriction on patentability is nonobviousness. United States patent law requires that the invention not be obvious to one ordinarily skilled in the relevant art at the time the invention was made. A hypothetical individual is constructed and the question is asked, "Would this invention be obvious to her?" If it would be obvious to this imaginary individual then the patent claim fails the test.[19]

In return for public disclosure and the ensuing dissemination of information that supposedly contributes to social utility, the patent holder is granted the right to make, the right to use, the right to sell, and the right to authorize others to sell the patented item.[20] Unlike copyright, patent law protects the totality of the idea, expression, and implementation. Moreover, the bundle of rights conferred by a patent excludes others from making, using, or selling the invention regardless of independent creation. For twenty years the owner of a patent has a complete monopoly over any expression of the idea(s). Like copyright, patent rights lapse after a given period of time. But unlike copyright protection, these rights preclude others who independently invent the same process or machine from being able to patent or market their invention. Thus, obtaining a patent on a new machine excludes others from independently creating their own machine (similar to the first) and securing owner's rights.

Trade Secret

A trade secret is almost unlimited in terms of the content or subject matter that may be protected and typically relies on private measures, rather than state action, to preserve exclusivity.

> A trade secret is any information that can be used in the operation of a business or other enterprise and that is sufficiently valuable and secret to afford an actual or potential economic advantage over others.[21]

As long as certain definitional elements are met, virtually any type of information or intellectual work is eligible for trade secret protection. It may be a formula for a chemical compound, a process of manufacturing, a method of treating or preserving materials, a pattern for a machine or other device, or a list of customers.

The two major restrictions on the domain of trade secrets are the requirements of secrecy and competitive advantage. Secrecy is determined in reference to the following three rules of thumb: an intellectual work is not a secret (1) if it is generally known within the industry; (2) if it is published in trade journals, reference books, or elsewhere; or (3) if it is readily copyable from products on the market. If the owner of a trade secret distributes a product that discloses the secret in any way, then trade secret protection is lost. Imagine that Coke's secret formula could be deduced from a simple taste test. If this were the case, then Coca-Cola would lose trade secret protection for its recipe. Competitive advantage is a weaker requirement and is satisfied so long as a company or owner obtains some benefit from the trade secret.

Although trade secret rights have no built-in sunset, they are extremely limited in one important respect. Owners of trade secrets have exclusive rights to make use of the secret but only as long as the secret is maintained.[22] If the secret is made public by the owner, then trade secret protection lapses and anyone can make use of it. Moreover, owner's rights do not exclude independent invention or discovery. Within the secrecy requirement, owners of trade secrets enjoy management rights and are protected from misappropriation. This latter protection is probably the most important right, given the proliferation of industrial espionage and employee theft of intellectual works.

Moral Rights: Continental Systems of Intellectual Property

Article 6 *bis* of the Berne Convention articulates the notion of "moral rights" that are included in continental European intellectual property law. It says,

> Independently of the author's economic rights, and even after the transfer of the said rights, the author shall have the right to claim authorship of the work and to object to any distortion, mutilation or other modification of, or other derogatory action in relation to, the said work, which would be prejudicial to his honor or reputation.

The doctrine protects the personal rights of creators, as distinguished from their economic rights, and is generally known in France as *droits morals* or "moral rights." These moral rights consist of the right to create and to publish in any form desired, the creator's right to claim the authorship of his work, the right to prevent any deformation, mutilation or other modification thereof, the right to withdraw and destroy the work, the prohibition against excessive criticism, and the prohibition against all other injuries to the creator's personality.[23] Much of this doctrine has been incorporated in the Berne Convention:

> When the artist creates, be he an author, a painter, a sculptor, an architect or a musician, he does more than bring into the world a unique object having only exploitive possibilities; he projects into the world part of his personality and subjects it to the ravages of public use. There are possibilities of injury to the creator other than merely economic ones; these the copyright statute does not protect.[24]

It should be noted that granting moral rights of this sort goes beyond a mere expansion of the rights conferred on property holders within the Anglo-American tradition (see table 1.1). While many of the moral rights listed above could be incorporated into copyright and patent law, the overall content of these moral rights suggests a new domain of intellectual property protection. The suggestion is that individuals can have intellectual property rights involving their personality, name, and public standing. This new domain of moral rights stands outside of the economic- and utilitarian-based rights granted within the Anglo-American tradition. This is to say that independent of social and economic utility, and sometimes in conflict with it, authors and inventors have rights to control the products of their intellectual efforts.

Overview of This Volume

The articles contained in this volume center on the ethical, legal, and applied issues surrounding the ownership of intellectual property. Part I, The Moral Foundations of Intellectual Property, begins with "Justifying

Table 1.1 Systems of Property

Property regime	Subject matter	Restrictions on subject matter	Rights conferred on property holders	Limitations on rights
Copyright	expression: writings, photos, music, computer software	fixation, originality, nonutility	rights to: reproduce, adapt, distribute copies, display, and perform publicly	limited term: rights lapse after author's lifetime plus 50 years, allows independent creation, fair use, first sale rule
Patent	inventions, processes, compositions of matter, articles of manufacture	usefulness, novelty, nonobviousness	exclusive rights to: make use of, sell, and produce	limited term: rights lapse after twenty years, excludes independent creation
Trade secret	expressions, inventions, processes, compositions of matter, articles of manufacture, words, ideas	secrecy, competitive advantage	rights to: use, manage, derive income, capital, and no term limits, rights against misappropriations	does not exclude independent creation
Trademark	words, symbols, marks, or combinations thereof	common use restriction (i.e, generic or merely descriptive symbols are excluded)	exclusive rights to: use, manage, security, transmissibility, (no term limits on rights)	no limitations on rights so long as the word or symbol does not become generic
Law of ideas	ideas or collections of ideas	novel and original, mature or concrete, misappropriated	rights to: use, manage, derive income, security, transmissibility, and no term limits	owner's rights lapse when idea becomes common knowledge; does not exclude independent creation
Tangible/physical property	individual physical or tangible items	separability or distinctness, dangerous weapons, hazardous materials	full ownership rights, including liability to execution	eminent domain, taxation on income, inheritance tax

Note: Obviously within the Anglo-American tradition there are a number of exceptions to the subject matter, rights, and limitations found in this table. For example, a corporation may receive a patent on a nuclear device but not obtain a right to use the device. For a more precise account of the rights conferred on property holders within each system, please see the relevant statute or code along with Hohfeld and Honoré's analysis of rights (see note 10 below).

Intellectual Property" (chapter 2) by Edwin Hettinger. Hettinger criticizes a number of mainstream attempts to justify intellectual property and argues that the non-exclusive nature of intellectual works grounds a case against ownership. "Why should one person have the exclusive right to use and possess something which all people could possess and use concurrently?" The well-known Lockean labor and desert arguments, as well as arguments based on privacy and sovereignty, are found to be problematic and are ultimately rejected as justifications of intellectual property. Hettinger also examines the utilitarian argument based on providing incentives which he considers to be only partially successful. He concludes with the claim that justifying intellectual property is a daunting task and we should think more imaginatively about alternative methods of stimulating intellectual labor short of granting full-blown property rights.

Lynn Sharp Paine, in "Trade Secrets and the Justification of Intellectual Property" (chapter 3), criticizes and replies to a number of problems raised by Hettinger. Paine develops a defense of intellectual property, and in particular trade secrets, that focuses on the privacy and sovereignty of individuals. She argues that in general individuals have initial disclosure rights with respect to the ideas, opinions, plans, and knowledge found within their own minds. These rights are grounded in respect for individual privacy and autonomy. While Paine acknowledges that this kind of justification has limits and may not work at all beyond trade secrets, she argues that some kinds of intellectual property may be justified along these lines.

James Child in "The Moral Foundations of Intangible Property" (chapter 4) argues that rights to intangible property can be justified on Lockean grounds. He finds fault with the "zero-sum" (more for some means less for others) conception of property that has led many to conclude that any appropriation violates John Locke's proviso that acquisitions leave "enough and as good" for others. Child argues that while the acquisition of tangible property may be zero-sum and therefore does not leave "enough and as good," this is not obviously the case for intangible property like owning shares in business enterprises.

In the next selection, "Toward a Lockean Theory of Intellectual Property" (chapter 5), Moore continues the themes introduced by Child and argues that rights to intellectual property can be justified given a suitable reading of Locke's "enough and as good" proviso. Locke claimed that so long as the proviso is satisfied, an acquisition can be of prejudice to no one. This can be understood as a version of a "no harm, no foul" principle. If the appropriation of an unowned object leaves enough and as good for others, then the acquisition is justified. Moore offers a defense of this moral principle and argues that it grounds a case for the ownership of intellectual works.

Part II, Intellectual Property Issues and the Law, begins with "The Philosophy of Intellectual Property" (chapter 6) by Justin Hughes. Hughes provides an analysis of Lockean and Hegelian justifications of intellectual property with respect to Anglo-American and European legal institutions. He argues that both theories have shortcomings and a combination is needed to justify intellectual property. For example, Locke's labor theory cannot account for the idea whose creation has nothing to do with labor and Hegel's personality theory is "inapplicable to valuable innovations that do not contain elements of what society might recognize as personal expression." Hughes provides a basis for both labor theories and personality theories within Anglo-American systems of intellectual property.

Tom Palmer, in "Intellectual Property: A Non-Posnerian Law and Economics Approach" (chapter 7), argues that the Anglo-American systems of copyright and patent protection are "constructivistic," "interventionistic," and "utilitarian," and attempt to reorder economic institutions to attain a particular end. He claims that copyrights and patents are forms "not of legitimate property rights, but of illegitimate state-granted monopoly" and should be dismantled in favor of market forces. In place of copyrights and patents, Palmer proposes a number of free market–based mechanisms to protect the intellectual effort of authors and inventors. Contracts, technological fencing (restricted access), tie-ins with complementary goods, and certain marketing strategies are possible market solutions for protection that do not rely on illegitimate government-granted monopolies.

Next, Michael Krauss argues in "Property, Monopoly, and Intellectual Rights" (chapter 8) that Palmer's view of copyrights and patents is mistaken. As well as challenging Palmer's claim that "constructivistic," "interventionistic," and "utilitarian" justifications of protections are somehow illicit, Krauss argues that free market–based fencing will not provide adequate coverage. Moreover, the question of fencing presupposes that those who engage in these activities have rights to control what they fence. Krauss asks, "Are patent and copyright the legal backdrops required to *allow for* subsequent fencing, or are they analogous to the *destruction of competitor's* fences?" The former would allow for protection of rights that already existed while the latter would create rights. Krauss argues that if copyright and patent institutions merely provide legal mechanisms for protection of *already existing* rights, then Palmer's criticisms are largely nullified.

According to Marci Hamilton, the Agreement Involving Trade-Related Aspects of Intellectual Property Rights, TRIPS for short, attempts to remake global and specific cultural perspectives about owning intellectual property in the image of Western copyright law. In "The TRIPS Agreement" (chapter 9), Hamilton claims that, if successful, TRIPS will become "one of the most effective vehicles of Western imperialism in history." The problem she finds with the agreement and the emerging global information infrastructure is that the war between information access and copyright protection is being won by the latter. This movement is particularly troubling as we move to an on-line age where the free-use zones of "first sale" and "fair use" are in danger of being abandoned because of protection-enforcement problems. Hamilton concludes that the copyright protections found in TRIPS should be tempered to ensure the widest possible dissemination of information consistent with fair remuneration to authors and inventors.

Hugh Hansen, in "International Copyright" (chapter 10), continues the discussion of the international aspects of copyright protection. He draws an analogy between the defenders of Anglo-American copyright protection and religious missionaries. The TRIPS agreement can be understood as an attempt to convert newly industrialized and developing countries to Western views about copyright protection. Given what is at stake, Hansen argues that voluntary conversion probably will not suffice, prompting those who would defend copyright protection to rely on sanctions or involuntary conversion.

Part III, Information and Digital Technology, begins with "Why Software Should Be Free" (chapter 11) by Richard Stallman, who argues that software ownership and hoarding is "one form of our general willingness to disregard the welfare of society for personal gain." Stallman claims the fencing of software has led to a number of harms, which include the restricted use of programs, the inability to adapt or fix programs, the loss of educational benefits for programmers, and what he calls "psychosocial" harm. The latter kind of harm refers to the loss of social cohesion and altruistic spirit that would prevail if ownership were eliminated. He concludes by arguing that the free software movement will contribute to sending the right message—that a good individual is one who cooperates, "not one who is successful in taking from others."

David Carey considers in "The Virtues of Software Ownership" (chapter 12) how a virtue-centered ethics in the Aristotelian-Thomistic tradition might aid Stallman's call for the elimination of software ownership. Carey maintains that computer software should be privately owned, but at the same time property holders should be encouraged to share and widely distribute their works. In such an environment, Carey argues, incentives to produce are optimized and virtuous character traits are cultivated.

In chapter 13, Eugene Spafford examines computer ethics ("Are Computer Hacker Break-ins Ethical?") as well as other on-line problems such as Internet viruses and programs designed to invade and damage other software. He argues that computer break-ins are only justified in extreme cases and criticizes many of the reasons given in support of computer intrusions.

Charles Meyer, in "National and International Copyright Liability for Electronic System Operators" (chapter 14), claims that the international aspects of the on-line age have led to new problems in protecting intellectual property for both authors and system operators. He argues that "the need of users for access must be balanced against the need to protect creator's rights in order to maximize the benefits of creation and access for society." System operators are caught in the middle and may be held liable for infringements that occur on their systems. Meyer presents an ideal copyright system and attempts to balance these issues in light of the new transnational information age.

In the final chapter, "The Economy of Ideas," John Barlow of the Electronic Frontier Foundation argues that the traditional legal institutions of copyright and patent cannot accommodate the "galloping digitization of everything not obstinately physical." Rather than trying to "patch" or "retrofit" these legal institutions, Barlow claims that digital property must be protected by moral norms and new technological mechanisms such as encryption.

Conclusion

With the proliferation of the Internet and the World Wide Web into everyday life, along with the corresponding international concerns of the information "haves" and "have-nots," the ranks of those with a vested interest in the control of intellectual property and digital information have swelled. In large part, this is why the ownership of intellectual property is currently one of the hottest areas of applied ethics. As we move further into the information age, marked by the shift from an industrial economy to an information-based economy, clarity is needed at the philosophical level so that morally justified policies and institutions can be adopted with respect to intellectual property. It is my hope that this volume will facilitate and further philosophical inquiry in this important area.

Notes

1. It should be noted that the restrictions on both the subject matter and the rights of property holders in each of these systems are intimately tied to how the systems are justified.

2. Trademark, the law of ideas, stock options, and the like are areas of intellectual property not included in this overview.

3. The 1990 Architectural Works Copyright Protection Act amended the 1976 Copyright Act to afford explicit protection to works of architecture; see also Copyright Act, 17 U.S.C. sec. 102 (1988).

4. See *Bleistein v. Donaldson Lithographing Co.*, 188 U.S. 239 (1903), and *Time Inc. v. Bernard Geis Associates*, 293 F. Supp. 130 (S.D.N.Y. 1968). In *Feist Publications, Inc. v. Rural Telephone Service Company* (1991), the United States Supreme Court made it clear that the originality requirement is a crucial prerequisite for copyrightability. "The *sine qua non* of copyright is originality. To qualify for copyright protection, a work must be original to the author" (499 U.S. 340 [1991]).

5. Infringement is determined often by substantial similarity tests. See *Nichols v. Universal Pictures Corp.*, 45 F.2d 49 (2d Cir. 1930), and *Sheldon v. Metro-Goldwyn Pictures Corp.*, 81 F.2d 49 (2d Cir.), *cert. denied*, 298 U.S. 669 (1936).

6. See *Baltimore Orioles, Inc. v. Major League Baseball Players Ass'n*, 805 F.2d 663 (7th Cir. 1986), *cert. denied*, 480 U.S. 941 (1987), and *National Football League v. McBee & Bruno's, Inc.*, 792 F.2d 726 (8th Cir. 1986). It should be noted that state, or common law, copyright still protects unfixed works.

7. 17 U.S.C. sec. 102(b) (1988).

8. This kind of worry is, in part, the basis for the moral rights championed by the European continent. See the section on moral rights below.

9. For more about the merger doctrine, see *Morrissey v. Procter & Gamble Company*, 379 F.2d 675 (1st Cir. 1967), and *Kregos v. Associated Press*, 937 F.2d 700 (2d Cir. 1991).

10. For a lucid account of "rights" see W. N. Hohfeld, *Fundamental Legal Conceptions* (New Haven: Yale University Press, 1919); A. M. Honoré, "Ownership" in *Oxford Essays in Jurisprudence*, edited by A. G. Guest (Oxford: Clarendon Press, 1961), 107–47; and Lawrence Becker, *Property Rights, Philosophic Foundations* (London: Routledge & Kegan Paul, 1977), 19.

11. Copyright Act, 17 U.S.C. sec. 106. For certain types of works, works of "visual art," recent amendments to the Copyright Act provide a sixth category of rights—the moral rights of attribution and integrity. See 17 U.S.C. sec. 106(a) (as amended 1990).

12. 17 U.S.C. sec. 201(d).

13. See 17 U.S.C. sec. 109(a).

14. S. Halpern, D. Shipley, and H. Abrams, *Copyright: Cases and Materials*, (St. Paul, Minn.: West Publishing, 1992), 216.

15. The limited term of copyright, and patent as well, is required by the Consti-

tution. Article I, Section 8 empowers Congress to "promote the Progress of Science and useful Arts, by securing *for limited Times* to Authors and Inventors the exclusive Right to their respective Writings and Discoveries" [emphases mine]. Currently there is a bill in Congress that would increase the term of copyright protection by twenty years.

16. Patent Act, 35 U.S.C. sec. 101 (1988). The 1995 version of the Patent Act has added three years to the term of patent protection—from seventeen to twenty. See 35 U.S.C. sec. 154(a)(2).

17. 35 U.S.C. sec. 101 (1988).

18. 35 U.S.C. sec. 101-4 (1988). See also *Christie v. Seybold*, 55 Fed. 69 (6th Cir. 1893), *Hull v. Davenport*, 24 C.C.P.A. 1194, 90 F.2d 103, 33 USPQ 506 (1937).

19. 35 U.S.C. sec 103. See also *Ryko Manufacturing Co. v. Nu-star, Inc.*, 950 F.2d 714 (Fed. Cir. 1991); *Environmental Designs, LTD. v. Union Oil Company of California*, 713 F.2d 693 (Fed. Cir. 1983); *ACS Hospital Systems, Inc. v. Montefiore Hospital*, 732 F.2d 1572 (Fed. Cir. 1984); and *In Re Oetiker*, 977 F.2d 1443 (Fed. Cir. 1992).

20. 35 U.S.C. sec. 154 (1984 and Supp. 1989).

21. The Restatement (Third) of Unfair Competition, sec. 39 (1995).

22. See *Forest Laboratories, Inc. v. Pillsbury Co.*, 452 F.2d 621 (7th Cir. 1971), and *E. I. duPont deNemours & Co., Inc. v. Christopher*, 431 F.2d 1012 (5th Cir. 1970).

23. Generally these moral rights are not recognized within the Anglo-American tradition. See *Crimi v. Rutgers Presbyterian Church*, 194 Misc. 570 (N.Y.S. 1949). Recently, given the inclusion of the United States in the Berne Convention treaty, there has been a move toward indirect recognition. See note 12 above, *Gilliam v. American Broadcasting Companies, Inc.*, 538 F. 2d 14 (2d Cir. 1976), *Wojnarowicz v. American Family Association*, 745 F. Supp. 130 (S.D.N.Y. 1990), and the Berne Convention Implementation Act of 1988.

24. M. A. Roeder, "The Doctrine of Moral Right: A Study in the Law of Artists, Authors, and Creators," *Harvard Law Review* 53 (1940): 554.

Part I

The Moral Foundations of Intellectual Property

2

Justifying Intellectual Property*

Edwin C. Hettinger

Property institutions fundamentally shape a society. These legal relationships between individuals, different sorts of objects, and the state are not
easy to justify. This is especially true of intellectual property. It is difficult
enough to determine the appropriate kinds of ownership of corporeal
objects (consider water or mineral rights); it is even more difficult to determine what types of ownership we should allow for noncorporeal, intellectual objects, such as writings, inventions, and secret business information. The complexity of copyright, patent, and trade secret law reflects
this problem.

According to one writer "patents are the heart and core of property
rights, and once they are destroyed, the destruction of all other property
rights will follow automatically, as a brief postscript."[1] Though extreme,
this remark rightly stresses the importance of patents to private competitive enterprise. Intellectual property is an increasingly significant and
widespread form of ownership. Many have noted the arrival of the "post-
industrial society"[2] in which the manufacture and manipulation of physical goods is giving way to the production and use of information. The
result is an ever-increasing strain on our laws and customs protecting intellectual property.[3] Now, more than ever, there is a need to carefully
scrutinize these institutions.

As a result of both vastly improved information-handling technologies

---

*This essay was originally published as "Justifying Intellectual Property," by
Edwin C. Hettinger, in *Philosophy & Public Affairs* 18 (winter 1989): 31–52.
Copyright © 1989 by Princeton University Press. Reprinted with permission of
Princeton University Press.

and the larger role information is playing in our society, owners of intellectual property are more frequently faced with what they call "piracy" or information theft (that is, unauthorized access to their intellectual property). Most readers of this chapter have undoubtedly done something considered piracy by owners of intellectual property. Making a cassette tape of a friend's record, videotaping television broadcasts for a movie library, copying computer programs or using them on more than one machine, photocopying more than one chapter of a book, or two or more articles by the same author—all are examples of alleged infringing activities. Copyright, patent, and trade secret violation suits abound in industry, and in academia, the use of another person's ideas often goes unacknowledged. These phenomena indicate widespread public disagreement over the nature and legitimacy of our intellectual property institutions. This chapter examines the justifiability of those institutions.

Copyrights, Patents, and Trade Secrets

It is commonly said that one cannot patent or copyright ideas. One copyrights "original works of authorship," including writings, music, drawings, dances, computer programs, and movies; one may not copyright ideas, concepts, principles, facts, or knowledge. Expressions of ideas are copyrightable; ideas themselves are not.[4] While useful, this notion of separating the content of an idea from its style of presentation is not unproblematic.[5] Difficulty in distinguishing the two is most apparent in the more artistic forms of authorship (such as fiction or poetry), where style and content interpenetrate. In these mediums, more so than in others, *how* something is said is very much part of *what* is said (and vice versa).

A related distinction holds for patents. Laws of nature, mathematical formulas, and methods of doing business, for example, cannot be patented. What one patents are inventions—that is, processes, machines, manufactures, or compositions of matter. These must be novel (not previously patented); they must constitute nonobvious improvements over past inventions; and they must be useful (inventions that do not work cannot be patented). Specifying what sorts of "technological recipes for productions"[6] constitute patentable subject matter involves distinguishing specific applications and utilizations from the underlying unpatentable general principles.[7] One cannot patent the scientific principle that water boils at 212 degrees, but one can patent a machine (for example, a steam engine) that uses this principle in a specific way and for a specific purpose.[8]

Trade secrets include a variety of confidential and valuable business information, such as sales, marketing, pricing, and advertising data, lists of customers and suppliers, and such things as plant layout and manufacturing techniques. Trade secrets must not be generally known in the industry, their nondisclosure must give some advantage over competitors, and attempts to prevent leakage of the information must be made (such as pledges of secrecy in employment contracts or other company security policies). The formula for Coca-Cola and bids on government contracts are examples of trade secrets.

Trade secret subject matter includes that of copyrights and patents: anything that can be copyrighted or patented can be held as a trade secret, though the converse is not true. Typically a business must choose between patenting an invention and holding it as a trade secret. Some advantages of trade secrets are (1) they do not require disclosure (in fact they require secrecy), whereas a condition for granting patents (and copyrights) is public disclosure of the invention (or writing); (2) they are protected for as long as they are kept secret, while most patents lapse after seventeen years; and (3) they involve less cost than acquiring and defending a patent. Advantages of patents include protection against reverse engineering (competitors figuring out the invention by examining the product that embodies it) and against independent invention. Patents give their owners the *exclusive* right to make, use, and sell the invention no matter how anyone else comes up with it, while trade secrets prevent only improper acquisition (breaches of security).

Copyrights give their owners the right to reproduce, to prepare derivative works from, to distribute copies of, and to publicly perform or display the "original work of authorship." Their duration is the author's life plus fifty years. These rights are not universally applicable, however. The most notable exception is the "fair use" clause of the copyright statute, which gives researchers, educators, and libraries special privileges to use copyrighted material.[9]

Intellectual Objects as Nonexclusive

Let us call the subject matter of copyrights, patents, and trade secrets "intellectual objects."[10] These objects are nonexclusive: they can be at many places at once and are not consumed by their use. The marginal cost of providing an intellectual object to an additional user is zero, and though there are communications costs, modern technologies can easily make an intellectual object unlimitedly available at a very low cost.

The possession or use of an intellectual object by one person does not preclude others from possessing or using it as well.[11] If someone borrows your lawn mower, you cannot use it, nor can anyone else. But if someone borrows your recipe for guacamole, that in no way precludes you, or anyone else, from using it. This feature is shared by all sorts of intellectual objects, including novels, computer programs, songs, machine designs, dances, recipes for Coca-Cola, lists of customers and suppliers, management techniques, and formulas for genetically engineered bacteria that digest crude oil. Of course, sharing intellectual objects does prevent the original possessor from selling the intellectual object to others, and so this sort of use is prevented. But sharing in no way hinders *personal* use.

This characteristic of intellectual objects grounds a strong prima facie case against the wisdom of private and exclusive intellectual property rights. Why should one person have the exclusive right to possess and use something that all people could possess and use concurrently? The burden of justification is very much on those who would restrict the maximal use of intellectual objects. A person's right to exclude others from possessing and using a physical object can be justified when such exclusion is necessary for this person's own possession and unhindered use. No such justification is available for exclusive possession and use of intellectual property.

One reason for the widespread piracy of intellectual property is that many people think it is unjustified to exclude others from intellectual objects.[12] Also, the unauthorized taking of an intellectual object does not feel like theft. Stealing a physical object involves depriving someone of the object taken, whereas taking an intellectual object deprives the owner of neither possession nor personal use of that object—though the owner is deprived of potential profit. This nonexclusive feature of intellectual objects should be kept firmly in mind when assessing the justifiability of intellectual property.

Owning Ideas and Restrictions on the Free Flow of Information

The fundamental value our society places on freedom of thought and expression creates another difficulty for the justification of intellectual property. Private property enhances one person's freedom at the expense of everyone else's. Private intellectual property restricts methods of acquiring ideas (as do trade secrets), it restricts the use of ideas (as do patents), and it restricts the expression of ideas (as do copyrights)—restrictions undesirable for a number of reasons. John Stuart Mill argued that free thought and speech are important for the acquisition of true beliefs and for individual growth and developments.[13] Restrictions on the free flow and use of ideas not only stifle individual growth, but impede the advancement of technological innovation and human knowledge generally.[14] Insofar as copyrights, patents, and trade secrets have these negative effects, they are hard to justify.

Since a condition for granting patents and copyrights is public disclosure of the writing or invention, these forms of intellectual ownership do not involve the exclusive right to possess the knowledge or ideas they protect. Our society gives its inventors and writers a legal right to exclude others from certain uses of their intellectual works in return for public disclosure of these works. Disclosure is necessary if people are to learn from and build on the ideas of others. When they bring about disclosure of ideas that would have otherwise remained secret, patents and copyrights enhance rather than restrict the free flow of ideas (though they still restrict the idea's widespread use and dissemination). Trade secrets do not have this virtue. Regrettably, the common law tradition, which offers protection for trade secrets, encourages secrecy. This makes trade secrets undesirable in a way in which copyrights or patents are not.[15]

Labor, Natural Intellectual Property Rights, and Market Value

Perhaps the most powerful intuition supporting property rights is that people are entitled to the fruits of their labor. What a person produces with her own intelligence, effort, and perseverance ought to belong to her and to no one else. "Why is it mine? Well, it's mine because I made it, that's why. It wouldn't have existed but for me."

John Locke's version of this labor justification for property derives property rights in the product of labor from prior property rights in one's body.[16] A person owns her body and hence she owns what it does, namely, its labor. A person's labor and its product are inseparable, and so ownership of one can be secured only by owning the other. Hence, if a person is to own her body and thus its labor, she must also own what she joins her labor with—namely, the product of her labor.

This formulation is not without problems. For example, Robert Nozick wonders why a person should gain what she mixes her labor with instead of losing her labor. (He imagines pouring a can of tomato juice into the ocean and asks whether he thereby ought to gain the ocean or lose his tomato juice.)[17] More important, assuming that labor's fruits are valuable, and that laboring gives the laborer a property right in this value, this would entitle the laborer only to the value she added, and not to the total value of the resulting product. Though exceedingly difficult to measure, these two components of value (that attributable to the object labored on and that attributable to the labor) need to be distinguished.

Locke thinks that until labored on, objects have little human value, at one point suggesting that labor creates 99 percent of their value.[18] This is not plausible when labor is mixed with land and other natural resources. One does not create 99 percent of the value of an apple by picking it off a tree, though some human effort is necessary for an object to have value for us.

What portion of the value of writings, inventions, and business information is attributable to the intellectual laborer? Clearly authorship, discovery, or development is necessary if intellectual products are to have value for us: we could not use or appreciate them without this labor. But it does not follow from this that all of their value is attributable to that labor. Consider, for example, the wheel, the entire human value of which is not appropriately attributable to its original inventor.[19]

The value added by the laborer and any value the object has on its own are by no means the only components of the value of an intellectual object. Invention, writing, and thought in general do not operate in a vacuum; intellectual activity is not creation *ex nihilo*. Given this vital dependence of a person's thoughts on the ideas of those who came before her, intellectual products are fundamentally social products. Thus, even if one assumes that the value of these products is entirely the result of human labor, this value is not entirely attributable to *any particular laborer* (or small group of laborers).

Separating out the individual contribution of the inventor, writer, or manager from this historical/social component is no easy task. Simply identifying the value a laborer's labor adds to the world with the market value of the resulting product ignores the vast contributions of others. A person who relies on human intellectual history and makes a small modification to produce something of great value should no more receive what the market will bear than should the last person needed to lift a car receive full credit for lifting it. If laboring gives the laborer the right to receive the market value of the resulting product, this market value should be shared by all those whose ideas contributed to the origin of the product. The fact that most of these contributors are no longer present to receive their fair share is not a reason to give the entire market value to the last contributor.[20]

Thus, an appeal to the market value of a laborer's product cannot help us here. Markets work only after property rights have been established and enforced, and our question is what sorts of property rights an inventor, writer, or manager should have, given that the result of her labor is a joint product of human intellectual history.

Even if one could separate out the laborer's own contribution and determine its market value, it is still not clear that the laborer's right to the fruits of her labor naturally entitles her to receive this. Market value is a socially created phenomenon, depending on the activity (or nonactivity) of other producers, the monetary demand of purchasers, and the kinds of property rights, contracts, and markets the state has established and enforced. The market value of the same fruits of labor will differ greatly with variations in these social factors.

Consider the market value of a new drug formula. This depends on the length and the extent of the patent monopoly the state grants and enforces, on the level of affluence of those who need the drug, and on the availability and price of substitutes. The laborer did not produce these. The intuitive appeal behind the labor argument—"I made it, hence it's mine"—loses its force when it is used to try to justify owning something others are responsible for (namely, the market value). The claim that a laborer, in virtue of her labor, has a "natural right" to this socially created phenomenon is problematic at best.

Thus, there are two different reasons why the market value of the product of labor is not what a laborer's labor naturally entitles her to. First, market value is not something that is produced by those who produce a product, and the labor argument entitles laborers only to the products of their labor. Second, even if we ignore this point and equate the fruits of labor with the market value of those fruits, intellectual products result from the labor of many people besides the latest contributor, and they have claims on the market value as well.

So even if the labor theory shows that the laborer has a natural right to the fruits of labor, this does not establish a natural right to receive the full market value of the resulting product. The notion that a laborer is naturally entitled as a matter of right to receive the market value of her product is a myth. To what extent individual laborers should be allowed to receive the market value of their products is a question of social policy; it is not solved by simply insisting on a moral right to the fruits of one's labor.[21]

Having a moral right to the fruits of one's labor might also mean having a right to possess and personally use what one develops. This version of the labor theory has some force. On this interpretation, creating something through labor gives the laborer a prima facie right to possess and personally use it for her own benefit. The value of protecting individual freedom guarantees this right as long as the creative labor and the possession and use of its product do not harm others.

But the freedom to exchange a product in a market and receive its full market value is again something quite different. To show that people have a right to this, one must argue about how best to balance the conflicts in freedoms that arise when people interact. One must determine what sorts of property rights and markets are morally legitimate. One must also decide when society should enforce the results of market interaction and when it should alter those results (for example, with tax policy). There is a gap—requiring extensive argumentative filler—between the claim that one has a natural right to possess and personally use the fruits of one's labor and the claim that one ought to receive for one's product whatever the market will bear.

Such a gap exists as well between the natural right to possess and personally use one's intellectual creations and the rights protected by copyrights, patents, and trade secrets. The natural right of an author to personally use her writings is distinct from the right, protected by copyright, to make her work public, sell it in a market, and then prevent others from making copies. An inventor's natural right to use the invention for her own benefit is not the same as the right, protected by patent, to sell this invention in a market and exclude others (including independent inventors) from using it. An entrepreneur's natural right to use valuable business information or techniques that she develops is not the same as the right, protected by trade secret, to prevent her employees from using these techniques in another job.

In short, a laborer has a prima facie natural right to possess and personally use the fruits of her labor. But a right to profit by selling a product in the market is something quite different. This liberty is largely a socially created phenomenon. The "right" to receive what the market will bear is a socially created privilege, and not a natural right at all. The natural right to possess and personally use what one has produced is relevant to the justifiability of such a privilege, but by itself it is hardly sufficient to justify that privilege.

Deserving Property Rights Because of Labor

The above argument that people are naturally entitled to the fruits of their labor is distinct from the argument that a person has a claim to labor's fruits based on desert. If a person has a natural right to something—say her athletic ability—and someone takes it from her, the return of it is something she is *owed* and can rightfully demand. Whether or not she deserves this athletic ability is a separate issue. Similarly, insofar as people have natural property rights in the fruits of their labor, these rights are something they are *owed*, and not something they necessarily deserve.[22]

The desert argument suggests that the laborer deserves to benefit from her labor, at least if it is an attempt to do something worthwhile. This proposal is convincing, but does not show that what the laborer deserves is property rights in the object labored on. The mistake is to conflate the created object that makes a person deserving of a reward with what that reward should be. Property rights in the created object are not the only possible reward. Alternatives include fees, awards, acknowledgment, gratitude, praise, security, power, status, and public financial support.

Many considerations affect whether property rights in the created object are what the laborer deserves. This may depend, for example, on what is created by labor. If property rights in the very things created were always an appropriate reward for labor, then as Lawrence Becker notes, parents would deserve property rights in their children.[23] Many intellectual objects (scientific laws, religious and ethical insights, and so on) are also the sort of thing that should not be owned by anyone.

Furthermore, as Becker also correctly points out, we need to consider the purpose for which the laborer labored. Property rights in the object produced are not a fitting reward if the laborer does not want them. Many intellectual laborers produce beautiful things and discover truths as ends in themselves.[24] The appropriate reward in such cases is recognition, gratitude, and perhaps public financial support, not full-fledged property rights, for these laborers do not want to exclude others from their creations.

Property rights in the thing produced are also not a fitting reward if the value of these rights is disproportional to the effort expended by the laborer. "Effort" includes (1) how hard someone tries to achieve a result, (2) the amount of risk voluntarily incurred in seeking this result, and (3) the degree to which moral considerations played a role in choosing the result intended. The harder one tries, the more one is willing to sacrifice, and the worthier the goal, the greater are one's deserts.

Becker's claim that the amount deserved is proportional to the value one's labor produces is mistaken.[25] The value of labor's results is often significantly affected by factors outside a person's control, and no one deserves to be rewarded for being lucky. Voluntary past action is the only valid basis for determining desert.[26] Here only a person's effort (in the sense defined) is relevant. Her knowledge, skills, and achievements insofar as they are based on natural talent and luck, rather than effort expended, are not. A person who is born with extraordinary natural talents, or who is extremely lucky, *deserves* nothing on the basis of these characteristics. If such a person puts forward no greater effort than another, she deserves no greater reward. Thus, two laborers who expend equal amounts of effort deserve the same reward, even when the value of the resulting products is vastly different.[27] Giving more to workers whose products have greater social value might be justified if it is needed as an incentive. But this has nothing to do with giving the laborer what she deserves.

John Rawls considers even the ability to expend effort to be determined by factors outside a person's control and hence a morally impermissible criterion for distribution.[28] How hard one tries, how willing one is to sacrifice and incur risk, and how much one cares about morality are to some extent affected by natural endowments and social circumstances. But if the ability to expend effort is taken to be entirely determined by factors outside a person's control, the result is a determinism that makes meaningful moral evaluation impossible. If people are responsible for anything, they are responsible for how hard they try, what sacrifices they make, and how moral they are. Because the effort a person expends is much more under her control than her innate intelligence, skills, and talents, effort is a far superior basis for determining desert. To the extent that a person's expenditure of effort is under her control, effort is the proper criterion for desert.[29]

Giving an inventor exclusive rights to make and sell her invention (for seventeen years) may provide either a greater or a lesser reward than she deserves. Some inventions of extraordinary market value result from flashes of genius, while others with little market value (and yet great social value) require significant efforts.

The proportionality requirement may also be frequently violated by granting copyright. Consider a five-hundred-dollar computer program. Granted, its initial development costs (read "efforts") were high. But once it has been developed, the cost of each additional program is the cost of the disk it is on—approximately a dollar. After the program has been on the market several years and the price remains at three or four hundred dollars, one begins to suspect that the company is receiving far more than it deserves. Perhaps this is another reason so much illegal copying of software goes on: the proportionality requirement is not being met, and people sense the unfairness of the price. Frequently, trade secrets (which are held indefinitely) also provide their owners with benefits disproportional to the effort expended in developing them.

The Lockean Provisos

We have examined two versions of the labor argument for intellectual property, one based on desert, the other based on a natural entitlement to the fruits of one's labor. Locke himself put limits on the conditions under which labor can justify a property right in the thing produced.

One is that after the appropriation there must be "enough and as good left in common for others."[30] This proviso is often reformulated as a "no loss to others" precondition for property acquisitions.[31] As long as one does not worsen another's position by appropriating an object, no objection can be raised to owning that with which one mixes one's labor.

Under current law, patents clearly run afoul of this proviso by giving the original inventor an exclusive right to make, use, and sell the invention. Subsequent inventors who independently come up with an already patented invention cannot even personally use their invention, much less patent or sell it. They clearly suffer a great and unfair loss because of the original patent grant. Independent inventors should not be prohibited from using or selling their inventions. Proving independent discovery of a publicly available patented invention would be difficult, however. Nozick's suggestion that the length of patents be restricted to the time it would take for independent invention may be the most reasonable administrative solution.[32] In the modern world of highly competitive research and development, this time is often much shorter than the seventeen years for which most patents are currently granted.

Copyrights and trade secrets are not subject to the same objection (though they may constitute a loss to others in different ways). If someone independently comes up with a copyrighted expression or a competitor's business technique, she is not prohibited from using it. Copyrights and trade secrets prevent only mimicking of other people's expressions and ideas.

Locke's second condition on the legitimate acquisition of property rights prohibits spoilage. Not only must one leave enough and as good for others, but one must not take more than one can use.[33] So in addition to leaving enough apples in the orchard for others, one must not take home a truckload and let them spoil. Though Locke does not specifically mention prohibiting waste, it is the concern to avoid waste that underlies his proviso prohibiting spoilage. Taking more than one can use is wrong because it is wasteful. Thus Locke's concern here is with appropriations of property that are wasteful.

Since writings, inventions, and business techniques are nonexclusive, this requirement prohibiting waste can never be completely met by intellectual property. When owners of intellectual property charge fees for the use of their expressions or inventions, or conceal their business techniques from others, certain beneficial uses of these intellectual products are prevented. This is clearly wasteful, since everyone could use and benefit from intellectual objects concurrently. How wasteful private ownership of intellectual property is depends on how beneficial those products would be to those who are excluded from their use as a result.

Sovereignty, Security, and Privacy

Private property can be justified as a means to sovereignty. Dominion over certain objects is important for individual autonomy. Ronald Dworkin's liberal is right in saying that "some sovereignty over a range of personal possessions is essential to dignity."[34] Not having to share one's personal possessions or borrow them from others is essential to the kind of autonomy our society values. Using or consuming certain objects is also necessary for survival. Allowing ownership of these things places control of the means of survival in the hands of individuals, and this promotes independence and security (at least for those who own enough of them). Private ownership of life's necessities lessens dependence between individuals, and takes power from the group and gives it to the individual. Private property also promotes privacy. It constitutes a sphere of privacy within which the individual is sovereign and less accountable for her actions. Owning one's own home is an example of all of these: it provides privacy, security, and a limited range of autonomy.

But copyrights and patents are neither necessary nor important for achieving these goals. The right to exclude others from using one's invention or copying one's work of authorship is not essential to one's sovereignty. Preventing a person from personally using her own invention or writing, on the other hand, would seriously threaten her sovereignty. An author's or inventor's sense of worth and dignity requires public acknowledgment by those who use the writing or discovery, but here again, giving the author or inventor the exclusive right to copy or use her intellectual product is not necessary to protect this.

Though patents and copyrights are not directly necessary for survival (as are food and shelter), one could argue that they are indirectly necessary for an individual's security and survival when selling her inventions or writings is a person's sole means of income. In our society, however, most patents and copyrights are owned by institutions (businesses, universities, or governments). Except in unusual cases where individuals have extraordinary bargaining power, prospective employees are required to give the rights to their inventions and works of authorship to their employers as a condition of employment. Independent authors or inventors who earn their living by selling their writings or inventions to others are increasingly rare.[35] Thus, arguing that intellectual property promotes individual security makes sense only in a minority of cases. Additionally, there are other ways to ensure the independent intellectual laborer's security and survival besides copyrights and patents (such as public funding of intellectual workers and public domain property status for the results).

Controlling who uses one's invention or writing is not important to one's privacy. As long as there is no requirement to divulge privately created intellectual products (and as long as laws exist to protect people from others taking information they choose not to divulge—as with trade secret laws), the creator's privacy will not be infringed. Trying to justify copyrights and patents on grounds of privacy is highly implausible given that these property rights give the author or inventor control over certain uses of writings and inventions only after they have been publicly disclosed.

Trade secrets are not defensible on grounds of privacy either. A corporation is not an individual and hence does not have the personal features privacy is intended to protect.[36] Concern for sovereignty counts against trade secrets, for they often directly limit individual autonomy by preventing employees from changing jobs. Through employment contracts, by means of gentlemen's agreements among firms to respect trade secrets by refusing to hire competitors' employees, or simply because of the threat of lawsuits, trade secrets often prevent employees from using their skills and knowledge with other companies in the industry.

Some trade secrets, however, are important to a company's security and survival. If competitors could legally obtain the secret formula for Coke, for example, the Coca-Cola Company would be severely threatened. Similar points hold for copyrights and patents. Without some copyright protection, companies in the publishing, record, and movie industries would be severely threatened by competitors who copy and sell their works at lower prices (which need not reflect development costs). Without patent protection, companies with high research and development costs could be underpriced and driven out of business by competitors who simply mimicked the already developed products. This unfair competition could significantly weaken incentives to invest in innovative techniques and to develop new products.

The next section considers this argument that intellectual property is a necessary incentive for innovation and a requirement for healthy and fair competition. Notice, however, that the concern here is with the security and survival of private companies, not of individuals. Thus, one needs to determine whether, and to what extent, the security and survival of privately held companies is a goal worth promoting. That issue turns on the difficult question of what type of economy is most desirable. Given a commitment to capitalism, however, this argument does have some force.

The Utilitarian Justification

The strongest and most widely appealed to justification for intellectual property is a utilitarian argument based on providing incentives. The constitutional justification for patents and copyrights—"to promote the progress of science and useful arts"[37]—is itself utilitarian. Given the shortcomings of the other arguments for intellectual property, the justifiability of copyrights, patents, and trade secrets depends, in the final analysis, on this utilitarian defense.

According to this argument, promoting the creation of valuable intellectual works requires that intellectual laborers be granted property rights in those works. Without the copyright, patent, and trade secret property protections, adequate incentives for the creation of a socially optimal output of intellectual products would not exist. If competitors could simply copy books, movies, and records, and take one another's inventions and business techniques, there would be no incentive to spend the vast amounts of time, energy, and money necessary to develop these products and techniques. It would be in each firm's self-interest to let others develop products, and then mimic the result. No one would engage in original development, and consequently no new writings, inventions, or business techniques would be developed. To avoid this disastrous result, the argument claims, we must continue to grant intellectual property rights.

Notice that this argument focuses on the users of intellectual products, rather than on the producers. Granting property rights to producers is here seen as necessary to ensure that enough intellectual products (and the countless other goods based on these products) are available to users. The grant of property rights to the producers is a mere means to this end.

This approach is paradoxical. It establishes a right to restrict the current availability and use of intellectual products for the purpose of increasing the production and thus future availability and use of new intellectual products. As economist Joan Robinson says of patents, "A patent is a device to prevent the diffusion of new methods before the original investor has recovered profit adequate to induce the requisite investment. The justification of the patent system is that by slowing down the diffusion of technical progress it ensures that there will be more progress to diffuse. . . . Since it is rooted in a contradiction, there can be no such thing as an ideally beneficial patent system, and it is bound to produce negative results in particular instances, impeding progress unnecessarily even if its general effect is favorable on balance."[38] Although this strategy may work, it is to a certain extent self-defeating. If the justification for intellectual property is utilitarian in this sense, then the search for alternative incentives for the production of intellectual products takes on a good deal of importance. It would be better to employ equally powerful ways to stimulate the production and thus use of intellectual products that did not also restrict their use and availability.

Government support of intellectual work and public ownership of the result may be one such alternative. Governments already fund a great deal of basic research and development, and the results of this research often become public property. Unlike private property rights in the results of intellectual labor, government funding of this labor and public ownership of the result stimulate new inventions and writings without restricting their dissemination and use. Increased government funding of intellectual labor should thus be seriously considered.

This proposal need not involve government control over which research projects are to be pursued. Government funding of intellectual labor can be divorced from government control over what is funded. University research is an example. Most of this is supported by public funds, but government control over its content is minor and indirect. Agencies at different governmental levels could distribute funding for intellectual labor with only the most general guidance over content, leaving businesses, universities, and private individuals to decide which projects to pursue.

If the goal of private intellectual property institutions is to maximize the dissemination and use of information, to the extent that they do not achieve this result, these institutions should be modified. The question is not whether copyrights, patents, and trade secrets provide incentives for the production of original works of authorship, inventions, and innovative business techniques. Of course they do. Rather, we should ask the following questions: Do copyrights, patents, and trade secrets increase the availability and use of intellectual products more than they restrict this availability and use? If they do, we must then ask whether they increase the availability and use of intellectual products more than any alternative mechanism would. For example, could better overall results be achieved by shortening the length of copyright and patent grants, or by putting a time limit on trade secrets (and on the restrictions on future employment employers are allowed to demand of employees)? Would eliminating most types of trade secrets entirely and letting patents carry a heavier load produce improved results? Additionally, we must determine whether and to what extent public funding and ownership of intellectual products might be a more efficient means to these results.[39]

We should not expect an across-the-board answer to these questions. For example, the production of movies is more dependent on copyright than is academic writing. Also, patent protection for individual inventors and small beginning firms makes more sense than patent protection for large corporations (which own the majority of patents). It has been argued that patents are not important incentives for the research and innovative activity of large corporations in competitive markets.[40] The short-term advantage a company gets from developing a new product and being the first to put it on the market may be incentive enough.

That patents are conducive to a strong competitive economy is also open to question. Our patent system, originally designed to reward the individual inventor and thereby stimulate invention, may today be used as a device to monopolize industries. It has been suggested that in some cases "the patent position of the big firms makes it almost impossible for new firms to enter the industry"[41] and that patents are frequently bought up in order to suppress competition.[42]

Trade secrets as well can stifle competition, rather than encourage it. If a company can rely on a secret advantage over a competitor, it has no need to develop new technologies to stay ahead. Greater disclosure of certain trade secrets—such as costs and profits of particular product lines—would actually increase competition, rather than decrease it, since with this knowledge firms would then concentrate on one another's most profitable products.[43] Furthermore, as one critic notes, trade secret laws often prevent a former employee "from doing work in just that field for which his training and experience have best prepared him. Indeed, the mobility of engineers and scientists is often severely limited by the reluctance of new firms to hire them for fear of exposing themselves to a lawsuit."[44] Since the movement of skilled workers between companies is a vital mechanism in the growth and spread of technology, in this important respect trade secrets actually slow the dissemination and use of innovative techniques.

These remarks suggest that the justifiability of our intellectual property institutions is not settled by the facile assertion that our system of patents, copyrights, and trade secrets provides necessary incentives for innovation and ensures maximally healthy competitive enterprise. This argument is not as easy to construct as one might at first think; substantial empirical evidence is needed. The above considerations suggest that the evidence might not support this position.

Conclusion

Justifying intellectual property is a formidable task. The inadequacies of the traditional justifications for property become more severe when applied to intellectual property. Both the nonexclusive nature of intellectual objects and the presumption against allowing restrictions on the free flow of ideas create special burdens in justifying such property.

We have seen significant shortcomings in the justifications for intellectual property. Natural rights to the fruits of one's labor are not by themselves sufficient to justify copyrights, patents, and trade secrets, though they are relevant to the social decision to create and sustain intellectual property institutions. Although intellectual laborers often deserve rewards for their labor, copyrights, patents, and trade secrets may give the laborer much more or much less than is deserved. Where property rights are not what is desired, they may be wholly inappropriate. The Lockean labor arguments for intellectual property also run afoul of one of Locke's provisos—the prohibition against spoilage or waste. Considerations of sovereignty, security, and privacy are inconclusive justifications for intellectual property as well.

This analysis suggests that the issue turns on considerations of social utility. We must determine whether our current copyright, patent, and trade secret statutes provide the best possible mechanisms for ensuring the availability and widespread dissemination of intellectual works and their resulting products. Public financial support for intellectual laborers and public ownership of intellectual products is an alternative that demands serious consideration. More modest alternatives needing consideration include modifications in the length of intellectual property grants or in the strength and scope of the restrictive rights granted. What the most efficient mechanism for achieving these goals is remains an unresolved empirical question.

This discussion also suggests that copyrights are easier to justify than patents or trade secrets. Patents restrict the actual usage of an idea (in making a physical object), while copyrights restrict only copying an expression of an idea. One can freely use the ideas in a copyrighted book in one's own writing, provided one acknowledges their origin. One cannot freely use the ideas a patented invention represents when developing one's own product. Furthermore, since inventions and business techniques are instruments of production in a way in which expressions of ideas are not, socialist objections to private ownership of the means of production apply to patents and trade secrets far more readily than they do to copyrights. Trade secrets are suspect also because they do not involve the socially beneficial public disclosure that is part of the patent and copyright process. They are additionally problematic to the extent that they involve unacceptable restrictions on employee mobility and technology transfer.

Focusing on the problems of justifying intellectual property is important not because these institutions lack any sort of justification, but because they are not so obviously or easily justified as many people think. We must begin to think more openly and imaginatively about the alternative choices available to us for stimulating and rewarding intellectual labor.

Notes

1. Ayn Rand, *Capitalism: The Unknown Ideal* (New York: New American Library, 1966), 128.
2. See, for example, John Naisbitt's *Megatrends* (New York: Warner Books, 1982), chap. 1.
3. See R. Salaman and E. Hettinger, *Policy Implications of Information Technology*, NTIA Report, 84–144 (Washington, D.C.: U.S. Department of Commerce, 1984), 28–29.
4. For an elaboration of this distinction see Michael Brittin, "Constitutional Fair Use," in *Copyright Law Symposium*, no. 28 (New York: Columbia University Press, 1982), 142ff.
5. For an illuminating discussion of the relationships between style and subject, see Nelson Goodman's *Ways of Worldmaking* (Indianapolis: Hackett, 1978), chap. 2, esp. sec. 2.
6. This is Fritz Machlup's phrase. See his *Production and Distribution of Knowledge in the United States* (Princeton: Princeton University Press, 1962), 163.
7. For one discussion of this distinction, see Deborah Johnson, *Computer Ethics* (Englewood Cliffs, N.J.: Prentice-Hall, 1985), 100–101.
8. What can be patented is highly controversial. Consider the recent furor over patenting genetically manipulated animals or patenting computer programs.
9. What constitutes fair use is notoriously bewildering. I doubt that many teachers who sign copyright waivers at local copy shops know whether the packets they make available for their students constitute fair use of copyrighted material.
10. "Intellectual objects," "information," and "ideas" are terms I use to char-

acterize the "objects" of this kind of ownership. Institutions that protect such "objects" include copyright, patent, trade secret, and trademark laws, as well as socially enforced customs (such as sanctions against plagiarism) demanding acknowledgment of the use of another's ideas. What is owned here are objects only in a very abstract sense.

11. There are intellectual objects of which this is not true, namely, information whose usefulness depends precisely on its being known only to a limited group of people. Stock tips and insider trading information are examples.

12. Ease of access is another reason for the widespread piracy of intellectual property. Modern information technologies (such as audio and video recorders, satellite dishes, photocopiers, and computers) make unauthorized taking of intellectual objects far easier than ever before. But it is cynical to submit that this is the major (or the only) reason piracy of information is widespread. It suggests that if people could steal physical objects as easily as they can take intellectual ones, they would do so to the same extent. That seems incorrect.

13. For a useful interpretation of Mill's argument, see Robert Ladenson, "Free Expression in the Corporate Workplace," in *Ethical Theory and Business*, 2d ed., edited by T. Beauchamp and N. Bowie (Englewood Cliffs, N.J.: Prentice-Hall, 1983), 162–69.

14. This is one reason the recent dramatic increase in relationships between universities and businesses is so disturbing: it hampers the disclosure of research results.

15. John Snapper makes this point in "Ownership of Computer Programs," available from the Center for the Study of Ethics in the Professions at the Illinois Institute of Technology. See also, Sissela Bok, "Trade and Corporate Secrecy," in *Ethical Theory and Business*, 176.

16. John Locke, *Second Treatise of Government*, chap. 5. There are several strands to the Lockean argument. See Lawrence Becker, *Property Rights* (London: Routledge and Kegan Paul, 1977), chap. 4, for a detailed analysis of these various versions.

17. Robert Nozick, *Anarchy, State, and Utopia* (New York: Basic Books, 1974), 175.

18. Locke, *Second Treatise*, chap. 5, sec. 40.

19. Whether ideas are discovered or created affects the plausibility of the labor argument for intellectual property. "I discovered it, hence it's mine" is much less persuasive than "I made it, hence it's mine." This issue also affects the cogency of the notion that intellectual objects have a value of their own not attributable to intellectual labor. The notion of mixing one's labor with something and thereby adding value to it makes much more sense if the object preexists.

20. I thank the editors of *Philosophy & Public Affairs* for this way of making the point.

21. A libertarian might respond that although a natural right to the fruits of labor will not by itself justify a right to receive the market value of the resulting product, that right plus the rights of free association and trade would justify it.

But marketplace interaction presupposes a set of social relations, and parties to these relations must jointly agree on their nature. Additionally, market interaction is possible only when property rights have been specified and enforced, and there is no "natural way" to do this (that is, no way independent of complex social judgments concerning the rewards the laborer deserves and the social utilities that will result from granting property rights). The sorts of freedoms one may have in a marketplace are thus socially agreed-upon privileges rather than natural rights.

22. For a discussion of this point, see Joel Feinberg, *Social Philosophy* (Englewood Cliffs, N.J.: Prentice-Hall, 1973), 116.

23. Becker, *Property Rights*, 46.

24. This is becoming less and less true as the results of intellectual labor are increasingly treated as commodities. University research in biological and computer technologies is an example of this trend.

25. Becker, *Property Rights*, 52. In practice, it would be easier to reward laborers as Becker suggests, since the value of the results of labor is easier to determine than the degree of effort expended.

26. This point is made nicely by James Rachels in "What People Deserve," in *Justice and Economic Distribution*, edited by J. Arthur and W. Shaw (Englewood Cliffs, N.J.: Prentice-Hall, 1978), 150–63.

27. Completely ineffectual efforts deserve a reward provided that there were good reasons beforehand for thinking the efforts would pay off. Those whose well-intentioned efforts are silly or stupid should be rewarded the first time only and then counseled to seek advice about the value of their efforts.

28. See John Rawls, *A Theory of Justice* (Cambridge: Harvard University Press, 1971), 104: "The assertion that a man deserves the superior character that enables him to make the effort to cultivate his abilities is equally problematic; for his character depends in large part upon fortunate family and social circumstances for which he can claim no credit." See also 312: "the effort a person is willing to make is influenced by his natural abilities and skills and the alternatives open to him. The better endowed are more likely, other things equal, to strive conscientiously."

29. See Rachels, "What People Deserve," 157–58, for a similar resistance to Rawls's determinism.

30. Locke, *Second Treatise*, chap. 5, sec. 27.

31. See Nozick, *Anarchy*, 175–82, and Becker, *Property Rights*, 42–43.

32. Nozick, *Anarchy*, 182.

33. Locke, *Second Treatise*, chap. 5, sec. 31.

34. Ronald Dworkin, "Liberalism," in *Public and Private Morality*, edited by Stuart Hampshire, (Cambridge: Cambridge University Press, 1978), 139.

35. "In the United States about 60 per cent of all patents are assigned to corporations" (Machlup, *Production*, 168). This was the case twenty-five years ago, and I assume the percentage is even higher today.

36. Very little (if any) of the sensitive information about individuals that corporations have is information held as a trade secret. For a critical discussion of the

attempt to defend corporate secrecy on the basis of privacy, see Russell B. Stevenson, Jr., *Corporations and Information* (Baltimore: Johns Hopkins University Press, 1980), chap. 5.

37. U.S. Constitution, art. 1, sec. 8, para. 8.

38. Quoted in Dorothy Nelkin, *Science as Intellectual Property* (New York: Macmillan, 1984), 15.

39. Even supposing our current copyright, patent, and trade secret laws did maximize the availability and use of intellectual products, a thorough utilitarian evaluation would have to weigh all the consequences of these legal rights. For example, the decrease in employee freedom resulting from trade secrets would have to be considered, as would the inequalities in income, wealth, opportunity, and power that result from these socially established and enforced property rights.

40. Machlup, *Production*, 168–69.

41. Machlup, *Production*, 170.

42. See David Noble, *America by Design* (New York: Knopf, 1982), chap. 6.

43. This is Stevenson's point in *Corporations*, 11.

44. Stevenson, *Corporations*, 23. More generally, see chap. 2, for a careful and skeptical treatment of the claim that trade secrets function as incentives.

*This essay was originally published as "Trade Secrets and the Justification of Intellectual Property," by Lynn Sharp Paine, in *Philosophy & Public Affairs* 20 (summer 1991): 247–63. Copyright © 1991 by Princeton University Press. Reprinted with permission of Princeton University Press.

3

Trade Secrets and the Justification of Intellectual Property: A Comment on Hettinger[*]

Lynn Sharp Paine

In chapter 2 Edwin Hettinger considers various rationales for recognizing intellectual property.[1] According to Hettinger, traditional justifications for property are especially problematic when applied to intellectual property because of its nonexclusive nature.[2] Since possessing and using intellectual objects does not preclude their use and possession by others, there is, he says, a "strong prima facie case against the wisdom of private and exclusive intellectual property rights" (p. 20). There is, moreover, a presumption against allowing restrictions on the free flow of ideas (p. 33).

After rejecting several rationales for intellectual property, Hettinger finds its justification in an instrumental, or "utilitarian,"[3] argument based on incentives (p. 30).[4] Respecting rights in ideas makes sense, he says, if we recognize that the purpose of our intellectual property institutions is to promote the dissemination and use of information (p. 31). To the extent that existing institutions do not achieve this result, they should be modified.[5] Skeptical about the effectiveness of current legal arrangements, Hettinger concludes that we must think more imaginatively about structuring our intellectual property institutions—in particular, patent, copyright,

*This essay was originally published as "Trade Secrets and the Justification of Intellectual Property," by Lynn Sharp Paine, in *Philosophy & Public Affairs* 20 (summer 1991): 247–63. Copyright © 1991 by Princeton University Press. Reprinted with permission of Princeton University Press.

and trade secret law—so that they increase the availability and use of intellectual products. He ventures several possibilities for consideration: eliminating certain forms of trade secret protection, shortening the copyright and patent protection periods, and public funding and ownership of intellectual objects (p. 31).

Hettinger's approach to justifying our intellectual property institutions rests on several problematic assumptions. It assumes that all of our intellectual property institutions rise or fall together—that the rationale for trade secret protection must be the same as that for patent and copyright protection.[6] This assumption, I will try to show, is unwarranted. While it may be true that these institutions all promote social utility or well-being, the web of rights and duties understood under the general heading of "intellectual property rights" reflects a variety of more specific rationales and objectives.[7]

Second, Hettinger assumes that the rights commonly referred to as "intellectual property rights" are best understood on the model of rights in tangible and real property. He accepts the idea, implicit in the terminology, that intellectual property is like tangible property, only less corporeal (p. 17). This assumption leads him to focus his search for the justification of intellectual property on the traditional arguments for private property. I will try to show the merits of an alternative approach to thinking about rights in ideas—one that does not depend on the analogy with tangible property and that recognizes the role of ideas in defining personality and social relationships.

The combined effect of these assumptions is that trade secret law comes in for particularly serious criticism. It restricts methods of acquiring ideas (p. 20); it encourages secrecy (p. 21); it places unacceptable restrictions on employee mobility and technology transfer (p. 33); it can stifle competition (p. 32); and it is more vulnerable to socialist objections (p. 33). In light of these deficiencies, Hettinger recommends that we consider the possibility of "eliminating most types of trade secrets entirely and letting patents carry a heavier load" (p. 31). He believes that trade secrets are undesirable in ways that copyrights and patents are not (p. 21).

Without disagreeing with Hettinger's recommendation that we reevaluate and think more imaginatively about our intellectual property institutions, I believe we should have a clearer understanding of the various rationales for these institutions than is reflected in Hettinger's chapter. If we unbundle the notion of intellectual property into its constituent rights,[8] we find that different justifications are appropriate for different clusters of rights.[9] In particular, we find that the rights recognized by trade secret law are better understood as rooted in respect for individual liberty, confidential relationships, common morality, and fair competition than in the promotion of innovation and the dissemination of ideas. While trade secret law may serve some of the same ends as patent and copyright law, it has other foundations that are quite distinctive.[10]

In this chapter, I am primarily concerned with the foundations of trade secret principles. However, my general approach differs from Hettinger's in two fundamental ways. First, it focuses on persons and their relationships rather than property concepts. Second, it reverses the burden of justification, placing it on those who would argue for treating ideas as public goods rather than those who seek to justify private rights in ideas. Within this alternative framework, the central questions are how ideas *may* be legitimately acquired from others, how disclosure obligations arise, and how ideas become part of the common pool of knowledge. Before turning to Hettinger's criticisms of trade secret principles, it will be useful to think more broadly about the rights of individuals over their undisclosed ideas. This inquiry will illustrate my approach to thinking about rights in ideas and point toward some of the issues at stake in the trade secret area.

The Right to Control Disclosure

If a person has any right with respect to her ideas, surely it is the right to control their initial disclosure.[11] A person may decide to keep her ideas to herself, to disclose them to a select few, or to publish them widely. Whether those ideas are best described as views and opinions, plans and intentions, facts and knowledge, or fantasies and inventions is immaterial. While it might in some cases be socially useful for a person to be generous with her ideas, and to share them with others without restraint, there is no general obligation to do so. The world at large has no right to the individual's ideas.[12]

Certainly, specific undertakings, relationships, and even the acquisition of specific information can give rise to disclosure obligations. Typically, these obligations relate to specific types of information pertinent to the relationship or the subject matter of the undertaking. A seller of goods must disclose to potential buyers latent defects and health and safety risks associated with the use of the goods. A person who undertakes to act as an agent for another is obliged to disclose to the principal information she acquires that relates to the subject matter of the agency. Disclosure obligations like these, however, are limited in scope and arise against a general background right to remain silent.

The right to control the initial disclosure of one's ideas is grounded in respect for the individual. Just as a person's sense of herself is intimately connected with the stream of ideas that constitutes consciousness, her public persona is determined in part by the ideas she expresses and the ways she expresses them. To require public disclosure of one's ideas and thoughts—whether about "personal" or other matters—would distort one's personality and, no doubt, alter the nature of one's thoughts.[13] It would seriously interfere with the liberty to live according to one's chosen life plans. This sort of thought control would be an invasion of privacy and personality of the most intrusive sort. If anything is private, one's undisclosed thoughts surely are.[14]

Respect for autonomy, respect for personality, and respect for privacy lie behind the right to control disclosure of one's ideas, but the right is also part of what we mean by freedom of thought and expression. Frequently equated with a right to speak, freedom of expression also implies a prima facie right not to express one's ideas or to share them only with those we love or trust or with whom we wish to share.[15] These observations explain the peculiarity of setting up the free flow of ideas and unrestricted access as an ideal. Rights in ideas are desirable insofar as they strengthen our sense of individuality and undergird our social relationships. This suggests a framework quite different from Hettinger's, one that begins with a strong presumption against requiring disclosure and is in favor of protecting people against unconsented-to acquisitions of their ideas.[16] This is the moral backdrop against which trade secrecy law is best understood.

Consequences of Disclosure

Within this framework, a critical question is how people lose rights in their ideas. Are these rights forfeited when people express their ideas or communicate them to others? Surely this depends on the circumstances of disclosure. Writing down ideas in a daily journal to oneself or recording them on a cassette should not entail such a forfeiture. Considerations of individual autonomy, privacy, and personality require that such expressions not be deemed available for use by others who may gain access to them.[17]

Likewise, communicating an idea in confidence to another should not render it part of the common pool of knowledge. Respect for the individual's desire to limit the dissemination of the idea is at stake, but so is respect for the relationship of trust and confidence among the persons involved. If A confides in B under circumstances in which B gives A reason to believe she will respect the confidence, A should be able to trust that B will not reveal or misuse the confidence and that third parties who may intentionally or accidentally discover the confidence will respect it.[18]

The alternative possibility is that by revealing her ideas to B, A is deemed to forfeit any right to control their use or communication. This principle is objectionable for a couple of reasons. First, it would most certainly increase reluctance to share ideas since our disclosure decisions are strongly influenced by the audience we anticipate. If we could not select our audience, that is, if the choice were only between keeping ideas to ourselves and sharing them with the world at large, many ideas would remain unexpressed, to the detriment of individual health as well as the general good.

Second, the principle would pose an impediment to the formation and sustenance of various types of cooperative relationships—relationships of love and friendship, as well as relationships forged for specific purposes such as education, medical care, or business. It might be thought that only ideas of an intimate or personal nature are important in this regard. But it is not only "personal" relationships, but cooperative relationships of all types, that are at stake. Shared knowledge and information of varying types are central to work relationships and communities—academic departments and disciplines, firms, and teams—as well as other organizations. The possession of common ideas and information, to the exclusion of those outside the relationship or group, contributes to the group's self-definition and to the individual's sense of belonging. By permitting and protecting the sharing of confidences, trade secret principles, among other institutions, permit "special communities of knowledge" that nurture the social bonds and cooperative efforts through which we express our individuality and pursue common purposes.[19]

Of course, by disclosing her idea to B, A runs the risk that B or anyone else who learns about the idea may use it or share it further. But if B has agreed to respect the confidence, either explicitly or by participating in a relationship in which confidence is normally expected, she has a prima facie obligation not to disclose the information to which she is privy.[20] Institutions that give A a remedy against third parties who appropriate ideas shared in confidence reduce the risk that A's ideas will become public resources if she shares them with B. Such institutions thereby support confidential relationships and the cooperative undertakings that depend on them.

Yet another situation in which disclosure should not be regarded as a license for general use is the case of disclosures made as a result of deceit or insincere promises. Suppose A is an entrepreneur who has created an unusual software program with substantial sales potential. Another party, B, pretending to be a potential customer, questions A at great length about the code and other details of her program. A's disclosures are not intended to be, and should not be deemed, a contribution to the general pool of knowledge, nor should B be permitted to use A's ideas.[21] Respect for A's right to disclose her ideas requires that involuntary disclosures—such as those based on deceit, coercion, and theft of documents containing expressions of those ideas—not be regarded as forfeitures to the common pool of knowledge and information. In recognition of A's right to control disclosure of her ideas and to discourage appropriation of her ideas against her wishes, we might expect our institutions to provide A with a remedy against these sorts of appropriation. Trade secret law provides such a remedy.

Competitive fairness is also at stake if B is in competition with A. Besides having violated standards of common morality in using deceit to gain access to A's ideas, B is in a position to exploit those ideas in the marketplace without having contributed to the cost of their development. B can sell her version of the software more cheaply since she enjoys a substantial cost advantage compared to A, who may have invested a great deal of time and money in developing the software. Fairness in a competitive economy requires some limitations on the rights of firms to use ideas developed by others. In a system based on effort, it is both unfair and ultimately self-defeating to permit firms to have a free ride on the efforts of their competitors.[22]

Problematic Issues

Respect for personal control over the disclosure of ideas, respect for confidential relationships, common morality, and fair competition all point toward recognizing certain rights in ideas. Difficult questions will arise within this system of rights. If A is not an individual but an organization or group, should A have the same rights and remedies against B or third parties who use or communicate information shared with B in confidence? For example, suppose A is a corporation that hires an employee, B, to develop a marketing plan. If other employees of A reveal in confidence to B information they have created or assembled, should A be able to restrain B from using this information to benefit herself (at A's expense)? Does it matter if A is a two-person corporation or a corporation with 100,000 employees? What if A is a social club or a private school?

Hettinger seems to assume that corporate A should not have such rights—on the grounds that they might restrict B's employment possibilities. It is certainly true that giving A a right against B if B reveals information communicated to B in confidence could rule out certain jobs for B. However, the alternative rule—that corporate A should have no rights in ideas they reveal in confidence to others—has problems as well.

One problem involves trust. If our institutions do not give corporate A certain rights in ideas they reveal in confidence to employees, A will seek other means of ensuring that competitively valuable ideas are protected. They may contract individually with employees for those rights, and if our legal institutions do not uphold those contracts, employers will seek to hire individuals in whom they have personal trust. Hiring would probably become more dependent on family and personal relationships and there would be fewer opportunities for the less well connected. Institutional rules giving corporate A rights against employees who reveal or use information given to them in confidence are a substitute for personal bonds of trust. While such rules are not cost free and may have some morally undesirable consequences, they help sustain cooperative efforts and contribute to more open hiring practices.

Contrary to Hettinger's suggestion, giving corporate A rights in the ideas they reveal in confidence to others does not always benefit the strong at the expense of the weak, or the large corporation at the expense of the individual, although this is surely sometimes the case.[23] Imagine three entrepreneurs who wish to expand their highly successful cookie business. A venture capitalist interested in financing the expansion naturally wishes to know the details of the operation—including the prized cookie recipe—before putting up capital. After examining the recipe, however, he decides that it would be more profitable for him to sell the recipe to CookieCo, a multinational food company, and to invest his capital elsewhere. Without money and rights to prevent others from using the recipe, the corporate entrepreneurs are very likely out of business. CookieCo, which can manufacture and sell the cookies much more cheaply, will undoubtedly find that most of the entrepreneurs' customers are quite happy to buy the same cookies for less at their local supermarket.

Non-Property Foundations of Trade Secret Law

To a large extent, the rights and remedies mentioned in the preceding discussion are those recognized by trade secret law. As this discussion showed, the concept of property is not necessary to justify these rights. Trade secret law protects against certain methods of appropriating the confidential and commercially valuable ideas of others. It affords a remedy to those whose commercially valuable secrets are acquired by misrepresentation, theft, bribery, breach or inducement of a breach of confidence, espionage, or other improper means.[24] Although the roots of trade secret principles have been variously located, respect for voluntary disclosure decisions and respect for confidential relationships provide the best account of the pattern of permitted and prohibited appropriations and use of ideas.[25] As Justice Oliver Wendell Holmes noted in a 1917 trade secret case, "The property may be denied but the confidence cannot be."[26] Trade secret law can also be seen as enforcing ordinary standards of morality in commercial relationships, thus ensuring some consistency with general social morality.[27]

It may well be true, as Hettinger and others have claimed, that the availability of trade secret protection provides an incentive for intellectual labor and the development of ideas. The knowledge that they have legal rights against those who "misappropriate" their ideas may encourage people to invest large amounts of time and money in exploring and developing ideas. However, the claim that trade secret protection promotes invention is quite different from the claim that it is grounded in or justified by this tendency. Even if common law trade secret rights did not promote intellectual labor or increase the dissemination and use of information, there would still be reasons to recognize those rights. Respect for people's voluntary disclosure decisions, respect for confidential relationships, standards of common morality, and fair competition would still point in that direction.

Moreover, promoting the development of ideas cannot be the whole story behind trade secret principles, since protection is often accorded to information such as customer data or cost and pricing information kept in the ordinary course of doing business. While businesses may need incentives to engage in costly research and development, they would certainly keep track of their customers and costs in any event. The rationale for giving protection to such information must be other than promoting the invention, dissemination, and use of ideas. By the same token, trade secret principles do not prohibit the use of ideas acquired by studying products available in the marketplace. If the central policy behind trade secret protection were the promotion of invention, one might expect that trade secret law, like patent law, which was explicitly fashioned to encourage invention, would protect innovators from imitators.

The fact that Congress has enacted patent laws giving inventors a limited monopoly in exchange for disclosure of their ideas without at the same time eliminating state trade secret law may be a further indication that trade secret and patent protection rest on different grounds.[28] By offering a limited monopoly in exchange for disclosure, the patent laws implicitly recognize the more fundamental right not to disclose one's ideas at all or to disclose them in confidence to others.[29]

Reassessing Hettinger's Criticisms of Trade Secret Law

If we see trade secret law as grounded in respect for voluntary disclosure, confidential relationships, common morality, and fair competition, the force of Hettinger's criticisms diminishes somewhat. The problems he cites appear not merely in their negative light as detracting from an ideal "free flow of ideas," but in their positive role as promoting other important values.

a. Restrictions on Acquiring Ideas. Hettinger is critical, for example, of the fact that trade secret law restricts methods of acquiring ideas. But the prohibited means of acquisition—misrepresentation, theft, bribery, breach of confidence, and espionage—all reflect general social morality. Lifting these restrictions would undoubtedly contribute to the erosion of important values outside the commercial context.

How much trade secrecy laws inhibit the development and spread of ideas is also open to debate. Hettinger and others have claimed that trade secrecy is a serious impediment to innovation and dissemination because the period of permitted secrecy is unlimited. Yet, given the fact that trade secret law offers no protection for ideas acquired by examining or reverse-engineering products in the marketplace, it would appear rather difficult to maintain technical secrets embodied in those products while still exploiting their market potential. A standard example used to illustrate the problem of perpetual secrecy, the Coke formula, seems insufficient to establish that this is a serious problem. Despite the complexity of modern technology, successful reverse-engineering is common. Moreover, similar technical advances are frequently made by researchers working independently. Trade secret law poses no impediment in either case. Independent discoverers are free to exploit their ideas even if they are similar to those of others.

As for nontechnical information such as marketing plans and business strategies, the period of secrecy is necessarily rather short since implementation entails disclosure. Competitor intelligence specialists claim that most of the information needed to understand what competitors are doing is publicly available.[30] All of these considerations suggest that trade secret principles are not such a serious impediment to the dissemination of information.

   b. Competitive Effects. Hettinger complains that trade secret principles stifle competition. Assessing this claim is very difficult. On one hand, it may seem that prices would be lower if firms were permitted to obtain cost or other market advantages by using prohibited means to acquire protected ideas from others. Competitor access to the Coke formula would most likely put downward pressure on the price of "the real thing." Yet, it is also reasonable to assume that the law keeps prices down by reducing the costs of self-protection. By giving some assurance that commercially valuable secrets will be protected, the law shields firms from having to bear the full costs of protection. It is very hard to predict what would happen to prices if trade secret protection were eliminated. Self-protection would be more costly and would tend to drive prices up, while increased competition would work in the opposite direction. There would surely be important differences in morale and productivity. Moreover, as noted, any price reductions for consumers would come at a cost to the basic moral standards of society if intelligence gathering by bribery, misrepresentation, and espionage were permitted.

   c. Restrictions on Employee Mobility. Among Hettinger's criticisms of trade secret law, the most serious relate to restrictions on employee mobility. In practice, employers often attempt to protect information by overrestricting the postemployment opportunities of employees. Three important factors contribute to this tendency: vagueness about which information is confidential; disagreement about the proper allocation of rights to ideas generated by employees using their employers' resources; and conceptual difficulties in distinguishing general knowledge and employer-specific knowledge acquired on the job. Courts, however, are already doing what Hettinger recommends, namely, limiting the restrictions that employers can place on future employment in the name of protecting ideas.[31] Although the balance between employer and employee interests is a delicate one not always equitably struck, the solution of eliminating trade secret protection altogether is overbroad and undesirable, considering the other objectives at stake.

   d. Hypothetical Alternatives. Hettinger's discussion of our intellectual property institutions reflects an assumption that greater openness and sharing would occur if we eliminated trade secret protection. He argues that trade secret principles encourage secrecy. He speaks of the "free flow of ideas" as the ideal that would obtain in the absence of our intellectual property institutions. This supposition strikes me as highly unlikely. People keep secrets and establish confidential relationships for a variety of reasons that are quite independent of any legal protection these secrets might have. The psychology and sociology of secrets have been explored by others. Although much economic theory is premised on complete information, secrecy and private information are at the heart of day-to-day competition in the marketplace.

In the absence of something like trade secret principles, I would expect not a free flow of ideas but greater efforts to protect information through contracts, management systems designed to limit information access, security equipment, and electronic counterintelligence devices. I would also expect stepped-up efforts to acquire intelligence from others through espionage, bribery, misrepresentation, and other unsavory means. By providing some assurance that information can be shared in confidence and by protecting against unethical methods of extracting information and undermining confidentiality, trade secret principles promote cooperation and security, two important conditions for intellectual endeavor. In this way, trade secret principles may ultimately promote intellectual effort by limiting information flow.

The Burden of Justification

We may begin thinking about information rights, as Hettinger does, by treating all ideas as part of a common pool and then deciding whether and how to allocate to individuals rights to items in the pool. Within this framework, ideas are conceived on the model of tangible property.[32] Just as, in the absence of social institutions, we enter the world with no particular relationship to its tangible assets or natural resources, we have no particular claim on the world's ideas. In this scheme, as Hettinger asserts, the "burden of justification is very much on those who would restrict the maximal use of intellectual objects" (p. 20).

Alternatively, we may begin, as I do, by thinking of ideas in relation to their originators, who may or may not share their ideas with specific others or contribute them to the common pool. This approach treats ideas as central to personality and the social world individuals construct for themselves. Ideas are not, in the first instance, freely available natural resources. They originate with people, and it is the connections among people, their ideas, and their relationships with others that provide a baseline for discussing rights in ideas. Within this conception, the burden of justification is on those who would argue for disclosure obligations and general access to ideas.

The structure of specific rights that emerges from these different frameworks depends not only on where the burden of justification is located, but also on how easily it can be discharged.[33] It is unclear how compelling a case is required to overcome the burden Hettinger sets up and, consequently, difficult to gauge the depth of my disagreement with him.[34] Since Hettinger does not consider the rationales for trade secret principles discussed here, it is not clear whether he would dismiss them altogether, find them insufficiently weighty to override the presumption he sets up, or agree that they satisfy the burden of justification.

One might suspect, however, from the absence of discussion of the personal and social dimension of rights in ideas that Hettinger does not think them terribly important, and that his decision to put the burden of justification on those who argue for rights in ideas reflects a fairly strong commitment to openness. On the assumption that our alternative starting points reflect seriously held substantive views (they are not just procedural devices to get the argument started) and that both frameworks require strong reasons to overcome the initial presumption, the resulting rights and obligations are likely to be quite different in areas where neither confidentiality nor openness is critical to immediate human needs. Indeed, trade secrecy law is an area where these different starting points would be likely to surface.

The key question to ask about these competing frameworks is which is backed by stronger reasons. My opposition to Hettinger's allocation of the burden of justification rests on my rejection of his conception of ideas as natural resources and on different views of how the world would look in the absence of our intellectual property institutions. In contrast, my starting point acknowledges the importance of ideas to our sense of ourselves and the communities (including work communities) of which we are a part. It is also more compatible with the way we commonly talk about ideas. Our talk about disclosure obligations presupposes a general background right not to reveal ideas. If it were otherwise, we would speak of concealment rights. To use the logically interesting feature of nonexclusiveness as a starting point for moral reasoning about rights in ideas seems wholly arbitrary.

Conclusion

Knives, forks, and spoons are all designed to help us eat. In a sense, however, the essential function of these tools is to help us cut, since without utensils, we could still consume most foods with our hands. One might be tempted to say that since cutting is the essential function of eating utensils, forks and spoons should be designed to facilitate cutting. One might even say that insofar as forks and spoons do not facilitate cutting, they should be redesigned. Such a modification, however, would rob us of valuable specialized eating instruments.

Hettinger's train of thought strikes me as very similar. He purports to examine the justification of our various intellectual property institutions. However, he settles on a justification that really only fits patent and, arguably, copyright institutions. He then suggests that other intellectual property rights be assessed against the justification he proposes and redesigned insofar as they are found wanting. In particular, he suggests that trade secret principles be modified to look more like patent principles. Hettinger fails to appreciate the various rationales behind the rights and duties understood under the heading "intellectual property," especially those recognized by trade secret law.

I agree with Hettinger that our intellectual property institutions need a fresh look from a utilitarian perspective.[35] The seventeen-year monopoly granted through patents is anachronistic given the pace of technological development today. We need to think about the appropriate balance between employer and employee rights in ideas developed jointly. Solutions to the problem of the unauthorized copying of software may be found in alternative pricing structures rather than in fundamental modifications of our institutions. Public interest considerations could be advanced for opening access to privately held information in a variety of areas. As we consider these specific questions, however, I would urge that we keep firmly in mind the variety of objectives that intellectual property institutions have traditionally served.[36] If, following Hettinger's advice, we single-mindedly reshape these institutions to maximize the short-term dissemination and use of ideas, we run the risk of subverting the other ends these institutions serve.

Notes

1. Edwin C. Hettinger, "Justifying Intellectual Property," reprinted in this volume (chapter 2), was originally published in *Philosophy & Public Affairs* 18 (winter 1989): 31–52. Subsequent page references to this chapter appear in parentheses in the text.

2. Thomas Jefferson agrees. See Jefferson's letter to Isaac McPherson, 13 August 1813, in *The Founder's Constitution* 3, edited by Philip B. Kurland and Ralph Lerner (Chicago: University of Chicago Press, 1987), 42.

3. Hettinger uses the term *utilitarian* in a very narrow sense to refer to a

justification in terms of maximizing the use and dissemination of information. Some utilitarians might see intellectual property institutions as promoting objectives other than information dissemination. My discussion of the roots of trade secret principles is perfectly consistent with a utilitarian justification of those principles. Indeed, a utilitarian could argue (as many economists do) that giving people certain rights in ideas they generate through their own labor advances social well-being by promoting innovation. See, for example, Robert U. Ayres, "Technological Protection and Piracy: Some Implications for Policy," *Technological Forecasting and Social Change* 30 (1986): 5–18.

4. In Hettinger's chapter and in mine, the terms *justification, goal, purpose, rationale,* and *objective* are used loosely and somewhat interchangeably. But, of course, identifying the purpose or goal of our intellectual property institutions does not automatically justify them. Some further legitimating idea or ultimate good, such as the general welfare or individual liberty, must be invoked. A difficulty with Hettinger's argument is that he identifies an objective for our intellectual property institutions—promoting the use and dissemination of ideas—and concludes that he has justified them. However, unless maximizing the use and dissemination of ideas is an intrinsic good, we would expect a further step in the argument linking this objective to an ultimate good. Hettinger may think this step can be made or is self-evident from his terminology. However, it is not clear whether he calls his justification "utilitarian" because of its consequentialist form or because he means to appeal to social well-being or some particular good he associates with utilitarianism.

5. Hettinger seems to think that he has provided a clear-cut objective against which to measure the effectiveness of our intellectual property institutions. Yet, a set of institutions that maximized the "dissemination and use of information" (p. 31) would not necessarily be most effective at "promoting the creation of valuable intellectual works" or promoting " 'the progress of science and the useful arts' " (p. 30). A society might be quite successful at disseminating information, but rather mediocre at creating valuable intellectual works.

There is an inevitable tension between the objectives of innovation and dissemination. The same tension is present in other areas of law concerned with rights in information—insider trading, for example. For discussion of this tension, see Frank H. Easterbrook, "Insider Trading, Secret Agents, Evidentiary Privileges, and the Production of Information," *Supreme Court Review* (1981), 309. While we struggle to piece together a system of information rights that gives due consideration to both objectives, we must be wary of the notion that there is a single optimal allocation of rights.

Indeed, the very idea of a "socially optimal output of intellectual products" (p. 30) is embarrassingly imprecise. What is a socially optimal output of poems, novels, computer programs, movies, cassette recordings, production processes, formulations of matter, stock tips, business strategies, etc.? How we allocate rights in ideas may affect the quality and kinds of intellectual products that are produced as well as their quantity and dissemination. Hettinger seems concerned primarily with quantity (p. 30). The use of general terms like *intellectual product* and *socially optimal output* obscures the complexity of the empirical assessment that Hettinger proposes.

6. Hettinger mentions trademark as another of our intellectual property institutions, along with our social sanction on plagiarism, but his central discussion focuses on copyright, patent, and trade secret concepts. Neither trademark principles nor the prohibition on plagiarism fits comfortably with his justification in terms of increasing the dissemination and use of ideas. Both are more closely related to giving recognition to the source or originator of ideas and products.

7. It may be helpful to think of two levels of justification: (1) an intermediate level consisting of objectives, purposes, reasons, and explanations for an institution or practice; and (2) an ultimate level linking those objectives and purposes to our most basic legitimating ideas such as the general good or individual liberty. Philosophers generally tend to be concerned with the ultimate level of justification while policymakers and judges more frequently operate at the intermediate level. Hettinger has, I think, mistaken an intermediate-level justification of patents and copyrights (promoting the dissemination and use of ideas) for an ultimate justification of intellectual property institutions.

8. Hettinger, of course, recognizes that various rights are involved. He speaks of rights to possess, to personally use, to prevent others from using, to publish, and to receive the market value of one's ideas. And he notes that one might have a natural right to possess and personally use one's ideas even if one might not have a natural right to prevent others from copying them (p. 23). But he does not consider the possibility that the different rights involved in our concept of intellectual property may rest on quite varied foundations, some firmer than others.

9. It is generally accepted that the concept of property is best understood as a "bundle of rights." Just as the bundle of rights involved in home ownership differs substantially from the bundle of rights associated with stock ownership, the bundle of rights involved in patent protection differs from the bundle of rights involved in trade secret protection.

10. Today we commonly speak of copyright protection as providing incentives for intellectual effort, while at the same time ensuring widespread dissemination of ideas. As Hettinger notes, the effectiveness of copyright protection in achieving these aims may depend partly on the period of the copyright grant. Historically, at least before the first English copyright act, the famous 1710 Act of Anne, it appears that the dissemination of ideas was not so central. The common law gave the author an exclusive first right of printing or publishing her manuscript on the grounds that she was entitled to the product of her labor. The common law's position on the author's right to prohibit subsequent publication was less clear. See generally *Wheaton v. Peters*, 8 Pet. 591 (1834), reprinted in *The Founders' Constitution* 3: 44–60.

11. Hettinger recognizes a right not to divulge privately created intellectual products (p. 29), but he does not fit this right into his discussion. If the right is

taken seriously, however, it will, I believe, undermine Hettinger's own conclusions.

12. We would hope that the right to control disclosure would be exercised in a morally responsible way and that, for example, people with socially useful ideas would share them and that some types of harmful ideas would be withheld. But the potential social benefits of certain disclosures cannot justify a general requirement that ideas be disclosed.

13. Here, I am using the term *personal* to refer to ideas about intimate matters, such as sexual behavior.

14. The right to control disclosure of one's thoughts might be thought to be no more than a reflection of technical limitations. Enforcing a general disclosure requirement presupposes some way of identifying the undisclosed thoughts of others. Currently, we do not have the technology to do this. But even if we did—especially if we did—respect for the individual would preclude any form of monitoring people's thoughts.

15. On the relation between privacy and intimate relationships, see Charles Fried, "Privacy," *Yale Law Journal* 77 (1968): 475–93. Below, I will argue that confidentiality is central to other types of cooperative relationships as well.

16. Whether the presumption is overcome will depend on the importance of the objectives served by disclosure, and the degree of violence done to the individual or the relationship at stake.

17. Technically, of course, others have access to ideas that have been expressed whereas they do not have access to undisclosed thoughts. But ease of access is not the criterion for propriety of access.

18. This is the fundamental principle behind the prohibition on insider trading.

19. The phrase "special communities of knowledge" comes from Kim Lane Scheppele, *Legal Secrets* (Chicago: University of Chicago Press, 1988), 14.

20. In practice, this prima facie obligation may sometimes be overridden when it conflicts with other obligations, for example, the obligation to prevent harm to a third party.

21. An actual case similar to this was litigated in Pennsylvania. See *Continental Data Systems, Inc. v. Exxon Corporation*, 638 F. Supp. 432 (D.C.E.D. Pa. 1986).

22. For the view that fair and honest business competition is the central policy underlying trade secret protection, see Ramon A. Klitzke, "Trade Secrets: Important Quasi-Property Rights," *Business Lawyer* 41 (1986): 557–70.

23. It appears that Hettinger is using the term *private company* in contrast to individuals rather than to public companies—those whose shares are sold to the public on national stock exchanges. If one wishes to protect individuals, however, it might be more important to distinguish small, privately held companies from large, publicly held ones than to distinguish individuals from companies. Many individuals, however, are dependent on large, publicly held companies for their livelihood.

24. *Uniform Trade Secrets Act* with 1985 Amendments, sec. I, in *Uniform Laws Annotated* 14 (1980 with 1988 Pocket Part). The Uniform Trade Secrets Act seeks

to codify and standardize the common law principles of trade secret law as they have developed in different jurisdictions.

25. See Klitzke, "Trade Secrets." Different theories of justification are discussed in Ridsdale Ellis, *Trade Secrets* (New York: Baker, Voorhis, 1953). Kim Lane Scheppele is another commentator favoring the view that breach of confidence is what trade secret cases are all about (see *Legal Secrets*, 241). In their famous article on privacy, Warren and Brandeis find the roots of trade secret principles in the right to privacy (Samuel D. Warren and Louis D. Brandeis, *Harvard Law Review* 4 [1890]: 212).

26. *E. I. DuPont de Nemours Powder Co. v. Masland*, 244 U.S. 100 (1917).

27. One commentator has said, "The desire to reinforce 'good faith and honest, fair dealing' in business is the mother of the law of trade secrets" (Russell B. Stevenson, Jr., *Corporations and Information* [Baltimore: Johns Hopkins University Press, 1980], 19).

28. Support for this interpretation is found in Justice Thurgood Marshall's concurring opinion in *Kewanee Oil Co. v. Bicron Corp.*, 416 U.S. 470, 494 (1974). The court held that the federal patent laws do not preempt state trade secret laws.

29. Congress may have realized that trying to bring about more openness by eliminating trade secret protection, even with the added attraction of a limited monopoly for inventions that qualify for patent protection, would be inconsistent with fundamental moral notions such as respect for confidential relationships, and would probably not have worked anyway.

30. See, for example, the statement of a manager of a competitor surveillance group quoted in Jerry L. Wall, "What the Competition Is Doing: Your Need to Know," *Harvard Business Review* 52 (November–December 1974): 34. See generally Leonard M. Fuld, *Competitor Intelligence: How to Get It—How to Use It* (New York: John Wiley and Sons, 1985).

31. See, for example, John Burgess, "Unlocking Corporate Shackles," *Washington Business*, 1 December 1989.

32. Hettinger speaks of ideas as objects, and of rights in ideas as comparable to water or mineral rights. Indeed, according to Hettinger, the difficulty in justifying intellectual property rights arises because ideas are not in all respects like tangible property, which he thinks is more easily justified.

33. The editors of *Philosophy & Public Affairs* encouraged me to address this point.

34. His argument from maximizing the production and dissemination of ideas suggests that the presumption in favor of free ideas is not terribly strong: it can be overridden by identifying some reasonable objective likely to be served by assigning exclusive rights.

35. That is, we should look at the effects of these institutions on social well-being in general and select the institutions that are best on the whole.

36. A utilitarian assessment will also include consideration of the various interests that would be affected by alternative allocations of intellectual property rights. For example, denying authors copyright in their works may increase the

power and profit of publishers and further impair the ability of lesser-known writers to find publication outlets. One scholar has concluded that America's failure to recognize the copyrights of aliens before 1891 stunted the development of native literature. For fifty years before the passage of the Platt-Simmonds Act, publishing interests vigorously and successfully opposed recognition of international copyright. This is understandable since the works of well-known British authors were available to publishers free of charge. Publishers were not terribly concerned with the artistic integrity of these works. They sometimes substituted alternative endings, mixed the works of different authors, and edited as economically necessary. There were few reasons to take the risks involved in publishing the works of unknown and untested American writers who might insist on artistic integrity. See generally Aubert J. Clark, *The Movement for International Copyright in Nineteenth Century America* (Westport, Conn.: Greenwood Press, 1973).

4

The Moral Foundations of Intangible Property*

James W. Child

John Locke believed that each person has a natural right to hold property, particularly the fruits of his own labor.[1] It is through the mixing of one's own labor with land and its products that a right to appropriate and own property arises. But that right, as we all know, was subject to what Robert Nozick called—and what has since become familiar as—"Locke's Proviso."[2] Thus, an integral part of Locke's defense of private property turned on its omnipresent availability for appropriation in the state of nature. That is, there must be unclaimed land, as well as the produce of land, free for the taking. The original appropriation of property by one person can be just only if "enough and as good" is available to the rest of humanity.[3]

"Enough and as Good": The Proviso in the State of Nature

What did Locke mean by his proviso? More specifically, how egalitarian was it meant to be? For the more egalitarian its purpose was in the state of nature, the less it would seem able to justify unequal property rights under conditions of scarcity.[4]

---

*This essay was originally published as "The Moral Foundations of Intangible Property," by James W. Child, in *The Monist* 73 (October 1990): 578–600. Copyright © 1990 by The Hegeler Institute. Reprinted with permission of publisher.

Locke puts forward his proviso in at least three places in his famous chapter 5. In the first appearance, he says:

> (1) For this labour being the unquestionable Property of the Labourer, no man but he can have a right to what that is once joined to, at least where *there is enough and as good* left in common for others.[5] (emphasis added)

In the second, he says:

> (2) Nor was this *appropriation* of any parcel of *land* by improving it, any prejudice to any other man since there was still enough and as good left; and more *than* the yet unprovided could use.[6] (emphases in original)

The third version is much less often identified and discussed, but is nonetheless a clear formulation of the proviso. A "Man" could appropriate property by mixing his labor with it:

> (3) . . . so that it was impossible for any Man, this way, to entrench upon the right of another, or acquire, to himself, a property, to the prejudice of his neighbor who would still have room, *for as good and as large possession* (after the other had taken out his) as before it was appropriated.[7] (emphasis added)

Do these three formulations imply that individuals in the state of nature must be equal in property holdings, however we interpret "property holdings"? Some writers suggest that a condition of equality in the stock of land (and produce of the land) must exist after an appropriation. (In all cases, hereafter, I mean by an "appropriation" of land a Lockean appropriation performed by mixing one's labor with it.) Alan Ryan follows other contemporary commentators and translates the proviso as requiring "as much and as good" being left to others, even though Locke never uses such a formulation.[8] Vincent Barry requires that in the state of nature, two conditions exist: (1) "the supply of land is inexhaustible" and (2) "individuals are equal," where this second condition clearly refers to some sort of equality of resources.[9]

Could Locke have meant by "enough and as good" that equal amounts of property must be available to each person to appropriate in the state of nature? Could he have meant that people actually must appropriate and thereafter own equal amounts of property? For, if either requirement were part of Locke's starting point, equality of resources looms far larger as a desideratum for Locke than we might otherwise think. This, in turn, might weaken a broadly Lockean commitment to strong property rights in post-state-of-nature conditions of relative scarcity—that is, where the proviso does not hold. This is precisely the direction taken by Virginia Held, Vincent Barry, and others, as we shall see.

What, then, could Locke have meant by "enough and as good"? "Enough," whatever else, cannot mean "an equal amount." It refers to some other characteristic of what is left and not its comparative quantity to that held by he who has already appropriated land (or goods of the land). It seems to compare what others have *before* an appropriator (call him A) appropriates and what those same others have after A's appropriation, and whether their position has been worsened. It could mean that there must be enough left that those who have not yet appropriated land do not have so little left as to make them suffer physical deprivation for lack of property. But there is no textual evidence for this.

A more demanding requirement would be that others are *no worse off* for the appropriation. This, I believe, is clearly what Locke means. In the second formulation of the proviso (2), Locke adds a strong conjunct to "enough and as good." That is, there must still be more left than *those who have not yet appropriated could use.* So if they had more than they could use before an appropriation and more than they could use after, then relative amounts as between the appropriator (A) and those yet to appropriate are irrelevant.[10]

The third formulation gives added credibility to this reading because it requires "as large a possession" left to be appropriated. And, clearly here, Locke means not as large as that appropriated by A but as large as was there before the appropriation. But how could as large a possession be left after some of it had been appropriated? Obviously, only if the amount of land and its produce was practically unlimited, so that a single appropriation makes no practical difference to the amount still available. Indeed, Locke tells us just this in a passage following the second formulation:

> So that in effect there was never less left for others because of his enclosure for himself. For he that leaves as much as another can make use of, *does as good as take nothing at all.*[11] (emphasis added)

A few lines later he compares such "enclosure" of land to taking a drink out of a river. Does it make any practical sense to say that there is less there for others to drink?

What could Locke mean by "as good," which appears in all three formulations of the proviso? It cannot mean "as much" as A has appropriated, since then the force of "enough," or "as large" in the third formulation, would be nugatory. The preposition "as" must compare *ex ante* and *ex post* situations of those having not yet appropriated (all those except A). It seems a simple requirement that the *quality* of the land that is left be the same. This makes an important point, because Locke believes in the enormous multiplicative effect of labor upon land. One reason why the proviso can plausibly be effective in the state of nature in addition to the vast amount of land available is that mixing labor with land so increases its value and the rewards reaped from it.

Locke begins by saying labor can increase the value of land tenfold, then a hundredfold,[12] and, at one point, a thousandfold.[13] The point is that the value produced by labor is a far greater source of inequality than any slight discrepancies in size of original appropriation. If you appropriate two acres while I appropriate only one and we both leave our land unimproved, you have twice what I do.[14] But, if I get maximum value out of my land by great industry and application of reason, I might end up with five hundred *times* your wealth while owning only half your original amount of property. Locke, however, makes clear that he is totally indifferent to even such radical disparities in wealth, so that equality *per se* must be completely irrelevant to him.[15]

The remarkable power of labor to produce so vast a multiplication of wealth might help explain the force of "as good." Locke clearly thinks of property in chapter 5 as real property and its products. Thus, he must require that the acreage left is as responsive to labor inputs as it was before an appropriation, else the overwhelming force of labor inputs to create wealth could be lost. I submit, then, that by "as good" he means abstractly providing the same ratio of original value to labor improved value. Concretely, for agriculture he means "as fertile and arable."

There is yet another way that labor improvement can make up for relatively slight inequalities in sizes of original appropriation. While there is no money and thus no sophisticated commerce, we can assume that there is barter, and there is some textual evidence of wage employment.[16] Locke makes clear that the labor-mixing appropriators are net benefactors to the rest of mankind. Barter and wage labor are probably the mechanisms he has in mind.[17] In a simple pre-money economy, barter allows some specialization to emerge, producing at least some gains from trade and the division of labor. This improves the lot of all.

It therefore seems clear that Locke's concerns within the state of nature are Paretian. That is, "Am I better off or left the same after A appropriates his land, or does his appropriation make me worse off?" Locke's concerns are not egalitarian. He is not concerned with the question "Do I have as much as A?" This bears powerfully upon arguments that use the force of the proviso outside the state of nature. Let us see how this is so.

A Moral Problem in the Acquisition of Property outside the State of Nature

Needless to say, the state of nature is a fiction; in most societies there is no longer a frontier that constitutes such a source of unclaimed property. It would surely seem, then, that there is no source of unclaimed new property. If this is correct, we can only acquire property from some fixed, finite stock, all of which is already claimed by our fellows. It may seem that I can accumulate property (ultimately becoming wealthy) only by getting that additional property from others. The means of obtaining such increments of wealth may have to be somehow illicit. We shall investigate that possibility below. But ignoring that problem for the moment, it would still seem that such accumulation of property might deny others their "fair share," that is, access to "enough and as good." Locke points out that after the invention of money, I can accumulate property beyond my own ability to use or consume it.[18] So far as this accumulation of property might deny others "enough and as good," as it appears it could without a source of free unappropriated property, it violates Locke's proviso.[19]

Indeed, this argument has been made both against the notion of private property as a right, and against capitalism as a system dependent upon that right. Virginia Held says:

> Even more serious for this attempt to justify moral rights to property is the difficulty that the Lockean proviso, in the contemporary world of overpopulation and scarce resources, can almost never be met. Instead, *more property for some will almost always bring about less for others.*[20] (emphasis added)

Vincent Barry has taken the same position:

> As they (capitalists) accumulate more and more property, there is less and less for others. The relative positions of the parties with respect to property is not equal, *for as one has gained the other has, of necessity, lost.* . . . Perhaps Locke provided an adequate defense of property in a hypothetical state of nature *in which supply is inexhaustible and individuals are equal,* but that blissful Eden does not exist. And yet, modern capitalism seemingly operates as if it does.[21] (emphases added)

Note the *zero-sum* nature of property accumulation assumed by both Held and Barry. I acquire more property only by taking property from you and all others. Similar positions, which suggest but do not explicitly state this argument, are taken by Lawrence Becker[22] and A. M. Honoré.[23]

This analysis, if it can be maintained, constitutes a devastating moral argument against private property. If Held and Barry are correct, there are only two kinds of transfers of property. The first are the sort of justice-preserving transfers of entitlements to property envisioned by Nozick. However, for Held and Barry, these transactions must be for equal value and cannot explain the unequal accumulation of property. Thus, you swap something to which you are justly entitled for something of equal value, to which your transactant is justly entitled.[24] Such transfers are zero-sum in the sense that neither of us gained or lost: that is, gains and/or losses equaled zero.[25] The kind of transfers that Held and Barry describe are also zero-sum (the law calls them "conversions"). "More property for some brings about less for others," Held tells us. "As one has gained, the other has lost," says Barry. That is, I get something from you for nothing; they are zero-sum because I am ahead some amount and you lose an equal amount.[26]

With the exception of the unusual case of an intentional gift, this kind of transfer is, by definition, wrongful, presumably carried out by force or fraud or, at least, exploitation of mistake or imprudence. Thus, any inequality in a free-market society—and there is undeniably a great deal—condemns the source of the inequality as the result of something morally very similar to theft. Thus, this line of argument proceeds, the system of property rights and the economic organization it underpins must constitute the source of this inequality. *Ergo*, the system is based upon immoral (or at the very least morally unjustified) conversions. One reason why it seems clear that Held and Barry assume this zero-sum theory is the one example adduced by both. Barry gives the enclosure movement as a case of capitalists getting rich by taking from others. It is the perfect historical example of their theory of inequality being produced by zero-sum transfer.[27] Indeed, that Barry chooses the enclosure movement as the primary example of property accumulation reveals how deep the zero-sum notion is in this view.

Let us set out briefly and roughly how the enclosure movement transpired.[28] Under feudal tenure, much of the land in a manor was "common." That is, tenants could use it for pasturage, and in some cases for crops, subject to various feudal duties owed to the lord. All of the rights, duties, and privileges involved were deeply feudal in character. The peasants' "rights" were either customary or practically enforceable only in the lord's court.[29] As the notion of legal title evolved toward modern *fee simple,* the lord's ownership became more absolute and less burdened with these customary peasant claims. At the same time, a huge market for wool developed. Thus, it became profitable for the lord to "enclose" these commons and run his own sheep, thereby ignoring the peasants' customary rights.[30] Generally, the newly emerging law of property supported this revocation of old and often only customary rights. Indeed, during the eighteenth century, private acts of Parliament expedited the process.[31]

Note that it takes only a small abstraction from this example to reach something like a Lockean state of nature. Heretofore, the commons was owned "in common" (though with unequal privileges and benefits). Then, Lord Bad encloses (appropriates) the land as his exclusive property, denying its use to Peasants Good, Nice, and Kind. Antecedently, Bad, Good, Nice, and Kind had (let us say) three hundred acres to use. Now, Bad is ahead three hundred acres and Good, Nice, and Kind are out three hundred acres (*ex ante* owned in common).

I think we must agree with Barry (if we assume custom can be a source of rights, which I do) that the enclosure movement, at least as here simplistically represented, constitutes a wrongful—as well as a zero-sum—taking. But what would make Barry (and Held as well) believe that the enclosure movement is characteristic of capitalist property acquisition or accumulation? Indeed, *prima facie*, it seems dramatically atypical. Property usually changes hands for valuable consideration. How could they arrive at this conclusion? Let us see.

What is the nature of the wrong in such conversions as the enclosure movement? It may well be that the wrong is deontological in nature, a violation of a right to property. Where Nozick sees such conversions, this is the only reason for their wrongfulness, although, for Nozick, the class of wrongful conversions is much narrower than for Held and Barry.[32] But there are at least two consequentialist moral objections as well as rights-based ones. First, such transfers will lead to relative inequality. This would be a problem for Held and Barry, but not for Locke, as we saw, nor for Nozick, nor for the author.[33] Held and Barry are egalitarians with respect to transactions. Locke, Nozick, and the author are Paretians.

However, most would agree, Held and Barry included, that there is a second and more serious consequential wrong in a world without the frontier, that is, with a closed and finite stock of property. That is, *sufficient inequality might well lead to physical deprivation and suffering*, as it will not in Locke's state of nature, since sufficient land and its produce was always present there to prevent it. Thus, on this account, in the closed, finite property case, I can accumulate two more units of property only by denying them to you and to everyone else, on the assumption that antecedently you had their use and enjoyment. Think of the enclosure example, where great physical privation and poverty did result. If most property is denied you and very little—or none—left for you, then you might well have so little that you suffer. It is the physical deprivation and poverty that results from this kind of unequal distribution that virtually everyone finds objectionable. That Locke found it so is illustrated by his proviso requiring *enough*—viz., at least, to avoid deprivation. While we interpreted Locke to mean something much stronger than this by "enough," it certainly includes a prohibition on physical deprivation.

Let us now state their view explicitly and concisely:

> The *Held-Barry Thesis:* The accumulation of property outside the state of nature in the hands of one person logically requires the denial of an equal amount of property to others, lessening their stock of property by the amount accumulated by the first person. This accumulation and denial, pursued far enough, will lead to deprivation and suffering.

The Real-Property Paradigm

The Held-Barry thesis logically depends upon what we might call a "zero-sum" characteristic of property. This zero-sum characteristic is best exemplified by real property: that is, land outside the state of nature (where there is no frontier). All of Locke's thought seems to be based on the identification of property with land (and the agricultural products of land, although this distinction is not always made clear). Other early modern discussions of property also depend upon its identification with land.[34]

What are the zero-sum characteristics of land as archetypal property? There are three salient, logical characteristics of real property. First, if I own a one-acre piece of property—Blackacre, let us call it—I have a right to prevent you (and all others) from owning or using *that specific parcel of land.* Second, without a practically unlimited source of property—that is, a frontier—there is a finite and limited amount of land.[35] The amount is *fixed:* that is, it will neither grow nor shrink. As my farmer neighbors in Ohio say, "They ain't makin' any more of it." Third, from the first and second characteristics, it follows that my acquiring Blackacre reduces the total stock of land *by one acre,* which is available to you to use or acquire without payment. These three characteristics together create a zero-sum conception of property. I gain one acre; you (and everyone else) lose one. That just is zero-sum in the very same sense as Lord Bad's appropriation denied the appropriated land to Peasants Good, Nice, and Kind in the enclosure case set out above. Thus, it is your being excluded in this way from enough land, where there isn't unappropriated land for you to acquire, which might lead to your suffering physical deprivation. The kind of transfers of property contemplated by Held and Barry, being based on the real-property paradigm, are zero-sum.

What logical prerequisites must exist in order to have private property characterized by the real-property paradigm? Any property that can be held in private must be *excludable*, as we saw with Blackacre above. That is, it must be possible to exclude others from its use and enjoyment. Indeed, economists frequently choose nonexcludability as a necessary characteristic of pure public goods, those things that are not subject to privatization: for example, clean air.[36] Excludability seems to be entailed by the very nature of the economic conception of private property. It is also central to the legal conception of private property.[37] Of course, the economist's and the lawyer's notions differ in that the former concerns the *practical physical ability* (and therefore the cost) to exclude, while the latter has to do with the *normative power* to exclude.

As we saw above, there is a closely related but distinct characteristic entailed by the zero-sum conception of property, which is often confused with excludability. If I claim Blackacre as my own, excludability will insure that no one else can own, use, or enjoy (without suitable permission) *that particular piece of land*—Blackacre. But a conceptually separate thing happens as well as a result of that property claim. *The total stock of land available to be used or appropriated is decreased by one acre.* This notion is sometimes referred to as *rivalry of consumption.*[38] Yet, Held and Barry conflate my denying you Blackacre with my denying you one acre, lessening the stock available to you by one. That is, they treat them as the same thing.[39] In the real-property paradigm, they *are* the same thing, but only within that paradigm.

Let us see if we can make these conditions explicit. Spelled out formally, we may say that the zero-sum characteristics of property are defined by:

1. The *exclusion condition:* Ownership of P (a specific, individually identifiable piece of property, i.e., 'P' is a name) by A implies that all others (those not A) are excluded from possession and use of P without the permission of A.

2. The *finitude condition:* There are only n things of type P (of which P is a token) in the world, where n is a practically finite number—that is, small enough to offer genuine constraint (scarcity in the economist's sense).

From (1) and (2), we get (3):

3. The *zero-sum condition:* A's ownership of P implies that there exists only
$(n - 1)$ other things of P's type for all others to own.

As one would expect, the real-property paradigm using these three conditions works extremely well for land with no frontier (outside the state of
nature). Indeed, the stipulation of "no frontier" or "outside the state of
nature" just is the introduction of the finitude condition.

How well do these three conditions work for other sorts of property?
Nonrenewable resources are by definition finite in quantity, and that
makes all tangible personal property—in some very abstract sense—
limited. However, that finitude often makes little difference in dividing up
the world, so to speak. The stock of many (though not all) nonrenewable
resources is indefinitely large, far more like land in the frontier case than
in the modern nonfrontier case. For, even on the frontier, there is a
knowledge that the total amount of land is ultimately finite, even if practically unbounded.

Moreover, science, technology, and human ingenuity generally can
multiply the effective quantity of a given resource many times, through
more efficient use in production processes and product design. The market is an enormously effective mechanism for sending signals that a given
material resource grows more dear. The consequent price increase then
drives the aforesaid technology to find replacements or technologies that
use less.

Nonetheless, there is the thesis, heard more often in the 1970s than
today, that we are fast running through our nonrenewable resources.
Soon, if not now, we will find all these resources practically limited. If
this is the case, then all tangible personal property manufactured from
those resources is, or soon will be, practically limited in amount. For the
reasons cited above, this claim may not be very realistic. Nonetheless, we
shall assume that all tangible personal property is practically limited. This
constitutes a very strong (and, I would say, highly artificial) presumption
in favor of Held's and Barry's use of Locke's proviso. We shall make it
for the sake of the argument. Thus, tangible personal property is subject
to the objection that accumulation leads to deprivation, that is, I can only
get more by denying an equal amount to others.

The kinds of property most important to modern Western capitalism,
however, are intangible. The traditional legal distinction between tangible
and intangible property is that the former is "corporeal" and therefore
"subject to physical dominion," while intangible property is "incorporeal
and abstract."[40] Intangible property includes patents, copyrights, trademarks, common law trade secrets, and the vastly important domain of
financial assets such as stocks and bonds.

Now comes the central question in this chapter: *Is it possible that for certain sorts of intangible property the exclusion condition may not entail the zero-sum condition* (and, thus, the attendant zero-sum conception of property)? Held and Barry implicitly answer this question no. Indeed, to sustain their thesis, they must. For they implicitly assume that all types of property outside the state of nature are characterized by the three conditions of the zero-sum notion of property, which we set out above. This, they believe, necessarily causes the violation of Locke's proviso. They reach this conclusion by ignoring the possible independence of the finitude condition (2) and, thus, by conflating the exclusion condition (1) with the zero-sum condition (3).

But, what if for certain sorts of intangible property, the excludability condition was independent of the finitude condition and did not by itself entail the zero-sum condition? Put the question in a different way: might there exist intangible property that is at once excludable but inexhaustible in amount? If excludable, it could be private property, that is, one could exercise control over it. If inexhaustible, it could meet Locke's proviso. It would satisfy Locke's proviso in that, never mind how much some have already, there exists "enough and as good" for all others. In other words, I might have a piece of property from which I can exclude you, but there being an unlimited amount of this kind of property available for your appropriation, you need never suffer privation. You merely go appropriate some for yourself. And this would be true regardless of how much I already have appropriated for myself. Thus, the Held-Barry thesis would fail for such a kind of property. The existence of an inexhaustible source of property would have vast moral implications for the justice or injustice of the institution of private property, the accumulation of property as wealth, and the distribution of that wealth. Let us see how this might be so.

The Patent Paradigm

The most obvious, if not the most important, example of intangible property of this sort is the idea.[41] An inventor of my acquaintance holds seventeen patents. These patents are his property every bit as much as my house is mine. True, he holds rights to them for a term of years, and that makes his ownership a bit more like a leasehold right. But in all other relevant particulars, his patents have the salient earmarks of being his property.

The most interesting thing about my friend's ideas as property—

indeed, I consider it amazing—is that he created them *ex nihilo*. Property was created out of nothing but mental labor.[42] He didn't even need raw materials—as the farmer needs land and seed, or the potter needs clay. Of course, he needed a pencil, paper, a drafting board, and a slide rule (my friend is an old-fashioned inventor). But these are more like tools. He needed no "stuff" with which to mix his labor.

Do my friend's patented ideas meet the *exclusion condition*, required of all private property? Yes, they do, for no one can use his invention without his approval, for which he will normally charge a fee (a royalty rather than rent, but logically identical to one). So exclusion is both practically possible and normatively effective. Indeed, the machinery of the patent law is created precisely to enable him to exclude others from the appropriation or use of any of an inventor's patented ideas. That is, his ownership of a particular idea precludes others' ownership, or use of *that* idea without his permission. However, even in virtue of his exclusion of me from his ideas, does it make sense to say there are fewer ideas out there that I now can think up, appropriate by a patent, and then use? Another way of asking this question is: do my friend's patents fit the last two parts of the zero-sum conception of property? What about the *finitude condition*? Let us assume a simple-minded Platonism in which all ideas thought of and not yet thought of, appropriated through the patent law and not yet appropriated, exist. To be sure, there are seventeen fewer unappropriated ideas available for me to appropriate than before my friend started thinking. But has that lowered the stock of unthought-of and unappropriated ideas still to be thought up at all? Certainly not. The number of both not-yet-thought-of and not-yet-appropriated ideas is at least practically unbounded, if not infinite. It wasn't ever *n* and it isn't now *n* − 17, where *n* is some identifiable whole number, offering real constraint. Indeed, subtracting seventeen from the number of all the ideas that I could still think up and appropriate does not seem to decrease the total number. This makes the arithmetic of ideas seem very similar to the arithmetic of aleph zero.[43] Thus, the *finitude condition* is violated.

What about the *zero-sum condition* itself? Excludability is enough to ensure that I cannot appropriate and cannot use without permission any *presently extant* and patented ideas. Moreover, if I do receive a patent on an idea, there is one fewer idea out of the finite number already thought up and in existence for others to own and use. If we limit ourselves to the presently extant patented (appropriated) ideas, they behave exactly like Blackacre, that is, in accord with the real-property paradigm. However, patented ideas are not like real property without a frontier, just because (as we have seen) there is a source of an infinite (or indefinitely large) number of new ideas that can be thought of and, thus, created (or discovered) and appropriated *ex nihilo*, merely by hard (and creative) thought. I do not have to pay anyone for those new ideas and, more important, when I come up with one, the number available to you is not thereby decreased. Thus, the *zero-sum condition* is not met. Perhaps most important, you are not *deprived*, so long as you remain able and willing to exert mental labor.

As it is with patents, so it is with copyrights and trademarks. Moreover, courts have decided that a number of other sorts of highly abstract things, unbounded in quantity or number, are property. One interesting example is a Supreme Court decision that held that the Associated Press had a property right in the news it had gathered.[44] All of these kinds of property share the characteristic that, while I can exclude you from the use of mine, there is not thereby a smaller amount upon which you can draw to use or own. Moreover, as with Locke's real property in the state of nature, you have only to mix labor with it (here, the mental labor of thinking) to appropriate it. It is otherwise free, as it should be if there is an inexhaustible supply presently unclaimed.

Of course, issues of distributive justice, implicit in the concerns of Held and Barry, are not thereby solved, for not all of us are intelligent enough (or intelligent in the right way) to think up ideas of sufficient novelty and value to be worth protection by patent or copyright. Thus, we cannot all be equal in access to resources. What is even more disturbing for most of us, if ideas so construed are the only inexhaustible source of wealth produced by labor, is that some of us willing to "labor" might nonetheless have so little as to suffer physical privation. Held and Barry might also, quite rightly, point out that there are substantial transaction costs connected with obtaining patents and copyrights. Theoretically, this can be construed as part of the cost of *recording title* rather than the cost of actually creating and appropriating the property itself. From their perspective, however, it makes very little difference, since such transaction costs do represent a hurdle to the poor.

There is no simple answer to the Held-Barry challenge. The availability of intellectual property may favor the industrious, as Locke and the author prefer. But it also favors the intelligent, and that is not obviously fair. Moreover, as intelligence can be magnified by education and, as the transaction cost of recording title to ideas can be high, there is some tendency for such property to be more available to the rich or, at least, the well-off. There is a response, however, for there is another source of unappropriated property that seems to be even more available to all than intellectual property.

Ownership in Business Enterprises

There is no doubt that the notions of the patent or the copyright constitute a different paradigm of property from that of real property in a nonfrontier situation. There also is no doubt that it fits the Lockean notion, including the proviso, far better than the real-property paradigm does in a nonfrontier situation. Thus, the Held-Barry thesis fails with respect to it. Yet we assumed, *for the sake of argument only,* that other kinds of tangible property, at least in theory, fit the real-property paradigm better. The numbers of bulldozers or bicycles or beer bottles are not unbounded in quite the same way as is intellectual property.[45]

Certainly, patents and copyrights are important in our economy, but are they *more important* than all *forms* of tangible property, both real and personal? No, they are not. But ownership shares in business enterprises (e.g., common stock in corporations), along with many similar kinds of property, constitute the single most important kind of property interests in our economic system.[46] At the very least, they constitute the sort of property that capitalism *must* have in order to be capitalist, that is, which allows us to accumulate and exchange capital. I wish to claim that the patent paradigm characterizes these most important kinds of property in modern capitalism far better than the real-property paradigm.

For the sake of brevity, we shall limit our discussion to common stock of corporations, although I believe a similar analysis could be made of any financial asset. An ownership interest in an enterprise is abstract and intangible in the way required by the patent paradigm. There is excludability in the sense necessary for all private property. That is, there are a finite number of ownership shares of corporations presently extant; further, if I acquire one share of stock, my having it denies ownership of that share to any other. Thus, if I own all the stock of XYZ Corporation, then neither you nor anyone else can own any of it. If I own nine thousand of the ten thousand shares outstanding, then you can own—at most—one thousand. But, of course, the salient feature of the patent paradigm is that, even as I exclude you from ownership of XYZ Corporation, there are not fewer shares of enterprises in general out there for you to own. Why not? Because in an exactly analogous way to patented ideas, you can create your own business enterprise through your own efforts and thereby create property *ex nihilo* (or you can purchase the shares of someone who has done this).

To see how this is so, we have only to trace the evolution of such an enterprise. Let us assume that you open a hot-dog stand. You use none of your own money; instead, you rent all of the fixed assets and borrow from a bank to finance the working capital. You are your sole employee. On day one, you have zero equity in the business. You have a bit of luck with your location and build a large and faithful clientele. You work hard, selling many hot dogs. At the end of a year of work, you have made a profit of $10,000 after paying yourself a meager salary. You then plow all the profits back into the business (probably by making principal payments on the bank loan or by buying some of the fixed assets).[47] In the second and third year, you make $20,000 per year profit, again putting it all back into the business. At the end of three years you have property worth $50,000.[48] Where did this property come from? From your original idea, your efforts, and your entrepreneurial activity as much as the ideas covered by the patents came from my friend's head. Moreover, your $50,000 in property did not, nor does it, lower the stock of the total worth of enterprises out there to be built by others (or the value of any other property they may hold).

From here, one can take the story in a variety of directions. Our entrepreneur might sell his business and then hold $50,000 in cash or passive investments. He might expand and soon have a business worth $100,000. Whatever the *dénouement,* we have seen that Held and Barry are wrong for this case. More property for our entrepreneur did not mean less for anyone else. He has gained and no one has lost. His greater stake of property has come from some source that, if we have not yet shown that it is inexhaustible or unlimited, was unappropriated and did not obviously detract from opportunities others might have for obtaining more property. It is not zero-sum in character.

But how does this "creation" of intangible property work? Does it really bring such property within the ambit of Locke's proviso? Let us see. An extremely simplified (and somewhat simplistic) version of the contemporary macroeconomic account of how this "creation" of value occurs might run something like this. We assume you didn't misrepresent your product or defraud your customers—by using cheap fillers, for example. Thus, each time you sold a hot dog you made a customer better off to the extent that their use value for the hot dog was higher than (or, at the limit, at least as high as) the exchange value you set on it (the price). So long as you keep answering needs or wants for hot dogs at a lower price than what peoples' use values for hot dogs are, but that remain higher than your costs, you are making a profit by making other people better off.[49]

This account may seem to describe a mysterious process, but a moment's reflection will show that it does not. It does, however, require a commitment to a subjective theory of value.[50] If I value something you have more than something I have and you attribute reciprocal values to the two things, the potential for a trade exists in which we are both better off (and no one else is worse off), thus creating a Pareto improvement. The exchange of one hot dog with one customer at a price both you (the hot-dog entrepreneur) and she (the customer) find acceptable is just such a transaction. Such transactions are the paradigm market phenomena of modern microeconomics.[51]

Profit, then, occurs when the entrepreneur-producer takes his share of the gain from trade, his part of the Pareto improvement. As he accumulates these gains, he measures profit in his business. Wealth in the form of intangible property (the ownership of a company) is just the accumulated profit. Indeed, modern accounting makes this point explicit by identifying the "net worth" of this company with its "earned surplus" or "retained earnings."[52]

Conclusion

Business profit and business growth is (or can be, if business is transacted ethically) *value creating*, which, as shares of business enterprises, means property creating.[53] We have an inexhaustible "frontier" from which we can continue to appropriate such property without denying anything to our fellow human beings. Indeed, the accumulation of wealth in this manner can (and should) be a Pareto-improving process, in that it makes some better off while making no one worse off. As regards the most important kinds of property in a capitalist economic system, Locke's proviso is completely satisfied. Contrary to the Held-Barry thesis, nowhere does the accumulation of this kind of property by some necessarily require less property for others.

Notes

1. John Locke, "The Second Treatise of Government," *Two Treatises of Government* (Cambridge: Cambridge University Press, 1960), chap. 5.

2. Robert Nozick, *Anarchy, State and Utopia* (New York: Basic Books, 1974), 174–82. In fact, Locke really provides two "provisos" that limit appropriations. The first, identified by Nozick, requires that "enough and as good" be available to all. The second, set out in Locke, sec. 32, p. 332, prohibits the accumulation without use of goods that will spoil. No one has a right to waste the bounty of the earth, for "Nothing was made by God for Man to spoil or destroy" (Nozick, *Anarchy*). See Ellen Frankel Paul's discussion of both provisos in *Property Rights*

and Eminent Domain (New Brunswick, N.J.: Transaction Books, 1987), chap. 3, esp. 202–7.

As we shall see, the invention of money obviates much of the limiting effect of this second proviso. Hereinafter, we shall mean by "the proviso" Locke's requirement that enough and as good be available to others.

3. Locke, chap. 5, sec. 27, 33.

4. We shall consider one such argument that turns on this point below.

5. Locke, sec. 27, 329.

6. Locke, sec. 33, 333.

7. Locke, sec. 36, 334.

8. *Property and Political Theory* (Oxford: Basil Blackwell, 1984), 17.

9. *Moral Issues in Business,* 3d ed. (Belmont, Calif.: Wadsworth Publishing, 1986), 86–87.

10. Nozick, 175, makes a distinction between two versions of this reading of the proviso. There are two possible things that could be as large after as before an appropriation. The stringent requirement is that there is as much land for others to *appropriate.* The weaker requirement is that there is as much land to *use* where this means use in the state of nature, that is, without mixing one's labor or improving or cultivating the land. For his own purposes, Nozick interprets Locke as specifying the weaker one. I believe the text of versions (1) and (2) of the proviso squares with Nozick's interpretation. In (1), Locke talks about as much being left "in common for others," i.e., unappropriated by mixed labor and, thus, held in common. In (2), he specifically refers to amounts available "to use." However, in (3), a version not cited by Nozick, Locke specifically says "as large a possession" must be available for "the neighbor" after (a single) "Man" (our friend, A) has appropriated his portion. So the textual evidence is mixed and it is probable that Locke was confused on this point.

As the reader shall see, unlike Nozick, we can live with the stringent requirement. It gives the strongest cards to those whose arguments about problems outside the state of nature we wish to defeat. We can give them those cards and still beat them. This is true in large measure because we shall demonstrate that there exists a situation *outside* the state of nature, wherein all can have as much property *to appropriate as their own* as they can while leaving a practically unlimited amount available to all others for their *appropriation.*

11. Locke, sec. 33, 333.

12. Locke, sec. 37, 336 and sec. 40, 338.

13. Locke, sec. 43, 340.

14. Obviously, I am using a very un-Lockean kind of appropriation, perhaps by declaration of some kind. However, the point being made is not vitiated by this change. In the name of consistency with a purely Lockean form of appropriation, we might imagine the case in which each of us has only marginally improved our land by mixing our labor, just enough to come to own it. We might then compare that case to the one set out below in which one of us has intensively improved our land.

15. Locke has *no* patience at all with lazy persons, either indolent landholders having done the minimum necessary for appropriation or those still in the state of nature who have not even done this. "Fancy or covetousness," presumably about others' wealth gained from hard work, renders one "quarrelsome and contentious" (Locke, sec. 34). Such people wish to benefit from "another's pains."

16. In a famous passage in section 28 (Locke, 330), he makes reference to his servant cutting hay for a horse. Obviously, this is deep water and I make these suggestions knowing that establishing them could be difficult. For an interesting discussion of possible protoeconomies, some of which require money, in Lockean near states-of-nature or early phases thereafter, see Andrew Reeve, *Property* (London: Macmillan, 1986), 127–32.

17. Locke, sec. 37, 336, tells us that appropriators "increase the *common* stock of mankind." That is what *we all* hold.

18. Locke, sec. 45–50, 341–45.

19. Virginia Held uses Locke's proviso and its apparently redistributive consequences to criticize Nozick's more libertarian reading of Locke and Nozick's own theory of entitlement that issues from it. Virginia Held, "John Locke on Robert Nozick," *Social Research* 43 (spring, 1976): 169–95.

20. Virginia Held, *Rights and Goods* (Glencoe, Ill.: The Free Press, 1984), 172.

21. Barry, *Moral Issues,* 86–87.

22. Becker, *Property Rights* (London: Routledge and Kegan Paul, 1977), chap. 4, esp. 42–43.

23. A. M. Honoré, "Property, Title and Redistribution," first published in *Equality and Freedom,* edited by Carl Wellman (Wiesbaden: Franz Steiner Verlag, 1977), reprinted in *Property, Profits and Economic Justice,* edited by Virginia Held (Belmont, Calif.: Wadsworth, 1980), 84–92, esp. 87–88.

24. Nozick, of course, places no requirement of equal value on these transactions. He only requires that they be free of fraud and force. For his treatment of entitlements and their transfer, see Nozick, 150–82. I introduced the notion of "equal value"; Held and Barry do not. For reasons that will emerge below, however, I believe that their argument crucially depends upon a concept of equal (and, more basically, objective) value, very like a just price. Obviously, this opens up another line of counterargument, one related to, but distinct from, that which we follow here. See also note 25 below.

25. It may strike the reader that such a notion of economic transactions is radically at odds with modern microeconomics and provides the parties with no rational motive to transact. Both these charges are quite true. Nonetheless, this objective value/just price/zero-sum theory of transactions lies at the root of both Aristotle's and Marx's theory of transactions and was never fully overthrown until the subjectivist revolution in the mid-nineteenth century (see Nicholas Georgescu-Roegen, "Utility and Value in Economic Thought," in *Dictionary of the History of Ideas* [New York: Scribner's, 1973], vol. 4, 450–58). As we shall see more clearly as we go forward, Held and Barry seem to presuppose such an objective value/zero-sum theory.

26. There is, of course, the possibility of hybrid cases of transfers for partial value. Yet, these also cannot be accounted for except as a partial conversion, also wrongful.

27. Barry, *Moral Issues,* 84–85.

28. I have used Lacey Baldwin Smith, *This Realm England,* 3d ed. (Lexington, Mass.: Heath, 1976), chap. 4, and William B. Willcox and Walter Arnstein, *The Age of Aristocracy,* 4th ed. (Lexington, Mass.: Heath, 1983), chaps. 3 and 9.

29. See J. H. Baker, *An Introduction to English Legal History,* 2d ed. (London: Butterworth, 1979), chaps. 12 and 15. Not all peasants were so badly off. Those who held some sort of recorded legal title fared much better than those having only customary or copyhold estates (see Smith, 71–72 and Baker, 259–60).

30. See S. T. Bindoff, *Tudor England* (Harmondsworth, England: Penguin, 1950), 22–24.

31. Willcox and Arnstein, *Age of Aristocracy,* 171.

32. See note 24 above.

33. Held says explicitly that she finds it morally problematic even if only the *relative positions* of the parties change due to the transaction, presumably because such change sacrifices equality. Thus, if A gains 2 units and B gains 1, each starting with 0, this is relative inequality, though both are better off. Held finds such inequality objectionable. But she does clearly distinguish the case of change to relative inequality from the true zero-sum transfer, where one party is made absolutely worse off while the other party is made absolutely better off. Barry never explicitly confronts the problem of relative positions and inequality *per se,* although the general tenor of his discussion leads one to conclude that he would agree with Held that even relative inequality is objectionable.

34. The other signal example of a real-property paradigm with the zero-sum characteristics clearly delineated is in the work of Jean-Jacques Rousseau (see "A Discourse on the Origin of Inequality," *The Social Contract and Discourses* [New York: E. P. Dutton, 1950], 234–44). The real-property paradigm is still implicitly assumed in many contemporary discussions of property (see A. M. Honoré, "Property, Title and Redistribution").

35. The reader will note that we *do not* assume that all land is held in private hands. To make the Held-Barry picture of property accumulation at all plausible, we must assume that there is some land that is either held in common and subject to appropriation or genuinely unowned, in no one's title. That is why the enclosure movement is such a good example for their thesis. In fact, outside of cases of warfare and conquest (e.g., the Norman Conquest), it may be nearly the only example.

Note also, however, we *do not* assume that there is an *unlimited* amount of such land, as in Locke's state of nature or a true frontier. To take an acre of land in our case practically reduces what is left by an acre. To go back to Locke's example in the state of nature (sec. 33), it is *not* like taking a drink from a river.

In the more realistic case, where all land is in private hands, it is hard to see quite how illicit appropriation or accumulation occurs without unlawful force or fraud. Just where are these zero-sum conversions of property? This dearth of examples, in the most realistic case of a stable lawful order, constitutes a major point against the Held-Barry thesis. Perhaps they would make the move made by many critics of capitalism. That is, force and fraud are too narrow to capture the "real" ways that zero-sum conversions occur in capitalist societies. They might occur through subtle misrepresentation, manipulation of preferences, coercive offers, and so on. Needless to say, the author would not agree, but a discussion would take us too far afield.

36. See Yew-Kwang Ng, *Welfare Economics* (New York: John Wiley and Sons, 1980), 188, and Robert Sugden, *The Political Economy of Public Choice* (New York: John Wiley and Sons, 1981), 23.

37. *Corpus Juris Secundum* defines property as *(inter alia)* "that dominion or indefinite right to use . . . generally to the exclusion of others" *(CJS,* vol. 73, 166). It holds further that an essential attribute of property is a "right of exclusion," which, it is frequently held, "may be exercised to the exclusion of all others, freely and without restriction" *(CJS,* vol. 73, 168–69).

Of the many, more theoretical discussions of the legal conception of property ownership, one of the best is A. M. Honoré, "Ownership," *Oxford Essays in Jurisprudence,* edited by A. G. Guest, reprinted in Becker and Kipnis, eds., *Property* (Englewood Cliffs, N.J.: Prentice-Hall, 1984), 78–87. Honoré adduces eleven incidences of ownership. While the right to exclude is not one of them, it appears explicitly as a constituent of two: the right to possess and the right to security.

38. Ng, *Welfare Economics,* 187.

39. Economists may be as inclined to confuse these two things also. Compare Ng's definition of non-excludability of a public good with Jack Hirshleifer's in *Price Theory and Applications,* 3d edition (Englewood Cliffs, N.J.: Prentice-Hall, 1984), 493.

40. See Roy Andrews Brown, *The Law of Personal Property,* 2d ed. (Chicago: Callaghan and Co., 1955), 13; and Crossley Vaines, *Personal Property* (London: Butterworth, 1967), 12–16. We now have introduced two pairs of legal terms referring to property:

Real	*Personal*
land	all other

Tangible	*Intangible*
corporeal and subject to physical dominion	incorporeal and abstract

All real property is tangible. Personal property comes in both tangible and intangible forms.

41. In patent law, ideas generally—especially purely abstract ideas and scientific principles—are not patentable. For an idea to be subject to patent protection

it must incorporate a "product or a process." That is, it must contain its own practical application (see Arthur Miller and Michael Davis, *Intellectual Property* [St. Paul, MN: West Publishing, 1983], 18–19). We use this restricted notion of an "idea" in what follows.

It is interesting that A. M. Honoré, in "Property, Title and Redistribution," uses, as his example of property, the idea (and invention) of a fishhook in a primitive society. However, at no time does he discuss the crucial, logical differences between this kind of property and the real-property paradigm, much less the moral consequences that flow from those differences. He treats an idea exactly as if it were an example of the real-property paradigm.

42. This is, of course, not creation *ex nihilo* in the physical sense, for that would violate the law of conservation of energy (and perhaps the second law of thermodynamics). But it is surely creation *ex nihilo* in the sense of economic value.

43. This refers to transfinite arithmetic and the lowest order of infinity—namely, denumerable or countable infinity within that theory. A set is countable if it can be put in one-to-one correspondence with the natural numbers. Aleph zero, or the set of natural numbers, does not behave as does a finite number. Subtracting a finite number, here 17, from a denumerably infinite set does not change the number in the set. It is still denumerably infinite, that is, the same size as the set of natural numbers.

44. *International News Service vs. Associated Press*, 248 U.S.C. sec. 215 (1918).

45. While this last line is literally true, the reader must not underestimate the magnitude of the concession I make here to Held and Barry. There is a very real sense in which the uses to which tangible property can be put are unlimited. There is also an apparently unlimited number of ways in which tangible property can be blended, assembled, and reassembled to make new artifacts. All of this is guided by human ideas and human invention informing matter with value and use. All tangible property but the rawest of raw material is as much intellectual as physical property. This would include even plant and animal material that is the product of selective breeding. Maize, as raised today, is as much an artifactual product of human reason as is the automobile tire or the microprocessor. Indeed, both Ellen Frankel Paul and Israel Kirzner (in somewhat different ways) see the value we put upon *any* physical thing, however unimproved, as a human creation of mental process, so that *anything* that we designate as property is already human creation (see Ellen Frankel Paul, *Property Rights and Eminent Domain*, 224–39, and Israel Kirzner, "Entrepreneurship, Entitlement and Economic Justice," in *Reading Nozick*, edited by Jeffrey Paul [Totowa, NJ: Rowman and Littlefield, 1981]).

I would add to their view that there is an unlimited feature of tangible property or that, if limited, it is only by the amount of matter in the universe. Still, there is a limitation on the creation of tangible property not existing upon intellectual property. I cannot go into my studio to sculpt a statue without stone (or some other material). The ownership of the stone is, at least, an issue. I take nothing when I go into my study to concoct an idea. There is no analogue of the stone, the title to which could be contested.

46. Keep in mind that such abstract, intangible property is represented not only by the common stock of corporations (and shares of partnerships) but by all evidences of the existence of indebtedness (or its availability) as well. These would include credit cards, personal checks, checking accounts, savings accounts, and promissory notes and bonds, including those of governments as well as corporations. Indeed, it includes paper currency. In modern capitalist economies, far more wealth is represented by such abstract intangible property than by all tangible property, both real and personal.

47. I have assumed that the entrepreneur has put no capital of his own into the business. This is simply for accounting convenience. However, it might be objected that this makes availability to entrepreneurial opportunity, and thus capitalist social justice, seem more fairly distributed than it really is. Three points should be made in rejoinder. First, starting a business without initial capital is not all that uncommon, especially where a bank knows the entrepreneur and his record of skill and reliability. In our example, perhaps our entrepreneur has worked many years for a successful hot-dog stand owner and has a record of managerial success. Remember also, the bank does not just give the entrepreneur a line of credit without security. It takes liens on his working capital (here, hot dogs, buns, etc.), which secure the loan. Second, many small and relatively poor entrepreneurs can make some small amount of capital available through savings, personal borrowings, and so on. Third, there is a vigorous venture-capital market available for entrepreneurs, at least in the United States. Of course, none of this obviates the fact that the rich have more access to capital than the poor, but it must ameliorate it to some extent. For probably half of the most successful entrepreneurs are self-made women and men who started on a shoestring.

48. Those versed in finance will notice that I have tacitly assumed that the market value of the business is identical with its book or accounting value. This is, of course, not always the case, but the assumption is harmless here.

49. Professor Hillel Steiner has pointed out in private correspondence that there is a potential inconsistency with my thesis in this "entrepreneurial success story." In a purely competitive market, profit will tend to fall to zero. It is perhaps avoided here by the fortunate location the hot-dog vendor has chosen, giving him a sort of local monopoly. However, if this is true, the proviso is violated for lack of a frontier, that is, similarly fruitful entrepreneurial opportunities are finite and fixed in number. It is those finite opportunities that are zero-sum in character.

This is a trenchant point, one that I don't have the space to answer completely. Indeed, candor requires that I admit that I am not sure that I *can* fully answer it. It surely deserves far more thought. However, a first pass at an answer is available. To be sure, in any one market, at any one time, such temporary local monopolies and other bottlenecks (e.g., curable inefficiencies, etc.) are practically finite. Thus, among hot-dog stands in this area, this location might constitute a zero-sum opportunity. But over all markets and long periods of time, it is not clear that such opportunities are practically finite. Thus, if I am a would-be entrepreneur, I have, in principle, available to me all possible entrepreneurial opportunities, a number that is at least indefinitely large, if not infinite. This sounds like an Austrian conception of the market as process and of the entrepreneurial function. To some extent it is. It is influenced by Hayek, Schumpeter, and Kirzner but also by Knight and Stigler, who are not Austrians.

See, for example, F. A. Hayek, "Competition as a Discovery Procedure," in *New Studies* (Chicago: University of Chicago Press, 1978), 179–90; Israel Kirzner, *Perception, Opportunity and Profit* (Chicago: University of Chicago Press, 1979), chaps. 1, 2, 3, and esp. 6, and *Discovery and the Capitalist Process,* chaps. 2, 3, and esp. 4; Frank Knight, *Risk, Uncertainty, and Profit* (Chicago: University of Chicago Press, 1971), chaps. 7 and 9; G. J. Stigler, "Imperfections in the Capital Market," *Journal of Political Economy* 75 (June 1967): 287–92.

One further way of answering Steiner is that profits tend to fall to zero only in the neoclassical or general equilibrium model. It is precisely the *dynamic,* discovery-oriented nature of the market that prevents this from happening. This is a key lesson the Austrian economists have to teach us. For our hot-dog vendor, this means that he will not continue to succeed unless he seeks more opportunities to modify or change his business and, thus, retain its profitability.

50. See note 26 above, on the relation of this sort of property to the theory of subjective value as compared to an objective theory of value and a zero-sum conception of economic transactions.

51. This presentation utilizes a very simplistic, but here untroublesome, analysis of exchange, using the antedated notions of use value and exchange value and presupposing the interpersonal comparison of utilities. It is more technically proper to deal with exchange using more advanced notions from microeconomics. Exchange is often explicated in terms of consumer and producer surplus (see William J. Baumol, *Economic Theory and Operations Analysis,* 4th ed. [Englewood Cliffs, N.J.: Prentice-Hall, 1977], 496–500). Even more common is the use of the Edgeworth Box and contract curve (see Kenneth Boulding, *Economic Analysis,* 4th ed., vol. 1 [New York: Harper & Row, 1966], 627–29). However it is handled, two points remain. First, there is an *exchange surplus.* Second, the exchange is *Pareto improving.* Thus (excepting the limit), both transactants share the surplus and are made better off.

Note also that I have concentrated exclusively on the *gains from trade.* There may as well be *productive efficiencies,* which will contribute to the transaction surplus, providing our hot-dog entrepreneur with wealth and therefore property not taken from others (including his customers). Indeed, if competition drives the price of hot dogs down, it will be the customers, not the entrepreneur, who will be the primary beneficiaries of his productive efficiency.

52. This identification of "net worth" with "retained earnings" is possible in our example only because the "initial capital" or "capital stock" with which our entrepreneur began was equal to zero. Remember, he contributed none of his own money. Had he done so, "net worth" would equal "initial capital" plus "retained earnings."

53. One crucial disclaimer is in order. Nothing in the argument contained

herein constitutes a sanction for a notion of the absolute ownership of property thus created by the individual who created it. The individual (or individuals) who created this property did so against a social background. They learned from their society. They had the protection of property and person necessary to engage in intellectual or entrepreneurial activities. This might well justify a partial claim by society upon the proceeds of such property. Indeed, our society does make such claims. In the patent case, the inventor holds the patent rights for a term of years, after which it belongs to all, that is, it is "in the public domain." Moreover, royalty income is taxed as is any other income. In the business enterprise case, income from the business is taxed and so is the "capital gain" at the time the business is sold (or the appreciation in capital otherwise realized). Indeed, on top of that, many states have an "intangible property tax," directly taxing the property itself.

This theory, then, is consistent both with a strict libertarian notion of near absolute property rights or one inclined to a more welfare capitalist model. But, if property is *created* in this way and, following Locke's proviso, denies nothing to others in its creation, property rights must garner substantial new moral weight.

5

Toward a Lockean Theory of Intellectual Property

Adam D. Moore

Nor was this appropriation of any parcel of land by improving it any prejudice to any other man, since there was still enough and as good left, and more than the yet unprovided could use. So that, in effect, there was never the less left for others because of his enclosure for himself; for he that leaves as much as another can make use of does as good as take nothing at all.

—John Locke, *The Second Treatise of Government*

Introduction

Most of us would recoil at the thought of shoplifting a ballpoint pen from the campus bookstore and yet many do not hesitate to copy software worth thousands of research dollars without paying for it.[1] When challenged, replies like "I wouldn't have purchased the software anyway" or "they still have their copy" are given to try to quell the sinking feeling that something ethically wrong has occurred. Moreover, with the arrival of the information age, where digital formats make copying simple and virtually costless, this asymmetry in attitudes is troubling to those who would defend Anglo-American institutions of property protection.

One way of understanding these replies is to take them to suggest a real difference between intellectual property and physical or tangible property. As noted by Hettinger in chapter 2, my use of your intellectual property does not interfere with your use of it, whereas this is not the case for most tangible goods. Justifying intellectual property in light of this feature raises deep questions and has led many to abandon the romantic image of "Lockean labor mixing" in favor of incentives-based rule-utilitarian justifications. Labor-mixing theories of acquisition may work well when the objects of property can be used and consumed by only one person at a time, but they seem to lose force when the objects of property can be used and consumed by many individuals concurrently.

In what follows, a Lockean theory of intellectual property rights will be explained and defended. In part, I will argue that the non-rivalrous nature of intellectual property, mentioned above, does not pose an insurmountable problem for the Lockean. The first part will consist of a protracted argument, grounded in the Lockean proviso, that seeks to justify individual acts of intellectual property appropriation. In the second part, I will examine how an institution or system of intellectual property might be justified, rather than justifying individual instances of intellectual property acquisition directly.[2] Finally, if successful, my theory will support the original intuition that something ethically wrong has occurred when computer software, music, or other intellectual works are pirated.

Lockean Intellectual Property

Anglo-American systems of intellectual property are typically justified on rule-utilitarian grounds. Rights are granted to authors and inventors of intellectual property "to promote the progress of science and the useful arts."[3] Society seeks to maximize utility in the form of scientific and cultural progress by granting limited rights to authors and inventors as an incentive toward such progress. This approach is, in a way, paradoxical. In order to enlarge the public domain permanently society protects certain private domains temporarily. In general, patents, copyrights, and trade secrets are devices created by statute to prevent the diffusion of information before the author or inventor has recovered profit adequate to induce such investment. The justification typically given for Anglo-American systems of intellectual property "is that by slowing down the diffusion of information these systems ensure that there will be more progress to diffuse."[4]

Many Lockeans, including myself, would like to provide a more solid foundation for intellectual property. Defenders of robust rights to property, be it tangible or intangible property, argue that something has gone awry with rule-utilitarian justifications. Rights, they claim, stand athwart considerations of utility-maximization or promoting the social good.[5] Thus, in generating rights to intellectual property on utilitarian grounds, we are left with something decidedly less than what we typically mean when we say someone has a right.[6] In fact, it may be argued that what has been justified is not a right but something less, something dependent solely on considerations of the overall social good. Alas, if conditions change it may be the case that granting control to authors and inventors over what they produce diminishes overall social utility, and thus, on utilitarian grounds, society should eliminate systems of intellectual property.[7]

Before proceeding toward a Lockean theory of intellectual property, I would like to discuss two important differences between intellectual property and physical property. As noted in the opening, intellectual property is non-rivalrous in the sense that it can be possessed and used by many individuals concurrently. Unlike my car or computer, which can only be used by one person at a time, my recipe for spicy Chinese noodles can be used by many individuals simultaneously. A second major difference between physical and intellectual property is the characterization of their respective pools of appropriatable items. While all matter, owned or unowned, already exists, the same is not true of intellectual property. Putting aside Platonic models, the set of unowned intellectual works is both practically infinite and nonactual. But this commons of intellectual property does not include privately owned intellectual works, and outside of limitations on independent creation (patent law), the same intellectual work may be created and owned by two or more individuals. Thus, in determining what can be legitimately acquired, we must include the set of privately owned intellectual works along with the practically infinite set of nonactual ideas or collections of ideas. Only the set of publicly owned ideas or those ideas that are a part of the common culture are not available for acquisition and exclusion. I take this latter set to be akin to a public park—that is, a commons created and maintained by statute or convention.[8]

Original Acquisition

It is generally the case that individuals acquire property rights via a transfer from previous owners. When assessing the moral status of a property transfer, it is necessary to examine the justification of the previous owner's rights to the object. Ultimately, all current rights to property rest on the acquisition of formerly unowned objects. But under what conditions can removing objects from an unowned state be justified? This is known as the problem of original acquisition.

A common response to this problem is given by John Locke. "For this labor being the unquestionable property of the laborer, no man but he can have a right to what that is once joined to, at least where there is *enough and as good left for others.*"⁹ Moreover, Locke claims that so long as the proviso that enough and as good is left for others is satisfied, an acquisition is of "prejudice to no man."¹⁰ The proviso is generally interpreted as a necessary condition for legitimate acquisition, but I would like to examine it as a sufficient condition.¹¹ If the appropriation of an unowned object leaves enough and as good for others, then the acquisition and exclusion is justified. Suppose that mixing one's labor with an unowned object creates a prima facie claim against others not to interfere that can only be overridden by a comparable claim. The role of the proviso is to stipulate one possible set of conditions where the prima facie claim remains undefeated. This view is summed up nicely by Clark Wolf:

> On the most plausible interpretation of Locke's theory, labor is neither necessary nor sufficient for legitimate appropriation. Mixing labor with an object merely supports a presumptive claim to appropriate. The proviso functions to stipulate conditions in which this presumptive claim will be undefeated, or overriding, and will therefore impose duties of noninterference on others.¹²

Whether or not Wolf has interpreted Locke correctly, this view has strong intuitive appeal. Individuals in a pre-property state are at liberty to use and possess objects. Outside of life or death cases, it is plausible to maintain that laboring on an object creates a weak presumptive possession and use claim against others. Minimal respect for individual sovereignty and autonomy would seem to support this claim. The proviso merely indicates the conditions under which presumptive claims created by labor, and perhaps possession, are not overridden by the competing claims of others. Another way of stating this position is that the proviso in addition to X, where X is labor or first occupancy or some other weak claim generating activity, provides a sufficient condition for original appropriation.

Suppose Fred appropriates a grain of sand from an endless beach and paints a lovely, albeit small, picture on the surface. Ginger, who has excellent eyesight, likes Fred's grain of sand and snatches it away from him. On this interpretation of Locke's theory, Ginger has violated Fred's weak presumptive claim to the grain of sand. We may ask, what legitimate reason could Ginger have for taking Fred's grain of sand rather than picking up her own grain of sand? If Ginger has no comparable claim, then Fred's prima facie claim remains undefeated. An undefeated prima facie claim can be understood as a right.¹³

A Pareto-Based Proviso

The underlying rationale of Locke's proviso is that if no one's situation is worsened, then no one can complain about another individual appropriating part of the commons. Put another way, an objection to appropriation, which is a unilateral changing of the moral landscape, would focus on the impact of the appropriation on others. But if this unilateral changing of the moral landscape makes no one worse off, there is no room for rational criticism.

The proviso permits individuals to better themselves so long as no one is worsened (weak Pareto-superiority). The base-level intuition of a Pareto improvement is what lies behind the notion of the proviso.[14] If no one is harmed by an acquisition and one person is bettered, then the acquisition ought to be permitted. In fact, it is precisely because no one is harmed that it seems unreasonable to object to a Pareto-superior move. Thus, the proviso can be understood as a version of a "no harm, no foul" principle.

It is important to note that compensation is typically built into the proviso and the overall account of bettering and worsening.[15] Gauthier echoes this point in the following case:

> In acquiring a plot of land, even the best land on the island, Eve may initiate the possibility of more diversified activities in the community as a whole, and more specialized activities for particular individuals with ever-increasing benefits to all.[16]

Eve's appropriation may actually benefit her fellows and the benefit may serve to cancel the worsening that occurs from restricted use. Moreover, compensation can occur both at the level of the act and at the level of the practice. This is to say that Eve herself may compensate or that the system in which specific property relations are determined may compensate.

This leads to a related point. Some have argued that there are serious doubts whether a Pareto-based proviso on acquisition can ever be satisfied in a world of scarcity. Given that resources are finite and that acquisitions will almost always exclude, your gain is my loss (or someone's loss). On this model, property relations are a zero-sum game.[17] If this were an accurate description, then no Pareto-superior moves could be made and no acquisitions justified on Paretian grounds. But this model is mistaken. An acquisition by another may worsen your position in some respects but it may also better your position in other respects. Minimally, if the bettering and worsening cancel each other out, a Pareto-superior move may be made and an acquisition justified. Locke recognizes this possibility when he writes,

> Let me add, that he who appropriates land to himself by his labour, does not lessen, but increase the common stock of mankind: for the provisions serving to the support of human life, produced by one acre of enclosed and cultivated land, are ten times more than those which are yielded by an acre of land of equal richness lying waste in common.[18]

Furthermore, it is even more of a stretch to model intellectual property as zero-sum. Given that *intellectual* works are non-rivalrous—they can be used by many individuals concurrently and cannot be destroyed—my possession and use of an intellectual work does not preclude your possession and use of it. This is just to say that the original acquisition of intellectual or physical property does not necessitate a loss for others. In fact, if Locke is correct, such acquisitions benefit everyone.

Before continuing, I will briefly consider the plausibility of a Pareto-based proviso as a moral principle.[19] First, to adopt a less-than-weak Pareto principle would permit individuals, in bettering themselves, to worsen others. Such provisos on acquisition are troubling because at worst they may open the door to predatory activity and at best they give anti-property theorists the ammunition to combat the weak presumptive claims that labor and possession may generate. Part of the intuitive force of a Pareto-based proviso is that it provides little or no grounds for rational complaint. Moreover, if we can justify intellectual property rights with a more stringent principle, a principle that is harder to satisfy, then we have done something more robust, and more difficult to attack, when we reach the desired result.

To require individuals, in bettering themselves, to better others is to require them to give others free rides. In the absence of social interaction, what reason can be given for forcing one person, if she is to benefit herself, to benefit others?[20] If, absent social interaction, no benefit is required, then why is such benefit required within society? Moreover, those who are required to give free rides can rationally complain about being forced to do so, while those who are left (all things considered) unaffected have no room for rational complaint. The crucial distinction that underlies this position is between worsening someone's situation and failing to better it,[21] and I take this intuition to be central to a kind of deep moral individualism.[22] Moreover, the intuition that grounds a Pareto-based proviso fits well with the view that labor and possibly the mere possession of unowned objects create a prima facie claim to those objects. Individuals are worthy of a deep moral respect and this fact grounds a liberty to use and possess unowned objects. Liberty rights to use and possess unowned objects, unmolested, can be understood as weak presumptive claims to objects.

I am well aware that what has been said so far does not constitute a conclusive argument. Rather, I have attempted to show that a Pareto-based proviso is a plausible moral principle. Minimally, those who agree that there is something deeply wrong with requiring some individuals, in bettering themselves, to better others (anything more than weak Pareto-superiority) should find no problem with a Pareto-based proviso on original acquisition. If you do not share my intuitions on this matter, then take the plausibility of the proviso as an assumption.

Bettering, Worsening, and the Baseline Problem

Assuming a just initial position and that Pareto-superior moves are legitimate, there are two questions to consider when examining a Pareto-based proviso.[23] (1) What are the terms of being worsened? This is a question of scale, measurement, or value. An individual could be worsened in terms of subjective preference satisfaction, wealth, happiness, freedoms, opportunities, and so on. Which of these count in determining bettering and worsening (or do they all)? (2) Once the terms of being worsened have been resolved, which two situations are we going to compare to determine if someone has been worsened? Is the question one of how others are now, after my appropriation, compared to how they would have been were I absent, or if I had not appropriated, or some other state? This is known as the baseline problem.

In principle, the Lockean theory of intellectual property rights being developed is consistent with a wide range of value theories.[24] So long as the preferred theory has the resources to determine bettering and worsening with reference to acquisitions, then Pareto-superior moves can be made and acquisitions justified on Lockean grounds. The following sketch of a theory of value is offered as a plausible contender for the correct account of bettering and worsening and should be taken as an assumption. Moreover, aside from being intuitive in its general outlines, the theory fits well with the moral individualism that grounds both a Pareto-based proviso and the view that liberty rights entail weak presumptive claims to objects.

Human well-being or flourishing is the sole standard of intrinsic value. There are at least two reasons to accept this view: first, happiness or flourishing is what is generally aimed at by everyone; and second, it seems absurd to ask what someone wants happiness or well-being for. Although the fact that everyone aims at well-being or flourishing does not establish it as the sole standard of intrinsic value, it does lend credibility to the claim that flourishing is valuable. Moreover, given that well-being is not merely an instrumental good, it is plausible to maintain that it is intrinsically good.[25] Finally, well-being or flourishing is general in scope, meaning that it can accommodate much of what seems intuitively correct about other candidates for intrinsic value (e.g., pleasure, love, friendship).

Human persons are rational project pursuers, and well-being or flourishing is attained through the setting, pursuing, and completion of life goals and projects. Both of these claims are empirical in nature. Humans just are the sort of beings that set, pursue, and complete life goals and projects. Project pursuit is one of many distinguishing characteristics of humans compared to nonhumans—this is to say that normal adult humans are, by nature, rational project pursuers. The second empirical claim is that only through rational project pursuit can humans flourish—a necessary condition for well-being is rational project pursuit where both the process of attaining the goal is rational and the goal itself is rational. Certainly this view is plausible. A person who does not set, pursue, or complete any life goals or projects cannot be said to flourish in the sense of leading a good life—in much the same way that plants are said not to flourish when they are unhealthy or when they do not get enough sunlight or nourishment.[26] Finally, whatever life project or goal is chosen, within certain constraints, individuals will need to use physical and intellectual objects.[27] This should not be taken as an argument for private property, but rather as a claim that material relations and opportunities to better oneself in terms of material relations are objectively, though instrumentally, valuable. So far, the scope and form of the material relations and opportunities are left open.

Any adequate account of bettering and worsening will include an individual's level of material well-being and opportunity costs as part of the measure.[28] Consider the following case. Suppose Fred appropriates all of the land on an island and offers Ginger a job at slightly higher earnings than she was able to achieve by living off of the commons. Although Ginger is worse off in terms of liberties to freely use, she has secured other benefits that may serve to cancel out *this* worsening. So far so good. But now suppose in a few months Ginger would have independently discovered a new gathering technique that would have augmented her earnings fivefold. Having achieved this success, she would have gone on to discover even better techniques ultimately ending in a fully satiated life in the commons. Instead, Ginger spends her life working in quiet drudgery and Fred becomes fully satiated.[29] If Fred does not offer Ginger compensation in the form of a wage most would think that she has been worsened by Fred's appropriation. As it stands, though, Fred has left her at the same level of material well-being but has failed to compensate her for lost opportunities to better herself. It would seem, then, that both one's material advantages and opportunities to better oneself should be included in any account of bettering and worsening.[30]

Opportunity costs are, for the economist, simply the benefits of alternative actions that are forgone when some action is performed, where the outcomes are known with certainty. If Ginger chooses B, then she loses the opportunity to do C and the benefits C would have given her. If she chooses C, then she loses the opportunity to do B and the benefits B would have given her.[31] This is an odd result because if both B and C yield the same outcome (suppose the outcome for both is n) and are mutually exclusive, what is lost? The outcomes are the same, so if B is chosen it seems the only thing that is lost is the bare opportunity to do C. But given the exclusivity of B and C, we cannot even claim to have lost a bare opportunity, because we never had the opportunity to do both. Minimally, and less controversially, we might claim that B (assuming our original example where the payoff of C was $n + 1$ and the payoff of B was n) has an opportunity cost for Ginger of $+1$.

In addressing opportunity costs, it could be argued that the value of an opportunity is a function of the probability and the value of the payoff. The value of an opportunity is a probabilistically weighted value of the various outcomes—this will include the probability that the action in question will produce the outcome, but also the probability that the action in question is available. If it is certain that the outcome of opportunity B is n, then the value or worth of opportunity B is the value of n (assuming that the opportunity is certain). If there is a .5 chance that a noncontingent opportunity B will yield n, then the value of B is half of the value of n.[32] There is a monotonic relationship between the probability of an opportunity (and its results) and the value of the opportunity. This is to say as the probability goes up so does the value and vice versa. In a world of uncertain opportunities (and uncertain results), opportunities are not worth their results; they are worth something less. Compensation for lost opportunities may cost less than it would otherwise appear.[33]

While it is probably the case that there is more to bettering and worsening than an individual's level of material well-being including opportunity costs, I will not pursue this matter further at present. Needless to say, a full-blown account of value will explicate all the ways in which individuals can be bettered and worsened with reference to acquisition.

The Baseline of Comparison

Lockeans, as well as others who seek to ground rights to property in the proviso, generally set the baseline of comparison as the state of nature. The commons or the state of nature is characterized as that state where the moral landscape has yet to be changed by formal property relations. Indeed, it would be odd to assume that individuals come into the world with complex property relations already intact—that individuals or groups have property rights to the universe or parts of the universe. Prima facie, the assumption that the world is initially devoid of such property relations seems much more plausible.[34] The moral landscape is barren of such relations until some process occurs. It is not assumed that the process for changing the moral landscape that the Lockean would advocate is the only justified means to this end.[35]

For now, assume a state-of-nature situation where no injustice has occurred and where there are no property relations in terms of use, possession, or rights. All anyone has in this initial state are opportunities to increase her material standing because it is assumed that there are no current property relations of any sort. Each individual in this state has a specific level of well-being based on legitimate opportunities to increase her standing. Suppose Fred creates an intellectual work and does not worsen his fellows—alas, all they had were contingent opportunities and Fred's creation and exclusion adequately benefits them in other ways. After the acquisition, Fred's level of well-being has changed. Now he has a possession that he holds legitimately, as well as all of his previous opportunities.[36] Along comes Ginger, who creates her own intellectual work and considers whether her exclusion of it will worsen Fred. But what two situations should Ginger compare? Should the acquisitive case (Ginger's acquisition) be compared to Fred's initial state (where he had not yet legitimately acquired anything) or to Fred's situation immediately before Ginger's taking? It seems clear that because an individual's level of well-being changes, the baseline must also change. If bettering and worsening are to be cashed out in terms of an individual's level of well-being with opportunity costs, and this measure changes over time, then the baseline of comparison must also change. In the current case we compare Fred's level of material well-being when Ginger possesses and excludes an intellectual work to Fred's level of well-being immediately before Ginger's acquisition.[37]

The result of this lengthy discussion of material well-being, opportunity costs, and the baseline problem is the following proviso on original acquisition:

If an acquisition makes no one worse off in terms of her level of well-being (including opportunity costs) compared to how she was immediately before the acquisition, then the taking is permitted.[38]

If correct, this account justifies rights to intellectual property. When an individual creates an original intellectual work and fixes it in some fashion, then labor and possession create a prima facie claim to the work. Moreover, if the proviso is satisfied, the prima facie claim remains undefeated and rights are generated.

Suppose Ginger, who is living off of the commons, creates, through a painstaking process, a new gathering technique that allows her to live better with less work. The set of ideas that she has created can be understood as an intellectual work. Given that Ginger has labored to create this new gathering technique, it has been argued that she has a weak presumptive claim to the work. Moreover, it looks as if the proviso has been satisfied given that her fellows are left, all things considered, unaffected by her acquisition. This is to say that they are free to create, through their own efforts, a more efficient gathering system, or even one that is exactly the same as Ginger's.

So far I have been pursuing a kind of top-down strategy in explicating certain moral principles and then arguing that rights to intellectual works can be justified in reference to these principles. In the next section I will pursue a bottom-up strategy by presenting certain cases and then examining how the proposed theory fits with these cases and our intuitions about them.

Test Cases

Suppose Fred, in a fit of culinary brilliance, scribbles down a new recipe for spicy Chinese noodles and then forgets the essential ingredients. Ginger, who loves spicy Chinese food, sees Fred's note and snatches it away from him. On this interpretation of Locke's theory, the proviso has been satisfied and Ginger has violated Fred's right to control the collection of ideas that comprise the recipe. We may ask, what legitimate reason could Ginger have for taking Fred's recipe rather than creating her own? If Ginger has no comparable claim, then Fred's prima facie claim remains undefeated.

We can complicate this case by imagining that Fred has perfect memory and so Ginger's theft does not leave Fred deprived of that which he created. It could be argued that what is wrong with the first version of this case is that Fred lost something that he created and may not be able to recreate. Ginger still betters herself, without justification, at the expense of Fred. In the second version of the case, Fred has not lost and Ginger has gained and so there is nothing wrong with her actions. But from a moral standpoint, the accuracy of Fred's memory is not relevant to his rights to control the recipe and so this case poses no threat to the proposed theory. That intellectual property rights are hard to protect has no bearing on the existence of the rights themselves. Similarly, that it is almost impossible to prevent a trespasser from walking on your land has no bearing on your rights to control, although such concerns will have relevance when determining legal issues. In creating the recipe and not worsening Ginger, compared to the baseline, Fred's presumptive claim is undefeated and thus creates a duty of noninterference on others. One salient feature of rights is that they protect the control of value and the value of control. As noted in the introduction to this anthology, a major difference between rights to intellectual property and rights to physical property is that the former, but not the latter, are rights to types. Having intellectual property rights yields control of the type and any concrete embodiments or tokens, assuming that no one else has independently created the same set of ideas.

Rather than creating a recipe, suppose Fred writes a computer program and Ginger simultaneously creates a program that is, in large part, a duplicate of Fred's. To complicate things further, imagine that each will produce and distribute his or her software with the hopes of capturing the market and that Fred has signed a distribution contract that will enable him to swamp the market and keep Ginger from selling her product. If opportunities to better oneself are included in the account of bettering and worsening, then it could be argued that Fred violates the proviso because in controlling and marketing the software he effectively eliminates Ginger's potential profits. The problem this case highlights is that what individuals do with their possessions can affect the opportunities of others in a negative way. If so, then worsening has occurred and no duties of noninterference have been created. In cases of competition, it seems that the proviso may yield the wrong result.

This is just to say that the proviso is set too high or that it is overly stringent. In some cases where we think that rights to property should be justified, it turns out, on the theory being presented, that they are not. But surely this is no deep problem for the theory. In the worst light it has not been shown that the proviso is not sufficient but only that it is overly stringent.[39] And given what is at stake (the means to survive, flourish, and pursue lifelong goals and projects), stringency may be a good thing. Nevertheless, the competition problem represents a type of objection that poses a significant threat to the theory being developed. If opportunities are valuable, then any single act of acquisition may extinguish one or a number of opportunities of one's fellows. Obviously this need not be the case every time, but if this worsening occurs on a regular basis, then the proposed theory will leave unjustified a large set of acquisitions that we intuitively think should be justified.

Even so, it has been argued that in certain circumstances individual acts of original acquisition can be justified. Protection at this level could proceed along the lines of contracts and licensing agreements between specific individuals. But I think that when pushed, systems or institutions of intellectual property protection will have to be adopted, both to explicate what can be protected legally and to solve competition problems and the like. As was noted early in this chapter, compensation for worsening could proceed at two levels. In acquiring some object, Ginger, herself, could better Fred's position, or the system that they both operate within could provide compensation. This is just to say that it does not matter whether the individual compensates or the system compensates, the agent in question is not worsened.

Justifying an Institution

It has been argued that in determining what it means to be better off and worse off, an "all things considered" notion of well-being should be used, that includes both compensation at the level of the act (micro level) and at the level of the system or practice (macro level). When an individual creates an intellectual work, she may, herself, bring about greater opportunities and wealth for her fellows that serve to compensate them for lost opportunities. But as systems or institutions of property relations arise, the systems themselves may confer benefits that serve to cancel out apparent worsenings. Institutions of property relations may arise that augment everyone's wealth while initiating new opportunities to increase well-being. An example of macro compensation is the possibility of diversified activities that systems of property relations provide for everyone. If macro compensation can and does occur, the question becomes what justifies institutions or systems of property relations.

Rather than trying to justify every particular appropriation by appealing to a Pareto-based version of the proviso, we might try to justify an institution or system. This is similar to the account given by many rule-utilitarians where actions are justified by appealing to rules and rules are justified by appealing to the principle of utility. Consider the following macro proviso (MP) on systems or institutions of property relations.

> MP: If a system of property relations does not worsen any individual in terms of her level of well-being (including opportunity costs), then the system is permitted.

Bettering and worsening are, as before, cashed out in terms of an individual's level of well-being with opportunity costs. At some point in a culture's advancement, a legal system will be developed in part to uphold and defend a system of property relations.[40] Within the Anglo-American tradition the regimes of patent, copyright, and trade secret each serve to protect and maintain private property relations in intellectual works. By adopting a specific institution of property relations, an individual may suffer instances of worsenings that are compensated by the benefits and increased opportunities provided by the system as a whole. This is to say that where micro compensation fails, macro compensation may succeed. The context of the baseline is the chosen system (or the system arrived at by convention) compared to the state-of-nature situation where there is no system of property relations. Since the comparison situation (the state-of-nature situation) includes opportunity costs, we must consider how individuals may have been under alternative systems of property relations.

Problems with assigning probabilities to opportunities in the macro case are more acute than before. The question is, what are the chances that some individual would have been better off under some justified alternative system of property relations? Imagine Ginger's opportunities and level of well-being under a system of property relations where use is based on need compared to her actual situation where she is middle-class and living in Ohio.[41] In assigning probabilities to Ginger's chances for wealth under some justified alternative system of property relations, we use our best empirical information about the alternative system, its average level of material well-being, how it handles tragedy of the commons problems, and so on. If the probabilities cannot be determined because of lack of information, then until such information arises and worsening is determined, the system is permitted. In cases of uncertainty, the shadow of the proviso will hang over both rights to particular items and the system itself.

Suppose there is some alternative system of property relations, Z, that yields Ginger $n + 1$ benefit where the system she finds herself engaged in, R, only nets her n benefit. R would then seemingly violate MP (a macro proviso). If $n + 1$ is certain for Ginger, meaning that if Z had been adopted she would have obtained $n + 1$, then R is illegitimate unless compensation is paid. But as we have seen, it is more likely the case that Ginger would have only had a chance to obtain $n + 1$—she would have had an opportunity to achieve a certain level of well-being under an alternative system of property relations. If opportunities are worth less than the results they promise, then compensation will be some percentage of the $+ 1$ benefit Z would have produced over R for Ginger.

This is a welcome result. The system of property relations that produces the highest level of well-being and opportunities for each individual will satisfy MP. Suppose some system of property relations, R, provides more opportunities and well-being than any competing system. Moreover, suppose R manages what we might generally call tragedy of the commons problems as well as or better than other systems. A tragedy of the commons occurs when unrestricted access and scarcity lead to the destruction of some common resource. In this case R will provide benefits and opportunities over and above its competitors and will most likely satisfy MP. Individual acquisitions may worsen one's fellows so long as the institution provides compensation in the form of opportunities and benefits. This, in a way, solves the competition problem and similar problems (outside of providing compensation) mentioned earlier. The opportunities that Ginger loses when Fred markets his software are dependent on the institution of property relations that they both operate within. It would be illicit for Ginger to complain about lost opportunities that were themselves dependent on competition and private ownership.

It could be argued that there can be no tragedy of the commons in relation to intellectual property. Given that intellectual property cannot be destroyed and can be concurrently used by many individuals, there can be no ruin of the commons.[42] And since there can be no tragedy of the intangible-commons, it is illegitimate to appeal to the benefits that institutions of intellectual property protection would provide on this score.

First, I would like to note that even if this is true it does not undermine the Paretian case for intellectual property institutions. It can still be argued that in providing spiraling opportunities and wealth, systems of intellectual property protection are Pareto-superior when compared to alternative systems. This is just to say that, outside of managing tragedy of the commons problems, systems of intellectual property are still better than competing property arrangements.

Furthermore, upon closer examination I think there can be a tragedy of the commons with respect to intellectual property. To begin, we may ask, "What is the tragedy?" Generally it is the destruction of some land or other object, and the cause of the destruction is scarcity and common access. But the tragedy cannot be the destruction of land or some physical object because, as we all well know, matter is neither created nor destroyed. The tragedy is the loss of value, potential value, or opportunities. Where there was once a green field capable of supporting life for years to come, there is now a plot of mud, a barren wasteland, or a polluted stream. It is claimed that if access is not restricted to valuable and scarce resources the tragedy will keep occurring. A prime example is the Tongan coral reefs that are currently being destroyed by unsavory fishing practices.[43] It seems that the quickest and cheapest way to catch the most fish along the reef is to pour bleach into the water, bringing the fish to the surface and choking the reef.

The tragedy in such cases is not only the loss of current value but of future value. Unless access is restricted in such a way that promotes the preservation or augmentation of value, a tragedy will likely result. Now suppose that intellectual works were not protected—that if they "got out" anyone could profit from them. In such cases, individuals and companies seek to protect their intellectual efforts by keeping them secret. Secrecy was the predominant form of protection used by guilds in the Middle Ages and the result can be described as a tragedy or a loss of potential value. If authors and inventors can be assured that their intellectual efforts will be protected, then the information can be disseminated and licenses granted so that others may build upon the information and create new intellectual works. The tragedy of a complete intellectual commons is secrecy, restricted markets, and lost opportunities.

We are now in a position to examine a seemingly serious objection raised by G. A. Cohen in "Self-Ownership, World-Ownership, and Equality" concerning the baseline. Cohen argues, "When assessing A's appropriation we should consider not only what would have happened had B appropriated, but also what would have happened had A and B cooperated under a socialist economic constitution."[44] B may be better off in a socialistic system of property relations than in a system of private property. And since we are building in opportunity costs, this alternative system would be reflected in B's baseline. So A's appropriation would be unjustified even though he has bettered her situation in relation to a baseline grounded in the commons. Moreover Cohen claims,

> And since a defensibly strong Lockean proviso on the formulation and retention of economic systems will rule that no one should be worse off in the given economic system than he would have been under some unignorable alternative, it most certainly follows that not only capitalism but every eco-

nomic system will fail to satisfy a defensibly strong Lockean proviso, and that one must therefore abandon the Lockean way of testing the legitimacy of economic systems.[45]

If Cohen is correct, any proviso that includes opportunity costs will be set too high to justify property rights—that is, any system of appropriation will make someone worse off.

Cohen's general attack on the context of the baseline will be examined first. His conclusion, "it most certainly follows that not only capitalism but every economic system will fail to satisfy a defensibly strong Lockean proviso, and that one must therefore abandon the Lockean way of testing the legitimacy of economic systems" is mere speculation.[46] Moreover, our discussion of the Lockean proviso has centered around what justifies individual acts of appropriation and systems of property relations, not what legitimates economic systems. Cohen writes as if there is a necessary connection between a system of private property and capitalism. This is clearly false. A system of private property is compatible with many economic arrangements that would not be considered capitalistic (individuals can do what they want with their property and this includes giving it to the collective). That B is better off in some other economic arrangement is not necessarily an indictment against private property, although it may be an indictment against an economic system.

In challenging the context or baseline of any proviso, Cohen might have argued that we must compare alternative systems of property relations (not economic arrangements). Maybe B would be better off under a system of property where need determined use rights and important needs were determined by committee. Only when such a theory is worked out can it be compared to a system of private property, along with tragedy of the commons considerations, which include incentive and efficiency arguments. And even if such an alternative system of property relations yields an individual better prospects, it cannot be concluded that she has been worsened, so long as compensation is allowed.

Institutions of private property are generally beneficial because the internalization of costs discourages value-decreasing behavior. Moreover, by internalizing benefits,

> property rights encourage the search for, the discovery of, and the performance of "socially" efficient activities. Private property rights greatly increase people's incentives to engage in cost-efficient conservation, exploration, extraction, invention, entrepreneurial alertness, and the development of personal and extra-personal resources suitable for all these activities . . .

These rights engender a vast increase in human-made items, the value and usefulness of which tend, on the whole, more and more to exceed the value and usefulness of the natural materials employed in their production.[47]

If this is true, the upshot of this discussion is that the Paretian has the resources to argue for specific institutions of property relations. We have good reason to conclude that the institution of private property can be justified on Paretian grounds. It is likely, especially in light of tragedy of the commons problems and the like, that the institution of private property yields individuals better prospects than any competing institution of property relations.[48] The general strategy has been to argue that institutions of private property are strongly Pareto-superior when compared to their competitors. If this conclusion is probable, and since strong Pareto-superiority greatly overdetermines and entails weak Pareto-superiority, we have good reason to think that the weaker test has been satisfied (see note 14 below).

Conclusion

While the preceding discussion has been sketchy, I think that important steps have been taken toward a Lockean theory of intellectual property. If no one is worsened by an acquisition, then there seems to be little room for rational complaint. The individual who takes a good long drink from a river does as much as to take nothing at all. The same may be said of those who acquire intellectual property. Given allowances for independent creation and that the frontier of intellectual property is practically infinite, the case for Locke's water-drinker and the author or inventor are quite alike. What is objectionable with the theft and pirating of computer software, musical CD's, and other forms of digital information is that in most cases a right to the control of value or the value of control has been violated without justification. Although the force of this normative claim is easily clouded by replies like "but they still have their copy" or "I wouldn't have purchased the information anyway," it does not alter the fact that a kind of theft has occurred. Authors and inventors who better our lives by creating intellectual works have rights to control what they produce. We owe a creative debt to individuals like Aristotle, Joyce, Jefferson, Tolkien, Edison, and Jimi Hendrix.

Notes

1. Adapted from a case in David Carey's *The Ethics of Software Ownership* (Ph.D. Dissertation 1989, University of Pittsburgh). Two examples come from

Lotus and Apple Computers. Lotus claims to lose approximately $160 million a year (over half of the program's potential sales) due to piracy and casual copying of 1–2–3. Apple Computer claims similar losses for MacPaint and MacWrite (see John Gurnsey, *Copyright Theft* [London: The Association For Information Management, 1995], 111–21).

2. My goal in this chapter is not to defend current property holdings or Anglo-American systems of intellectual property as they now stand. As noted by Eric Mack in "Self-Ownership and the Right of Property" (*The Monist* 73 [October 1990]: 539, n2), "One should expect that any philosophical account of the justice of private holdings will undercut rather than sustain certain actual current holdings. Those whose holdings are engorged through impermissible interference with others' free exercise of their property rights have not just claim on their gains."

3. U.S. Constitution, art. 1, sec. 8, para. 8.

4. Joan Robinson, *Science as Intellectual Property* (New York: Macmillan, 1984), 15.

5. There is a kind of global inconsistency to utilitarian justifications of rights within the Anglo-American tradition. Why should my rights to physical property be somehow less subject to concerns of social utility than my rights to intellectual property? Within the Anglo-American tradition, "rights" (to physical property, life, the pursuit of happiness) are typically deontic in nature.

6. For exegetical reasons I will continue to talk of utilitarian-justified "rights" even though what is being justified is, in a deep sense, decidedly different from traditional deontic conceptions of rights.

7. Furthermore, over the past three decades rule-utilitarian moral theory, as well as utilitarian-based justifications for systems of intellectual property, have come under a sustained and seemingly decisive attack. See J. J. C. Smart's "Extreme and Restricted Utilitarianism," in *Theories of Ethics*, edited by Philippa Foot (London: Oxford University Press, 1967); David Lyons, *Forms and Limits of Utilitarianism* (Oxford: Oxford University Press, 1965); R. B. Brandt, *Ethical Theory* (Englewood Cliffs, N.J.: Prentice-Hall, 1959), 396–400; "Toward a Credible Form of Utilitarianism," in *Morality and the Language of Conduct*, edited by H. Castaneda (Detroit: Wayne State University Press, 1963), 107–40; E. Hettinger, "Justifying Intellectual Property," chapter 2 in this volume; and Fritz Machlup, *Production and Distribution of Knowledge in the United States* (Princeton: Princeton University Press, 1962).

8. Although I have claimed that the set of publicly owned ideas or collections of ideas cannot be acquired and held as private property, it could be argued that this need not be so. If an author or inventor *independently* reinvents the wheel and satisfies some rights-generating process, then it may be argued that she has private property rights to her creation. The trouble is, given that the set of ideas that comprise "the wheel" is public property, each of us has current rights to use and possess those ideas. Thus, the inventor in this case may indeed have moral rights to exclude others and to control his idea, but given that we all have similar

rights to the very same collection of ideas, such control and exclusion are meaningless.

9. John Locke, *The Second Treatise of Government*, edited by Thomas P. Peardon (Indianapolis: The Bobbs-Merrill Company, 1952), sec. 27 (italics mine).

10. Locke, *Second Treatise*, sec. 33, 34, 36, 39.

11. Both Jeremy Waldron, "Enough and as Good Left for Others," *Philosophical Quarterly* 29 (1979): 319–28, and Clark Wolf, "Contemporary Property Rights, Lockean Provisos, and the Interests of Future Generations," *Ethics* 105 (July 1995): 791–818, maintain that Locke thought of the proviso as a sufficient condition and not a necessary condition for legitimate acquisition.

12. Wolf, "Contemporary Property Rights," 791–818.

13. For a defense of this view of rights see G. Rainbolt, "Rights as Normative Constraints," *Philosophy and Phenomenological Research* 53 (1993): 93–111; and Joel Feinberg, *Freedom and Fulfillment: Philosophical Essays* (Princeton, N.J.: Princeton University Press, 1986).

14. One state of the world, S_1, is Pareto-superior to another, S_2, if and only if no one is worse off in S_1 than in S_2, and at least one person is better off in S_1 than in S_2. S_1 is *strongly* Pareto-superior to S_2 if everyone is better off in S_1 than in S_2, and *weakly* Pareto-superior if at least one person is better off and no one is worse off. State S_1 is Pareto-optimal if no state is Pareto-superior to S_1: it is *strongly* Pareto-optimal if no state is *weakly* Pareto-superior to it, and *weakly* Pareto-optimal if no state is *strongly* Pareto-superior to it. Throughout this chapter, I will use Pareto-superiority to stand for *weak* Pareto-superiority (adapted from G. A. Cohen's "The Pareto Argument for Inequality," in *Social Philosophy & Policy* 12 [winter 1995]: 160). The term "Pareto" comes from the Italian economist Vilfredo Pareto; see *Manual of Political Economy*, trans. by M. Kelley (New York: John Wiley and Sons, 1966), and William Jaffé's "Pareto Translated: A Review Article," *Journal of Economic Literature* (December 1972).

15. Consider the case where Ginger is better off, all things considered, if Fred appropriates everything than she would have been had she appropriated everything (maybe Fred is a great manager of resources). Although Ginger has been worsened in some respects, she has been compensated for her losses in other respects.

16. Gauthier, *Morals By Agreement* (Oxford: Oxford University Press, 1986), 280.

17. For a more precise analysis of the zero-sum model of property, see James Child's article, "The Moral Foundations of Intangible Property," chapter 4 in this volume.

18. Locke, *Second Treatise*, sec. 37.

19. This minimal defense rests on an underlying moral theory that includes a theory of value and a view of persons as ends in themselves—topics that will concern us later.

20. I have in mind Nozick's Robinson Crusoe case in *Anarchy, State, and Utopia* (New York: Basic Books, 1974), 185.

21. The distinction between worsening someone's position and failing to better it is a hotly contested moral issue. See Gauthier, *Morals by Agreement*, 204; Shelly Kagan, *The Limits of Morality* (Oxford: Oxford University Press, 1989), chap. 3; John Harris, "The Marxist Conception of Violence," *Philosophy & Public Affairs* 3 (1973–74): 192–220; John Kleinig, "Good Samaritanism," *Philosophy & Public Affairs* 5 (1975–76): 382–407; and Eric Mack's two articles, "Bad Samaritanism and the Causation of Harm," *Philosophy & Public Affairs* 9 (1979–80): 230–59, and "Causing and Failing To Prevent Harm," *Southwestern Journal of Philosophy* 7 (1976): 83–90. This distinction is even further blurred by my account of opportunity costs.

22. This view is summed up nicely by A. Fressola. "Yet, what is distinctive about persons is not merely that they are agents, but more that they are rational planners—that they are capable of engaging in complex projects of long duration, acting in the present to secure consequences in the future, or ordering their diverse actions into programs of activity, and ultimately, into plans of life" (Anthony Fressola, "Liberty and Property," *American Philosophical Quarterly* [October 1981]: 320).

23. One problem with a Pareto condition is that it says nothing about the initial position from which deviations may occur. If the initial position is unfair, then our Pareto condition allows that those who are unjustly better off remain better off. This is why the problem of original acquisition is traditionally set in the state of nature or the commons. The state of nature supposedly captures a fair initial starting point for Pareto improvements.

24. It has been argued that subjective preference satisfaction theories fail to give an adequate account of bettering and worsening. See D. Hubin and M. Lambeth's "Providing for Rights," *Dialogue* 27 (1989): 489–502.

25. Mill's proof in *Utilitarianism*, chap. 4, considered to be very contentious, is supposed to establish this claim.

26. For similar views see Rawls, *A Theory of Justice* (Cambridge: Harvard University Press, 1971), chap. 7; Aristotle, *Nicomachean Ethics*, bks. 1 and 10 (New York: Bobbs-Merrill Company, Inc., 1962); Kant, *The Fundamental Principles of the Metaphysics of Morals* (New York: Bobbs-Merrill Company, Inc., 1965); Sidgwick, *Methods of Ethics*, 7th ed. (London: Macmillan, 1907); R. B. Perry, *General Theory of Value* (New York: Longmans, Green, 1926); and Loren Lomasky, *Persons, Rights, and the Moral Community* (New York: Oxford University Press, 1987).

27. A life of both intellectual and physical activity is necessary for human flourishing. Minimally, the claim is that the individual who does not develop her intellectual capacities or engage in an active intellectual life cannot be said to flourish. Similarly, the individual who does not develop her physical capacities or engage in a robust life of physical activity (including material relations) cannot be said to flourish. Life projects that do not accommodate these general facts are irrational. A complete picture of what counts as a rational lifelong project will depend on the underlying moral theory and a refined theory of human nature.

28. Crudely, it is not how you fare *vis-à-vis* some particular object that determines your legitimate wealth, income, and opportunities to obtain wealth. Imagine someone protesting your acquisition of a grain of sand from an endless beach, claiming that she can now no longer use *that* grain of sand and has thereby been worsened. What is needed is an "all things considered view" of material well-being or wealth, income, and opportunities to acquire wealth.

29. Another case similar to the exploited worker case is where Ginger, because she is temporarily sick, has limited capacities to use things. Fred appropriates everything and compensates Ginger for her "sickly capacities" to use rather than her "healthy capacities" to use.

30. At a specific time each individual has a certain set of things she can freely use and other things she owns, but she also has certain opportunities to use and appropriate things. This complex set of opportunities along with what she can now freely use or has rights over constitutes her position materially—this set constitutes her level of material well-being.

31. See Heinz Kohler, *Scarcity And Freedom* (Lexington, Mass.: Heath and Company, 1977), or H. G. Heymann and Robert Bloom, *Opportunity Cost In Finance And Accounting* (New York: Quorum Books, 1990).

32. As a fallback position, we can claim that it is plausible to discount potential benefits if the opportunity or result in question is contingent. It may be sufficient to show that opportunities that have probabilities attached, to either the result or the opportunity itself, are worth less than noncontingent opportunities with results that are certain.

33. The assumption is that, if it were the case that *A* then it might be that *B*. When determining, epistemically, what some probability would be, it is proposed that we proceed as we normally do when assigning probabilities. Historical facts, previous analogous situations, physical laws, and the like should be used in assigning the probability of the consequent of a "might" conditional.

34. One plausible exception is body rights, which are similar to, if not the same as, many of the rights that surround property.

35. There may be many others such as consent theories, consequentialist theories, social contract theories, theories of convention, and so on.

36. Minus the opportunity to acquire the object he just acquired. But then again, his acquisition and exclusion of some object may create other opportunities as well.

37. The case compared to the acquisitive case is assumed to be a situation where no injustice has occurred.

38. The proviso permits the use, exclusion, and augmentation of an object. Although this does not give us a complete theory of property relations, it begins the process. I would argue that the proviso, whatever other forms of property relations it might allow, permits private property relations.

39. In its present state it will be fairly hard to find a problem with sufficiency because of the sketchy status of the account of bettering and worsening presented.

40. I take a virtue of this theory to be that the system adopted will be chosen

on empirical grounds. The system that provides the most opportunities and benefits for each will likely satisfy MP in terms of compensation—in providing spiraling opportunities and benefits a system will compensate those individuals who had the opportunity to be better off in an alternative system. Note: we are not justifying distributions of property within a system, we are justifying the systems or relations themselves.

41. It may be the case that Ginger would not have existed if another system of property relations had been in place. Maybe her parents would have never met if an alternative system had developed. For now, assume that Ginger would have existed in this alternative system of property relations.

42. While intellectual works cannot be destroyed, they may be lost or forgotten—for example, consider the number of Greek or Mayan intellectual works that were lost.

43. The example comes from D. Schmidtz, "When Is Original Acquisition Required?" in *The Monist* 73 (October 1990): 513.

44. G. A. Cohen, "Self-Ownership, World-Ownership, and Equality," in *Justice and Equality Here and Now,* edited by F. Lucash (Ithaca, N.Y.: Cornell University Press, 1986), 132.

45. Cohen, "Self-Ownership," 133.

46. Cohen, "Self-Ownership," 133.

47. Eric Mack, "The Self-Ownership Proviso: A New and Improved Lockean Proviso," *Social Philosophy & Policy* 12 (winter 1995): 207–8.

48. Harold Demsetz in "Toward a Theory of Property Rights," *American Economic Review* 47 (1967): 347–59, argues that an institution of property rights is the answer to the negative externalities that befall the commons. For general discussions, outside of Demsetz, of externalities, see Garrett Harden, "The Tragedy of the Commons," *Science* 162 (1968): 1243–48; Anderson and Hill, "The Evolution of Property Rights: A Study of the American West," *Journal of Law and Economics* 18 (1975): 163–79; N. Scott Arnold, "Economists and Philosophers As Critics of the Free Enterprise System," *The Monist* 73 (October, 1990): 621–639; and Allen Buchanan, "Efficiency Arguments For and Against the Market," in *Justice and Economic Distribution,* edited by John Arthur and William Shaw (Englewood Cliffs, N.J.: Prentice-Hall, 1991).

Part II

Intellectual Property Issues and the Law

6

The Philosophy of Intellectual Property[*]

Justin Hughes

As a slogan, "property" does not have the siren's call of words like "freedom," "equality," or "rights." The Declaration of Independence speaks boldly of liberty, but only obliquely of property—through the imagery of the "pursuit of Happiness."[1] This, however, should not obscure the fact that ideas about property have played a central role in shaping the American legal order. For every Pilgrim who came to the New World in search of religious freedom, there was at least one colonist who came on the promise of a royal land grant or one slave compelled to come as someone else's property.

In the centuries since our founding, the concept of property has changed dramatically in the United States. One repeatedly mentioned change is the trend towards treating new things as property, such as job security and income from social programs.[2] A less frequently discussed trend is that historically recognized but nonetheless atypical forms of property, such as intellectual property, are becoming increasingly important relative to the old paradigms of property, such as farms, factories, and furnishings. As our attention continues to shift from tangible to intangible forms of property, we can expect a growing jurisprudence of intellectual property.

The foundation for such a jurisprudence must be built from an under-

*This essay was originally published as "The Philosophy of Intellectual Property," by Justin Hughes, in the *Georgetown Law Journal* 77 (1988): 287–366. Copyright © 1988 by the Georgetown Law Journal and Georgetown University. Reprinted with permission of publisher. Parts of the text and notes of this article have been omitted.

standing of the philosophical justifications for property rights to ideas—a subject that has never been addressed systematically in American legal literature. Rights in our society cannot depend for their justification solely upon statutory or constitutional provisions. As Justice Stewart said in *Board of Regents v. Roth*, "property interests . . . are not created by the Constitution. Rather they are created and their dimensions are defined by existing rules and understandings that stem from an independent source."[3] This chapter analyzes the "independent sources" that apply to intellectual property by testing whether traditional theories of property are applicable to the very untraditional field of intellectual goods.

Part I of this chapter maps out this field by describing intellectual property. It then explores and explains the justifications for ascribing ownership of such property. The first justification it presents is the Lockean "labor theory," which informed our Constitution's vision of property. This labor justification can be expressed either as a normative claim or as a purely incentive-based, instrumental theory. Both of these aspects of the labor theory are examined in Part II.

The main alternative to a labor justification is a "personality theory" that describes property as an expression of the self. This theory, the subject of Part III, is relatively foreign to Anglo-Saxon jurisprudence. Instead, its origins lie in continental philosophy, especially the work of Georg Wilhelm Friedrich Hegel.[4] Part III argues, however, that more familiar civil rights doctrines, specifically rights of expression and privacy, also can provide a foundation for personality theory in intellectual property. This civil rights justification serves, in large part, as a bridge from American legal doctrines to the more abstract personality justification.

When I say "justification," I do not mean that every aspect of our system of intellectual property should be tortured on some rack of theoretical validity. Instead, I hope to show that the existing law supports, to varying degrees, the credibility of different theories of property and that these theories support, to varying degrees, the validity of existing laws. Some might call this a funhouse epistemology: two things becoming more acceptable by mirroring one another. In fact, this metaphor of "mirroring" is a powerful one that recently has inspired both philosophers and legal thinkers.[5] The latter usually have been concerned with the *normative* question of when and how the law should mirror reality. This chapter's concern differs in two respects. First, its reflection is between law and philosophical theory, not between law and pragmatic reality. Second, this chapter is intended mainly to be descriptive and not prescriptive. It is concerned primarily with answering one question: Does the law of intellectual property reflect general theories of property? In answering this question, however, I invariably fall into discussions motivated by an image of what the theory should be and, reflecting from that image, of what the law should be.

In the end, I suspect that many people who think about property rights are propelled by the same forces that provoked Proudhon to proclaim that "all Property is theft."[6] His slogan, however, is incoherent if taken literally: the idea of theft presupposes that someone else holds legitimate title.[7] If Proudhon meant to exempt certain property from his indictment, then the original dilemma is merely pushed back to the question of defining and justifying the exemption. One of this chapter's fundamental propositions is that property can be justified on either the labor or personality theories and that it should be justified with both. Properly elaborated, the labor and personality theories together exhaust the set of morally acceptable justifications of intellectual property. In short, intellectual property is either labor or personality, *or* it is theft.

I. What Counts as Intellectual Property?

In many quarters, property is viewed as an inherently conservative concept—a social device for the maintenance of the status quo. In the eighteenth century, Edmund Burke argued that property stabilized society and prevented political and social turmoil that, he believed, would result from a purely meritocratic order.[8] Property served as a counterweight protecting the class of persons who possessed it against competition from nonpropertied people of natural ability and talent. To Burke, the French National Assembly—dominated by upstart lawyers from the provinces— exemplified the risk of disorder and inexperience of an unpropertied leadership.[9] In contrast, the British parliament, a proper mix of talented commoners and propertied lords, ruled successfully.[10]

The conservative influence of property does not, however, depend on primogeniture or even inheritance—features that gave property a valuable role in Burke's political system as well as in the political theories advanced by Hegel and Plato.[11] Within a single lifetime, property tends to make the property owner more risk-averse. This aversion applies both to public decisions affecting property, such as taxes, and to personal decisions that might diminish one's property, such as investment strategies and career choices. Inheritance and capital appreciation are only additional characteristics of traditional notions of property that tend to stabilize social stratification.

Intellectual property is far more egalitarian. Of limited duration and obtainable by anyone, intellectual property can be seen as a reward, an empowering instrument, for the talented upstarts Burke sought to restrain. Intellectual property is often the propertization of what we call "talent." It tends to shift the balance toward the talented newcomers whom Burke mistrusted by giving them some insurance against the predilections of the propertied class that had been their patrons. But this is only part of the truth. Much intellectual property is produced only after considerable financial investment, whether it be in the research laboratory or in the graduate education of the scientist using the facility. It would not be surprising if historical studies showed that most holders of copyrights and patents come from at least middle-class backgrounds. For every Abraham Lincoln or Edmonia Lewis who lifted him- or herself from a simple background, there is a Wittgenstein or Welty who enjoyed comfort during his or her formative years.[12] One cannot call the history of intellectual property a purely proletarian struggle. While ancient Roman laws afforded a form of copyright protection to authors, the rise of Anglo-Saxon copyright was a saga of publishing interests attempting to protect a concentrated market and a central government attempting to apply a subtle form of censorship to the new technology of the printing press.[13]

    In the final analysis, intellectual property shares much of the origins and orientation of all forms of property. At the same time, however, it is a more neutral institution than other forms of property: its limited scope and duration tend to prevent the very accumulation of wealth that Burke championed.[14] Because such accumulation is less typical, the realm of intellectual property has less of the laborer/capitalist hierarchy of Marxist theory. The breakthrough patent that produces a Polaroid company is more the exception than the rule. The rule is the modestly successful novelist, the minor poet, and the university researcher—all of whom may profit by licensing or selling their creations. Furthermore, intellectual property may be a liberal influence on society inasmuch as coming to own intellectual property is often tied to being well educated. If people become increasingly progressive with increasing education, intellectual property confers economic power on men and women of talent who generally tend to reform society, not because they are haphazard Burkian goblins, but because they have well-informed convictions.

    At the most practical level, intellectual property is the property created or recognized by the existing legal regimes of copyright, patent, trademark, and trade secret.[15] We also must include property recognized by similar legal regimes. For example, federal law now protects original semiconductor masks.[16] "Gathered information" is another genre of intellectual property. Copyright law protects the particular arrangement of the contents of telephone directories and reference works, while other forms of gathered information may have quasi-property status under *International News Service v. Associated Press.*[17] Like most subjects, intellectual property has gray zones on the periphery, such as the right to publicity—whether, in property style, someone can control his public image.[18]

While this chapter is devoted to American intellectual property, a positivist's definition of intellectual property need not be limited to citations to the United States Code. First, several well-subscribed international treaties create international standards for what counts as intellectual property.[19] At the level of national laws, even socialist economies either have recognized roughly similar parameters to intellectual property or at least have averred their subscription to the general idea of legal regimes for copyright, trademark, and patent.[20] This does not mean that there is international uniformity in the protection granted to intellectual property, only that there are generally accepted baselines of protection. Some countries extend protection well beyond these baselines, while others benignly ignore enforcing or intentionally cut back these general principles.

There is good reason to think that these differences among national legal systems do not represent profound differences in the underlying notions of what intellectual property is all about. Developing countries may fail to promulgate or enforce intellectual property laws simply because these laws are not critical to maintaining immediate social order. Other developing countries intentionally deny protection to intellectual property as part of their official development strategy. Taiwan's long-standing refusal to honor copyrights is an infamous case, but usually the failure to protect intellectual property rights has been more limited and tailored to particular fears of foreign economic domination. Such elimination of intellectual property protection does not reflect a different conception of intellectual property so much as a countervailing social policy. In the final tally, there is at least as much continuity in different societies' understandings of intellectual property as in their respective conceptions of freedom of expression, equality, and property in general.

A universal definition of intellectual property might begin by identifying it as nonphysical property that stems from, is identified as, and whose value is based upon some idea or ideas. Furthermore, there must be some additional element of novelty. Indeed, the object, or *res,* of intellectual property may be so new that it is unknown to anyone else. The novelty, however, does not have to be absolute. What is important is that at the time of propertization, the idea is thought to be *generally* unknown. The *res* cannot be common currency in the intellectual life of the society at the time of propertization.

The *res* is a product of cognitive processes and can exist privately, known only to its creator. This private origin is a reasonable means to distinguish the *res* of intellectual property from the *res* of other intangible properties such as stock or stock options. Although the "inputs" for the *res* of intellectual property are social—the education and nurture of the creator—the assembling of the idea occurs within the mind of the creator, which produces something beyond those inputs. Sometimes the addition is more effort than creativity, as in compilations of information or number-crunching. Some people disfavor describing such efforts as "ideas," but I will use "idea" to refer to this broad notion of the *res*, understanding "idea" to be shorthand for the unique product of cognitive effort.

Intellectual property also may be thought of as the use or the value of an idea. Where X is the idea, intellectual property is defined by the external *functions* of X. The creator introduces the idea into society and, like Henry Higgins, he seeks to control the social calendar of his creation. This Pygmalion story is more apropos than first meets the eye. The creator's control is never complete and he may find himself—like Pygmalion, Higgins, or Dr. Frankenstein—fighting to control that which he has introduced into the world. The most interesting areas of intellectual property law tend to be just those places in which people are trying to hold on to their creations against those who want the creation unfettered from its master. For example, in 1985, Samuel Beckett challenged the Harvard American Repertory Theater's controversial production of Beckett's *Endgame*.[21] The playwright screamed about the integrity of his art; the actors screamed about the freedom of their art, and there was much public debate about constitutional protection of speech, theater versus film, and the evilness of publishing houses.[22]

Even without such debates, intellectual property—like all property—remains an amorphous bundle of rights. However, there are some clear limits to the bundle of rights we will drape around an idea. First, these rights invariably focus on physical manifestations of the res. In the words of one commentator, "a fundamental principle common to all genres of intellectual property is that they do not carry any exclusive right in mere abstract ideas. Rather, their exclusivity touches only the concrete, tangible, or physical embodiments of an abstraction."[23]

Even regarding physical embodiments, there are limitations on intellectual property rights. Copyrighted materials may be copied within the broad limits of statutorily recognized "fair use."[24] "Fair use" focuses on personal use or use that is *not* directly for profit. Yet such uses can be public, such as quoting another's work. Although patents do not have a similar exemption for personal use, patent protection is subject to a judicially created exception: the patent holder has no right against the person whose "use is for experiments for the sole purposes of gratifying a philosophical taste or curiosity or for instruction and amusement."[25] Such limitations are motivated, in part, by pragmatic considerations as to the difficulty of policing such infringements. These limitations, however, also serve the perhaps primary objective of intellectual property: to "promote the Progress of Science and useful Arts" by increasing society's stock of knowledge.[26] Both concerns are best served by limiting property rights over ideas.

Yet even these limited rights are not draped over all ideas. Everyday ideas, like thinking to walk the dog on a shorter leash or to go to the top of the Eiffel Tower on a first date, are not the subject of intellectual property rights. At the opposite extreme, the most extraordinary ideas or discoveries are also beyond the ken of legal protection: the calculus, the Pythagorean theorem, the idea of a fictional two-person romance, the cylindrical architectural column, or a simple algorithm. These extraordinary ideas usually are broadly applicable concepts, but they can be very specific—as in the case of accurate details on a navigation map. I will show how justifications of intellectual property can account for denying the creators of these sorts of ideas property rights over them.

These limits might lead one to conclude that intellectual property is especially positivist in origin, at least compared to property rights over land and chattels. That conclusion may be myopic. Many physical objects also are beyond appropriation, like navigable rivers, beaches, and the airspace in congested urban areas. The use of physical property is circumscribed by laws on easements, zoning, and nuisance. Even the apparent ability to enforce exclusivity over physical property may pose less of a difference than one would think. It is certainly easier for me to enforce my exclusivity over my apartment than over my short story, but what about my ability to exclude others from a ten-thousand-acre Colorado ranch? Is the patent holder worse off than the holder of distant and extensive real estate parcels?

Perhaps the greatest difference between the bundles of intellectual property rights and the bundles of rights over other types of property is that intellectual property always has a self-defined expiration, a built-in sunset. Imagine how different Western society would be if it had developed on the basis of a 100 percent inheritance tax. This difference powerfully distinguishes intellectual property from other property. The remainder of the chapter explains, at various junctures, how this sunset enhances the social neutrality of intellectual property rights and improves the fit between these laws and the theories by which they can be justified.

II. A Lockean Justification

Reference to Locke's *Two Treatises of Government* is almost obligatory in essays on the constitutional aspects of property. For Locke, property was a foundation for an elaborate vision that opposed an absolute and irresponsible monarchy.[27] For the Founding Fathers, Locke was a foundation for an elaborate vision opposed to a monarchy that was less absolute, but seemed no less irresponsible.

Locke's theory of property is itself subject to slightly different interpretations. One interpretation is that society rewards labor with property purely on the instrumental grounds that we *must* provide rewards to get labor. In contrast, a normative interpretation of this labor theory says that labor *should* be rewarded. This part of the chapter argues that Locke's labor theory, under either interpretation, can be used to justify intellectual property without many of the problems that attend its application to physical property.

A. Locke's Property Theory

The general outline of Locke's property theory is familiar to generations of students. In chapter 5 of the *Second Treatise of Government*, Locke begins the discussion by describing a state of nature in which goods are held in common through a grant from God.[28] God grants this bounty to humanity for its enjoyment but these goods cannot be enjoyed in their natural state. The individual must convert these goods into private property by exerting labor upon them. This labor adds value to the goods, if in no other way than by allowing them to be enjoyed by a human being.

Locke proposes that in this primitive state there are enough unclaimed goods so that everyone can appropriate the objects of his labors without infringing upon goods that have been appropriated by someone else.[29] Although normally understood as descriptive of the common, the *enough and as good condition* also is conceptually descriptive of human beings.[30] In other words, this condition is possible because the limited capacities of humans put a natural ceiling on how much each individual may appropriate through labor.

The enough and as good condition protects Locke's labor justification from any attacks asserting that property introduces immoral inequalities. Essentially the enough and as good condition is an equal opportunity provision leading to a desert-based, but *noncompetitive* allocation of goods: each person can get as much as he is willing to work for without creating meritocratic competition against others. What justly can be reduced to property in this primitive state also is limited by Locke's intro-duction of the *non-waste* condition. This condition prohibits the accumu-lation of so much property that some is destroyed without being used.[31] Limited by this condition, Locke suggests that even after the primitive state there sometimes can be enough and as good left in the common to give those without property the opportunity to gain it. Spain and America, he says, illustrate the continuing applicability of this justifica-tion of property.[32]

Until this point in his exposition, Locke does not explore the notion of labor and the desert it creates. His theory is largely a justification by negation: under his two conditions there are no good reasons for not granting property rights in possessions. This has led scholars such as Richard Epstein to a possession-based interpretation of Locke. Epstein argues that "first possession" forms the basis for legal title and believes that this is the heart of Locke's position. For Epstein, the talk of labor is a smoke screen hiding the fundamental premise of Locke's argument that a person possesses his own body:

> Yet if that possession is good enough to establish ownership of self, then why is not possession of external things, unclaimed by others, sufficient as well? The irony of the point should be manifest. The labor theory is called upon to aid the theory that possession is the root of title; yet it depends for its own success upon the proposition that the possession of self is the root of title to self.[33]

It is unclear why Epstein should reach this conclusion. Locke never mentions one's *possession* of one's body as the basis for one's property in one's body; he begins simply by asserting one's body is one's property.[34] Yet Epstein connects property to possession by saying, "the obvious line for justification is that each person is in possession of himself, if not by choice or conscious act, then by a kind of natural necessity."[35]

Epstein directly, albeit unknowingly, points out a critical difference: we are not in possession of any particular external objects by a kind of natural necessity. If we were, the need for property laws would be greatly diminished. Each person, like a tree, would be rooted to his own parcel of external objects; this would be "of natural necessity," and no one would try to displace another from his natural and necessary attachments. Precisely because "natural necessity" goes no further than the mind/body link, reliance upon the "possession" of body as a foundation for a posses-sion-based justification of property is a bit disingenuous.[36]

Epstein's possession-based theory also seems inaccurate because Locke offers a positive justification for property that buttresses his labor theory. He suggests that granting people property rights in goods procured through their labor "increase[s] the common stock of mankind," a utilitarian argument grounded in increasing mankind's collective wealth.[37]

This justification is called into question by an obvious problem. If the new wealth remains the private property of the laborer, it does not increase the common stock. If it can be wantonly appropriated by the social mob, the laborer will realize quickly that he has no motivation to produce property and increase the common stock. One solution would be to rely upon the laborer's donations to the common, but increasing the common stock cannot be made to depend on supererogatory acts. The better solution—one that Locke in fact advocated—is to make this added value *potentially* part of the common stock by introducing the money economy.[38]

In depicting the transition to a money economy, Locke assumes that: (1) the individual is capable of appropriating more than she can use; (2) the individual will be motivated to do so; and (3) nothing is wrong with this other than waste. Locke condemned waste as an unjustified diminution of the common stock of potential property. To allow goods to perish after appropriating them—and thereby removing them from a state in which others could have made use of them—violates "the Law of Nature."[39] Stripped of its Lockean vestments, this non-waste principle can also be understood as an impulse to avoid labor when it produces no benefits. The waste is not just spoiled food, but the energy used gathering it. The non-waste condition, however, allows the individual to barter for things which he can enjoy, which may be more durable, and which have been gathered as surplus by other individuals similarly motivated.

Finally, Locke justifies the allocation of property in this more-advanced money economy by tacit consent. For Locke, positive laws that manifest "disproportionate and unequal possession of the Earth" derive their authority from the tacit consent that people have given to be governed.[40] Modern writers have debated how much importance should be put on this hypothetical consent.[41] In the final analysis, Locke's overall scheme for property can be viewed as an alloy of the labor and tacit consent theories.[42] Yet it is the labor justification that has always been considered uniquely Lockean. Accordingly, when I refer to a "Lockean" theory of property, I will be referring to his labor justification.

We can justify propertizing ideas under Locke's approach with three propositions: first, that the production of ideas requires a person's labor; second, that these ideas are appropriated from a "common," which is not significantly devalued by the idea's removal; and third, that ideas can be made property without breaching the non-waste condition. Many people implicitly accept these propositions. Indeed, the Lockean explanation of intellectual property has immediate, intuitive appeal: it seems as though people *do* work to produce ideas and that the value of these ideas—especially since there is no physical component—depends solely upon the individual's mental "work." The following sections of this chapter test the strength of such a vision.

B. Labor and the Production of Ideas

A society that believes ideas come to people as manna from heaven must look somewhere other than Locke to justify the establishment of intellectual property. The labor theory of property does not work if one subscribes to a pure "eureka" theory of ideas. Therefore, the initial question might be framed in two different ways. First, one would want to determine if society believes that the production of ideas requires labor. Second, one might want to know whether or not, regardless of society's beliefs, the production of ideas *actually does* require labor. This second question is the metaphysical one; in its shadow, society's belief may appear superficial. It is not. We are concerned with a justification of intellectual property, and social attitudes—"understandings," as Justice Stewart said—may be the only place to start.

Some writers begin with the assumption that ideas always or usually are the product of labor. For example, Professor Douglas Baird assumes that although one cannot physically possess or occupy ideas, property in ideas is justified because people "have the right to enjoy the fruits of their labor, even when the labors are intellectual."[43] He believes the great weakness in this justification is that others also need free access to our ideas.[44] In Lockean terms, this is an "enough and as good" problem. Baird, however, never considers the prospect that idea-making may not involve labor.

Of course, there are clear instances in which ideas seem to be the result of labor: the complete plans to a new suspension bridge, the stage set for a Broadway show, a scholar's finished dissertation involving extensive research, or an omnibus orchestration of some composer's concertos. The peripheral realms of intellectual property also provide examples in which the object immediately seems to be the product of tremendous work: news stories gathered and disseminated by wire services, or stock indexes calculated by a financial house. The images of Thomas Edison inventing the lightbulb and George Washington Carver researching the peanut come to mind as examples of laborious idea-making. As society has moved toward more complicated technologies, the huge scales of activity required by most research, involving time, money, and expertise, have made the autonomous inventor a rarity. This trend strengthens the image of idea-making as labor akin to the mechanical labor that operates industrial assembly lines.

Yet as we move toward increasingly large research laboratories that produce patentable ideas daily, we should not be so entranced by the image of a factory that we immediately assume there is labor in Silicon Valley. Locke, after all, begins his justification of property with the premise that initially only our bodies are our property.[45] Our handiwork becomes our property because our hands—and the energy, consciousness, and control that fuel their labor—are our property. The point here is not validation of Epstein's link of property with bodily self-possession but rather the more general observation that Locke linked property to the product of the individual person's labor. We must examine the production of ideas more fully if we expect to show that their creation involves Lockean labor.

1. The "Avoidance" View of Labor

If we surveyed people on their attitudes toward idea-making, what might we find? First, we would probably find that many people who spend time producing ideas prefer this activity to manual labor. It probably also is true that many manual laborers would rather spend time producing ideas than performing manual labor. That an idea-maker prefers idea-making to farming, roofing, or putting screws in widgets suggests that idea-making may not be viewed as laboring the same way that the latter activities are. It may share this distinction with such professions as competitive sports. Yet at least at some level of desires, the idea-maker probably prefers to be on vacation than to be in his office or laboratory. For most people creation is less fun than recreation. Although "idea work" is often exhilarating and wonderful, it is something we generally have to discipline ourselves to do, like forcing oneself to till the fields or work the assembly lines.

This discussion depicts labor in one particular way: something that people avoid or want to avoid, something they don't like, an activity they engage in because they must. Lawrence Becker aptly has described Locke's view of labor as a "proposal that labor is something unpleasant enough so that people do it only in the expectation of benefits."[46] In fact, Locke himself refers to labor as "pains."[47]

One commentator has observed that this concept of labor is more likely the product of experience than logical rigor:

[Comparing labor and property] is complicated by an equivocation about the idea of labor, which is dominated by the metaphor of sweat on the brow.

Hence it is that the least imaginative work counts most securely as labor. The squires and merchants of the seventeenth century were far from idle men, but administration and entrepreneurship do not so obviously qualify for the title of labor as the felling of trees and the planting of corn.[48]

In an understanding of labor based on the notion of "avoidance," labor is defined as an unpleasant activity not desirable in and of itself and even painful to some degree.

At this point we can separate the normative proposition of the labor theory from the instrumental argument with which it is usually identified.[49] The normative proposition states: *the unpleasantness of labor should be rewarded with property.* In this proposition, the "should" is a moral or ethical imperative, which is not based on any consideration of the *effects* of creating property rights. In comparison, the instrumental argument is directly concerned with those effects. It proposes that the unpleasantness of labor should be rewarded with property *because people must be motivated to perform labor.* In principle, the two propositions can coexist but neither requires acceptance of the other. In practice, however, the two not only coexist, but the instrumental argument often seems to be treated as a "proof" of the normative argument. The instrumental claim has a utilitarian foundation: we want to promote labor because labor promotes the public good. Once we recognize that property is needed to motivate work for the public good, we may transform the reward into a right just as we often convert systematically granted benefits into rights *deserved* by the recipients. Perhaps we do this because it would be inconsistent and disconcerting to say that some systematically granted benefit is not deserved. Perhaps we just make the transition from instrumental to normative propositions through lack of attention. For example, in the 1954 case *Mazer v. Stein,* the Court said:

> The economic philosophy behind the clause empowering Congress to grant patents and copyrights is the conviction that *encouragement* of individual effort by personal gain is the best way to advance public welfare through the talents of authors and inventors. . . . Sacrificial days devoted to such creative activities *deserve* rewards commensurate with the services rendered.[50]

As *Mazer* demonstrates, it is strikingly easy to move from an instrumental discussion of consequences to an assumption of just rewards.

Indeed, when the normative proposition emerges in court opinions it is usually used as an adjunct to the instrumental argument. The instrumental argument clearly has dominated official pronouncements on American copyrights and patents. Even the Constitution's copyright and patent clause is cast in instrumental terms. Congress is granted the power to create intellectual property rights in order "To promote the Progress of Science and useful Arts."[51] As President Lincoln remarked, "the inventor had no special advantage from his invention [under English law prior to 1624]. The patent system changed this. . . . It added the fuel of interest to the fire of genius in discovery and production of new and useful things."[52] In almost all of its decisions on patents, the Supreme Court has opined that property rights are needed to motivate idea-makers. This instrumental justification is the heart of what Judge Easterbrook has called the Supreme Court's "Ex Ante Perspective on Intellectual Property."[53]

The wide acceptance of the instrumental argument suggests wide acceptance of the premise that idea-making is a sufficiently unpleasant activity to count as labor that requires the inducement of reward. Admittedly, this hardly is a tight argument. Idea-making just as easily could be a neutral activity or even a pleasant activity whose pursuit individuals covet. The issue is not whether idea-making is an absolutely unpleasant activity, but whether it is comparatively less pleasant and less desirable than other activities. As Peter Rosenberg writes in his treatise on patent law, "while necessity may be the mother of invention, the quest for new products and technologies must fiercely compete against the demands for current consumption."[54] The judgments we make about most forms of labor are not that they are absolutely unpleasant, but that they are *relatively* unpleasant. For most people, raking leaves is relatively unpleasant compared to sitting and watching them fall. Similarly, there is a widespread attitude that idea-making is not such a pleasant activity that people will choose it, by itself, over recreation. At least, people will not choose it in sufficient numbers to meet our collective needs. This same characterization applies to labor in the fields, the forests, and the factories. That is our best grounds for assuming that idea-making is a form of labor.

If we believe that an avoidance theory of labor justifies intellectual property, we are left with two categories of ideas: those whose production required unpleasant labor and those produced by enjoyable labor. Are the latter to be denied protection? This strange result applies to all fruits of labor, not just intellectual property.

2. The "Value-Added" Labor Theory

Another interpretation of Locke's labor justification can be called the "labor-desert" or "value-added" theory. This position "holds that when labor produces something of value to others—something beyond what morality requires the laborer to produce—then the laborer deserves some benefit for it."[55] This understanding of property does not require an analysis of the idea of labor. Labor is not necessarily a process that produces value to others. It is counterintuitive to say labor exists only when others value the thing produced. It also would be counter to Locke's example of the individual laboring and appropriating goods for himself *alone*. The "labor-desert" theory asserts that labor often creates *social* value, and it is this production of social value that "deserves" reward, not the labor that produced it.

The legal history of intellectual property contains many allusions to the value-added theory. The legislative histories of intellectual property statutes refer repeatedly to the value added to society by investors, writers, and artists. Indeed, those judicial or legislative statements that appear to fuse the normative and instrumental propositions of the labor justification are perhaps based, unknowingly, on the value-added theory. In *Mazer v. Stein*, the Court appeared to be saying that the enhancement of the public good through the efforts of intellectual laborers made the creators of intellectual property *worthy* of reward.[56] In other words, their contribution to the public good justified the reward of property rights. Earlier I noted that the Constitution's copyright and patent clause is an instrumental provision. More precisely, it is an instrumentalist provision aimed at rewarding people who bring added value to the society. Little else could have been meant by giving people "the exclusive Right to their respective Writing and Discoveries" in order "to promote the Progress of Science and useful Arts."[57]

The value-added theory usually is understood as an instrumentalist or consequentialist argument that people will add value to the common if some of the added value accrues to them personally. Paralleling the discussion of the avoidance theory of labor, it is possible also to treat the value-added theory as a normative proposition: people *should* be rewarded for how much value they add to other people's lives, regardless of whether they are motivated by such rewards.

Some kinds of intellectual property have appeared only in contexts in which the property represents a value added to the society. *International News Service v. Associated Press* inaugurated "quasi-property" protection for gathered information.[58] The opinion merged unfair competition doctrine and property arguments to prohibit one party's appropriation of the product of another party's labor. Such appropriations occur only when the party taking the product believes it to have some value. To state the proposition differently, one could not argue that it is *unfair competition* to take away someone's *worthless* labor.

Unfair competition is the purloining of another's competitive edge—an "edge" that has social value. Insofar as protection of gathered information rests on an unfair competition model, it necessarily relies on the value-added justification. If the fruits of labor have no prospective value, stealing those fruits may be socially unkind, but not competitively unfair. Similarly, trade secret infringement cases result from claimed losses of social value by the petitioner. No court has ever had to face a test case of a vigorously defended but worthless trade secret.

There is a very simple reason why the legal doctrines of unfair competition and trade secret protection are inherently oriented toward the value-added theory: they are court-created doctrines and people rarely go to court unless something valuable is at stake. When intellectual property is created more systematically, such as through legislation, the resulting property doctrines seem less singularly oriented toward rewarding social value.

Indeed, patents provide a vexing example of conflicting reliance on the value-added theory. To receive patent protection, a new invention must meet a standard of "usefulness" or "utility," a criterion that suggests that the invention must manifest some value added to society.[59] On closer inspection, the meaning of this criterion is not so clear. At one extreme, it has been expressed as being devoid of a "value-added" requirement and as only mandating that the invention not be, on its face, wholly valueless. In *Lowell v. Lewis* Justice Story eloquently expressed this position:

> All that the law requires is, that the invention should not be frivolous or injurious to the well-being, good policy, or sound morals of society. The word "useful", therefore, is incorporated into the act in contradistinction to mischievous or immoral. . . . But if the invention steers wide of these objections, whether it be more or less useful is a circumstance very material to the interests of the patentee, but of no importance to the public. If it be not extensively useful, it will silently sink into contempt and disregard.[60]

While this standard was incorporated into nineteenth-century American patent jurisprudence, modern tests for the utility criterion support a value-added interpretation.[61] Most courts now hold that a "step forward" or an "advance over prior art" is a critical part of the utility requirement. But these tests seem to blur the utility criterion with the "novelty," "obviousness," and "operability" requirements of patent grants.

It is not necessary to separate these modern standards in order to appreciate how they generally bear on the value-added question. Stated succinctly, they require that an invention be enough of an advance over the previous art so that the average person schooled in the art would not consider the advance immediately obvious, but also would understand how the invention improves upon previously available technology. The invention need not function perfectly, but it must operate effectively enough that a person schooled in the art could make it perform the tasks described in the patent application.

To require that something be an "advance" over existing technology clearly demands that there be new value in this item; that the invention be "nonobvious" raises the threshold of the additional value requirement. Obvious improvements add some value to existing art, but it is only modest value because anyone trained in the art can see the improvement almost as a matter of intuition. The patent law requires that the new value be greater than that derived from "tinkering" with known technology.[62]

Those standards seem conclusively to manifest a value-added requirement. There are, however, some complexities. In discussing the operability criteria, Peter Rosenberg aptly describes a well-accepted patent doctrine that seems to pose a strong counterargument to the value-added requirement:

> To satisfy the operability standard, an inventor need not establish that his invention is better than, or that it is even as good as, existing means for accomplishing the same result. . . . The law does not ask *how* useful is the invention. A device that may not operate well may nevertheless be operative.[63]

An invention that is not as effective or efficient as the existing means for accomplishing the same result does not add value to society—at least not in a direct and straightforward way.[64] Nonetheless, the patent law covers such inventions. For example, one could patent an advance in vacuum tube computers although it is hard to imagine a technology so completely replaced by its successor. Usually a succeeding technology leaves the older technology with peripheral or special area applications, but chip technologies have replaced vacuum tubes so thoroughly in computer applications that any value added by a vacuum tube advance would be minimal or nonexistent.

Similarly, patent scholars have not agreed with the presumed patentability of items that are technological "advances" without any *imaginable* value. A good hypothetical is a new vote-counting machine that errs by up to 10 percent in any vote tabulation. Not only is this worse than existing technology, but its operation has absolutely *no value*. People will count votes by hand before they will entrust it to a machine erring 10 percent. If this kind of "operable" machine is not patentable, it is evidence of the value-added justification. If it is patentable, that patent clearly is granted without any consideration of added value.

A patentee is not required to exploit his patent; indeed, there is universal recognition that the patentee may shelve his invention and use his patent only to prevent others from utilizing the patented process or invention. This hardly seems to mesh with the requirement that there be value delivered to the society as a prerequisite for granting property rights.

Copyright law also seems to defy value-added reasoning. As with patents, one can register a writing for copyright protection without ever planning to publish the work. For copyrighted works, no statutory provision demands "value." Indeed, thousands of worthless works are probably copyrighted every month. Bad poetry, box office failures, and redundant scholarly articles are not denied copyright protection because they are worthless or, arguably, a net loss to society.

The interesting issue of proportional contributions further evinces the degree to which the value-added justification underpins intellectual property law. Modern industry depends on equipment and machines utilizing multiple patents to carry out a single activity. Through patent-licensing schemes, patent owners share proportionally in the aggregate value of the intellectual property in such machines. However, the same ability to distribute value has eluded the copyright system.

A modest copyright apportionment doctrine was established in *Sheldon v. Metro-Goldwyn Pictures*.[65] In *Sheldon,* both Judge Hand and Justice Hughes upheld the apportionment of only 20 percent of the profits to the plaintiff when the defendant's infringing film used only a small part of the plaintiff's play and expert testimony attributed the movie's success to its popular stars, not the script.[66] But even while making the award, Hand wrote of apportionment that, "strictly and literally, it is true that the problem is insoluble."[67] The common wisdom, with some scholarly debate, has been to follow the *Sheldon* dictum instead of attempting its result.

That the apportionment system has appeared as an ideal in copyright is homage to people's belief in the value-added theory as a normative standard: social value contributed *should* be rewarded. The fact that an apportionment system in copyright has remained only an ideal is explicable for several reasons. Certainly apportionment could produce uncertain shifts in incentives. It might encourage infringements and discourage originality by lowering the awards against infringers. On the other hand, it might strengthen enforcement by tempting judges to find infringements more often.

Apportionment may remain impractical in copyright for the same reason it would be impractical to have any value-added requirement in copyright law. The "insoluble" problem for apportionment is measuring the value of a copyrighted work when it forms part of a larger work whose value can be measured by objective criteria, such as box office receipts or number of copies sold. The corresponding problem for a preliminary value requirement in copyright is that it is much harder to predict whether a writing will have value than to do so for an invention. It is often startling to see what copyrighted works are ultimately judged valuable by society. Before the precocious judgment of history, a "step forward" in literature or in the arts is easily confused with a step sideways or backwards.

A value-added interpretation of intellectual property laws is easier to support by moving away from particular legal doctrines. Probably the best support for the value-added theory is an argument based upon "net gain." This rule-utilitarian argument for granting intellectual property rights finds it unnecessary that individual cases of copyright or patents be of social value. A very high percentage of protected works could be worthless so long as the system of property protection results in a net increase in social value beyond what would be produced without the system.

3. Labor and the Idea/Expression Distinction

The avoidance and value-added interpretations of the labor theory have very different foci. The avoidance theory argues that labor, by its nature, is unpleasant. The value-added theory places no limits on the general nature of labor; it can be pleasant or unpleasant, stupefying or invigorating. The value-added theory may explain why labor justifies property at the social level, while the avoidance theory makes the *individual* feel justified in receiving something for his "pains." But this still leaves unresolved the nettlesome question of whether or not producing intellectual property actually requires labor.

For the moment, let us treat the creation of a finished intellectual product as a two-step process. One step is thinking up the "idea," used here in the usual sense of the creative element or unique notion. The second step is the work necessary to employ the idea as the core of a finished product. In the case of an innovative suspension bridge, the engineer has an original idea and then spends months doing all the drawings and calculations necessary to produce the finished plans. Edison had the idea of a light source produced by electrons traveling through a filament within a vacuum. He and his workers then spent weeks finding the proper filament material, the proper vacuum, and the proper electrical charge.

These two steps represent the difference between idea and execution. Sometimes this difference is not readily visible or, when it does exist, the part we identify as the idea may seem the less important of the two components. *Sartoris* and *Absalom, Absalom!* have the "same" idea: the not too original notion of the saga of a Southern family.[68] The difference, the uniqueness, and the importance to society is in the execution. The idea of orchestrating *Pictures at an Exhibition,* Mussorgsky's 1874 composition for solo piano, is not worth much in itself, nor is the thought of doing a painting of the front of the Rouen Cathedral basked in sunlight. But each idea has proved to be a foundation for more than one significant execution.

In these examples, the distinction between idea and execution is drawn at a gross level. Although the distinction may seem intuitively right, it can be blurred and redrawn by focusing on different levels of detail. There is not just the idea of orchestrating a piano piece, but the more-detailed idea of using a particular motif in the third movement, and the even more detailed idea of using a particular percussion instrument in the forty-seventh stanza of that movement. The achievement in writing fiction or in composing may be in the execution precisely because each turn of phrase, musical or literally, is the result of a creative event.

The creativity we perceive in an intellectual product may be either in the core idea or in the core idea's execution. I suggest that when we readily can separate the two, execution always seems to involve labor, but it is not always clear that the creation of the idea involves labor. Ideas often seem to arrive like Athena—suddenly they are here, full and complete. Like Zeus, we may have a headache in the process, but it is some unseen Minerva who puts in the labor.

Yet our inability to formulate any clear separation between idea and execution suggests that we should treat them as one. This apparent inability is reinforced by occasions in which the "execution" step begins before the idea. In many fields, one has to do extensive research to create a necessary launching pad for a new idea. A graduate law student writing his doctoral paper made the telling comment, "If I had six more months to work on this paper, it would be an original idea."[69]

The Lockean conception of idea-making provides another ground for treating idea and execution as a single event. Viewing new ideas as plucked from some Platonic common may be reification in the extreme. Yet in that view, the ideas already exist and the chief labor is transporting them from the ethereal reaches of the idea world to the real world where humanity can use them.[70] If ideas are thought of as such preexistent Platonic forms, the *only* activity possible is execution, which consists of transporting, translating, and communicating the idea into a form and a location in which humans have access to it.

Existing intellectual property regimes favor granting property rights only to those ideas that have received substantial execution. Patents are not granted for formulae disembodied from any technical applications; in some sense, such unapplied formulae may be thought of as unexecuted ideas. A book or dissertation receives copyright protection, not its underlying thesis statement. One might even point to the fact that federal copyright protection applies only to work put into some permanent, tangible form—which suggests a requirement of execution.

With products such as phone directories or some news stories, execution—a product of labor—is all that realistically can be required because there is no original idea. *Time, Inc. v. Bernard Geis Associates,* in which the Zapruder film of the Kennedy assassination was recognized as copyrightable property, provides an interesting application of this same standard.[71] Clearly, Zapruder had no original idea—most people in his position and equipped with a camera would have filmed that tragic event. Zapruder's case is a dramatic example of copyright protection in the category of nonartistic photos and films of public events and places. It demonstrates that a unique *product* of one's labor can receive property protection even if there is no unique underlying *idea.*

The case law of section 102 of the 1976 Copyright Act has developed what has been called "the idea/expression dichotomy." Under this doctrine, "expressions" are protected but the underlying "ideas" are not. Not surprisingly, the courts have never developed a clear distinction between the two, relying instead on comparisons such as between the idea of a male nude and the expression of the *David.* When one replicates a series of *scènes à faire* to make a story, there is no copyright problem; when one reproduces sets and production techniques, there is.[72] Illicit copying is copying an expression, "the total concept and feel" of a work, not just the idea.

The idea/expression dichotomy is frequently explained in terms of balancing the need to reward artists with the need for free access to ideas, or as a tension between the copyright clause and the first amendment. Although this theory has never been explicitly considered by the Supreme Court, Justice Douglas was one of its adherents. In a 1980 opinion, the Ninth Circuit also confidently stated this rationale: "The impact, if any, of the first amendment on copyright has not been discussed by the Court. We believe this silence stems not from neglect but from the fact that the idea-expression dichotomy already serves to accommodate the competing interests of copyright and the first amendment."[73] While not abandoning this view, Professor Melville Nimmer showed that there are occasions in which the idea/expression distinction does not ensure access to all the expressions we might want freely available from a First Amendment perspective.[74] In a society that relies on freedom of expression, there is a constant demand that many "expressions" be part of the public domain, such as photographs and films of very important events.[75]

I suggest that the idea/expression dichotomy and the idea/execution dichotomy are the same.[76] At a minimum, the force behind the latter dichotomy—the concern for *labor*—significantly contributes to explaining the idea/expression division. The courts' ad hoc approach in this area suggests that copyrightability may be based as much on what we feel are people's deserts as on what we feel are society's informational needs. It has been said that the idea/expression issue is uniquely well suited for juries.[77] I suggest that this is so not because juries care about a doctrine that ameliorates copyright and First Amendment tensions and not because they know what idea-making is, but rather because jurors sense what *labor* is.

First Amendment considerations define the "idea" side of the copyright dichotomy—that which must be kept as a public preserve. Labor defines the "expression" side—that which must be rewarded because it is unpleasant activity. Protection of expression and not of ideas can be understood as protection for that part of the idea-making process that we are most confident involves labor. In a world in which we cannot definitely separate idea and execution, we still find ways to emphasize that property protection goes to execution and less to the ideas themselves.

In fact, these First Amendment concerns have a place in a Lockean theory. In a Lockean framework, First Amendment freedom manifests a problem with the "common." Stated simply, some ideas and facts cannot be removed from the common because there would not be the slightest chance of there being "enough and as good" afterwards. Imagine the absurdity of a political debate in which some people held copyrights over certain "new ideas." This leads to the second element of a Lockean theory of intellectual property: the common.

C. Ideas and the Common

It requires some leap of faith to say that ideas come from a "common" in the Lockean sense of the word. Yet it does not take an unrehabilitated

Platonist to think that the "field of ideas" bears a great similarity to a common.

The differences between ideas and physical property have been repeated often. Physical property can be used at any one time by only one person or one coordinated group of people. Ideas can be used simultaneously by everyone. Furthermore, people cannot be excluded from ideas in the way that they can be excluded from physical property. You may prevent someone from publicly using an idea, but preventing the private use of ideas may not be possible. These two basic differences between ideas and physical goods have been used by some writers to argue *against* intellectual property, but, if anything, they suggest that ideas fit Locke's notion of a "common" better than does physical property.[78]

The "field" of all possible ideas prior to the formation of property rights is more similar to Locke's common than is the unclaimed wilderness. Locke's common had enough goods of similar quality that one person's extraction from it did not prevent the next person from extracting something of the same quality and quantity. The common did not need to be infinite; it only needed to be practically inexhaustible. With physical goods, the inexhaustibility condition requires a huge supply. With ideas, the inexhaustibility condition is easily satisfied; each idea can be used by an unlimited number of individuals. One person's use of some ideas (prior to intellectual property schemes) cannot deplete the common in *any* sense. Indeed, the field of ideas seems to expand with use.

It may seem pointless to talk about how the field of possible ideas fulfills Locke's conception of the common prior to the creation of property, for the common is a concept discussed only in connection with the creation of property. The point is that Locke's treatment of the common implicitly concerns itself with the problems of distribution. This distribution problem also arises in pre-property uses of the physical common. When some starve in a pre-property world because others overconsume food or occupy all the tillable land, there is a problem of just distribution. Such distribution problems are not found in pre-property uses of the field of ideas.

1. The Common and Tempered Property Rights

How the creation of property affects distribution of the common depends on the extent of exclusion entailed in property rights. Existing forms of intellectual property do not countenance complete exclusion of the non-owner. Nor can one easily imagine systems of intellectual property that could completely exclude.

This complete exclusion is impossible for two reasons. First, any property scheme that completely excludes third parties from ideas must enforce its restrictions in ways incompatible with our notions of privacy and individual freedom. Second, successful policing of such exclusion probably would be impossible. This impossibility can be thought of in either technical or economic terms. For the foreseeable future, practical considerations will limit the ways in which people can be excluded from intellectual goods. By any standard, thought-police would look more like Keystone Kops than like the KGB. Such thought policing would certainly not be cost effective. Historically, the only time the cost effectiveness of policing has not been a controlling factor is when the police enforce the claims of the sovereign and not the claims of individuals. Police states guard the interests of the state, not those of persons.

As long as complete exclusion cannot or does not happen, ideas will be available to people in their own thoughts even though these ideas already have become someone else's property. Through this availability, one idea can lead to still more ideas. In other words, once a "new" idea has been put into intellectual commerce, once people know about it, it leads to an "expansion" of the common, or of the accessible common.[79] New idea X may be the key to a whole new range of ideas that would not have been thought of without X. Assuming the Platonic model, putting X into intellectual commerce does not increase the common so much as it enhances the abilities of people to take from the common; it gives people longer arms to reach the ideas on higher branches. In this view, X just makes new ideas Y and Z more easily discovered by a wider range of people. When the range of people and/or ease of discovery is dramatically improved, one can think of the common as being practically enlarged.[80]

Computer languages provide a good example of a case in which one contribution to the society makes other contributions possible. Embarking on an effort to create a new language is a considerably more ambitious and difficult project than writing programs in an existing language. It is not something most computer scientists would undertake. In that sense, it is more a unique idea than is a new program in an existing language. This new language may stimulate programming in a way that would not have been possible *but for* the language. Furthermore, this new language creates an incentive to write these programs. Thus, it is an addition to the "common," which gives many people new ability to create even more property and expand the common even further.

Finally, idea X may be genuinely necessary to new idea Y. Orchestrations and adaptions are examples of this. The movie *Cabaret* was adapted from the musical *Cabaret*, which was adapted from Isherwood's *Berlin*

Diaries. Parodies provide an even better example of such necessity. The *Mona Lisa, American Gothic, Whistler's Mother,* and Hemingway's prose all have inspired generations of parodies—cultural objects that would have neither humor nor sense without the object of comic adoration. The original is necessary as a preexisting part of the culture.

Robert Nozick has argued that a system of physical appropriation benefits society in a manner analogous to this expansion in the world of ideas.[81] Yet there is an important difference between the expansion of the physical common and of the idea common. According to Locke, the act by which physical object X is transformed into property is an act that creates new social value. This added value, however, goes directly into that property owner's possession. At least this characterization applies to Locke's example of cultivated land and the added grain it produces.[82] This new physical value—grain—adds to the commonweal only if the owner releases it, either through gifts or commerce. Locke relies upon the money economy to facilitate this.

Intellectual property systems release the added value of a new idea without requiring the property owner's active and intentional introduction of the idea into commerce. Take the situation in which Mr. Smith creates idea X and this idea makes possible ideas Y and Z. Ideas Y and Z are not possessed by Mr. Smith in the same way the grain is possessed by the farmer. Sequel ideas are not "attached" to their antecedent ideas as grain is attached to farmland. As long as idea X is known to other people, it can inspire ideas Y and Z.

New ideas, however, can be "attached" to idea X in the sense that they seem too derivative of X to be granted their own property status. Mr. Smith, the owner of idea X, may claim that Mr. Jones, the author of Y, really did not create anything independent and different from X. The claim here is that Mr. Jones has not added much value (or much labor) beyond idea X.

Intellectual property systems handle this situation of questionable added labor with a few general principles. First, if the idea is sufficiently separate from its "parent" idea to have required significant independent labor or creativity, it belongs to the laborer.[83] Conversely, if the new idea bears too much resemblance to its parent idea, the owner of the parent has a controlling interest in the new idea. Finally, the two principles are limited by situations in which the descendant idea includes the entire parent idea, as with a new machine that uses a patented process as one of several steps or a play that uses someone's concerto as its theme. In these cases, the owner's interests in the parent idea must be accommodated with much less balancing than that afforded by the first two principles.

The law regarding parodies exemplifies the balance struck between the first two principles. A copyright does not enable its holder to prevent parodies of the copyrighted work; as long as the parody has creativity and originality, it may use substantial elements of the original.[84] However, if reasonable people would easily mistake the parody for the original, the copyright holder would have an especially strong interest in stopping publication of the parody because it will probably appear to be a bad or erroneous production of the original.[85] The creator of such a parody, because of its resemblance to the original and the little labor employed in making the parody, would possess a lesser interest in his product. Under such balancing, the recognition of property rights in idea X still permits, indeed inspires, others to reach new ideas Y and Z.

Because creating property rights in an idea never completely excludes others from using the idea, it need not be justified by Locke's legerdemain that increases in privately produced goods necessarily benefit the commonweal. Nor does it require justification from Nozick's reconstitution of "the Lockean proviso."[86] Under Nozick's reconstruction, the public would be better off even if an intellectual property owner could completely exclude others from his idea because it could still buy the goods and services developed from that idea.[87] This might be true, but intellectual property need not be justified on such a thin reed. People are better off today because there are more ideas available to them, at least in part, that provide springboards to generate even more intellectual property. New ideas, even most that become private property, benefit the commonweal by *immediately* being known and, in some sense, available to all. There is no need to rely on property holders to actively introduce them into the common.

2. The Common and Ideas That Cannot Be Granted Property Status

Intellectual property systems also are more suitable for a Lockean justification than are physical property systems because a growing set of central ideas are never permitted to become private property and are held in a *permanent common*. By preventing private control of these particular ideas, intellectual property law resolves a major inequity often present in physical property systems. Even in a vast wilderness, an individual should not be permitted to claim certain physical goods as property because their extraction from the common will not leave "as good and as many" for the remaining individuals. The "New World" prior to its colonization may have been as close to a Lockean common as human history records, yet it is easy to make a list of things that the society could not allow to be appropriated as private property: the Amazon, St. Lawrence, and Ohio Rivers, the Cumberland Pass, or the St. George's Bank fisheries.

Earlier I described two broad categories of ideas to which ascription of private ownership is denied. The first is the category of common, "everyday" ideas, such as thinking to wash one's car, to add paprika to a quiche for coloring, or to tell mystery stories to your Cub Scout troop. The second is the category of extraordinary ideas like the Pythagorean theorem, the heliocentric theory of the solar system, or the cylindrical column in architecture.

One reason that we do not permit property rights in either category of ideas may be that doing so would involve tremendous reallocations of wealth toward the property holders of these ideas. If we had to pay a royalty each time we told a ghost story or walked the dog, unprecedented wealth would concentrate in the hands of those "holding" the most common ideas. These common, everyday ideas are too generically useful to allow someone to monopolize them. The common would not have "enough and as good" if they were removed.

The same is true of extraordinary ideas. This category, however, actually contains two distinct groups of ideas. First, there are ideas that are extraordinarily important because they disclose facts about the world, such as the Pythagorean theorem and the theory of electromagnetism. In the case of electromagnetism, the Supreme Court ruled that Samuel Morse could not monopolize the general idea of using galvanic current for long-distance communications, although he could monopolize his particular process for exploiting the idea.

A second group of extraordinary ideas—which contains ideas like the architectural columns—may not be monopolized because of their widespread public use. At first, this sounds like a poor argument: that the idea of a column is widely used may mean it is a "public idea," but that is hardly a self-evident reason why it *must* be public. Yet widespread use of something, like columns and vaulted ceilings, has another effect: it makes a particular idea *appear* to be a basic truth or process. At some point, one hardly can imagine the larger social organization without the lesser object. Columns would appear as a far less basic truth to cave dwellers than to those who inhabit a post-Hellenic world in which columns prevent our buildings from crumbling into impromptu pyramids.

In short, some ideas become "depropertized." Originally, they could have been subject to private ownership (unlike the first kind of extraordinary ideas), but the pressure to keep them in the common increases as the ideas become increasingly important to the society. As an idea becomes extraordinary, it is clear the common will not have "enough and as good" if the rights to the idea continue to be privately held.

Law itself provides an interesting example. Saul Levmore has adroitly observed that "the law does not normally offer intellectual property rights to lawyers who develop novel arguments and establish precedents."[88] Perhaps legal arguments could be fit within either of the two subcategories of extraordinary ideas. In one view, arguments adopted by a court become valuable (as precedent) precisely because the court believes that argument is a basic *truth* about the legal system or the world. For the legal realist who sees no truths, the novel argument still can become (like architectural columns) a necessary fixture in the social edifice. In fact, that is the basis for Benjamin Kaplan's criticism of *Continental Casualty v. Beardsley,* a 1958 case upholding the copyright on certain insurance forms.[89] Without reaching the broader issue of ideas beyond privatization, Kaplan observed that "the effect of the decision may be to force users to awkward and possibly dangerous recasting of the legal language to avoid infringement actions."[90] Kaplan's criticism is basically that the language in those forms had become necessary to the legal system and therefore should be beyond privatization.

Ideas that *can* be privatized fall between these extremes of common and extraordinary ideas. A new device to wash cars may be patentable; a quiche recipe with secret herbs and spices can be privatized as a trade secret; the original mystery story can be transferred from campfire to copyrighted novella. Even things that are related to extraordinary ideas may be privatized. While neither Leibniz nor Newton could copyright the calculus under today's copyright laws, each probably could copyright his own system of notation for calculus. The idea of a science fiction "space-empires-at-war" story cannot be copyrighted, but when *Battlestar Gallactica* is too much like *Star Wars,* the owner of *Star Wars* can drag the Galacticans into court with a credible claim of property infringement.[91] The Supreme Court has struggled with perhaps the most basic dilemma of this sort: When can an algorithm be made into property? Its present doctrine is that an algorithm closely linked to a specific technological application may qualify for patent protection. This provides an example of a specific application (the technology) being used to bring the general idea (the algorithm) into the field of protectable ideas.

What separates the everyday idea from the protectable idea is the former's relative unimportance and the latter's uniqueness; what separates the protectable idea from the extraordinary idea is that the extraordinary idea is uniquely important. One rule of thumb is that the more generally required by society an idea is, the more important and less subject to propertization it becomes. However, very detailed ideas or pieces of information also may be beyond privatization because monopolistic control of them would harm society. For example, in the eighteenth century, copyright over a navigation map was held not to preclude someone from copying its geographic details. In eighteenth-century navigation, these details provided the *only* safe way to proceed. There would not be "enough and as good" without free access to these details.

With ideas that *become* extraordinary, society's increasing dependency on them creates a pressure to remove them from private control. For example, a popular trademark that comes to serve a unique representational function loses some of its property protection under the doctrine of genericness.[92] Examples of trademarks that have or may have lost their property status because the words are so generally relied upon for communication include "thermos," "cellophane," "aspirin," and "xerox." At least one commentator has remarked that this can be an unfair penalty on one "who has made skillful use of advertising and has popularized his product."[93] Perhaps the loss of a trademark would seem less like a penalty if we view the situation as the owner lulling the society into a dependency on a privately owned word. When the society realizes that dependence it should place the word in the permanent common.

3. Augmenting the Common through Expiration of Property Rights

For those trademarks that have become generic words, their "condemnation" is a method of deprivatizing ideas. Other intellectual property regimes augment the idea common in another way: they require *all* idea property to return to the common automatically at some point. Copyrighted property enters the public domain fifty years after the death of the author. Patents expire after a maximum of thirty-four years. News becomes commonplace information, and the shadowy existence of its quasi-property status dissipates. Trade secrets may be the lone exception; they must be constantly defended, not only against real industrial espionage but as a legal requirement to maintain their protection. Trade secrets and "gathered information" property have no fixed expiration, but they tend to be self-extinguishing. At some point, the guard drops and the trade secret expires. This general occurrence of expiration marks a radical difference from physical property arrangements.

I find it helpful to think of two commons: a "common of ideas" and a "common of potential ideas." Perhaps progress is an inexorable movement of the former gobbling up more and more of the latter. When an individual augments the common of ideas, we recognize a property right. Yet at some point an individual's addition to the common of ideas appears to be part of the historic migration of ideas from the potential common to the actual common. At that point, the property right expires.

Robert Nozick hints at this point in his example of the scientist who stumbles upon a new substance. Nozick argues that this scientist does not deprive anyone of the substance by privatizing it and excluding others from its use. While this is certainly true at the moment of discovery, Nozick recognizes that limitations on the discoverer's rights may be justified later because, "as time passes, the likelihood increases that others would have come across the substance."[94] Nozick uses this reasoning to justify limitations on the bequest and inheritance of physical goods.[95] Expiration times in intellectual property regimes also seem inspired by this idea.

Expiration ensures that most ideas eventually reside in the common unfettered in any way. This new wealth cannot be retaken and privatized by someone else; it is material that will be held permanently in common. This new material will lead to new ideas, hence new property for as yet unidentified people. This condition is sufficient to show "enrichment" of the common even in those rare instances in which the public might be successfully and totally excluded from an idea during its period as privately held property. If the owners of new ideas could exclude everyone from the idea, social progress would be slow, but as long as those new ideas eventually become freely available, idea-based progress would continue.

The expiration of intellectual property rights may help a Lockean scheme of intellectual property overcome one general objection to Locke's theory. This objection is that Locke's vision of property rights justifies property for one generation, but cannot justify the subsequent property arrangements of future generations. Hillel Steiner has expressed one form of this attack:

> Consider, first, Locke's construction of individuals' original rights. The claim that for a limited (early) historical period each person was entitled to appropriate a quantitatively similar collection of natural resources is open to the unanswerable objection—noted by Nozick—that a right of historically limited validity and, thus, of less than universal incidence, cannot be constituted by any set of moral rules that extend the same kinds of rights to all persons. The titles thereby established can preclude historically later persons from exercising the same kind of right. Hence the set of rights constituted by Locke's rule fails the test of coherence.[96]

Nozick particularly addresses this problem with his discussion of the "Lockean proviso." Nozick has deftly interpreted Locke's condition that there must be "enough and as good left in common for others" as a principle meant "to ensure that the situation of others is not worsened" by the appropriations of property from the common.[97] Nozick says that Locke would justify privatization of things previously in the common unless "appropriation of an unowned object worsens the situation of others."[98] Assuming that acts of propertization do produce inequalities, Nozick's reformulation of Locke's "enough and as good" provision holds that inequalities of this sort always should be tolerated so long as they do not make the worse-off more badly off. To use the economist's jargon, Nozick is adopting the principle of Pareto-optimality. Whether or not this reformation is successful, both Locke and Nozick have used the original acceptability of initial property rights to lead to the acceptability of property rights for succeeding generations.

Intellectual property systems avoid these shoals. As long as there is an ever-growing common of ideas available for everyone's unlimited use, every person has at least as much opportunity to appropriate ideas as had the first man in the wilderness. There is an equilibrium between those ideas being removed from the common through privatization and those ideas that society relies heavily upon. What results is akin to John Rawls' treatment of justice between generations. Rawls argues that a fixed rate of savings between generations allows each generation to reap the same rewards and make the same investment in the future.[99] This effectively happens with intellectual property. The common of ideas grows like investment in an idea bank.

D. The Non-Waste Condition and Intellectual Property

Historians treat Locke's condition of non-waste as an ugly stepsister of the enough and as good condition—maligned, not for its own infirmity, but for how quickly Locke abandons it in his adoption of a money economy.[100] Nozick offers a criticism from another side: true application of Locke's "enough and as good" provision makes the non-waste condition superfluous.[101] This criticism attacks the *place* of the non-waste condition in Locke's theory, not the condition itself. Without entering this fray, I suggest that many systems of intellectual property neither embody nor require a non-waste condition.

1. Intellectual Property and the Money Economy

A "pure" Lockean account might dismiss the applicability of the non-waste condition on the grounds that intellectual property exists only in societies that have transcended the condition.[102] It is possible, however, to imagine intellectual property existing before the creation of a money society. Certainly the *subjects* of intellectual property exist in primitive states: the corkscrew method of raising water from the Nile, the varied means of tanning hides, or original straw weaving patterns. When the originator of one of these ideas shared it with others, he gave some value to the others by allowing them to remove property from the common with less labor.

This can produce paradoxical results depending on our understanding of Locke's theory of private property. For example, if what separates private property from the common is labor, then sharing a labor-saving idea with a friend actually may rob my friend of her Lockean title to those goods she extracts with my idea. This is especially true if more labor makes one's property claims stronger. My friend is, after all, laboring less for the thing she gets. A related question is whether use of the idea by another is equivalent to additional labor by its originator. If so, when a friend uses my idea to draw water from the Nile, it would be as if the friend and I drew the water together. Would we, therefore, have some type of joint title to the water?

There is a powerful argument that ideas cannot be subjects of Lockean property rights in the pre-money state. If so, this sharply distinguishes ideas from physical objects. In the state of nature, people take what they need for survival. Those who fail to appropriate enough perish. In this situation, giving a friend my labor-saving idea would likely produce one of two results: either it preserves her life when otherwise she would have perished for insufficient labor to appropriate enough or it allows her to accumulate surpluses with which to barter.[103]

The first possibility, that the idea preserves her life, runs counter to Locke's assumptions. If a person of average physical capability requires the idea to take enough from the common to survive there is something wrong either with the common or with human capacities. Before we even reach the question of "enough and as good," the common is not good enough.

The simplest cure is to say that the idea is part of the common—as something everyone needs to take the common's physical things—or that the idea is part of human capacities—an idea all humans should possess in the same way they would possess the idea of using their arms to climb trees. Either way, the idea could not be the subject of propertization. I prefer to view certain ideas as things Locke would consider basic to human capacities. These might include, for example, the use of simple tools—the club, the knife, the rope, and clothing. This would seem to fit Locke's description of the state of nature in which men do certain activities that entail the use of simple tools.

On the other hand, if the idea I give my friend allows her to accumulate a surplus for bartering, this idea exists in or begins the money economy. The idea can be treated as intellectual property precisely because it produces surplus value, which can be traded.[104]

2. The Non-Waste of Intellectual Property

Locke presents his non-waste condition most directly in the example of food spoilage, and this particular form of loss powerfully demonstrates the appeal of the non-waste condition. The waste of food is an absolute loss. Arguably, the moral force of the non-waste condition dissipates in a world in which all have enough or more than enough to meet their needs. This is the gist of Nozick's argument that Locke does not need the non-waste condition so long as he employs the "enough and as good" condition.[105]

But spoiled food can be viewed as waste in either of two ways: food that spoils is available neither for the *present* potential use of those who do not own the food nor for the *future* potential use of its owner. There is waste in others needing something that is not being used, and in consumption of the individual's labor without bringing any benefit to the individual. The first is waste in a social context; the second is waste for the individual organism.

Nozick's argument addresses only the former, and completely misses the latter. For although no one may need the food that spoils in the pre-economic state of natural bounty, the individual's labor that was used to produce and appropriate the spoiled food nevertheless has been "wasted"—it was used without creating any present or future value to society or to himself. In the realm of intellectual property, there are interesting differences between these two versions of waste. Unlike food, ideas are not perishable: they almost always retain future value. From an individual's perspective, it is much harder to say at a point in time, T_1, that the individual's investment in some idea is wasted. The investment may yield value at a later T_2. Of course, one can claim that intellectual goods actually are perishable: ideas go stale, new stories become "old," literature becomes dated, and patents become worthless as the technology on which they are based becomes obsolete. These are examples of good ideas being introduced into society too late to yield maximum return.

Yet the value lost by hoarding an idea until it becomes obsolete is a very different kind of loss than food spoilage. There is no internal deterioration in the idea and the loss in value is seen only against a social backdrop. The loss is speculative and may be reversible. Future trends may make the outdated idea fashionable again. Even with technology-based intellectual property—the property most prone to an objectively measurable loss in value—there may be a recovery of value. For example, new technical improvements in equestrian equipment and train engines can still be very profitable despite the appearance of automobiles and Boeing 757s.

While the social value of an idea may decline below an optimal point, the value of the idea, apart from its value to society, may remain constant. An unpublished story may still give an author joy when shared with intimates. The secret recipe for Kentucky Fried Chicken will taste as good to the creator whether or not it is shared with Madison Avenue. With intellectual property, there is no waste to the *individual* because the act of "consumption" is inseparable from the act of production. Intellectual property holds value derived solely from the act of creation.

In intellectual property systems, manifestations of a non-waste condition are few and far between. Perhaps the most explicit inclusion of the condition in intellectual property law was the publication requirement for copyright protection. Until the 1976 Copyright Act became effective, federal copyright protection for a work commenced upon publication.[106] Publication ensured that the literary work was not being wasted. Effectively, ideas could be monopolized through copyrights only when put to good use, that is, published. Yet since 1976, publication has not been required for federal copyright protection, and even before 1976, common law copyright or state statutes protected the author's unpublished work in the stages before federal statutory copyrights could have been granted.[107]

It is difficult to think of any other ways in which intellectual property schemes embody any notion of the non-waste condition. Patents, copyrights, and trade secrets are recognized whether or not the owner is squandering or has shelved the idea. In the case of quasi property, the legal right to waste a news story by nonpublication has not been clearly stated, but surely this is because of the news story's limited shelf life and not the law's limited protection.

E. Final Comments on a Lockean Justification

The absence of a non-waste condition in intellectual property systems does not weaken a Lockean justification for intellectual property. Locke, after all, declined to apply the non-waste condition to the advanced social conditions that are required by most intellectual property systems. However, it may be disconcerting to those of us who believe that applying the non-waste condition to advanced societies would produce a more moral justification for property. Intellectual property systems, however, do seem to accord with Locke's labor condition and the "enough and as good" requirement. In fact, the "enough and as good" condition seems to hold true *only* in intellectual property systems.[108] That may mean that Locke's unique theoretical edifice finds its firmest bedrock in the common of ideas.

My own view is that a labor theory of intellectual property is powerful, but incomplete. I believe we also need the support of a personality theory, such as the one proposed by Hegel, in which property is justified as an expression of the self. Some writers have suggested that Locke actually subscribed to such a personality theory in which "applying one's labor to a natural object . . . endow[s] it with certain features pertaining to one's own form of existence."[109] With this understanding of Locke, the difference between him and Hegel—at least as to the analysis of intellectual property—may be minimal.

III. A Hegelian Justification

In the preceding discussion, I argued that Locke's labor theory can serve as a powerful justification for intellectual property. But beyond intellectual property, a Lockean model thickens with the ingredients of modern life: financial markets, capital accumulation, service industries, inheritance, and the like. Those who try to apply Locke to all modern property end up multiplying distinctions like pre-Copernican astronomers calculating celestial orbits with their Ptolemaic epicycles. At some point, it becomes easier to reorient one's universe.

The most powerful alternative to a Lockean model of property is a personality justification. Such a justification posits that property provides a unique or especially suitable mechanism for self-actualization, for personal expression, and for dignity and recognition as an individual person. Professor Margaret Radin describes this as the "personhood perspective" and identifies as its central tenet the proposition that "to achieve proper self-development—to be a *person*—an individual needs some control over resources in the external environment."[110] According to this personality theory, the kind of control needed is best fulfilled by the set of rights we call property rights.

Like the labor theory, the personality theory has an intuitive appeal when applied to intellectual property: an idea belongs to its creator because the idea is a manifestation of the creator's personality or self. The best-known personality theory is Hegel's theory of property.[111] This section sketches his property theory, its application to intellectual property, and some problems of using the personality theory as a justification for intellectual property.

In the field of intellectual property, the personality justification is best applied to the arts. This is true both in theory and in European legal systems that have recognized a personality basis for property. Efforts to introduce the personality justification into American law frequently appeal to those European intellectual property laws.[112] As an alternative, I suggest ways to bring civil liberties doctrines to bear on intellectual property and, in so doing, inject the personality justification into American intellectual property law.

A. Hegelian Intellectual Property

1. The General Hegelian Philosophy

At the heart of Hegel's philosophy are his difficult concepts of human will, personality, and freedom. For Hegel, the individual's will is the core of the individual's existence, constantly seeking actuality *(Wirklichkeit)* and effectiveness in the world. Hegel perceives a hierarchy of elements in an individual's mental make-up in which the will occupies the highest position. As one of Hegel's biographers wrote, the Hegelian will is that in which thought and impulse, mind and heart, "are combined in freedom."[113]

We can identify "personality" with the will's struggle to actualize itself. Hence Hegel writes that "a person must translate his freedom into an external sphere in order to exist as an Idea" and that "personality is the first, still wholly abstract, determination of the absolute and infinite will."[114] For Hegel, "personality is that which struggles to lift itself above this restriction [of being only subjective] and to give itself reality, or in other words to claim that external world as its own."[115]

Invariably, writings on Hegel devote some attention to the difference between Hegelian "freedom"—as it appears in the passage above—and the conception of "freedom" that lies at the root of classical liberalism. However, these disparate conceptions of freedom need not greatly affect the acceptability of Hegel's justification for property.

To the classical liberal, true freedom is a freedom from external restraint. For Hegel, freedom is increasingly realized as the individual unites with and is expressed through a higher objective order: a unity that, to the classic liberal, is tantamount to drowning the individual in the larger "geist" of social groups. In the words of R. N. Berki, Hegel's notion of "*philosophical freedom* grows with comprehensiveness and with ever higher degrees of realized self-determination, thus, an animal is freer than a physical object, a man freer than an animal, the family freer than the individual, the State freer than the family, World-History freer than the State."[116] Berki's summary is instructive on the difference between liberal and Hegelian notions of freedom: this difference is more about the proper *receptacle* of freedom than about the *nature* of freedom. Both recognize freedom as involving expression and realization. The liberal reposes this freedom in the individual while Hegel discards the individual when he believes it is time to pursue freedom to new and dizzying heights.

In his property theory, however, Hegel focused on the immediate freedom of an individual.[117] So at this level the liberal's critique of Hegel should be most muted. The liberal still differs from Hegel by defining freedom as the absence of restraints, but this negative definition means little without the positive freedom to act upon things. In Camus' *Caligula,* the despotic Emperor declares himself to be the most free man in the world because no wish is denied him.[118] Caligula has few external restraints; he can manifest his will on anything within the reach of imperial legions or Roman sesterces.

Caligula's claim to be a model of freedom for his people is faint comfort to them because they frequently are the things upon which he manifests his will. At least at the level of individual freedom, Hegel denounced such manifestations of will upon others.[119] Caligula's material self-indulgence points to a weakness in both Hegelian and classical liberal theories: the need to sort out the effects upon other people of an individual's exercise of freedom over inanimate objects.[120] In Hegel's system, property is a genre of freedom and, like any other freedom, it may have deleterious effects on others.

2. The Property/Person Connection

Drawing upon his model of the hierarchy of elements in the individual's make-up, Hegel implies that the will holds the "inferior" elements of the self as if they were a type of property.[121] It is worth noting that this view is not very distant from Locke's initial premise that "every Man has a Property in his own Person."[122] Assuming that the self is a type of property, the difference between internal property of this sort and property external to the person is that the latter can be alienated. This reasoning can lead to an abandoning of barriers in both directions. As Dudley Knowles put it, "The contraction of the core of one's property into the sphere of personality (life, limb, and liberty) licenses the expansion of the concept of personality to cover those physical objects which are deemed to be property."[123]

According to Hegel, the will interacts with the external world at different levels of activity. Mental processes—such as recognizing, classifying, explaining, and remembering—can be viewed as appropriations of the external world by the mind.[124] Cognition and resulting knowledge, however, are the world imposing itself upon the mind. The will is not bound by these impressions. It seeks to appropriate the external world in a different way—by imposing itself upon the world. This is the true purpose of property and, perhaps to emphasize that purpose, Hegel explicitly disavows any need for the institution of property to satisfy physical wants.[125]

Acting upon things is an initial step in the ongoing struggle for self-actualization. Socially mandated property rights do not trigger this self-actualization; they are only a means to protect the individual's initial attempt to take command of the world. Once we accept that self-actualization is manifested in enduring objects as well as in fleeting acts, property rights acquire an important purpose in preventing men from forever being embroiled in an internecine conflict of each individual trying to protect his first forays at self-actualization from the predation of others. Property becomes expression of the will, a part of personality, and it creates the conditions for further free action.

Respect for property allows the will to continue abstraction and "objectification." With some property secure, people can pursue freedom in non-property areas or they may continue to develop themselves by using property to move themselves toward the person they wish to become. Knowles has clearly depicted the Hegelian interaction between property and personal development: "Imaginative conceptions of our future selves are indistinguishable from fantasy or day-dreams unless they are supported by acquisition, investment, or planned savings. . . . Anyone who wishes to conduct an inventory of his desires may profitably begin by walking round his own dwelling or looking into his wardrobe."[126]

Property is not just a matter of the physical world giving way to assertion of the self, for the society must acknowledge and approve property claims. Through society's acceptance of the individual's claims upon external objects, possession becomes property, and the expression of the individual becomes more objective.[127] For Hegel, increased objectivity is increased freedom in part because social recognition of a person's claims to private property demonstrates that the individual's claims comport with that social will.

The individual person comes to be manifested in some object through "occupation" and "embodiment."[128] Although much of Hegel's language seems to support either a "first possession" theory or a labor theory, neither accurately captures what he means by occupation. He characterized possession of the object as the initial step in property, but this is because the will can only occupy a *res nullius*—either a virgin object or something that has been abandoned.[129]

Abandonment occurs easily in the Hegelian system because the relationship between person and object is fluid. Being first in possession of an object is not sufficient to maintain title to it; the property relationship continues only so long as the will manifests itself in the object. Because "the will to possess something must express itself," a person who fails to reaffirm constantly this expression can "lose possession of property through prescription."[130] The individual also can actively withdraw his will; this is the basis of alienability.

Labor often is the means by which the will occupies an object. But while labor may be a sufficient condition for occupation, it is not a *necessary* one. For example, one may manifest one's will in a gift or in a natural object to which one becomes emotionally attached. There is a rock on my shelf from the coast of Corsica that reminds me of days spent there. My will occupies that rock without wishing to change it and without having labored upon it. This exemplifies another non-condition of occupation; Hegel specifically argues that an individual need not *use* an object to occupy it.

This is not to say that there are no objective indicia of the will's occupation. Hegel sets out three ways in which the will may occupy an object: physically seizing it, imposing a form upon it, and marking it. This would not appear to be an exhaustive list of events that signal possession, nor is Hegel precise in defining these three events. Thus he finds *use*, when aimed toward preservation of the object, equivalent to "marking it" because it shows the will's desire to make the object a permanent part of the inventory of things utilized and enjoyed by the individual.

Hegel seems to envision spatio-temporal proximity between the individual and the object, but that too is only indicia rather than a requirement. Unlike the labor theory, Hegel's personality justification

> focuses on where a commodity ends up, not where and how it starts out. . . . It focuses on the person with whom it ends up—on an internal quality in the holder or a subjective relationship between the holder and the thing, and not on the objective arrangements surrounding production of the thing.[131]

As Radin points out in this passage, the connection between personality and property is open-ended. A person could claim a personality stake in any material object, meaning that the personality justification is liable to excessive claims. It is a theory that allows Virginia Woolf to claim a room of her own, but also allows Louis XIV to claim the 2,697 rooms of Versailles.

This subjectivity causes unhealthy identifications with property that should not give rise to legitimate property claims. Early in his writings, Hegel hinted that certain self-identifications with property were destructive to the individual. For example, in the *Theologische Jugendschriften,* Hegel argues that the ownership of property can stand in the way of complete harmony between individuals in love.[132] "The dead object in the power of one of the lovers is opposed to both of them, and a union in respect of it seems to be possible only if it comes under the dominion of both."[133]

This destructive effect of property should be distinguished from the alienation that later came to propel Hegelian and Marxian social criticism. It differs from the problem of a laborer who attaches his existence to objects that he produces but does not own: the plight for such a laborer is that his identity is attached to something that is *not* his property. Nor is this the problem of a person owning things with which he does not identify.[134] In the *Jugendschriften,* the problem is that a person owns and identifies with some property to his own detriment; it prevents a greater happiness in the form of a love relationship.

Generalizing from this example, we might say that a person's identification with property is "unhealthy" when it prevents that person from maximizing self-actualization from other sources—lovers, friends, careers, peer groups, other property, and even feelings antithetical to the possession of property such as the flower-child freedom of the 1960s. The complexity of maximizing self-actualization usually makes us defer to the judgments of the individual. However, when the industrialist is inextricably in love with the flower child, we may conclude that his property is unhealthy for his present and future self-actualization.

Radin also has expressed concern about the adverse effects of property on self-actualization. However, she focuses concern on the detrimental impact of property on people other than the property owner. She distinguishes between "fungible" and "personal" property, the latter being property that increases self-actualization. She adopts the principle that property fungible to person X should be denied to X if giving that property to X would deny personal (that is, self-actualizing) property to Y.[135]

Radin's standard accords with Hegel's own reasoning. In addressing the severe inequality of property distribution in his own day, Hegel argued that his system required only equality as to the *possibility* of obtaining property.[136] Hegel implicitly endorses the view that property can be denied to person X if giving this property to X would deny Y the possibility of obtaining property. Under Radin's standard, whether an act of appropriation is "healthy" depends upon whether it has deleterious effects on others. This standard has a resemblance to Locke's "enough and as good" condition. As long as there is enough and as good potential property for the self-actualization of others, one may appropriate.

In fact, Radin's principle of "fungible" and "personal" property *is* the "enough and as good" condition unless we construe it in one of two ways. The first construction would require people to disgorge their fungible property, even when there is "enough and as good." This position does not make much sense if subjective judgments determine personal attachment to property. Property that objectively appears to be fungible may actually be personal; occasionally someone will have a personality stake in U.S. Savings Bonds or GM stock.

The second construction would *not* require people to disgorge personal property even when there is not "enough and as good" property available to all. This position makes some sense on a cost/benefit rationale: with truly personal property, we may be damaging the self-actualization of the property-loser as much as we would augment the self-actualization of those to whom the property is distributed. In a world of property shortage, some persons will be malnourished in their self-actualization. It is just a matter of who.

The fungible/personal distinction therefore renews the subjectivity dilemma, a problem recognized by Radin. "Fungible" and "personal" are strong intuitive guides in a culture enamored with economic analysis. Stock portfolios, mining rights, and tons of wheat are fungible; photos, diaries, and pets are not. Yet this leads us nowhere with the person willing to sell his grandmother or the person who keeps pet wheat. We are left with either an artificially constrained or an entirely subjective measure of when property actualizes the self.

3. Intellectual Property under Hegel

For Hegel, intellectual property need not be justified by analogy to physical property. In fact, the analogy to physical property may distort the status Hegel ascribes to personality and mental traits in relation to the will. Hegel writes:

> Mental aptitudes, erudition, artistic skill, even things ecclesiastical (like sermons, masses, prayers, consecration of votive objects), inventions, and so

forth, become subjects of a contract, brought on to a parity, through being bought and sold, with things recognized as things. It may be asked whether the artist, scholar, &c., is from the legal point of view in possession of his art, erudition, ability to preach a sermon, sing a mass, &c., that is, whether such attainments are "things." We may hesitate to call such abilities, attainments, aptitudes, &c., "things," for while possession of these may be the subject of business dealings and contracts, as if they were things, there is also something inward and mental about it, and for this reason the Understanding may be in perplexity about how to describe such possession in legal terms.[137]

Intellectual property provides a way out of this problem, by "materializing" these personal traits. Hegel goes on to say that "attainments, eruditions, talents, and so forth, are, of course, owned by free mind and are something internal and not external to it, but even so, by expressing them it may embody them in something external and alienate them."[138]

Hegel takes the position that one cannot alienate or surrender any universal element of one's self. Hence slavery is not permissible because by "alienating the whole of my time, as crystallized in my work, I would be making into another's property the substance of my being, my universal activity and actuality, my personality."[139] Similarly, there is no right to sacrifice one's life because that is the surrender of the "comprehensive sum of external activity."[140] This doctrine supplies at least a framework to answer the question of intellectual property that most concerns Hegel. It is a question we ignore today, but one that is not easy to answer: what justifies the author in alienating copies of his work while retaining the exclusive right to reproduce further copies of that work?

A sculptor or painter physically embodies his will in the medium and produces one piece of art. When another artist copies this piece Hegel thinks that the handmade copy "is essentially a product of the copyist's own mental and technical ability" and does not infringe upon the original artist's property.[141] The problem arises when a creator of intellectual property does not embody his will in an object in the same way the artist does. The writer physically manifests his will only "in a series of abstract symbols" that can be rendered into "things" by mechanical processes not requiring any talent. The dilemma is exacerbated by the fact that "the purpose of a product of mind is that people other than its author should understand it and make it the possession of their ideas, memory, thinking, &c."[142] This concern for the common of ideas is familiar.

In resolving this dilemma, Hegel says that the alienation of a single copy of a work need not entail the right to produce facsimiles because

such reproduction is one of the "universal ways and means of expression
. . . which belong to [the author]."[143] Just as he does not sell himself into
slavery, the author keeps the universal aspect of expression as his own.
The copy sold is for the buyer's own consumption; its only purpose is to
allow the buyer to incorporate these ideas into his "self."

Hegel also identifies the instrumentalist-labor justification as a consideration against granting full rights of reproduction to buyers of individual
copies of a work. Hegel admits that protecting intellectual property is
"the purely negative, though the primary, means of advancing the sciences and arts."[144] Beyond this, Hegel says little. He declares that intellectual property is a "capital asset" and explicitly links this label to a later
section in which he defines a "capital asset."[145] There is considerable literature on how Hegel did not develop the idea of "capital" to its logical
conclusions, but here "capital asset" can be understood as property that
has a greater tendency to permanence and a greater ability than other
property to give its own economic security.[146]

B. Problems in Applying the Personality Justification to Intellectual Property

A property system protecting personality will have difficulty finding
reliable indicia for when people do and do not have a "personality stake"
in particular objects. The personality justification also leaves some nag-
ging theoretical questions. Even if we reliably could detect when a person
possesses a "personality stake" in an object, we surely would find that
personality is manifested to varying degrees in different objects. This is
the personality counterpart to the varying amounts of labor one "puts"
into different objects. Neither personality nor labor is simply an on-off
proposition. The question is: Does more personality warrant more property protection?

This problem also has a "categorical" aspect—different categories of
intellectual property seem to lend themselves to different amounts of
"personality." Poetry seems to lend itself to personality better than trade
secrets, symphonies better than microchip masks. Should poetry as a category receive more protection than microchip masks? Should some categories receive no protection at all from the personality justification? Finally,
the theory suffers from internal inconsistency in its somewhat incoherent
account of alienation.

1. Varying Degrees of Personality in Intellectual Property

One of the problems with the labor theory discussed in Part II is that
some intellectual products have no apparent social value or require no

labor to produce, leaving these pieces of property unjustified by the labor theory. The personality justification has the same problem with those intellectual products that appear to reflect little or no personality from their creators. As with the labor theory, we can overcome this difficulty with a utilitarian principle that justifies property rights on the grounds that they protect the "net gain" of personality achieved by the entire system. This avoids the question of whether or not personality is present in every case of intellectual property. Yet the personality justification has this same "coverage" problem at a "categorical" level. With a controversial exception mentioned below, there seem to be no categories of intellectual property that are especially more or less hospitable to the labor theory. This is not true with the personality justification. Some categories of intellectual property seem to be receptacles for personality; others seem as if they do not manifest any "personality" of their creators.

Poems, stories, novels, and musical works are clearly receptacles for personality. The same can be said for sculpture, paintings, and prints. Justice Holmes aptly characterized such works as "the personal reaction of an individual upon nature."[147] Another receptacle for personality is the legal concept of an individual's "persona." The "persona" is an individual's public image, including his physical features, mannerisms, and history. In the United States, it is debated whether or not the personal should be considered intellectual property at all. The answer to this question may turn on what justification we use for intellectual property.

The persona is the one type of potential intellectual property that is generally thought of as *not* being a result of labor.[148] Even if the persona is considered to be a product of labor, people would work on their personas without any property rights being necessary to motivate them. Therefore, the instrumental labor justification is not necessary. In contrast, the persona is the ideal property for the personality justification. No intermediary concepts such as "expression" or "manifestation" are needed: the persona is the reaction of society and a personality. Property rights in the persona give the individual the economic value derived most directly from one's personality.[149] As long as an individual identifies with his personal image, he will have a personality stake in that image.[150]

The problems for the personality justification do not arise in justifying these obvious expressions or manifestations of personality, but with those kinds of intellectual property that do not seem to be the personal reaction of an individual upon nature. Even in the field of copyright these problems arise. While most of the personality-laden categories are protected by copyrights, copyrights protect more than just personality-rich objects. Atlases and maps are a good example. In the early days of oceanic explorations, mapmakers competed with one another on their claims of accuracy. Today, the same competition does not arise because the generic information is already there in the form of old maps and publicly held government materials.[151] The result is that maps have a tremendous uniformity. There may be personality galore in a map of Tolkien's Middle Earth, but not much in a roadmap of Ohio. That does not mean maps are absolutely devoid of personality. Certainly a new form of map manifests personal creativity, as in the case of Peter Arno's revisions of the Mercator projections.[152] Even in everyday maps, there can be artistic content or social commentary in the choices of color, identifying symbols, and information included.

More difficult problems for the personality justification are posed by copyrightable computer software and other technological categories of intellectual property: patents, microchip masks, and engineering trade secrets. These items usually embody strongly utilitarian solutions to very specific needs. We tend not to think of them as manifesting the personality of an individual, but rather as manifesting a raw, almost generic insight. In inventing the lightbulb, Edison searched for the filament material that would burn the longest, not a filament that would reflect his personality. Marconi chose to use a particular wavelength for his radio because that wavelength could travel much farther than waves slightly longer, not because that wavelength was his preferred form of expression.

In a report related to the recently enacted microchip mask protection law, the House Judiciary Committee discussed attempts by some microchip inventors to protect chip designs by copyrighting photographs of the chips' layout as artistic designs.[153] This clear attempt to use a system designed to protect personality-rich art for the protection of engineering designs exudes irony. The House Committee concluded, as most of us do, that engineering designs are characterless and without personality. As congressmen or consumers, we generally think that state of the art is not art.

Yet technology may not be categorically different from atlases and maps. The primary goal of computer programs is to produce a particular result using as little software and hardware as possible. But writing programs, like creating logical proofs, can involve a certain aesthetic vision. Within the constraints of efficiency, it is frequently possible to write a program a number of ways—some simpler, some more Byzantine; each depicts a particular style for resolving the problem. If there are ten ways to write a program of roughly the same efficiency, it seems perfectly reasonable to think that the choice among the ten may demonstrate personality.

It is an oversimplification to think that some genres of intellectual property *cannot* carry personality. This oversimplification avoids the true issue of the constraints of economy, efficiency, and physical environment that limit the range of personal expression. Such constraints exist to some degree in every genre. Few movies or plays can afford to ignore the average attention span of audiences or the limits of a budget; the artist in the plastic arts is constrained by the physical properties of the materials; the architect faces these material constraints with the additional limits of plot size, location, and zoning regulations. The computer programmer and the cartographer are further along the spectrum of constraint, but even they can embellish their works to suit at least some of their own predilections. The genetic researcher or the aerospace engineer is even more constrained; their slightest embellishments may be dangerous indeed.

The more a creative process is subject to external constraints, the less apparent personality is in the creation. At some point, these constraints on a particular form of intellectual property may be too great to permit meaningful expressions of personality. We may determine that the personality justification should apply only to some genres of intellectual property or that the personality generally present in a particular genre warrants only limited protection.[154]

In the ideal situation, before we made such a determination we would ask the creator what personality she sees in her creation. As mere consumers we may think a genre of intellectual property too constrained to permit expressions of personality, while the majority of creators in that genre may think that their works do express personality. Subtle manifestations of personality may be visible only to people knowledgeable in that field. Just as chess players can recognize particular moves as reflecting the personality of certain players, particular moves in a computer program or a chemical process may be characteristic of a particular inventor or group.

This subjective inquiry approaches personality stake as being a question of whether or not there is personality *in* the object. In other words, does the object show others an aspect of the creator's self? This aspect of the personality-property connection focuses on the *expression* of the creator's will through the *medium* of her creation. The creation itself is merely a conduit for the expression of personality. Another type of personality stake may exist, however.

A person may claim property so that others will *identify* him with the property. In this case, the creator claims his property in order to *create* (rather than *express*) a particular persona. This "externalization" accords with Hegel's theory. Hegel argues that recognizing an individual's property rights is an act of recognizing the individual as a person.[155] That same reasoning applies to the externalization connection: if X owns a patent, people will recognize him as a *particular* person—the inventor of a unique innovation.

There is a problem, however, with founding intellectual property rights upon such externalization. X can't just say "I want people to identify me with the World Trade Center" and expect this to justify his property claim to it. The individual must have some *internal* connection to the claimed property. This connection need not be that the object "expresses" the owner's personality. It may be simply that the owner *identifies* himself with the object. With inventions, the object may precede the personality stake, but with time the scientist or engineer comes to identify himself with his scientific or technological advances. Doppler became identified with certain principles of sound, Edison with the lightbulb and gramophone, Bell with his telephone. The personality inquiry cannot just examine the object. The *relationship* between object and creator is where personality is visible.

2. Alienation and the Personality Justification

Hegel regards alienation as the final element in the agenda of an individual's relationship to the propertized thing. Viewed as a single act, alienation is equivalent to abandonment: "The reason I can alienate my property is that it is mine only insofar as I put my will into it. Hence I may abandon . . . as a *res nullius* anything that I have or yield it to the will of another."[156]

There is some intuitive appeal in this view of alienation, especially in a barter-exchange framework.[157] Two people can exchange distinct objects if each thinks her own personality would be better expressed through the object presently owned by the other. Jessica can exchange her comic books for Ken's baseball cards if she has more interest in baseball than in the exploits of Spiderman. Ken will engage in the same transaction if he identifies with superheroes more than with the baseball heroes collecting dust in his closet. Each person increases the actualization of his or her personality.

In a money economy, however, the exchange may lose some of its intuitive appeal. An individual alienates his property for *value* that he can then invest in things that will increase self-actualization above what it would have been had he continued to own the alienated property. Depending upon the degree of development, however, the individual might not be able to increase self-actualization through future investment. One can no longer be as certain that one will receive a profitable return. A

fragile money economy—subject to inflation and shortages—threatens
the prospect of translating value received into increased self-actualization.
A stable economy strengthens the prospect.

The risk of unprofitable investment, however, is not the main problem.
Alienation is more than just "giving up" something. Like many of the
rights encompassed by property, the right to alienate X is the right partially to determine X's future. In an absolute sense, only the future decision maker—the transferee—for X is determined, but in practice an act
of alienation usually establishes clear probabilities as to the future of the
object itself. This is true whether the alienation conveys land to a developer, sends a horse to a glue factory, or sells weapons to terrorist organizations.

To better understand this, imagine a system of depositing or redepos-
iting objects in a "community bank" for which, upon deposit, one received value coupons. The property, once in the bank, becomes a *res nullius*, and the bank would dispose of this property on a first-come/first-
served basis, much as the government auctions newly acquired lands or
unclaimed postal freight.

The difference between alienation and this community bank is that
most alienation involves some degree of determining the object's future.
Imagine that Jessica can sell her new baseball card collection to David, an
avid collector, or to Nat, the restaurateur who is opening a sports version
of the Hard Rock Cafe and is looking for wall decorations. Now Jessica's
act of alienation involves the choice of where and how the property will
be used in the future.

This is the paradox of alienation under the personality model of property. The present owner maintains ownership because he identifies the
property as an expression of his self. Alienation is the denial of this personal link to an object. But if the personal link does not exist—if the
object does not express or manifest part of the individual's personality—
there is no foundation for property rights over the object by which the
"owner" may determine the object's future. An owner's present desire to
alienate a piece of property is connected to the recognition that the property either is not or soon will not be an expression of himself. Thus, the
justification for property is missing. This subtle control of the object's
future does not jibe with foreseen future denial of the personality stake.

One way to explain this paradox is to say that the personality justification is powerful for property *protection*, but that it fails to explain property exchange. Using Radin's terminology, the willingness to sell a piece
of property suggests that the property has moved from the "personal"
category to the "fungible" category. This follows because personal prop-

erty is defined as having an internal value for the property owner in excess of possible external value. When a buyer comes forward offering a price acceptable to the owner, there is an external valuation of the property commensurate to the owner's internal valuation and the personality justification for guarding rights to personal property vanishes.

Specific covenants and restrictions on property suffer in the same way. A restriction—covenant, servitude, or easement—acknowledges that the present owner has a limited personality interest continuing into the future. Restrictions on real property, such as preservation of particular natural features or prohibitions on particular uses, seem like very honest claims to future personality stakes in property. By using a restriction, a person retains the specific stick(s) in the bundle of property rights that will "contain" his continuing personality stake.

The restriction turns a present owner's freedom to choose from varying courses of action into a future static condition inherent in the property. A farm owner's right to cut down a woods in the corner of his farm is transformed into a static condition when he sells the farm with a restriction against destroying those trees. This conversion produces a static condition that continues regardless of the evolving wishes of either the original owner or the new owner. This static condition replaces both the original owner's right and the new owner's right. With alienation, the condition becomes subject to the new owner's right. The original owner alienated his property, betting only on the probability that the new owner would not pursue a course of action that offends him.

It is more difficult to defend a personality justification for restrictions than it is for complete alienation. We often use our property rights to alter an object to suit our personality. A restriction destroys the flexibility by which property becomes and continues to be a reflection of those who own it. This flexibility, of course, may not matter to an original owner seeking to preserve memories, but it will matter a great deal to the new owner seeking to maximize his personal expression. Perhaps it is no accident that even more so than covenants disallowed for violating public policy or constitutional provisions, covenants creating affirmative obligations on real property are generally limited and "a general restraint upon alienation is ordinarily invalid."[158] Such a restraint would be *ideal* for an owner who wishes to alienate *and* to control the object's future. It would permit him to choose the new owner (whose probable use of the property can be known) and restrict whom the new owner can alienate.

Alienation of intellectual property can take one of two basic forms. The first is its entire alienation by selling, at one time, all rights to the property. The second is the complete alienation of copies of the property with limitations on how those copies may be used: the selling of copies of copyrighted works, objects displaying trademarks, or licenses to use patented technology.[159]

Alienation of the entire intellectual property—all rights to a trademark, patent, or copyright—has the same paradoxical problems as does the alienation of physical objects. If a person genuinely has no personality stake in a work, why should she determine who publishes it, who markets it, or who dramatizes it? If an inventor foresees that an invention will neither manifest his vision of the world nor speak as an expression of his identity, why should he derive economic value from it? As with physical property, on most occasions the complete alienation of intellectual property is an exercise of rights over property in an act that, by its nature, denies the personality stake necessary to justify property rights.

This paradox of personality and alienation is more acute with intellectual property because, in the absence of any physically tangible *res* (other than the copy, which is not itself the entirety of the property) that is distinct from the creator's personality, it is difficult to conceive of abandonment. If there is no "thing" to abandon, how is alienation possible? Abandonment of an idea is arguably alienation of personality—a prohibited act in Hegel's system.[160]

When I take the rock from my shelf and toss it back onto the Corsican beach, I do so because I no longer identify with the memories the rock evokes and no longer see it as manifesting a part of my life. We go through this same process when we put old knickknacks in a garage sale or send old clothes to the Salvation Army. The *res* exists independent of our personality, so it is not incoherent to claim that there is no longer a personality stake in the *res*.

This abandonment of a personality stake will be incoherent if there is no recognizable *res* that exists beyond the individual's expression. The question is whether the created work exists independent of the creator: does the expression turn to artifact? Performing artists often war with writers and composers over this issue. Seeking maximum freedom, the performers view the particular play or musical composition they are using as a device for their own expression, a *res* through which they can express their personalities. Yet the writer or composer may not think the *res* is abandoned at all.

Playwrights versus actors, composers versus conductors and orchestras—these two sides will always be locked in one another's arms, in a grip that is both mortal combat and mutual need. It is possible to draw many comparisons and analogies to this issue. There is the familiar comparison to the rights of parents—the author having a parental stake in her work. A less-familiar analogy might be made to the questions of original intent and interpretivism in constitutional jurisprudence.

The "interpreters" believe that intellectual property can be, and usually is, abandoned. Their vision is reinforced by both popular notions of artistic development and philosophical notions of personal identity. A writer may simply no longer identify with something he previously wrote. A Picasso or a Le Corbusier may change radically the style of his work and, in the end, no longer identify with the works of the abandoned period. David Bowie can move beyond "Ziggy Stardust" and David Stockman can repudiate his doctrine of supply-side economics.[161] Philosophers are familiar with arguments that there is no reason to identify the works written by Jorge Luis Borges in 1956 as a manifestation of the personality of Jorge Luis Borges as of 1986. For Borges in 1986, his earlier works may indeed have seemed like a *res nullius*.

Hegel seems to have taken a contrary view, considering the complete alienation of intellectual property to be wrong—morally analogous to slavery or suicide because it is the surrender of a "universal" aspect of the self. Selling an entire piece of intellectual property seems like a lesser surrender of the self, but Hegel considered it too much a "universal" part of the individual to be permitted. He seemed to identify the intellectual object as an ongoing expression of its creator, not as a free, abandonable cultural object. Supporting Hegel's view, we can note that even when the creator thinks he has abandoned the object, he may still identify with it enough to oppose certain uses for it. Even after "abandoning" a visual image, the artist might oppose its use as a symbol by a fringe political or religious organization.

The alienation of copies of the intellectual property offers a different set of issues. An owner may or may not limit the uses to which the alienated copies may be put. However, in either case the original owner still retains rights over the property. This type of alienation does not fall prey to the paradox of complete alienation: there is no exercise of property rights (alienation) after an "owner" no longer has a personality stake in an object. It also is immune from Hegel's objection to the selling of a part of oneself. Unlike physical property, the owner can, in this way, alienate the intellectual property while keeping the "whole" of the property and himself.

Not only does Hegel's personality theory pose no inherent objection to this kind of alienation of intellectual property, it also provides affirmative justifications. Hegel focuses on one such justification—concern for the economic well-being of the intellectual property creator.

At first blush, this economic rationale seems far removed from the concerns of personality theory, yet it can be recast into the framework of the personality theory. From the Hegelian perspective, payments from intellectual property users to the property creator are acts of recognition. These payments acknowledge the individual's claim over the property, and it is through such acknowledgment that an individual is recognized by others as a person.[162] "Recognition" involves more than lip service. If I say "this forest is your property" and then proceed to flagrantly trespass, cut your timber, and hunt your deer, I have not recognized your property rights. Similarly, verbal recognition of an intellectual property claim is not equal to the recognition implicit in a payment. Purchasers of a copyrighted work or licensees of a patent form a circle of people recognizing the creator as a person.

Furthermore, this generation of income complements the personality theory inasmuch as income facilitates further expression. When royalties from an invention allow the inventor to buy a grand piano he has always wanted, the transaction helps maximize personality. But this argument tends to be too broad. First, much income is used for basic necessities, leading to the vacuous position that life-sustenance is "personally maximizing" because it allows the personality to continue. Second, this approach could justify property rights for after-the-fact development of personality interests without requiring such interests in the property at the time the property rights are granted.

The personality theory provides a better, more direct justification for the alienation of intellectual property, especially copies. The alienation of copies is perhaps the most rational way to gain exposure for one's ideas. This is a non-economic, and perhaps higher, form of the idea of recognition: respect, honor, and admiration. Even for starving artists, recognition of this sort may be far more valuable than economic rewards.

Two conditions appear essential, however, to this justification of alienation: first, the creator of the work must receive public identification, and, second, the work must receive protection against any changes unintended or unapproved by the creator. Hegel's prohibition of "complete" alienation of intellectual property appears to result from his recognition of the necessity for these two conditions. While he would permit alienation of copies, and even the rights to further reproduction, he disapproves alienation of "those goods, or rather substantive characteristics, which constitute . . . private personality and the universal essence of . . . self-consciousness."[163] Such alienation necessarily occurs if the recognition of the connection between a creator and his expression is destroyed or distorted. When the first condition is violated, this recognition is destroyed; when the second condition is violated, it is distorted.

C. The Personality Justification in U.S. Law

These two conditions are recognized in French and German intellectual property law under the general name of "moral rights."[164] For both copyright and patent owners, there is the right to be properly identified with one's creations. For copyright owners, there also exists an inalienable right to guard the integrity of a work against change that would damage the author's reputation or destroy his intended message.

Although this chapter will not critique these Continental laws in depth, a couple of observations are in order. First, even in these systems, there is no clear right for patent owners to protect the integrity of their creation, although they do enjoy a right to have their name attached to the patent. This may reflect an implicit social judgment that the degree of personality reflection in most patented works is different and smaller than in most copyrighted works. Second, by forbidding alienation of certain rights in intellectual property, these civil systems prevent the complete alienation of the property: "transfer of the copyright as a whole between living persons is basically precluded on account of the elements of the right of personality (*droit moral*)."[165]

There are no provisions in American copyright law giving an author "moral rights" to protect against distortion and to ensure recognition. It is interesting, however, to note how the personality justification has subtly affected American copyright doctrine.[166] The property interest in a work does not depend on any external measure of artistic, cultural, or social worth in any field covered by copyright. The world is full of bad, but nonetheless personal, poetry and of paintings that look like Rorschach images to everyone but the painter. Initially there seems to have been some confusion as to whether worth was a prerequisite to copyright—but this uncertainty was dispelled in the 1903 case of *Bleistein v. Donaldson Lithographing Co.*[167]

In *Bleistein* the plaintiff sought to protect three lithographs used as advertisements for a circus. Against the defendant's calls to require some level of artistic achievement before conferring copyright, the Supreme Court held that copyright of the prints was not barred because of their "limited pretensions." Writing for the majority, Justice Holmes wrote that "a very modest grade of art has in it something irreducible, which is one man's alone. That something he may copyright unless there is a restriction in the words of the act."[168] Holmes was prepared to cast a wide net to recognize tiny bits of individual personalities: "Personality always contains something unique. It expresses its singularity even in handwriting."[169]

Perhaps *Bleistein* marks only a momentary flirtation with the personality justification. Indeed, it is the Supreme Court's only intellectual property opinion that uses the word "personality" as a juridically significant concept. There are few cases inheriting—and explicitly averring—Holmes' reasoning.[170] Yet both the notions it exorcised from American law and the notions it enshrined are significant.

٭   ٭   ٭

D. Civil Rights Support for a Personality Justification

The most frequently attempted bridge from existing American law to more control over intellectual property has not been civil rights, but defamation claims. Common examples include a playwright suing when a director "degrades" the play, or a novelist suing the producer when the movie script focuses on sex and violence in a way the novel does not.

Defamation claims are perhaps the worst method of protecting personality interests within existing doctrine because any "distortion-as-defamation" doctrine will eventually have to be reconciled with *New York Times v. Sullivan* and its progeny.[171] These cases have established rigorous standards for proving libel and defamation in news stories and cartoons. Ultimately, they must stand as a bulwark against finding libel in printed material or copyrighted works in general. It would be very odd jurisprudence that had rigorous tests for defamation when the defamer was using his own words, but made it easier to show defamation when the victim used the victim's own expression.

In place of the defamation strategy, I suggest using two civil rights approaches to protect intellectual property. Although generally unrecognized, there are civil liberties arguments available that functionally can provide some "moral rights" that protect the personality of the creator as it is manifested in the creation.

1. The Privacy Right Argument

For centuries unpublished works have been protected by copyright, either statutorily or under common law. Copyright over unpublished works can be explained by economic considerations—allowing a person to retain the economic value in an unpublished work until he or she chooses to exploit that value. Yet the privacy of the individual also is at issue. We always allow people to shape their public images; this is part of having private and social selves. Similarly, an author should be able to guard a work until she is satisfied that the work warrants public consideration. It also is possible that a person may intend for his writings or art *never* to reach the public, having created the work solely for his private pleasure and that of his intimates. Seeing the personality issues involved, Samuel Warren and Louis Brandeis declared that the right to privacy should allow a person to prevent publication of private letters, even when the would-be publisher was the recipient of the letters.

∗   ∗   ∗

A series of cases have recognized, as a principle, that dissemination of a work under the author's name and against the author's wishes may infringe privacy rights. This principle, however, almost invariably remains dicta. In *Shostakovich v. Twentieth Century-Fox Film Corp.*,[172] the right was recognized, but the plaintiffs did not succeed in preventing the appearance of their names as the composers of the music used in an anti-Soviet film because their music already was in the public domain.[173] In *Geisel v. Poynter Products, Inc.,* Theodor Seuss Geisel could not succeed in a privacy action against those using "Dr. Seuss" attached to toy dolls because "Dr. Seuss" was judged to be his trade name, or *nom de plume,* not his proper name.[174]

It is instructive to note the posture of the privacy arguments made by both *Shostakovich* and *Geisel.* On the surface, the plaintiff in each case claimed that public use of his name against his will invaded his privacy. Interestingly, this is the reverse of the right to demand that one's name be used publicly with one's work.

∗   ∗   ∗

2. The Freedom of Expression Argument

First Amendment freedom of expression often is portrayed as the enemy of intellectual property rights. Proponents of cutting back copyright protection usually invoke free speech and the marketplace of ideas, if not a direct appeal to the First Amendment, as a "trump" over the copyright clause. Recent articles typify this approach. One argues that "a First Amendment defense to [copyright] infringement actions . . . would guarantee the free dissemination of ideas conveyed through visual media."[175] Another includes a milder observation that "our deep rooted tradition of free speech stemming from the first amendment's mandate requires the same balance of interests when a creator alleges violations of his personal, rather than pecuniary, rights."[176]

While these arguments may be persuasive, they face a potentially powerful pro-copyright First Amendment counterargument, which might be stated as follows: *freedom of expression is meaningless without assurances that the expression will remain unadulterated.*[177] Free speech requires that speech be guaranteed some integrity. It follows that if intellectual property is expression, it merits the same guarantee.

*   *   *

In *Gilliam v. American Broadcasting Companies, Inc.*, the British comedy show *Monty Python's Flying Circus* successfully enjoined the ABC network from broadcasting radically edited versions of the Monty Python comedy programs.[178] ABC had removed twenty-four minutes from each ninety-minute show. The Second Circuit found that "the truncated version at times omitted the climax of the skits . . . and at other times deleted essential elements in the schematic development of a story line."[179] The court concluded:

> We therefore agree with Judge Lasker's conclusion that the edited version broadcast by ABC impaired the integrity of appellants' work and represented to the public as the product of appellants what was actually a mere caricature of their talents. We believe that a valid cause of action for such distortion exists and that therefore a preliminary injunction may issue.[180]

Cases of this sort presently are treated as contract disputes or matters to be decided under equitable principles, but they could be collected and made the building materials for a First Amendment claim built into copyright protection. Justice Brennan's dissent in *Columbia Broadcasting System v. Democratic National Committee* touches the heart of the matter.[181] Although writing about access to media, the basic concern applies to copyright:

> In the absence of an effective means of communication, the right to speak would ring hollow indeed. And, in recognition of these principles, we have consistently held that the First Amendment embodies, not only the abstract right to be free from censorship, but also the right of an individual to utilize an appropriate and effective medium for the expression of his views.[182]

At issue is not just the right to use an appropriate and effective medium, but also to make a particular medium appropriate and effective. The goal is to ensure that printed and published materials effectively convey the creator's expression.

*   *   *

The rise of the printing press actually strengthened the author's ability to protect his work.[183] By centralizing the reproduction process, the printing press permits the author to deal with one person at one time, to insure the integrity of the text. Computerized systems offer both increased centralization and increased decentralization, undoubtedly forcing the author to do more ongoing surveillance. After a publisher has printed a book, the author can rest tranquil if he is satisfied with the text. Authors will rest less comfortably when their works are published on a computerized databank that at any time can be centrally altered.

New technology also raises new economic concerns that may increase the need for protection of the expression. Historically, the unauthorized publisher faced an unprofitable environment. First, the pirate faced publishing costs similar to those of the legitimate publisher—fixed costs that far exceeded the cost of royalty payments avoided by piracy. This meant that the pirate's ability to underprice authorized publishers was limited to his savings in royalties not paid. Furthermore, the original publisher usually enjoyed a market-introduction advantage. These "barriers to entry" have been steadily eroded by developments in the past decades. Scanning devices allow the pirate to create computer files of a book directly from an authorized copy, without retyping the text manually. This lowers the pirate's production costs and diminishes the time advantage enjoyed by the authorized publisher. Desktop printers allow nearly anyone to produce high quality reproductions of (possibly altered) texts, logos, and insignias.[184] The less sophisticated pirate might discover that these days it is frequently cheaper to photocopy a book than to buy a published copy. This is especially true with hardbound books of three hundred pages or less.

We know that the author has an interest in preventing such activities. *Society's* interest in preventing distortions and preserving original forms is less obvious. As Roberta Kwall writes, "protection for creators' personal rights . . . enables society to preserve the integrity of its cultural heritage. The public's right to enjoy the fruits of a creator's labors in original form and to learn cultural heritage from such creations has no time limit."[185]

The preservation of cultural works has become increasingly important to all modern societies, but what counts as effective preservation varies with the cultural object. It is not enough to preserve music scores in a library basement if no one plays them or no one knows the tempo at which they should be played. The level or degree to which an original will be preserved is proportional to available resources, but our society of relative abundance should preserve the original form of a work so that it may contribute effectively to our ongoing cultural discourse.

A system that actively protects expression guarantees that the most radical and unconventional voices will survive. The less respect a system accords particular expressions, the more likely that those expressions will disappear or will be altered to fit conventional thinking. Even if the quantity of expression remains the same, the content may be pasteurized into a dull conformity. Protection of expressive integrity advances systemic evolution by countering the conformist pressures that befall unusual messages.

*   *   *

IV. Conclusion

Twenty years ago, in a lecture at Columbia Law School, Benjamin Kaplan applied the pragmatist's lens to intellectual property and concluded as follows:

> Examining the view from the top of the hill, I find one temptation easy to resist, and that is to sum up copyright with just the word "property" or "personality" or any one of the other essences to which scholars, foreign and domestic, have been trying to reduce the subject. . . . Characterizations in grand terms then seem of little value: we may as well go directly to the policies actuating or justifying the particular determinations.[186]

This chapter has looked to the social policies and the judicial determinations underlying our system of intellectual property, but it has done so while testing two grand characterizations. There is a purpose to such characterizations. Husserl once observed that "tradition" meant only that the particulars of the past had been forgotten. Of course, it is inevitable that the details of the past will be lost. That means that we have a choice between unreflective tradition and grand theories; I find the latter a preferable way to capture and condense a history. The grand characterization can be tested, more thoroughly than the tradition, as it is used as a guide for new situations.

Both of the grand theories for intellectual property—labor and personality—have their own strengths and weaknesses. The labor justification cannot account for the idea whose inception does not seem to have involved labor; the personality theory is inapplicable to valuable innovations that do not contain elements of what society might recognize as personal expression. The personality justification has difficulty legitimating alienation, while the labor explanation may have to shuffle around Locke's non-waste condition.

At the same time, the two justifications seem to apply more readily to intellectual property than to the property they are usually called upon to legitimate. The Lockean labor theory applies more easily because the common of ideas seems inexhaustible. The Hegelian personality theory applies more easily because intellectual products, even the most technical, seem to result from the individual's mental processes. As for Hegel's interests in using property rights to secure recognition for the individual, intellectual property rights are a powerful instrument to this end because the *res* is not merely *seized* by the individual, but rather it is a *product of the individual.*

Earlier I suggested that the personality theory might justify rights to protect one's private property without justifying rights to alienate that property. I must add, as a possible corollary, that the labor justification, with its emphasis on value maximization, might legitimate alienation and value exchange without safeguarding rights to keep particular objects merely as "possessions." In this way, the two theories may compensate for each other's weaknesses.

There are two reasons to seek out such grand generalizations to explain the social institution of intellectual property. The first is that "labor" and "individuality" have much more populist appeal than "property." To return full circle, rights to labor and rights to individual expression *do* have much more of a siren's call than property rights. The second reason, applicable to all social institutions, is that we cannot avoid general characterizations. Our only course is to face such generalizations squarely and assemble them consciously.

Notes

1. The Declaration of Independence, paragraph 1 (U.S. 1776).
2. The heralding article on this subject is Reich, "The New Property," *Yale Law Journal* 73 (1964): 733.
3. 408 U.S.C. sec. 564, 577 (1972).
4. See generally, G. Hegel, *Philosophy of Right*, trans. by T. M. Knox (Oxford: Clarendon Press, 1965), paragraphs, 41–45 (individual demonstrates ownership of property by imposing his will on it and thereby "occupying" it); Stillman, "Property, Freedom, and Individuality in Hegel's and Marx's Political Thoughts," in *Property, Nomos XXII,* edited by J. Pennock and J. Chapman (New York: New York University Press, 1980), 130, 134.
5. Professor Richard Rorty argues that "mirror imagery" has been the foundation for the Cartesian and Kantian philosophical traditions (R. Rorty, *Philosophy and the Mirror of Nature* [Princeton, N.J.: Princeton University Press, 1979],

12). Professor Laurence Tribe has also used the mirror image to condemn the Supreme Court's narrow interpretation of the equal protection clause in recent decisions (L. Tribe, *Constitutional Choices* [Cambridge, Mass.: Harvard University Press, 1985], 238–45).

6. P. J. Proudhon, *What Is Property? An Inquiry into the Principles of Right and of Government*, trans. by B. R. Tucker (Paris, 1840; repr. 1966), 11–12.

7. Marx quickly grasped the fallacy of Proudhon's position. See Marx, "On Proudhon," reprinted in *Karl Marx and Frederick Engels, Selected Works* (Moscow: Progress Publishers, 1969), 25–26.

8. See E. Burke, "Reflections on the Revolution in France," in *The Works of Edmund Burke* (George Bell & Sons, 1905), 277, 324. Hegel similarly advocated an important role in social stability for the landed class. Hegel, *Philosophy of Right*, par. 313.

9. See Burke, "Reflections," 316 ("Whenever the supreme authority is vested in a body so composed, it must eventually produce the consequences of supreme authority placed in hands of men not taught habitually to respect themselves; who could not be expected to bear with moderation . . . a power, which they themselves . . . must be surprised to find in their hands").

10. Burke, "Reflections," 317.

11. See Burke, "Reflections," 324 ("the power of perpetuating our property in our families is one of the most valuable and interesting circumstances belonging to it"); see also Hegel, *Philosophy of Right*, par. 178 ("The natural dissolution of the family by the death of the parents, particularly the father, has inheritance as its consequence so far as the family capital is concerned").

In the eighth and ninth books of the *Republic*, Plato avers that the best government is an aristocratic state led by a propertied class. Yet the drive for property eventually produces an undesirable oligarchy with a propertyless underclass: "such a state is not one, but two states, the one of poor, the other of rich men; and they are living on the same spot and always conspiring against one another" (Plato, *Republic*, trans. by B. Jowett [Oxford: Clarendon Press, 1986], 303).

12. Lincoln applied for and was granted U.S. Patent No. 6,469 (22 May 1849). Lewis (1845–1890) was a Black American sculptress known for her neoclassical busts and medallions. She is an especially apt example because royalties from copies of her busts supported her move to Rome, where she established her studio (J. Porter, *Modern Negro Art* [New York: Arno Press, 1943], 58). Several of her works survive in the National Museum of American Art, Washington, D.C.

13. UNESCO, *The ABC of Copyright* (Paris: UNESCO, 1981), 12. See also, B. Kaplan, *An Unhurried View of Copyright* (New York: Columbia University Press, 1967), 2–9.

14. Denmark and Norway are the only countries that have granted perpetual rights in intellectual property. The ordinance that created these rights was somewhat less perpetual. It was adopted in 1741 and repealed in 1814 (UNESCO, *Copyright*, 15).

15. Copyright provisions are codified at 17 U.S.C. sec. 101–914 (1982 and

Supp. IV, 1986). The Patent Act is codified at 35 U.S.C. sec. 1–376 (1982 and Supp. IV, 1986). Federal trademark law is codified at 15 U.S.C. sec. 1051–1127 (1982 and Supp. IV, 1986). Trade secret protection is left to the states.

16. Semiconductor Chip Protection Act of 1984, 17 U.S.C. sec. 901–912 (Supp. IV, 1986).

17. 17 U.S.C. 103. See also, 248 U.S.C. sec. 215, 236–42 (1918) (one who expends time and resources for purposes of lucrative publication has a quasi-property interest in the results of the enterprise as against a rival in the same business; appropriation of those results to the damage of one and the profit of another constitutes unfair competition).

18. See notes 148–50 below (discussing the concepts of persona and property interest).

19. There are two international copyright conventions; a nation may belong to both without conflict. The Universal Copyright Convention, signed by the United States and more than fifty other countries, provides for reciprocity of rights extended to nationals, and also provides some substantive protections, including protection for "not less than the life of the author and twenty-five years" (Universal Copyright Convention [24 July 1971]). The Berne Convention, which the United States ratified in 1988, has over seventy signatories and provides more definite substantive requirements, such as protection "for the life of the author and fifty years."

There are also two major patent treaties, both of which the United States has signed. The Paris Convention for the Protection of Industrial Property (14 July 1967) and the Patent Cooperation Treaty (24 January 1978).

20. See generally S. Levitsky, *Copyright, Defamation, and Privacy in Soviet Civil Law* (Alphen aan den Rijn: Sijtheff & Noordhoff, 1979) (citing Soviet Union's acceptance in 1973 of the Universal Copyright Convention); Pavelic, "The Protection of Private Rights in a Socialist State: Recent Developments in Yugoslav Copyright Law," *Harvard International Law Journal* 14 (1973): 111, 117–26.

21. See Hughes, "Between Art and Law," *Harvard Crimson*, 21 January 1985.

22. Hughes, "Between Art and Law," *Endgame*'s stage direction called for a bare, gray stage. The Cambridge production set the play in a gutted, abandoned Boston subway station. In 1988, Beckett successfully opposed efforts by the Comédie-Française in Paris to do a production of *Endgame* on a set bathed in pink light (see *International Herald Tribune*, 14 October 1988).

23. P. D. Rosenberg, *Patent Law Fundamentals*, 2d ed. (New York: C. Boardman, 1985), sec. 1.03.

24. 17 U.S.C. sec. 107 (1982).

25. *Gayler v. Wilder*, 51 U.S. (10 How.) 477, 497 (1850). This exception, of course, is not useful to research laboratories that are pursuing developments that may have commercial applications. Accordingly, a problem has emerged in biomedical laboratories because the patenting of certain cell lines prevents other research labs from using these types of cells in their research (Weiner, "Universities,

Professors, and Patents: A Continuing Controversy," *Technology Review* February/March 1986: 32, 42–43).

26. U.S. Constitution, art. I, sec. 8, cl. 8.

27. See J. Locke, *Second Treatise of Government,* sec. 138–40, in *Two Treatises of Government,* edited by P. Laslett (New York: Cambridge University Press, 1963).

28. Locke, *Second Treatise,* sec. 25.

29. Locke, *Second Treatise,* sec. 33.

30. Locke, *Second Treatise,* sec. 27. See generally Mautner, "Locke on Original Acquisition," *American Philosophical Quarterly* 19 (1982): 259, 260 (claiming the "enough and as good" condition is not actually a premise in Locke's argument). Although some scholars agree with Mautner, most seem to treat the proposition as a central premise of Locke's argument. See, for example, C. B. MacPherson, *The Political Theory Of Possessive Individualism: Hobbes To Locke* (Oxford: Oxford University Press, 1962), 201; G. Parry, *John Locke* (London: G. Allen & Unwin, 1978). Perhaps even Mautner implicitly retreats from saying the "enough and as good" condition is not a premise by admitting that Locke makes an "assumption of original abundance" (Mautner, "Original Acquisition," 260).

31. Locke, *Second Treatise,* sec. 37.

32. Locke, *Second Treatise,* sec. 36, 37, and 41. An interesting problem raised by these examples is the geographical consideration in determining what counts as "enough and as good." For example, the Treaty of Paris left the new United States with the unsettled Northwest Territory (which became Ohio, Indiana, Illinois, Michigan, and Wisconsin). Does this mean the enough and as good condition would be satisfied for those within the territory? Would it be satisfied for everyone within the United States assuming unrestricted immigration? Would it be satisfied for all within the English-speaking world?

33. Epstein, "Possession as the Root of Title," *Georgia Law Journal* 13 (1979): 1221, 1227.

34. Locke, *Second Treatise,* sec. 27, cited in Epstein, "Possession," 1227.

35. Epstein, "Possession," 1227.

36. By definition, "possession" involves a relationship that includes domination. The possessor controls his possession. He is dominant over it. The mind-body connection, however, is not based upon unilateral domination. While it is said that the mind "controls" the body, we now know that the symbiosis between the two renders such a statement inaccurate. We cannot say that the mind controls the body any more than that the body controls the mind. There is an integration of the two—or perhaps the concept of two separate entities is itself misleading—but there is no possessory relationship.

37. Locke, *Second Treatise,* sec. 37.

38. Locke, *Second Treatise.*

39. Locke, *Second Treatise.*

40. Locke, *Second Treatise,* sec. 50.

41. Thomas Scanlon seems to consider this consent critical because "the origi-

nal moral foundation for property rights is no longer valid" once we have a money economy (Scanlon, "Nozick on Rights, Liberty, and Property," in *Reading Nozick* edited by J. Paul [Totowa: Rowman & Littlefield, 1981], 107, 126). But Nozick appears to disagree. See R. Nozick, *Anarchy, State, and Utopia* (New York: Basic Books, 1974), 18 (social contract not necessary for free exchange of goods).

42. Such an alloy exists if people were to give their tacit consent to the distribution of property because (1) they believed that the present distribution arose from an original distribution based on the labor justification and (2) they believed that the labor justification was indeed valid.

43. Baird, "Common Law Intellectual Property and the Legacy of *International News Service v. Associated Press*," *University Of Chicago Law Review* 50 (1983): 411, 413.

44. Baird, "Common Law," 415.

45. Locke, *Second Treatise*, sec. 27.

46. Becker, "The Labor Theory of Property Acquisition," *Journal of Philosophy* 73 (1976): 653, 655.

47. Locke, *Second Treatise*, sec. 34.

48. Minogue, "The Concept of Property and Its Contemporary Significance," in *Property, Nomos XXII*, edited by J. Pennock and J. Chapman (New York: New York University Press, 1980), 3, 10.

49. David Ellerman argues that the "labor theory of property has throughout its history been entwined with and often confused with the labor theory of value. . . . The admixture of the two labor theories [was] present even in Locke" (Ellerman, "Property and the Theory of Value," *Philosophical Forum* 16 [1985]: 293, 294). Ellerman writes of the confusion of normative propositions, but the same confusion can occur with the consequentialist arguments. For example, should we use property to give people incentives, or should we use some other measure of value?

50. 347 U.S.C. sec. 201 (1954); see also 347 U.S.C. sec. 219 (emphasis added).

51. U.S. Constitution, art. I, sec. 8, cl. 8.

52. A. Lincoln, "Second Lecture on Discoveries and Inventions," *The Collected Works of Abraham Lincoln*, edited by R. P. Basler (New Brunswick, N.J.: Rutgers University Press, 1953), 356, 363.

53. Easterbrook, "Foreword: The Court and the Economic System in the Supreme Court 1983 Term," *Harvard Law Review* 98 (1984): 4, 21–29.

54. Rosenberg, *Patent Law*, sec. 1.07.

55. Becker, "The Moral Basis of Property Rights," in *Property, Nomos XXII*, edited by J. Pennock and J. Chapman (New York: New York University Press, 1980), 187, 193.

56. 347 U.S.C. sec. 201 (1954).

57. U.S. Constitution, art. I, sec. 8, cl. 8.

58. 248 U.S.C. sec. 215 (1918).

59. See generally D. S. Chisum, *Patents* (1988), sec. 4.01–4.

60. 15 F. Cas. 1014, 1018 (C.C.D. Mass. 1819) (No. 8,568).

61. See *Brenner v. Manson*, 383 U.S. 519, 533–36 (1965) (requiring showing of positive social benefit to satisfy utility requirement).

62. See *Graham v. Jorn Deere*, 383 U.S. 1, 25 (1965).

63. Rosenberg, *Patent Law*, sec. 8.03, at 8–8.

64. Such an invention might indirectly produce value for society by improving a technology that, after further research and improvement, eventually surpasses existing technologies.

65. 106 F.2d 45 (2d Cir. 1939), *aff'd*, 309 U.S. 390 (1940).

66. 309 U.S. 390 (1940), 50 (stars were Joan Crawford and Robert Montgomery).

67. 309 U.S. 390 (1940), 48.

68. W. Faulkner, *Sartoris* (1929) and *Absalom, Absalom!* (1936).

69. Remark of Hadi Abu Shakra, LL.M. candidate, Harvard Law School (May 1985).

70. W. V. O. Quine recently put it another way: "If the fantasy of the universal library were realized, literary creativity would likewise reduce to discovery: the author's book would await him on the shelf" (Quine, *Quiddities* [Cambridge, Mass.: Belknap Press, 1987], 39).

71. 293 F. Supp. 130, 144 (S.D.N.Y. 1968).

72. *Scènes à faire* are elements (e.g., scene, character, plot component) of a genre of literature so common that they are customary. For example, in space-voyage science fiction, a battle scene and a non-human character would probably qualify as *scènes à faire*.

73. *Krofft Television*, 562 F.2d at 1170; see also *Triangle Publications, Inc. v. Knight-Ridder Newspapers, Inc.*, 626 F.2d 1171, 1178 (5th Cir. 1980) (Brown, J., concurring) ("The idea-expression dichotomy generally provides a workable balance between copyright and free speech interests").

74. Nimmer, "Does Copyright Abridge the First Amendment Guarantees of Free Speech and Press?" *U.C.L.A. Law Review* 17 (1970): 1180.

75. Nimmer, 1197–1200 (photographs of My Lai massacre and film of John F. Kennedy's assassination could not be censored from public by copyright owners). An audacious example of copyright over the expression of a public event is the television evangelist Jimmy Swaggart's claimed copyright over his public confession of relations with a prostitute. Swaggart claimed copyright in an effort to stop the Cincinnati Opera from using part of the confession in an advertisement for the opera *Susannah* (*Int'l Herald Tribune*, 18–19 June 1988). What other reason would Swaggart have to claim copyright than to chill the confession's use by others?

76. The two dichotomies may not be completely parallel. Under present law, when "idea" and "expression" merge, the creation is unprotected on the rationale that one could not express the idea any other way.

77. See *Krofft Television*, 562 F.2d at 1169 ("the intrinsic test for expression is uniquely suited for determination by the trier of fact").

78. See Prager, "The Early Growth and Influence of Intellectual Property,"

Journal of the Patent Office Society 34 (1952): 106, 108–9 (authors, unlike creators of tangible things, lose right to exclusive use of words and ideas after publication and public possession).

79. In fact, this addition to the common pool of ideas has been recognized as part of the "bargain" of patent law: "such additions to the general store of knowledge are of such importance to the public weal that the Federal Government is willing to pay the high price of 17 years of exclusive use for its disclosure, which disclosure, it is assumed, will stimulate ideas and the eventual development of further significant advances" (*Kewanee Oil Co. v. Bicron Corp.*, 416 U.S. 470, 481 [1974]). To some, society has the better bargain: "the purpose of disclosure to the public is to catalyze other inventors into activity . . . The inventor makes a truly Faustian bargain with the sovereign, exchanging secrecy of indefinite and of possibly perpetual duration, for ephemeral patent rights" (Rosenberg, *Patent Law*, sec. 1.02, 1–5).

80. Another point is that idea X may breathe new life into the common by making set of ideas Y worth developing. For example, L'Enfant's plans for Washington, D.C., made it viable for generations of architects to develop ideas to use the city's oddly shaped intersections.

81. See Nozick, *Anarchy*, 174–82 (social considerations favor establishment of private property and a free market system would not violate Locke's proviso that "enough and as good" remain in the common).

82. Locke, *Second Treatise*, sec. 32.

83. This is true even where the inventor of the "child" holds a license to the "parent" idea. Hence the pressure for "grant-backs" of offspring patents to the owner of the original patent.

84. Parody is considered a "fair use" of the copyrighted work and a parody's "fair use" of an original is usually more extensive than the "fair use" of an ostensibly rather unrelated work. At a minimum, a parody can "conjure up" an original for the sake of humor. See, for example, *Elsmere Music, Inc. v. National Broadcasting Co.*, 623 F.2d 252, 253 n.1 (2d Cir. 1980) (per curiam) (*Saturday Night Live* transformation of song "I Love New York" into "I Love Sodom" was fair use). A parody threatening to displace the original within the market may infringe. See *Warner Bros., Inc. v. American Broadcasting Co.*, 654 F.2d 204, 208 (2d Cir. 1981) (to determine whether similarity between original work and parody constitutes "substantial and hence infringing similarity," the court must decide whether similarities are "something more than mere generalized ideas or themes").

85. At the same time, the purported parody—no longer recognized as such—is not "complimenting" the original as a parody normally does by indicating that the original has reached a certain level of fame.

86. See Nozick, *Anarchy*, 175–82.

87. See Nozick, *Anarchy*, 180.

88. Levmore, "Explaining Restitution," *Virginia Law Review* 71 (1985): 65, 96.

89. 253 F.2d 702, 704 (2d Cir.), *cert. denied*, 358 U.S. 816 (1958).

90. Kaplan, *Copyright*, 65.

91. *Twentieth Century-Fox Film Corp. v. MCA, Inc.*, 715 F.2d 1327, 1329 (9th Cir. 1983) (vacating trial court's grant of pretrial summary judgment for MCA, creator of "Battlestar Galactica").

92. This is sometimes called the "aspirin and cellophane doctrine."

93. R. Callman, *The Law of Unfair Competition and Trademark*, 2d ed. (Chicago: Callaghan, 1950), 1149–50.

94. Nozick, *Anarchy*, 181.

95. Nozick, *Anarchy*.

96. Steiner, "Slavery, Socialism, and Private Property," in *Property, Nomos XXII*, edited by J. Pennock and J. Chapman (New York: New York University Press, 1980), 244, 251.

97. Nozick, *Anarchy*, 175.

98. Nozick, *Anarchy*.

99. J. Rawls, *A Theory Of Justice* (Cambridge, Mass.: Harvard University Press, 1971), 204–93.

100. Locke, *Second Treatise*, sec. 46–51.

101. Nozick, *Anarchy*, 176.

102. Locke, *Second Treatise*, sec. 46–51.

103. A third, less likely possibility is that the idea I give my friend allows her to labor less to survive and to loiter more. However, this does not seem to accord with Locke's view of human motives, for he assumed that people will inevitably strive to accumulate material objects (Locke, *Second Treatise*, sec. 46).

104. To attack the notion that there is no intellectual property in the pre-money economy, one might argue that we should make a distinction between a barter economy and a money economy. Locke does not draw any significant distinction between the two, but one could infer from Locke's discussion that the barter economy is a situation in which people are trying to acquire more of the "useful" goods they need without doing violence to the non-waste condition and without accumulating non-useful goods like gold. "First-order" bartering displays this kind of exchange: short-lived fruits bartered for more durable nuts. Such barters are useful things in Locke's scheme; the person receiving nuts avoids the non-waste condition and the person receiving the fruits adds variety to his diet. Given Locke's announced antipathy toward non-useful items that people value (gold, silver, baubles), as soon as these items enter the barter system, one has a money economy: an exchange system based on an unnatural, or at least less fundamental, second order of valuation.

105. Nozick, *Anarchy*, 175–76.

106. D. Johnston, *Copyright Handbook*, 2d ed. (New York: R. R. Bowker Co., 1982), 23–33.

107. Johnston, *Copyright Handbook*.

108. It has been argued that this condition never occurred with physical goods, or that it has not occurred during the known history of mankind (see MacPherson, *Possessive Individualism*). Others argue that even if this condition applied to

physical goods at one point in time, it cannot be used in a justification for property enduring past its original allocation (see Steiner, "Slavery, Socialism, and Private Property," 251–52 [eventually all land will be owned and non-landowners will be trespassers unless they obtain permission for use from owners, citing H. Spencer, *Social Statics* (1851) 114–15]; and Mautner, *Original Acquisition,* 267–68 [justification fails because claim that property was legitimately acquired can rarely be supported]).

109. Rapaczynski, "Locke's Conception of Property and the Principle of Sufficient Reason," *History Of Ideas* 42 (1981): 307.

110. Radin, "Property and Personhood," *Stanford Law Review* 34 (1982): 957.

111. This theory was most thoroughly developed in Hegel, *Philosophy of Right.*

112. See Kwall, "Copyright and the Moral Right: Is an American Marriage Possible?," *Vanderbilt Law Review* 38 (1985): 1, 5–16 (urging United States to adopt aspects of European copyright law that recognize moral and personal rights of the creator in the work produced, rather than mere pecuniary interests recognized under U.S. law); Katz, "The Doctrine of Moral Rights and American Copyright Law—A Proposal," *S. California Law Review* 24 (1951): 375, 391–409 (proposing that the United States incorporate the European concept of moral rights into copyright law); Roeder, "The Doctrine of Moral Rights: A Study in the Law of Artists, Authors and Creators," *Harvard Law Review* 53 (1940): 554, 558–65 (arguing that the United States should adopt European moral rights in copyrighted work, which includes right to publish, or not, in form desired and right to prevent deformation).

113. Acton, *The Encyclopedia of Philosophy,* "Hegel, Georg Wilhelm Friedrich" (R. N. Berki, 1967 ed.), 442.

114. Hegel, *Philosophy of Right,* par. 41.

115. Hegel, *Philosophy of Right,* par. 39.

116. Berki, "Political Freedom and Hegelian Metaphysics," *Political Studies* 16 (1968): 365, 376.

117. *The Philosophy of Right* is divided into three parts. Part I, "Abstract Right," is concerned with the individual agent as a person in relationships with other persons and things. Parts II and III are concerned with the higher development of the agent as an autonomous moral subject and as a member of the rational community ultimately manifested in the state (Hegel, *Philosophy of Right*).

118. A. Camus, *Caligula* (Paris: Gallimard, 1945).

119. For example, he attacks parents who treat their children as "things" (Hegel, *Philosophy of Right,* par. 43).

120. The first principle of Rawls' architectonic system addresses this concern: "Each person is to have an equal right to the most extensive total system of equal basic liberties compatible with a similar system of liberty for all" (Rawls, *Theory of Justice,* 250, 302).

121. Hegel, *Philosophy of Right,* par. 47–48.

122. Locke, *Second Treatise,* sec. 27.

123. Knowles, "Hegel on Property and Personality," *Philosophical Quarterly,* January 1983, 45, 48.

124. Acton, *Encyclopedia of Philosophy*, 446.

125. Hegel, *Philosophy of Right*, par. 24.

126. Knowles, "Hegel on Property," 52–53.

127. John Plamenatz has made this point nicely: "To make a claim is not to give vent to an appetite; it is not to be demanding in a way that even an animal can be. It is to make a moral gesture that has meaning only between persons who recognize one another as persons. . . . The creature that aspires to freedom is a social being and can get what it aspires to only in society—or, in the language of Hegel, it belongs to an ethical universe and can achieve freedom only inside it" ("History as the Realization of Freedom," in *Hegel's Political Philosophy*, edited by Z. Pelczynski [Oxford: Clarendon Press, 1971], 30, 40–41).

128. Hegel, *Philosophy of Right*, par. 51.

129. Hegel, *Philosophy of Right*, par. 50.

130. Hegel, *Philosophy of Right*, par. 64.

131. Radin, "Property and Personhood," 987.

132. Hegel, *Early Theological Writings*, trans. T. M. Knox (Chicago: Chicago University Press, 1977).

133. Hegel, *Early Theological Writings*, 308.

134. Note that this is also different from Marx's classic statement of alienation in which the laborer expends labor on the object he produces but neither identifies with it nor owns it (see K. Marx, *Economic And Philosophic Manuscripts of 1844*, edited by B. Struik [1964], 110–11).

135. Radin, "Property and Personhood," 989–91.

136. Hegel, *Philosophy of Right*, par. 49.

137. Hegel, *Philosophy of Right*, par. 43.

138. Hegel, *Philosophy of Right*.

139. Hegel, *Philosophy of Right*, par. 67.

140. Hegel, *Philosophy of Right*, par. 70. The oblique references to slavery and suicide in paragraphs 67 and 70 are made explicit in the additions, at paragraphs 44 and 45.

141. Probably because of the technology of his time, Hegel did not consider the possibility of mass production capable of imitating an artist's work.

142. Hegel, *Philosophy of Right*, par. 69.

143. Hegel, *Philosophy of Right*.

144. Hegel, *Philosophy of Right*.

145. Hegel, *Philosophy of Right*.

146. See generally, J. Hyppolite, *Studies on Marx and Hegel* (New York: Basic Books, 1969), 82–83; D. McLellan, *The Young Hegelians and Karl Marx* (London: Macmillan Press, 1969), 140–41; C. Taylor, *Hegel and Modern Society* (Cambridge: Cambridge University Press, 1979), 144–45.

147. *Bleistein v. Donaldson Lithographing Co.*, 188 U.S. 239, 250 (1903).

148. While some politicians and rock stars may work on their public images, the world is full of famous athletes, heroes, and actors who do not labor to create their public images.

149. Aspects of the persona have been given property or quasi-property protection in a series of cases throughout the country (see generally Shipley, "Publicity Never Dies; It Just Fades Away: The Right of Publicity and Federal Preemption," *Cornell Law Review* 66 [1981]: 673, 680 [citing several cases granting publicity rights]).

150. Indeed, it is hard to say whether an author's writing or an author's persona is the better medium for expressing personality. The persona may be more important because it represents a whole character, image, and lifestyle, while an author's written works consist of only specific expressions. On the other hand, a novel may be a more accurate representation of personality for some writers because the work is an intentional expression of the creator, while the persona is the individual's intentional and unintentional actions combined with popular reaction to these actions. Indeed, it is difficult to fit personas into both the labor and personality theories of intellectual property. They are sometimes the result of hard work toward securing a public image based on an internal vision. But quite often they are creations of pure chance, perhaps the only "intellectual property" without intentionality.

151. The privatization of space satellites, however, raises the specter of new geographic data being monopolized in the hands of private individuals and released only in copyrighted works.

152. Arno corrects for Mercator distortions that make the Northern Hemisphere, that is, First and Second World countries, appear larger in land area than they really are and that make the less-developed nations of the Southern Hemisphere look smaller (see P. Arno, *A New Map of the World* [1983]).

153. *Trademark Clarification Act of 1984*, Pub. L. No. 98–620, 98 Stat. 3335.

154. Refusing to grant property rights over discovered scientific facts may be a fitting example of insufficient personality association limiting property rights over a set of ideas.

155. Hegel, *Philosophy of Right,* par. 71.

156. Hegel, *Philosophy of Right,* par. 65.

157. See generally, Hegel, *Philosophy of Right,* par. 72–81.

158. *Dr. Miles Medical Co. v. Park & Sons Co.,* 220 U.S. 373, 404 (1910).

159. Licensing arrangements take either of two forms. One approach, common with patents, is to license an individual to use a patented process for her own work. This is directly analogous to alienation of single copies. "Licensing" might also take the form of giving a marketing company all rights to a copyright or patent in exchange for fixed royalties. This would seem more analogous to complete alienation of the *res.*

160. Hegel, *Philosophy of Right,* par. 66.

161. Compare Bowie, *The Rise and Fall of Ziggy Stardust and the Spiders from Mars* (RCA 1972) with Bowie, *Heroes* (RCA 1977). See D. Stockman, *The Triumph of Politics* (New York: Harper & Row, 1986).

162. A creator concerned only with economic return might allow radical brutal changes in his work if this produced the most profit. Personality considerations,

by contrast, cause owners to prohibit change, deletions, or misattributions during any reproduction. Indeed, a creator concerned purely with personality expression might allow free reproduction of his work as long as these restrictions were honored. Hegel, *Philosophy of Right*, par. 71.

163. Hegel, *Philosophy of Right*, par. 66, 69.

164. American intellectual property laws are often compared to their European counterparts, which are based on the concept of "moral rights" (see, for example, Merryman, "The Refrigerator of Bernard Buffet," *Hastings Law Journal* 27 [1976]: 1023, 1042 [discussing reasons for absence of moral rights doctrine in American copyright law]).

165. *Studies in Industrial Property and Copyright Law: German Industrial Property, Copyright, And Antitrust Laws*, vol. 6, edited by F. Beier, G. Schricker and E. Ulmer (Munich: Max Planck Institute, 1983), 114.

166. In late 1988, the United States became the seventy-eighth nation to join the Berne Copyright Convention. See note 19. The convention provides minimum standards of copyright protection in member states including a provision that protects "moral rights."

167. 188 U.S. 239 (1903).

168. 188 U.S. 239 (1903).

169. 188 U.S. 239 (1903).

170. In fact, LEXIS searches uncovered only one case that explicitly reasons with the "personality" model adopted by Holmes: *F. W. Woolworth Co. v. Contemporary Art Inc.*, 193 F.2d 162, 164 (1st Cir.) (artist's rendering of a cocker spaniel in show position reflected "something irreducible" about the artist and is therefore protected by copyright [citing *Bleistein*, 188 U.S. at 249–50], *aff'd*, 344 U.S. 228 [1951]).

171. 376 U.S. 254 (1964) (public official cannot recover damages for defamatory falsehood without a showing of actual malice). *Time, Inc. v. Hill*, 385 U.S. 374, 387–88 (1967) (under state statute providing remedy for "unwanted publicity," *New York Times* standard applicable not only to public officials, but also to matters of public interest); *Gertz v. Robert Welsh, Inc.*, 418 U.S. 323, 349 (1974) (private individuals must meet *New York Times* standard to recover presumed or punitive damages).

172. 196 Misc. 67, 80 N.Y.S. 2d 575 (1948), *aff'd*, 275 A.D. 692, 87 N.Y.S. 2d 430 (1949).

173. 196 Misc. 69, 80 N.Y.S.2d at 577.

174. 295 F. Supp. 331 (S.D.N.Y. 1968).

175. P. Krieg, note, "Copyright, Free Speech, and the Visual Arts," *Yale Law Journal* 93 (1984): 1565.

176. Kwall, "Copyright and the Moral Right," 68.

177. See generally D. Ladd, *Securing the Future of Copyright: A Humanist Endeavor* (1984).

178. 538 F.2d 14 (2d Cir. 1976).

179. 538 F.2d 25 (2d Cir. 1976).

180. 538 F.2d 25 (2d Cir. 1976).
181. 412 U.S. 94 (1973).
182. 412 U.S. 193 (Brennan, J., dissenting).
183. The limited reproduction process before the printing press revolutionized publication was very decentralized. An author could not police the scribes reproducing his book and catch all the intentional and unintentional mistakes they made.
184. The increasing quality of desktop "printing" has brought copyright issues to the fore already. The varying views are reflected in two editorials in *Publish: The How-To Magazine Of Desktop Publishing* (August 1987).
185. Kwall, "Copyright and the Moral Right," 69.
186. Kaplan, *Copyright*, 74.

7

Intellectual Property: A Non-Posnerian Law and Economics Approach[*]

Tom G. Palmer

This chapter is divided into four main sections: a brief description of the "Posnerian" approach to intellectual property rights; a historical look at the origins of intellectual property rights and of the relationship between property rights and technology; an examination of the economics of property rights and of public goods, and criticism of some typical applications of this theoretical machinery to intellectual property; and a description of the functioning of markets for non-tangible economic goods in the absence of intellectual property rights.

I. Posnerian Jurisprudence and Intellectual Property

Recent decades have seen an explosion in the number of new ways of creating, storing, transmitting, and manipulating "ideal objects," or non-tangible economic goods.[1] The new technologies include personal computers, digital encoding, optical storage, virtually instantaneous electronic communication, photocopying, optical scanning, computerized databases, and many more. Like the introduction of millions of other inventions before them, their arrival on the economic scene has brought to

---

[*]This essay was originally published as "Intellectual Property: A Non-Posnerian Law and Economics Approach," by Tom G. Palmer, in the *Hamline Law Review* 12 (1989): 261–304. Copyright © 1989 by Hamline University School of Law. Reprinted with permission of publisher.

many industries a storm of what economist Joseph Schumpeter called "creative destruction."

Not only have these new technologies radically changed many industries, they have contributed to the explosive growth of a new "industry" among economists and lawyers, as well. Much of this work is characterized by overtly utilitarian—even Benthamite—concerns. The assumption is that the principal or even sole criterion for evaluating intellectual property law is its contribution to aggregate utility, and that the legal regime governing ideal objects should aim explicitly at a utilitarian result, maximizing net utility by balancing off the welfare gain from innovations induced by intellectual property rights against the welfare losses resulting from the restrictions on the dissemination of such innovations.

One of the most explicit of the proponents of this view is Judge Richard Posner. In spite of his criticism of Jeremy Bentham, Posner remains in his jurisprudence strongly indebted to Bentham.[2] Although Posner significantly parts company with Bentham over the common law,[3] with Bentham he sees the law's function as maximization of some quantity: in place of the norm of utility maximization, Posner offers "wealth maximization."[4] This change, however, takes place within a framework that remains decidedly Benthamite; judges are still exhorted to aim at an explicit overall goal other than seeking justice in particular cases. Wealth is substituted for utility as the maximand, but the jurisprudential approaches remain consistent. As Posner remarks, "The basic function of law in an economic or wealth-maximization perspective is to alter incentives."[5] In other words, the role of law is constructivistic and interventionistic, an attempt to reorder economic institutions to attain a particular end.

Posner and his colleague William M. Landes have applied this model to the development of copyright in an attempt to explain "to what extent the principal features of copyright law can be explained as devices for promoting an efficient allocation of resources" and to show that "the principal legal doctrines" are "reasonable efforts to maximize the benefits from creating additional works minus both the losses from limiting access and the costs of administering and enforcing copyright protection."[6] Landes and Posner offer both explicit positive analysis of the law (purporting to show how it promotes economic efficiency) as well as exhortations to judges to apply the law so as to attain this end. For example, in discussing difficulties in applying the "idea versus expression" distinction central to copyright law to computer programs (to which the distinction is problematic), they state:

> We hope the debate will be resolved not by the semantics of the words 'idea' and 'expression' but by the economics of the problem, and specifically by

comparing the deadweight costs of allowing a firm to appropriate what has become an industry standard with the disincentive effects on originators if such appropriation is forbidden.[7]

As Jules Coleman responds, "The alternative and I believe common-sense view is that the responsibility of a judge is to determine which of the litigants in a dispute has a relevant legal right."[8] Further, "adjudication primarily—or always—concerns rights rather than the promotion of some useful social policy while at the same time it provides a substantial and meaningful role for economic argument."

In the course of this chapter, I will present a "non-Posnerian" law and economics approach to intellectual property rights; patents and copyrights are forms, not of legitimate property rights, but of illegitimate state-granted monopoly. Insofar as my approach is a law and economics approach, it is influenced by the more mainstream law and economics of the jurist Bruno Leoni[9] and the economist F. A. Hayek,[10] rather than by the "wealth maximization" approach of Judge Posner. Although the bulk of this chapter offers an alternative model of the development of intellectual property, it is implicitly a criticism of the Posnerian/Benthamite approach.

Preliminary Remarks

Intellectual property rights in the United States are generally classified into four kinds: patents, copyrights, trade secrets, and trademarks. Patents govern "any new and useful process, machine, manufacture, or composition of matter, or any new and useful improvement thereof." Patents may be granted when the subject matter satisfies the criteria of utility, novelty, and non-obviousness. Copyright protects the creative expression of ideas in tangible form; copyrights may be granted when a work is not a copy but originates with the creator; it need not be novel. Trade secrecy laws, like patents, also protect ideas but rely entirely on private measures, rather than on state action, to maintain exclusivity. Finally, trademark law protects words, marks, and symbols that serve to identify and differentiate goods and services in the market. The analysis in this chapter will focus on the first two categories of intellectual property rights, for reasons that should become clearer as the chapter proceeds. (The term "intellectual property rights" will also be reserved for patents and copyrights.) At this point, I will merely assume a contractual interpretation of the protections governing trade secrets and trademarks (e.g., in the former case the relationship between principal and agent, and in the latter between buyer and seller) to differentiate them from the clearly non-contractual protections governing patents and copyrights.[11]

II. Historical Origins of Intellectual Property Rights

American intellectual property law, while diverging in many respects from that of the United Kingdom, is rooted in the English system of patents and copyrights. Patents for new inventions were issued by the English Crown with the aim of raising funds through the granting of monopolies or of securing control over industries perceived to be of political importance, while copyrights functioned to ensure governmental control over the press in a time of great religious and political dissent. Monopoly privilege and censorship lie at the historical root of patent and copyright.[12]

Patents

Grants of monopoly over industrial processes were often used as inducements to the introduction of new arts to a realm (importation franchises), often with little or no concern for originality of invention.[13] To take a prominent example, Venice, in one of the earliest cited patents, in 1469 granted a monopoly over the art of printing itself to John of Speyer, awarding him exclusive rights to print books in Venetian territory and forbidding the importation of books into the realm.[14] Fortunately for the future growth of the Venetian printing industry, John of Speyer died the next year.

Such privileges often extended to the granting of exclusive rights to produce certain classes of items, regardless of whether the grantee had originated them (e.g., glass, printed works by specified classical authors, bibles and prayer books, ammunition, and so forth). This practice characterized England as much as it did the other European states awarding such privileges at the time. Even the prohibition on monopolies set forth in the Statute of Monopolies (1624), a significant influence on the development of intellectual property rights, in addition to exempting specified industries such as printing and glass and alum production, exempted from the prohibition grants to "any Corporations Companies or Fellowships of any Art Trade Occupation or Mistery, or to any Companies or Societies of Merchants within this Realme, erected for the mayntenance enlargement or ordering of any Trade of Merchandize."[15]

Some writers, taking a notably "Whiggish" view of the development of intellectual property law, have argued that the present system of granting property rights to originators of ideal objects emerged through a gradual winnowing process, whereby intellectual property emerged from a background of monopoly and privilege. As legal historian Bruce Bugbee writes:

> the ancient institution of monopoly, which was also used to reward royal favorites or to increase state treasuries through the sale of exclusive privileges to individuals, continued to flourish in spite of longstanding legal prohibitions. Such grants came to be confused with patents of invention when the latter appeared, and the onus of monopoly was unjustly shared. . . . The exclusive character of both monopolies and patents of invention, and the elaborate common procedure by which both were granted, notably in England, encouraged this confusion. Compounding the difficulty, importation franchises have also been mistaken for true patents of invention by writers on the subject, partly because the distinction was not always made clear at the time the grant was made.[16]

One might respond that if the grantors of such privileges saw no difference, then the distinction drawn by contemporary writers may be an imposition on the actual character of the legal institutions. An alternative interpretation would be to see the current system of intellectual property as the remnant of a system of monopoly privileges; rather than emerging spontaneously, like other property rights, as responses to scarcity, they could be seen as deliberate creations of scarcity through state action.

The identification of patent privileges with "property rights" has provided a powerful form of legitimation for these privileges. As Fritz Machlup and Edith Penrose write, "those who started using the word property in connection with inventions had a very definite purpose in mind: they wanted to substitute a word with a respectable connotation, 'property,' for a word that had an unpleasant ring, 'privilege.' "[17]

Copyright

Copyright, too, emerges from the exercise of state power, rather than from a concern with the property rights of authors. As Barbara Ringer (no enemy of intellectual property rights) has argued:

> The pro-copyright theologians argue that copyright as a natural property right emerged from the mists of the common law and took definite form as the result of the invention of the printing press and the increase in potential and actual piracy after 1450. They dismiss the historical ties between copy-

right and the Crown's grants of printing monopolies, its efforts to suppress heretical or seditious writing, and to exercise censorship control over all publications. This line of argument tends to infuriate the anti-copyright scholars who point out that the first copyright statute in history, the Statute of Anne of 1710, was a direct outgrowth of an elaborate series of monopoly grants, Star Chamber decrees, licensing acts, and a system involving mandatory registration of titles with the Stationers' Company.[18]

The chartering of the Company of Stationers by Queen Mary in 1557, with its monopoly over printing and the registration of titles with the company, was an attempt to exercise control over a threatening new technology, with the particular purpose of suppressing Protestantism.[19] The Star Chamber decree of 1586 called for the repression of the "greate enormities and abuses" of "dyvers contentyous and disorderlye persons professinge the arte or mystere of Pryntinge or sellinge of bookes."[20] In 1637, the Company of Stationers was authorized by a Star Chamber decree to seize and destroy unauthorized books and presses, eliminating both economic competition and threats to established political and religious authorities at one blow.

With the abolition of the Star Chamber by the Long Parliament in 1641, the basis for this monopolistic system of control was temporarily removed, only to be quickly replaced by a series of licensing acts, beginning in 1643. As one legal scholar has commented, the only real change was in the "political and religious biases of the licensers."[21] The last of the licensing acts expired in 1694, and with it the monopoly powers of the Company of Stationers.

The first significant mentions in English history of the rights of authors, in addition to the interests of the Crown and of its obedient company of printers, are found after the temporary lapsing of controls over the press in 1641. At that time, in a petition presented to Parliament, the Company of Stationers made their case for a renewal of their monopoly privileges. As Arnold Plant remarks, "the case against unregulated competition was argued by the Company with a skill which our present-day trade associations hardly excel."[22] Complaining of "Too great multitudes of presses" set up by "Drapers, Carmen and others," the stationers pointed to the resulting indiscriminate printing of "odious opprobrious pamphlets of incendiaries."[23] Buried among six economic reasons offered, including overproduction, underproduction, "confusion" and risk, securing the livelihood of the stationers' families, and preference of domestic products over imports, were found the following words: "Fourthly, Community as it discourages stationers, so it is a great discouragement to the authors of books also; many men's studies carry no other profit or recompense with them, but the benefit of their copies; and if this be taken away, many pieces of great worth and excellence will be strangled in the womb, or never conceived at all for the future."[24]

As the need to suppress dissenting religious and political literature abated, the Company of Stationers began to place greater weight on other reasons for perpetuation of their privileges. These included alleged authorial rights and the sad plight of their families at a time when country presses were issuing rival editions of works and cutting seriously into their trade. Thus, Lord Camden, in debate over the case of *Donaldson v. Beckett,* in which the Law Lords, sitting as the highest court of the land, rejected any common law right of copyright, remarked of the stationers' petition:

> They—the stationers (whose property by that time) consisted of all the literature of the Kingdom, for they had contrived to get all the copies into their own hands—came up to Parliament in the form of petitioners, with tears in their eyes, hopeless and forlorn, they brought with them their wives and children to excite compassion, and induce Parliament to grant them a statutory security.[25]

Parliament responded by passing the Statute of Anne in 1710, stating in the preamble that "Printers Booksellers and other Persons have of late frequently taken the Liberty of printing reprinting and publishing or causing to be pirated reprinted and published Books and other Writings without the Consent of the Authors or Proprietors of such Books and Writings to their very great Detriment and too often to the Ruin of them and their Families."[26] A shift in the legitimating argument for copyright monopolies had led to a subtle change in the law itself. The Statute of Anne shifted emphasis away from publishers to authors, thus feeding modern myths that copyright originated to secure the rights of authors and thereby to provide incentives for them to produce what would otherwise be a public good (and therefore underproduced on the market).[27]

As legal scholar Benjamin Kaplan has argued:

> Although references in the text of the statute to authors, together with dubious intimations in later cases that Swift, Addison, and Steele took some significant part in the drafting, have lent color to the notion that authors were themselves intended beneficiaries of parliamentary grace, I think it nearer the truth to say that publishers saw the tactical advantage of putting forward authors' interests together with their own, and this tactic produced some effect on the tone of the statute.[28]

Drawing on the English pattern, but with somewhat diminished emphasis on the usefulness of copyright and patent grants for furthering state power, the American colonies—and later states—awarded grants of monopoly to inventors and authors. This experience culminated in the writing and unanimous acceptance of Article 1, Section 8 of the Constitution at the Constitutional Convention of 1787 and the passage of the first Federal Copyright Act in 1790. As was made clear with the passage of the first copyright act, however, the statutory rights granted involved no claim of *natural rights* by originators of ideal objects. The rationale presented was purely one of incentives to "Promote the Progress of Science and useful Arts."

Two more issues deserve to be considered before leaving this brief historical examination of the origins of copyright. First is the issue of whether there existed a common law copyright that was statutorily superseded by the Parliament's action of 1710. Second is the relation between new technologies and the emergence of patent and copyright privileges.

Common Law Copyright

It is a commonplace that statutory rights to intellectual property merely superseded, and indeed limited, common law rights. (In this context, "common law rights" refer to more than the right generally recognized in the common law of an author to prevent publication of his or her *unpublished* manuscript and refer to rights allegedly retained *after* the act of publication.) As recent scholarship has shown, however, this commonplace is based on a misreading of the reporting procedures of the English court system.[29] The decision of *Millar v. Taylor*[30] by the Court of King's Bench did indeed declare a perpetual copyright to have existed in common law, a copyright that was not superseded by the Statute of Anne.[31] This decision was overturned, however, in the case of *Donaldson v. Beckett.*[32] The Law Lords, sitting as the highest court of appeal, voted by twenty-two to eleven against perpetual common law copyright. The practice of forbidding reporting of remarks made by members of the House of Lords has led to a confusion of the vote of the Lords with the advisory opinions solicited from eleven judges, whose remarks were submitted to the Lords and were legally reproducible.

Examination of the reports of the debates from the time shows, however, that the true import of the decision has been widely misunderstood. During the debate in the House of Lords, Lord Camden (who, in the words of Arnold Plant, "wiped the floor with the London booksellers") successfully argued against the claims of the booksellers, finding all claims of precedent for any common law right to be "founded on patents, privileges, Star-chamber decrees, and the bye laws of the Stationers' Company; all of them the effects of the grossest tyranny and usurpation; the very last places in which I would have dreamt of finding the least trace of the common law."[33] As Camden pointed out, during the fifteen years between the expiration of the last licensing act and the passage of the Statute of Anne, "no action was brought, no injunction obtained, although no illegal force prevented it; a strong proof, that at that time there was no idea of a common law claim."[34]

The confusion in this area stems from taking the merely advisory opinions of the judges to be the finding of the Law Lords. Thus, Bugbee confuses the two when he writes, "Although the perpetual common law copyright supported in *Millar v. Taylor* was again held to exist, and was held to be unaffected by mere publication, a majority of the eleven judges in *Donaldson v. Beckett* asserted that the Statute of Anne had terminated the common law right of action to enforce it."[35] Thus, the advisory opinions of the judges are conflated with the action and reasons of the Law Lords. A careful examination of the advisory answers to the questions placed by the Lords to the judges shows, however, that even the weaker claim that the advice of the judges supported a pre-existing common law right is highly questionable.[36]

Technology and Intellectual Property Rights

Critical discussion of patents and copyrights has focused too little attention on the historical interdependence of changing technologies and the legal concepts underlying intellectual property rights. One need not be a historical materialist or economic determinist to realize that not only the economic circumstances that might prompt movement toward recognition of "new" property rights, but also the very concepts by which these rights would be structured are contingent upon technology.[37]

The concept of personal and individual authorship, as we understand it today, was dependent upon the "invention" of the typographically fixed title page. Typographical fixity was also necessary to fix the density of the text itself. Before the introduction of printing, works were copied and recopied, often introducing a multiplicity of minor errors, additions, or deletions by scribes.[38] The proliferation of works attributed to classical authors (many now often cited with the prefix "Pseudo" before the name under which the work appeared) was a natural outcome of scribal culture.

Additional problems arise in ascribing modern notions of authorship to scribal culture. Thus, as Daniel Boorstin argues:

There were special problems of nomenclature when books were commonly composed as well as transcribed by men in holy orders. In each religious house it was customary for generation after generation of monks to use the same names. When a man took his vows, he abandoned the name by which he had been known in the secular world, and he took a name of one of the monastic brothers who had recently died. As a result, every Franciscan house would always have its Bonaventura, but the identity of "Bonaventura" at any time could only be defined by considerable research.

All this, as we have seen, gave a tantalizing ambiguity to the name by which a medieval manuscript might be known. A manuscript volume of sermons identified as *Sermones Bonaventurae* might be so called for any one of a dozen reasons. . . . Was the original author the famous Saint Bonaventura of Fidanza? Or was there another author called Bonaventura? Or was it copied by someone of that name? Or by someone in a monastery of that name? Or preached by some Bonaventura, even though not composed by him? Or had the volume once been owned by a Friar Bonaventura, or by a monastery called Bonaventury? Or was this a collection of sermons by different preachers, of which the first was a Bonaventura? Or were these simply in honor of Saint Bonaventura?[39]

As Elizabeth Eisenstein has demonstrated, "scribal culture could not sustain the patenting of inventions or the copyrighting of literary compositions. It worked against the concept of intellectual property rights."[40] With the typographical fixity and attribution made possible by printing, authorship became a matter of personal responsibility, and respect for the "wisdom of the ages" correspondingly declined.[41] Authorship and invention, the very acts to be rewarded by intellectual property law, may not be timeless concepts plucked from Heaven but may emerge in conjunction with—and be inextricably intertwined with—the technology that makes them possible.

The relationship between intellectual property rights and technology poses a very important question: If laws are dependent for their emergence and validation upon technological innovations, might not succeeding innovations require that those very laws pass back *out* of existence? Today this question should be considered in the context of drastically lowered costs of reproduction and transmission, increased costs of enforcement, problems arising from indeterminate or collective authorship due to new applications of computer technology, and similar issues. One need not conclude from such considerations that copyright did not emerge legitimately in a world of typography, but one should at least be led to question whether it fulfills a legitimate role in a world of electronics.

Further, as succeeding sections of this chapter should make clear, merely to point to the unsavory origins of an institution, or to its dependence on other factors, is not in itself a condemnation of that institution (in this case, intellectual property rights). Nor does such pointing tell us much about the actual operations, social function, or significance of the institution. These issues are raised simply to "demystify" the institution and to separate such issues of function and moral validity from any alleged historical validation of the institution.

III. Economics of Property Rights and Public Goods

The issues of property rights and of public goods are closely related. Since the publication in 1960 of Ronald Coase's essay on "The Problem of Social Cost," the attention of economists has been focused on the institution of property, previously taken as simply given in economic analysis.[42] Coase's work on externalities and transaction costs has brought the problem of property rights into focus, allowing greater attention to be paid to the *emergence* and structure of property rights. As Coase has shown, external (or third-party) effects can be "internalized" through the assignment of property rights. (As we shall see, public goods have been defined to be accompanied by external effects.)

Based on Coase's insight, Harold Demsetz has proposed a theory of the emergence of property rights. As Demsetz writes,

> what converts a harmful or beneficial effect into an externality is that the cost of bringing the effect to bear on the decisions of one or more of the interacting persons is too high to make it worthwhile. . . . 'Internalizing' such effects refers to a process, usually a change in property rights, that enables these effects to bear (in greater degree) on all interacting persons. . . . A primary function of property rights is that of guiding incentives to achieve a greater internalization of externalities.[43]

By making possible negotiations among parties whose actions create external effects, property rights allow them to attain higher levels of satisfaction (or lower levels of dissatisfaction) than would otherwise be possible.

Property rights can emerge when changes in technology, demand, or other factors create externalities that were previously absent. To use Demsetz's example, property rights in hunting territories emerged among certain North American Indian communities when greater demand for furs in European markets led to intensified hunting of certain animals. When one hunter or group of hunters captured a beaver, that meant fewer beavers for others. Without property rights in animals or their territories, no individual or group finds it worthwhile to invest in increasing the animal stock or in restricting the harvest. Before the rise in the demand for furs, "these external effects [diminution of the stock available to others] were of such small significance that it did not pay for anyone to take them into account." After the rise in demand and the concomitant increase in hunting, the significance of the externalities associated with hunting rose, triggering a process that led to the spontaneous evolution of property rights among competing claimants to the previously unowned resources.[44] Thus, in Demsetz's words, "property rights develop to internalize externalities when the gains of internalization become larger than the costs of internalization."[45]

Externalities also accompany public goods. Various approaches to the definition of public goods have been developed, but most share two related characteristics: jointness of consumption (also known as non-rivalrous consumption) and nonexcludability of would-be consumers.[46] Jointness of consumption means that one person's consumption of a good does not diminish another person's consumption of the same good.[47] (The applicability of this notion to ideas should be obvious.) Nonexcludability means that if one person consumes the good, it cannot feasibly be withheld from some other person(s).[48] For example, if a lighthouse sends out a beam of light, its services cannot be selectively withheld from nonpaying passersby. (In a somewhat weaker version, it is simply asserted that, given a good for which the marginal cost of exclusion is greater than the marginal cost of provision, it is *inefficient* to expend resources to exclude nonpurchasers.) Thus, the effect of these two attributes is that for goods so characterized each person has an incentive to "free-ride" off of the contributions toward the purchase of the good made by others. Under such conditions, consumers can be expected to under-reveal their "true" preferences for the good and an inadequate supply will be produced.

Both of these two characteristics are applied to ideal objects. My consumption of an idea or of a process, for example, does not in the least diminish the consumption of another, while, since the cost of reproduction of an idea is virtually zero (as it need only be thought), it can be very difficult, if not impossible, to exclude nonpurchasers from enjoying the benefits of their production. Thus, ideal objects may qualify as truly archetypical cases of pure public goods.[49] (Note, however, that the existence of opportunity costs to acquisition of ideas, for example, to learn organic chemistry or Sanskrit or to sit through a play, indicate that 1) there do exist costs of acquisition for ideas, 2) there often exist opportunities for exclusion [e.g., refusing to give Sanskrit lessons], and 3) such "public goods" are not equivalent to "free goods." Further, the "public" element of many goods must be "embedded" in a tangible substrate before they can be consumed or enjoyed, for example, the movie *Jaws* in a videocassette or the poems of John Donne on the pages of a book.)

Being a public good means that the production of ideal objects entails the creation of external effects. My act of publishing or in some other way revealing an idea, for instance, means that that ideal object is appropriable by any and all who wish to think it. They receive positive externalities from my act. According to many accounts, such positive externalities might be internalized either through provision by the state, which (some people persist in believing) has the interests of all at heart, or by assignment of property rights and negotiation among interested parties, bringing to bear upon one another the interests of both generators and recipients of the externalities in question. Most writers on intellectual property rights, to their credit, prefer the decentralized property rights approach, rather than the state provision approach, with all its attendant inefficiencies and horrors.

While much recent thinking on the subject is informed by the externalities and property rights analysis described above, such attempts to explain intellectual property rights fail to take into account adequately the central role of scarcity in the emergence of property rights and the difficulties inherent in any attempt to apply the economic notion of scarcity to ideal objects.[50] Further, too little attention is focused on alternative means of internalizing externalities; assignment of property rights is not the only means available to this end.

In the Landes-Posner model, for example, the assumption is made that "For a new work to be created the expected return—typically, and we shall assume exclusively, from the sale of copies—must exceed the expected costs."[51] As we shall see, this assumption (that the exclusive source of revenue is sale of copies) in effect rigs the game; had such an assumption been employed in attempting to understand the market for radio broadcasting, it would have overlooked the most significant form of income for broadcasters: advertising. This would have naturally led to the conclusion that either state monopoly or some system of coerced collection of tolls on radio sets was the only way to produce an "efficient" quantity of radio broadcasting. This would, in fact, have been the fate of broadcasting but for the serendipitous discovery of advertising.[52]

In what follows I will criticize the application of the legal category of property to ideal objects and will explore other methods of achieving internalization of externalities. In addition, some attention will be paid to the overly static approach taken by some proponents of intellectual property rights (e.g., attempts are made to mimic real market processes by constructing incentives that will equalize marginal social cost and marginal social benefit).

Objections to the Property Model for Ideal Objects

The first problem with applying the kind of property rights analysis described above to ideal objects is that such goods are not characterized by the same kind of scarcity as tangible goods, such as land, game animals, or water rights. As Thomas Jefferson wrote:

> If nature has made any one thing less susceptible than all others of exclusive property, it is the action of the thinking power called an idea, which an individual may exclusively possess as long as he keeps it to himself; but the moment it is divulged, it forces itself into the possession of everyone, and the receiver cannot dispossess himself of it. Its peculiar character, too, is that no one possesses the less, because every other possesses the whole of it. He who receives an idea from me, receives instruction himself without lessening mine; as he who lights his taper at mine, receives light without darkening me.[53]

The central element in the spontaneous emergence of property rights is scarcity, or the possibility of conflicting uses. As Arnold Plant observes, "It is a peculiarity of property rights in patents (and copyrights) that they do not arise out of the scarcity of the objects which become appropriated. They are not a *consequence* of scarcity. They are the deliberate creation of statute law; and, whereas in general the institution of private property makes for the preservation of scarce goods, tending (as we might somewhat loosely say) to lead us 'to make the most of them,' property rights in patents and copyright make possible the *creation* of a scarcity of the products appropriated which could not otherwise be maintained."[54]

According to Nobel laureate F. A. Hayek:

> The slow selection by trial and error of a system of rules delimiting individual ranges of control over different resources has created a curious position. Those very intellectuals who are generally inclined to question those forms of material property which are indispensable for the efficient organization of the material means of production have become the most enthusiastic supporters of certain immaterial property rights invented only relatively recently, having to do, for example, with literary productions and technological inventions (i.e., copyrights and patents).

The difference between these and other kinds of property rights is this: while ownership of material goods guides the use of scarce means to their most important uses, in the case of immaterial goods such as literary productions and technological inventions the ability to produce them is also limited, yet once they have come into existence, they can be indefinitely multiplied and can be made scarce only by law in order to create an inducement to produce such ideas. Yet it is not obvious that such forced scarcity is the most effective way to stimulate the human creative process.[55]

As will be shown later, there are means of internalizing the externalities involved in the creation of public goods other than through statutory grant of monopoly privileges over them. The mere existence of externalities, in the absence of scarcity, does not justify state creation of enforceable property rights.

Further, to the detriment of attempts to apply the Demsetz model of intellectual property rights, such rights are creatures of the state, and not the product of an evolutionary process of interaction among interested parties that is later ratified through legal sanctions.[56] (Trademark and trade secrecy laws, however, do emerge from the actions taken in the common law. While they are often lumped together with patents and copyrights, my approach would separate them and recognize their legitimacy in a market order.) While the work of Coase and his followers has highlighted the importance of the proper definition and enforcement of property rights for the solution of many externalities problems (notably pollution, land use patterns, and so on), this need not imply that the state can simply define property rights in any way at all and then let the market so defined perform its magic.

A definition of property rights that would require massive and continual state interference in the market, for example, is not consistent with a market system, the beauty of which is its self-governing character. State enforcement of intellectual property rights, especially in an age of high-speed electronics and computer technology, requires just such a pattern of state intervention into social processes.

Law in a liberal society is a "horizontal," rather than a "vertical," creation. It emerges out of contract and interaction among interested parties, and not as a result of state edicts handed down from on high, as in the case of intellectual property rights. As the noted jurist and early pioneer of law and economics Bruno Leoni pointed out, law is a matter of "individual claim": "The legal process always traces back in the end to individual claim. Individuals make the law, insofar as they make claims."[57] Rights are not creations of the state, bestowed as gifts upon the people by wise and beneficent legislators, but simultaneously the spontaneous product and the ground—both the *definiendum* and the *definiens*—of the system of voluntary interactions we call the market.[58]

Finally, any system of "property rights" that requires the violation of other property rights, for example, the right to determine the peaceful use in one's home of one's own videocassette recorder or to purchase blank tapes without paying a royalty to a third party, is no system of rights at all. In short, a system of intellectual property rights is not compossible with a system of property rights to tangible objects, especially one's own body, the foundation of the right to property in alienable objects.[59]

As journalist and Jacksonian political theorist William Leggett argued,

> The mental processes by which [the author] contrived those results are not, and cannot properly be tendered, exclusive property; since the right of a free exercise of our thinking faculties is given by nature to all mankind, and the mere fact that a given mode of doing a thing has been thought of by one, does not prevent the same ideas presenting themselves to the mind of another and should not prevent him from a perfect liberty of acting upon them.[60]

Proposals to ban or cripple entire technologies (i.e., technologies capable of rendering existing intellectual property rights nugatory) would wipe out whole areas of property rights altogether, and cannot be defended in the name of property rights.[61]

The immediate jump from identifying potential externalities to advocating creation of new property rights is unjustified, as has been indirectly shown by two prominent writers on intellectual property rights. Richard P. Adelstein and Steven I. Peretz have suggested a model for the evolution of property rights in ideal objects that draws on the Demsetz model but supplements it with an entrepreneurial evolutionary dynamic to explain the emergence of rights.[62] Adelstein and Peretz identify two dimensions of the process of market exchange: (1) identifying and exchanging information with prospective buyers, negotiating mutually agreeable terms of trade, and (2) transferring control over the resources, on the one hand, while on the other protecting "this channel of exchange with buyers against the constant threat of those who would, where possible, breach the channel so as to extract the value of the commodity being traded without purchasing it from the seller."[63] Thus, one element of the market process is the exclusion of potential "free riders" from enjoying the good without paying for it. Adelstein and Peretz see the process of technological innovation being driven, at least in part, by the competition between potential sellers and potential free riders either to fence the goods or to be free riders on their production: "hence the competition of technologies, in which entrepreneurs attempt simultaneously to overcome the obstacles separating them from willing buyers and to place corresponding impediments in the path of free riders, who are constantly in search of ways to dissipate them."[64] In the case of intellectual goods (or what I have called "ideal objects"), changes in technology may allow sellers to embed the good in tangible or "impure" goods (e.g., a book in the corporeal sense), at the same time that they may allow free riders to extract and "purify" the intellectual good from its tangible embodiment, or "host." The former reflects "the essential properties of private goods," while the latter takes on "some of the attributes of public goods." Thus, "intellectual goods can be traded in markets as private goods only so long as the governing technology renders them impure and . . . technological change which purifies the intellectual good will require some kind of collective action to ensure that the incentives to produce and purchase the good in markets are maintained."[65] This framework is used to explain the introduction of intellectual property rights when new technologies, such as movable type, made it easier to extract and reproduce intellectual goods than was the case under older methods, such as hand reproduction on animal skins (when it could take a full year to copy a single book).

Unfortunately, the authors are hoist on their own petard. In a paragraph that begins by suggesting that "the creation of new property rights favoring the seller may be the only way to ensure the continued production of intellectual goods in such a technological environment," the authors bring up the case of professional magicians, who

> successfully embed their intellectual good within an illusion. To reveal the trick is thus to enable consumers to produce their own illusions, reducing the 'magic' to mere physical dexterity, and so magicians have long refused to share their secrets freely with one another or with their audiences. Yet here, too, the relentless advance of technology takes its toll; the rapid spread of high resolution video recorders with slow motion capability threatens to drive magicians from television screens, depriving them of an important source of revenue and denying vast audiences the enjoyment of their talents.[66]

Adelstein and Peretz argue that the code that has "bound the fraternity of magicians for generations" no longer adequately protects the channel between sellers and buyers of such illusions. In cases where this channel has been breached, they argue for creation of property rights. But do they really want to create property rights to the illusions of magicians, and enforce them by restraining VCR owners from using the playback feature in slow motion? Surely, their own example illustrates the folly of creating property rights whenever the specter of free riding on externalities generated by others arises. In fact, as I demonstrate in the next major section of this chapter, there are many mechanisms other than enforceable property rights for internalizing externalities, many of which are already in current use.

Rethinking Public Goods Theory

In order to understand the manner in which public goods can be and are produced on the market, a short return to the theory of public goods is necessary. The first point, as Adelstein and Peretz hint, is that "publicness" is not a characteristic inherent to goods, but is a function of the manner in which they are produced, and even of the choice of the relevant marginal unit. As economist Tyler Cowen argues, "publicness is an attribute of institutions, not of abstract economic goods. Every good can be made more or less public by examining it in different institutional contexts."[67] The choice of the relevant marginal unit of analysis (e.g., the road in front of my house or "the interstate highway system") is a determining factor of whether something is a public good, as is the choice of the method of production. Thus, the choice of a production and distribution system that allows private consumption or of a system that allows public consumption antedates the classification of a good as private or as public. As economist Kenneth Goldin writes:

> The evidence suggests that we are *not* faced with a set of goods and services which have the inherent characteristics of public goods. Rather, we are faced with an unavoidable choice regarding every good or service: shall everyone have *equal access* to that service (in which case the service will be similar to a public good) or shall the service be available *selectively:* to some, but not to others? In practice, public goods theory is often used in such a way that one overlooks this important choice problem.[68]

Thus, the cost of producing any service or good includes not only labor, capital, marketing, and other cost components, but also fencing (or exclusion) costs as well. Movie theaters, for example, invest in exclusion devices like ticket windows, walls, and ushers, all designed to exclude noncontributors from enjoyment of service. Alternatively, of course, movie owners could set up projectors and screens in public parks and then attempt to prevent passersby from watching, or they could ask government to force all noncontributors to wear special glasses that prevent them from enjoying the movie. "Drive-ins," faced with the prospect of free riders peering over the walls, installed—at considerable expense—individual speakers for each car, thus rendering the publicly available visual part of the movie of little interest. (This may explain why pornographic movies are rarely shown at drive-in theaters.)

The costs of exclusion are involved in the production of virtually every good imaginable. There is no compelling justification for singling out some goods and insisting that the state underwrite their production costs through some sort of state-sanctioned collective action simply because of a decision to make the good available on a nonexclusive basis. This decision is itself the relevant factor in converting a potential private good into a public good.

The politicization of goods, that is, the decision to provide them on a nonexclusive and available-on-demand basis (for "free") in "exchange" for the payment of taxes, initiates a vicious cycle, creating free riders and then demonstrating that private market forces cannot satisfy their demands.[69] Further, state provision does not eliminate the costs of exclusion, although it can change the structure of their imposition. Tax collectors, state surveillance of economic transactions of every sort, and jails replace ticket booths and other voluntary arrangements.

Moreover, the argument for state provision of public goods or for enforcement of intellectual property rights is framed in purely static, rather than dynamic, terms: it is inefficient to expend resources to exclude nonpurchasers if the marginal cost of making a given good available to one more person is zero (or less than the cost of exclusion). But this begs the question. We do not live in a world where goods are given; they have to be produced. Therefore, the problem is how best to produce these goods, taking all of the relevant costs and benefits into account.[70] An argument for a method of provision that assumes that the good is already produced is no argument at all.

Exclusion devices should be seen as endogenous to the market, as a regular part of its operation. The introduction of barbed wire in the 1870s, for example, allowed the enforcement of property titles in the prairies, a process that proceeded rapidly despite a federal law of 1885 forbidding the erection of stretched fences upon the "public domain."[71] Similarly, encryption and encoding devices (economically roughly equivalent to "electronic barbed wire") and other mechanisms can serve to fence the "public domain" of ideas and should be considered endogenous elements of the production process.

Discussions of ideal objects reveal a failure to apply insights into dynamic market processes; these discussions assume that efficiency is a state of the market in which, among other things, marginal revenue and marginal cost are equalized.[72] Schedules of costs and benefits are hypostatized in such analyses, leading to very peculiar and often counterintuitive results, as well as to "constructivist" impulses to mimic the results of the market, rather than allow it to function.[73]

This discussion is not, however, meant to denigrate the very important problem of demand revelation implicit in discussions of public goods and their provision. Indeed, this is a problem in the production of all goods, and a challenge to the entrepreneurial abilities of potential producers. Textbook writers commonly offered the lighthouse as an example to demonstrate the necessity of government action to produce certain goods. Their writings were often prefaced by phrases such as "Even Adam Smith believed . . ." Such examples became more problematic, however, after the publication of Ronald Coase's examination of the history of lighthouse provision in the United Kingdom. It was shown that navigational services were in fact provided privately, funded by the fees charged for using ports served by lighthouses.[74] As Kenneth Goldin commented, "Lighthouses are a favorite textbook example of public goods, because most economists cannot imagine a method of exclusion. (All this proves is that economists are less imaginative than lighthousekeepers)."[75]

Decisions regarding the proper method of providing goods for market, including the appropriate means of exclusion of potential free riders, are, fortunately, made by entrepreneurs, who are alert to finding ways of exploiting such profit opportunities, rather than by economists, whose interest is often merely academic. The next section of this chapter will focus on means of providing ideal objects on the market without recourse to intellectual property rights or other forms of state intervention.

IV. Markets for Ideal Objects in the Absence of Intellectual Property Rights

That markets for ideal objects can and do function in the absence of enforceable intellectual property rights is demonstrated by the fact that many innovations that are not accorded copyright or patent protection are nevertheless produced on the market. Among the valuable ideal objects unprotected in the United States are fashions; business, accounting, management, and marketing strategies; discoveries of naturally occurring substances; scientific principles and mathematical formulae;[76] jokes and magic tricks; useful mental processes (e.g., techniques for discovering natural gas deposits); new words and slogans; and designs or applications for atomic weapons(!).[77] Included are also large classes of nonpatentable inventions, as well as works on which copyrights have expired or are not applicable (ranging from the poems of Sappho and Virgil to the works of Arthur Conan Doyle and even the congressional testimony of Lieutenant Colonel Oliver North).

Further, functioning markets existed in the nineteenth century in the United States for the works of foreign authors. This free market situation included payment of royalties to British writers, even though those authors received no copyright protection in the United States until the extension of copyright protection to foreigners in 1891. American publishers who paid royalties to British authors for their works in order to receive advance galleys also had no legal protection against competitors who could legally copy their products and sell them on the market without paying any royalty either to the author or to the first publisher. As the English author T. H. Huxley testified to the Royal Commission of 1876–1878, "I myself am paid upon books which are published there: my American publisher remits me a certain percentage upon the selling price of the books there, and that without any copyright which can protect him."[78] In the absence of state protectionism, both publishers and authors utilized a number of the voluntary and contractual mechanisms for internalization of externalities to be discussed below.

Thus, the problem shifts to one of marketing. As Armen Alchian remarked in a comment on a paper quite critical of copyright, "I am sure that most publishers are so used to operating with a copyright monopoly that they will think Hurt's analysis strikes at the foundations of the publishing business. Not at the foundation; just at the present selling methods."[79]

Technological Fences

Most performance arts, including musical concerts, plays, movies, and circuses, rely to one degree or another on fencing. Tickets are sold and checked at the door. Others, however, rely on different means to garner support. Street musicians, breakdancers, magicians, and puppeteers, for instance, pass the hat following their performances, relying on the donations of passersby. Still others perform for the simple pleasure of it, with little or no expectation of financial gain.

Most television programs are broadcast, meaning that anyone with a television can receive them. Revenues are generated by advertising, a method that will be discussed at greater length later. Other stations "narrowcast" their signals, sometimes in scrambled forms that require descrambling devices available from the station for a fee, and sometimes over dedicated cables, access to which is available only upon payment of a fee. Thus, television signals, which would seem to be a strong candidate for a pure public good, can be and are provided on the market without government protection.[80]

In the case of prerecorded videocassettes, technological fencing devices are available to prevent unauthorized reproduction. Thus, a firm in California has developed a process called "Macrovision," which tricks VCRs into making virtually unviewable copies of prerecorded cassettes carrying a certain code. The cassette tape is encoded with strong electronic pulses, which lead the recording mechanism to expect a stronger signal than is available from the cassette's audio and visual information. When played, the resulting copy has colored splotches cross it and becomes alternately too dim or too loud.[81]

Unauthorized photocopying can also be thwarted by use of a special uncopyable paper produced by Nicopi International of Canada. Boise, Cascade has developed a paper that, when photocopied, splashes "Unauthorized Copy" across the result.[82]

Some computer programs available on the market include "worms," which detect efforts to copy the program and erase the program or "counterattack" by erasing files on the copying computer's memory. (I am assured that such forms of protection are rapidly being removed from programs by software producers, due to consumer dissatisfaction. Merely to identify a possible solution to potential problems of "publicness" is not to assert that it will be widely adopted on the market.) Others simply place the words "Unauthorized Copy" in the resulting copy. Still other firms offer "dedicated" software, which can only be run on computers that they manufacture (an example of a "bundled" good, which will be discussed at greater length later).

Not all of these technological fencing mechanisms will prove effective at discouraging the dedicated copier, just as music concert promoters do not manage to exclude all fans from listening in with special eavesdropping devices or from simply standing outside of a concert hall in the hopes of hearing some of the music performed inside. In many cases, however, it is sufficient merely to exclude a large enough percentage of potential free riders to sell the good profitably on the market. In other cases, a particular technological fence may fail to achieve even that, and incentives will exist to come up with a better exclusion system. Additionally, some technological fences may be profitably employed only in conjunction with other devices, such as special marketing plans or contractual relations.

Tie-Ins and Complementary Goods

Another way to exclude nonpurchasers from enjoying a good is to "bundle" it together with another good, for which the costs of exclusion may be lower. This bundled good can either be complementary to the "public" good, such as program guides sold in conjunction with television broadcasts, or noncomplementary but appealing to market segments that are sufficiently coextensive, such as health insurance sold to farmers through the Farm Bureau, which also provides the "public good" of lobbying for programs that benefit all farmers.[83]

This method of providing collective goods is more common than one might at first think. Economist Daniel Klein points out:

> The price of a ticket to a ball game may be seen as the total payment for two goods, a seat in the stands (a noncollective good) and the spectacle on the playing field (a joint good). The ball park is like a one-day club, with members enjoying free and exclusive access to the game on the field. Similar tie-in interpretations can be given for shows, concerts, transportation services, recreation facilities, education, and cable television.[84]

Thus, television stations can tie one good, the broadcast of an electromagnetic signal, with another, the dissemination of information from (excludable) sellers to potential buyers (advertising).[85] Alternatively, sale of program guides, a product complementary to a television broadcast, can be used to finance television programs. This is often the case with noncommercial stations that do not accept advertising (except in their program guides). Many magazines and newspapers are also financed through advertising revenues. In the absence of copyright privileges, more goods might be provided in this way.

Computer programs may be "fenced" in the manner described above. They may also be (and very often are) "bundled" together with other goods, such as manuals, periodic updates, and toll-free numbers and passwords that give purchasers access to expert advice on the use of the program. As Ithiel de Sola Pool predicted, "Perhaps we should stop speaking about 'copyright' and start speaking about 'service-right.' The tie that makes it worthwhile for the customer to pay the vendor rather than try to copy a disk is the need for a continuing service relationship."[86] "Shareware" programs, produced with the intention of realizing a profit, are distributed with the explicit understanding and request that users copy them and give them to friends and colleagues. Users are then offered the opportunity to pay for the program and receive a manual and other complementary goods, as well as the knowledge (and satisfaction) of having paid for a useful good.

As with the other methods of goods provision discussed in this section, the possibilities for bundling of goods are not finite, but are subjects for human entrepreneurship and creativity. No one could have predicted that an early radio enthusiast in Pittsburgh in 1919 would have discovered that bundling advertising with radio broadcasts provides a successful method of satisfying consumer demands.[87] We are fortunate, however, that this discovery provided an effective means for provision of radio and television broadcasts at such an early stage in radio technology's development, thus saving Americans from the monotony, boredom, and tyranny of a state broadcast system (or from bogus property rights assignments to broadcast signals).[88]

Contractual Arrangements for Internalization of Externalities

Decentralized, private, contractual remedies are also available for the internalization of externalities. One means of using contract rather than monopoly privilege is through exploitation of other legal remedies for copying. For example, due to the often cumbersome nature of the patent system and the shortened product cycle of many new inventions, such as drugs, microelectronics, and biologically engineered "bugs," many producers are switching to other systems for protecting their interests in innovations.[89]

While some firms are expending more resources on exploiting other features of their product (such as being first to market, about which more later), others are relying on legal remedies rooted in the common law and utilizing their property rights in the tangible goods in which their "ideal objects" are instantiated. Thus, bailments are being more widely used by biotechnology firms. As Blackstone writes,

> Property may also be of a qualified or special nature, on account of the peculiar circumstances of the owner, when the thing itself is very capable of an absolute ownership. As in case of *bailment*, or delivery, of goods to another person for a particular use; as to a carrier to convey to London, to an innkeeper to secure in his inn, or the like. Here there is no absolute property in either the bailor or the bailee, the person delivering, or him to whom it is delivered: for the bailor hath only the right, and not the immediate possession; the bailee hath the possession, and only a temporary right. But it is a qualified property in them both; and each of them is entitled to an action, in case the goods be damaged or taken away: the bailee on account of his imme-

diate possession; the bailor, because the possession of the bailee is, immediately, his possession also.[90]

Thus, firms seeking to market new inventions may release them to others through a kind of lease, whereby the property title is retained by the originating firm (the bailor) while possession and use are transferred to the bailee. Remedies in the event of release of the goods to others or of unauthorized use can be contractually specified. In the case of biologically engineered products, ownership rights to both the "starter cells" and their progeny are retained by the originating firm. Thus, "Using a bailment not only ensures that the cells and their progeny will be returned once the license to use the process has run out, but it protects the company that developed the biological material in case its licensee runs into financial trouble."[91]

In addition, performance bonds can be posted by the bailee to ensure compliance with the terms of the mutually agreeable contract. If, for example, "bugs" licensed to the bailee for a specific use turn up in another use or in the hands of another firm, the bailee could be held liable for the resulting damages suffered by the bailor.

Such contractual remedies can be used in conjunction with trade secrecy law, which offers a broad spectrum of protection against unauthorized disclosure of any guarded or contractually governed secret "used in one's business and which gives him an opportunity to gain an advantage over competitors who do not know or use it."[92] While trade secrecy laws do not offer protection identical to patent or copyright law, there are many cases in which it is preferable to either.[93] The example of Coca-Cola, the formula for which was never patented, indicates one of the advantages of reliance on trade secret law, as opposed to patents. Had the Coca-Cola formula been patented, protection would have lasted only seventeen years, rather than the decades enjoyed by the firm's stockholders thanks to the protection of trade secrecy.

The objection is often heard, of course, that patents are preferable to trade secret protection because under patent protection the holder of the patent is induced to reveal the innovation to the public. Without patents, it is alleged, the process of scientific and technical advance would stall, with each innovator jealously guarding his or her secrets and refusing to share them with the world. Patents, thus, rather than retarding the spread of new knowledge, actually advance it.

This thinking rests, however, on dubious economic premises. Only in cases where one believes that a secret is unlikely to remain so would one trade the protection of trade secrecy for patent. Patent protection is sought only in cases where the patentee fears that the secret will become known. As Fritz Machlup comments, "the patent system cannot be said to serve the purpose of eliciting any secrets that would not in any event become known in the near future. People patent only what they cannot hope to keep secret."[94] Indeed, patents may discourage the spread of knowledge, not only by granting monopolies, but by discouraging innovators from collaborating during the period prior to the filing of a patent. A small time lead on one's competitors leading to an earlier filing date can mean the difference between winning or losing the entire monopoly right to exploit the technology. It is an advantage one would be less likely to trade for the advantages of cooperation, given the all-or-nothing character of patent protection. Patents may, in fact, actually act to inhibit, rather than encourage, the spread of knowledge.

Another means of contractually securing the interests of innovators is through self-enforcing voluntary trade association agreements. Thus, though unprotected by any form of enforceable intellectual property rights, the Fashion Originator's Guild successfully campaigned against "style piracy" in the 1930s. The guild organized producers to refuse to sell to retail stores that also carried unauthorized copies of works created by their members. The guild also used an internal system of arbitration to penalize members of the guild who violated their contractual obligations. This system allowed guild members to protect their investments in innovative fashion designs, at the same time that free entry into the market allowed competition from nonmembers to restrain guild members from monopolizing the market.[95]

Finally, the example of pre–1891 America may illustrate how the use of retaliatory action functioned in markets for ideal goods unprotected by intellectual property rights. As mentioned earlier, prior to 1891, foreign authors and their publishers received no protection from American copyright law. American publishers, seeking to secure their interests in books by foreign authors, would occasionally issue "fighting editions" of such works to undercut editions of the same works published by rival houses. As T. H. Huxley explained to the Royal Commission of 1876–78, "the practice of all the great houses in America (there are some three or four large publishing houses with very great capital), if anybody publishes one of their books, is to publish a largely cheaper edition at any cost, and they would make any pecuniary sacrifice rather than not cut out a rival."[96] Such a policy, combined with the possibility of free entry, encouraged publishers to lower prices as a discouragement to competitors. Thus, "In such circumstances, the American public enjoyed cheap books, the American publishers found their business profitable, and the English authors received lump sums for their advance sheets and royalties on American sales."[97]

Marketing Strategies

Entrepreneurship extends to marketing just as it does to production techniques. Indeed, marketing is an integral part of the entire process of production; without some anticipation that goods will be successfully sold at prices yielding a profit, the act of production will not be undertaken in the first place. Here again the evidence indicates that marketing strategies can overcome many of the problems associated with the potential "publicness" of the final product.

To begin with, there is very often a substantial advantage to being "first to market" with a product, especially in the case of ideal objects. Currently, in the fields of microelectronics, biotechnology, and videocassettes, to take but a few examples, exploitation of the status of being first to market is often far more valuable than patent or copyright protection.[98]

Such exploitation of being first in the market with a product played an important role in the pre–1891 American market for books by foreign authors.[99] It also induced English authors to deliver manuscripts to American publishers prior to publication in England and only after contracts had been written securing their interest. As Sir Louis Mallet, a member of the Royal Commission of 1876–1878 concluded in his report, "it will always be in the power of the first publisher of a work so to control the value, by a skillful adaptation of the supply to the demand, as to avoid the risk of ruinous competition, and secure ample remuneration both to the author and to himself."[100]

Price discrimination provides another method of providing many goods. In the case of videocassettes, producers have been able to engage in temporal price discrimination, initially offering movies at high prices to enthusiasts (who desire copies immediately) or to rental-store owners (who will rent the tape many times), then dropping the price after several months to capture less enthusiastic segments of the market, followed by very low prices to capture the remainder of the market.[101] This form of temporal price discrimination also extends to the way movies are now marketed through theaters prior to being released on videocassette: the result has been an explosion in the number of new movies released and an increase in the genre once known as "art films" (e.g., *A Room with a View*).[102] Other forms of price discrimination currently being used by producers of ideal objects include the issuance of both hardcover and paperback editions of books, differential prices for magazines and journals sold to individuals or to libraries, and, in the case of the arts, special rates based on age, school enrollment, or ability to pay.

Such marketing strategies may also be combined with forward and backward market integration, allowing originators of ideal objects to ensure markets for their goods. Thus, publishers may arrange with bookstores (through contracts with individual stores or with chains, or through outright ownership of stores) to offer their works to the public on an exclusive basis. Movie producers and theaters may also make similar arrangements, and similarly for other goods.

Another marketing strategy that may be utilized is fairly simple: lower prices. The fixed costs of underwriting research or of paying royalties to authors can be "spread over" a larger number of copies if production is increased, diminishing any advantage that copiers might otherwise enjoy.[103] Subjecting producers of ideal objects to the ever-present possibility of entry by competitors has the added advantage of lowering prices for consumers, with a corresponding increase in the consumption of the ideal object. The possibility of competition and the rivalrous pursuit of temporary "monopolies," often based on creation of new products or markets, is one of the engines of the market system.[104] The granting of statutory monopolies tends to have, on the other hand, the effect of decreasing flexibility and alertness to consumer demand and production possibilities on the part of market participants.

Quality control and assurance offer another advantage to originators of new products and ideas. Milton Friedman, having come up with and publicly explained and defended a monetary theory of business cycles, did not thereby dissipate all of the rents accruing to this discovery. He still commands public speaking fees in the thousands of dollars to explain a theory that is publicly available and explainable by any of thousands of economists, most of whom would certainly charge far less. Nevertheless, organizers of conventions and other public events still demand Milton Friedman as a speaker, presumably because of the assurance of quality his "name brand" brings. Similar processes can be seen in markets for other goods, where innovators often enjoy advantages over copiers deriving from their position as innovators.

In addition, the introduction of copying technology can often increase the demand for originals, in some cases leading to unambiguous increases in profits for the producers of originals (when, for example, the publisher's marginal cost of producing originals exceeds the marginal cost of copying), indicating that "the interests of consumers and those of publishers may be congruent, rather than divergent, with respect to the effects of copying."[105] Congruence of benefits for producers and consumers is clearest in cases where purchasers of originals make copies for their own use, as in the case of recordings of telecasts for later viewing, known as "time shifting." In free markets, without state imposition of intellectual property rights, firms are able to arrange technological, marketing, and other factors to set the difficulty of copying so as to maximize the demand for originals. In the field of computer software, the enormous costs of state enforcement of intellectual property rights against individual copying has led to minimal state action against copiers. This has left software manufacturers to their own devices to thwart copying, and many firms, rather than increasing technological copy protection in response, have instead reduced it. This stems from a recognition that the demand for originals is often tied to the possibility of making copies.[106]

Yet another advantage innovators have over copiers that is related to their status of being first on the market is that they possess what amounts to "inside information" regarding their product. Anticipations of the value of their innovation may provide innovators with opportunities to invest in factors complementary to their innovation, thus reaping some of the benefits of the increased social product made possible by their creativity.[107] Indeed, the general problem of non-rivalrous consumption of information is a major factor in explaining the emergence of firms and of horizontal or vertical integration of production processes.

An integral element of marketing is the determination of consumer demand. The problem of demand revelation is present for every good, but it can be especially acute for some. Indeed, the central core of the older theory of public goods is the belief that in the absence of coercion consumers will "underreveal" their "true" preferences for goods and producers will "underinvest" in their production. This problem is intimately related to the possibility of exclusion, discussed in the section above on technological fences. Here the problem is taken up in relation to marketing techniques, such as pre-sale and other forms of pre-contract excludability.

The most obvious way to exclude a nonpurchaser from enjoyment of a good is not to produce the good. The standard response from orthodox public goods theory would be that pre-contract excludability would make no difference to a potential purchaser, as the good still either will or will not be produced, regardless of whatever course of action (purchasing or "free riding") the consumer takes. But as economist Earl Brubaker argues, given the benefits that will accrue to members of a group if the good is produced,

> The typical individual may decide . . . that he would, after all, be quite willing to make an offer reflecting the worth of the good to him, provided only that

he receive some assurance that the remainder of the community would make an appropriate 'matching' offer, so that he doesn't waste his own scarce resources supporting an ineffectual collective effort.[108]

Brubaker proposes an alternative to the "Free Rider" model, that is, the "Golden Rule" of model demand revelation, in which pre-contractual arrangements are made committing potential purchasers to the purchase of a collective good only in the event that a sufficient number of others also agree to contribute. This is precisely what happens in the event of pre-sale contracts for books and similar goods.[109] Book and record clubs also operate on this basis, and we could reasonably expect an increase in such forms of organization in markets without intellectual property rights.

The use of conditionally binding assurance contracts (CBACs) is already widespread in a number of fields, including charitable fund raising (e.g., "matching pledges") and magazine and book sales. Demand is "revealed" only in those cases where there is some assurance that at least a large enough number will "reveal" their demand to make production of the good worthwhile. Externalities are internalized by exploiting pre-contract excludability to include within the group enjoying the good a sufficient number to ensure its production.[110] In the absence of intellectual property rights, one might expect to see a greater use of such marketing devices.

Finally, complementary technological innovations may allow new marketing techniques to capture the residuals accruing to innovation. For example, the advent of digital audio technology (DAT) could lead to an entirely new system of distribution for musical recordings. Rather than selling "hard copies" of musical recordings (records, tapes, and compact disks) in stores, music recording firms could offer digitally encoded versions through electronic databases. Subscribers would pay a fee and in exchange would receive a personal identification code that they could use to access a database, perhaps through a toll-free number. Upon entering the code over the phone, they would be allowed to "download" some determinate number of musical works per month directly from the database to their DAT machines. (Alternatively, they could be charged on a per-use basis, through invoices or through credit cards.) The technology for such a distribution and marketing system already exists. The advantage to recording firms would be a reduction in inventory costs, one of their major costs of doing business, to virtually zero.

Another innovation, already being tested on the market, is to produce customized audio tapes in music stores. This system allows music sellers to cut into the "home recording" market composed largely of teenagers who create specialized tapes of songs from many different sources to match their own preferences. The machines that make this possible are the product of Personics Corporation of California. Drawing on a digitally recorded disk capable of storing up to fifteen thousand songs, the customer selects a mix of tunes, the machine is programmed, and a customized audiocassette is produced in one-eighth the normal playing time.[111] Thus, technological innovations at first believed to represent a grave threat to an industry may in fact represent new opportunities for profits, just as recording technology, rather than wiping out the incomes of performance artists, as was widely expected at the time, allowed them to soar to heights never before imagined.

Are Patents and Copyrights Efficient?

Having shown that voluntary mechanisms other than intellectual property rights are available to externalize the internalities of production of ideal objects, it is worthwhile at this point to review briefly the question of whether there is any strong evidence to suggest that patent and copyright protections in fact actually do result in an increase in innovation and creativity.

The available evidence is, by and large, ambiguous. As Fritz Machlup, reflecting an understandable caution, concluded his classic economic study of the patent system:

> No economist, on the basis of present knowledge, could possibly state with certainty that the patent system, as it now operates, confers a net benefit or a net loss upon society. . . . If one does not know whether a system 'as a whole' (in contrast to certain features of it) is good or bad, the safest 'policy conclusion' is to 'muddle through'—either with it, if one has lived long with it, or without it, if one has lived without it. If we did not have a patent system, it would be irresponsible, on the basis of our present knowledge of its economic consequences, to recommend instituting one. But since we have had a patent system for a long time, it would be irresponsible, on the basis of our present knowledge, to recommend abolishing it.[112]

Whether patents, on net, increase or suppress innovation is not at all clear. A recent survey of 650 research and development executives in 130 industries indicated that, when given a choice of patents to prevent duplication, patents to secure royalty income, secrecy, lead time, moving quickly down the learning curve, and sales and service efforts, "In general, patents were viewed by R&D executives as an effective instrument for protecting the competitive advantages of new technology in most chemical industries, including the drug industry, but patents were judged to be relatively ineffective in most other industries."[113] (Notably, the pharmaceutical industry could be one in which lead time would be more significant, were it not for the requirements of the 1962 amendments to the Pure Food and Drug Act, which require publication of information on new drugs years prior to their final approval for sale in the United States, thus giving foreign producers a healthy head start in the competition in foreign markets. The perceived usefulness of patents in the pharmaceutical industry may result from the competitive disadvantages imposed by federal drug regulations.)

Another study of data obtained from "a random sample of 100 firms in 12 manufacturing industries" indicated that:

> patent protection was judged to be essential for the development or introduction of one-third or more of the inventions during 1981-1983 in only 2 industries—pharmaceuticals and chemicals. On the other hand, in 7 industries (electrical equipment, office equipment, motor vehicles, instruments, primary metals, rubber, and textiles), patent protection was estimated to be essential for the development and in production of less than 10 percent of their inventions. Indeed, in office equipment, motor vehicles, rubber, and textiles, the firms were unanimous in reporting that patent protection was not essential for the development or introduction of any of their inventions during this period.[114]

Indeed, patents may in many cases present serious obstacles to innovation. The conflict between the Wright brothers and Glenn Curtis over patent rights to aircraft stabilizing devices, for example, may have seriously hampered the development of airplane design.[115] Patents can also create serious roadblocks to innovation, as monopoly claims are made in strategic areas.[116]

In addition, the incentives offered by patents for "inventing around" the protected intellectual property rights diminish the compatibility of manufactured goods.[117] The recently concluded (in the United States) fight between competing videocassette standards—JVC's "VHS" system and Sony's "Beta" system—was a direct result of the patents held by Sony on the Beta system and their initial reluctance to share their technology with rival producers.

Finally, it is clear that a good deal of great art would not have been produced under a strict copyright regime. William Shakespeare, for example, took the works of others and created greater works; under today's copyright regime, his legal bills would have been staggering.

Conclusion

Regimes that foster innovation and creativity can and do emerge through the market process without legislative or judicial intervention. The legal system of a free society, based on the right to self-ownership and the voluntary transference of alienable rights, allows entrepreneurs to generate solutions to problems that many theorists find intractable.[118] It may be difficult, for example, to imagine how entrepreneurs might create technological or contractual "fences" around their works, but create them they do. As in many other cases, the economic incentives facing actual market participants offer greater inducements to creativity than do the idle curiosity or speculation of the academics who study them. Violating those rights of self-ownership and control over tangible alienable property that ground the market system in pursuit of elusive efficiency gains is ultimately inconsistent with both economic efficiency and the free market.

A jurisprudence that claims to be based on "law and economics" but that would constructively assign or rearrange rights as part of a strategy to achieve some predetermined outcome (maximization of utility or of wealth, for example) overlooks the analogy between the spontaneous order of the market and the spontaneous order of a legal system. As Bruno Leoni remarked, *"there is much more than an analogy between the market economy and a judiciary or lawyers' law, just as there is much more than an analogy between a planned economy and legislation."*[119] Leoni could have included constructivistic judicial intervention with legislation as systemically inconsistent with the market economy.[120] By focusing on desirable specific outcomes (efficiency and wealth maximization), the "Posnerian" approach ignores the broader economic understanding of the legal system as an order derived from the adjudication of individual claims rather than from a public policy blueprint.[121] Patents and copyrights, both deliberately state-created monopolies that did not emerge through common law or otherwise spontaneous legal processes, are unjustifiable interventions into voluntary market processes.

Investigation of the real workings of markets shows how a voluntary regime based on rights to tangible property generates institutions and mechanisms—whether through technology, contract, or other means—of rewarding innovation and creativity. Patents and copyrights have no place in a regime based on individual rights and are insupportable on either the grounds of (utilitarian) efficiency or of a jurisprudence of law and economics.

Notes

1. Such goods include ideas and processes, lists and databases, algorithms and computer programs, and music and literary products and are contrasted with tangible objects like chairs, land, and apples in their capacity to be infinitely multiplied, or instantiated, without concomitant diminution of size or quality. Despite this difference from tangible goods, such ideal objects remain economic goods because they are scarce, that is, they must be produced, and they are valuable.

2. R. Posner, *The Economics of Justice* (Cambridge, Mass.: Harvard University Press, 1981), 13–47.

3. For Bentham's attitudes to the common law, see G. Postema, *Bentham and the Common Law Tradition* (Oxford: Clarendon Press, 1986).

4. Posner, *Economics of Justice*, 48–87, 88–115. For criticism of wealth maximization as a normative principle, see J. Coleman, *Markets, Morals, and the Law* (Cambridge: Cambridge University Press, 1988), 95–132. For a criticism (from a contractarian perspective) of the principle of wealth maximization as a descriptive principle, see K. Scheppelle, *Legal Secrets: Equality and Efficiency in the Common Law* (1988).

5. Posner, *Economics of Justice*, 75.

6. W. M. Landes and R. Posner, "An Economic Analysis of Copyright Law," *Journal of Legal Studies* 17 (June 1989).

7. Landes and Posner, "An Economic Analysis," 52. Landes and Posner also describe the distinction between standards in literary and musical copyright as being made by the courts "correctly from the economic standpoint" ("An Economic Analysis," 41).

8. Coleman, *Markets, Morals, and the Law*, 131.

9. B. Leoni, *Freedom and the Law* (Los Angeles: Nash Publishers, 1972). See also P. Aranson, "Bruno Leoni in Retrospect," *Harvard Journal of Law and Public Policy* 11 (1988): 661; and Liggio and Palmer, "Freedom and the Law: A Comment on Professor Aranson's Article," in *Harvard Journal of Law and Public Policy* 11 (1988): 714.

10. See, for example, Hayek and Leoni, *Law, Legislation, and Liberty* (Chicago: Chicago University Press, 1973, 1976, 1979). In contrast to Judge Posner's pursuit of the clearly articulated goal of wealth maximization, Hayek and Leoni argue that a liberal legal order is a spontaneous order that aims at no particular end, but rests on general rules that emerge out of the adjudication of specific claims.

11. Such hybrids as the Semiconductor Chip Protection Act, 17 U.S.C. sec. 901 (1984), which combines elements of both patents and copyright, will be subject to the same criticisms leveled at patents and copyrights.

12. Bruce W. Bugbee, in his *Genesis of American Patent and Copyright Law* (Washington, D.C.: Public Affairs Press, 1967), takes issue with the identification of patents and copyrights with monopoly. Bugbee cites Supreme Court decisions distinguishing between monopoly and patent, all of which rely ultimately on Lord

Coke, who wrote in his *Institutes of the Laws of England* (1628), "A monopoly is an institution, or allowance by the king by his grant, commission, or otherwise to any person or persons, bodies politique, or corporate, of or for the sole buying, selling, making, working, or using of any thing, whereby any person or persons, bodies politique, or corporate, are sought to be restrained of any freedome, or liberty that they had before, or hindered in their lawfull trade." Subsequent decisions placed great weight on the phrase "that they had before," arguing that no one had any freedom to use an invention prior to its invention, and that the granting of an exclusive right to use of such an invention therefore does not constitute a monopoly. It should be pointed out, however, that for economic purposes such distinctions are moot and that, further, the publication of Coke's work came just four years after the *Statute of Monopolies* (1624), which declared illegal all monopolies except for "patents and Graunts of Priviledge for the tearme of one and twentie yeares or under, heretofore made of the sole workinge or makinge of any manner of newe Manufacture within this Realme, to the first and true Inventor or Inventors of such Manufactures which others at the tyme of the making of such Letters Patents and Graunts did not use, soe they be not contrary to the Lawe nor mischievous to the State." Bugbee and others have seen this exemption as providing "a firmer legal basis for clearing away the bad company with which patents of invention had been forced to travel" (Bugbee, *Genesis*, 39–40).

It is notable, however, that also exempted from the prohibition of monopolies were defense-related activities, such as "the production of ordnance, shot, gunpowder, and saltpeter and such industries as the manufacture of glass, the production of alum, and—significantly enough—printing" (Bugbee, *Genesis*, 40). The last in the list provided the rationale for the continuing use of grants of privilege by the Crown to censor religious and political dissenters. Rather than distinguishing patents and copyrights from monopolies, then, they could be seen as a class of monopolies considered especially important to the maintenance of the power of the Crown, and therefore as exempted from the blanket condemnation of the *Statute of Monopolies*.

13. Thus, the traditional practice of granting monopoly right over industrial and other creative processes for multiples of seven years was based on the seven-year duration of apprenticeship, the time during which native craftsmen could learn the art newly introduced into the realm (Bugbee, *Genesis*, 34).

14. Bugbee, *Genesis*, 21–22.

15. Bugbee, *Genesis*, 40.

16. Bugbee, *Genesis*, 14.

17. Machlup and Penrose, "The Patent Controversy in the Nineteenth Century," in *Journal of Economic History* 10 (1950): 1, 16.

18. Ringer, "The Demonology of Copyright," in *Perspectives on Publishing*, edited by P. Altbach and S. McVay (Lexington, Mass.: Lexington Books, 1976), 38.

19. B. Bugbee, *Genesis*, 50.

As on the Continent, the tremendous power of the press in this period of religious controversy was appreciated by those in authority. Consciously or otherwise, Mary and her Spanish husband Philip were following Venetian precedent when they chartered the Stationers' Company in 1557. . . . All of England's printers and publishers were required to join this association, organized to facilitate the control of the press for the suppression of Protestant literature. As compensation for royal supervision, censorship and licensing of books to be printed, the approximately 100 members of the Company were given what amounted to a monopoly of all printing in England.

20. Quoted in J. Lawrence, "Copyright Law, Fair Use, and the Academy: An Introduction," in *Fair Use and Free Inquiry: Copyright Law and the Media*, edited by J. Lawrence and B. Timberg (Norwood, N.J.: Ablex Publishing Corp., 1980), 4.

21. Abrams, "The Historic Foundations of American Copyright Law: Exploding the Myth of Common Law Copyright," *Wayne State Law Review* 29 (1983): 1137, 1138.

22. Arnold Plant, "The Economic Aspects of Copyright in Books" (1934), in Plant, *Selected Economic Essays and Addresses* (1974), 64–65.

23. Plant, "Economic Aspects," 65.

24. Plant, "Economic Aspects," 67.

25. Quoted in U.S. Congress, Office of Technology Assessment, *Intellectual Property Rights in an Age of Electronics and Information* (1986).

26. Quoted in Bugbee, *Genesis*, 53–54.

27. The theme of underproduction due to the public nature of the good will be dealt with later at greater length.

28. B. Kaplan, *An Unhurried View of Copyright* (New York: Columbia University Press, 1967), 8.

29. Abrams, "Historic Foundations of American Copyright Law."

30. 4 Burr. 2303, 98 Eng. Rep. 201 (1769).

31. The inclusion of the word "perpetual" in this context is important, for if the common law truly recognized a property right in ideal objects, then such a right, like other property rights, would not be limited in duration by the Statute of Anne but would extend beyond the period specified in the statute.

32. 1 Eng. Rep. 837 (1774).

33. Quoted in Abrams, "Historic Foundations of American Copyright Law," 1162.

34. Abrams, "Historic Foundations of American Copyright Law."

35. Bugbee, *Genesis*, 55.

36. Abrams, "Historic Foundations of American Copyright Law," 1119–71.

37. Bugbee, *Genesis*, 43: "Rights of literary property remained legally unprotected until the fifteenth century, when the introduction of the printing press to Europe made the rewards of publishing—or plagiarism—far greater than ever before."

38. At one point in the copying of the Greek of Aristotle's *Posterior Analytics*, for example, *dia mesou*—"through the middle term"—became *di' amesou*—"through no middle term"—in the version used by St. Thomas to write his com-

mentary, a very small error that directly reversed the meaning of the text and led St. Thomas to some philosophical acrobatics to justify his reading.

39. D. Boorstin, *The Discoverers: A History of Man's Search to Know His World and Himself* (New York: Random House, 1985), 530.

40. E. Eisenstein, *The Printing Press As an Agent of Change* (1979), 229.

41. Eisenstein, 122: "The new forms of authorship and literary property-rights undermined older concepts of collective authority in a manner that encompassed not only biblical composition but also texts relating to philosophy, science, and law. Veneration for the wisdom of the ages was probably modified as ancient sages were retrospectively cast in the role of individual authors—prone to human error and possibly plagiarists as well."

42. Ronald H. Coase, "The Problem of Social Cost," in *Journal of Law and Economics* 3 (1960): 1.

43. Demsetz, "Toward a Theory of Property Rights," in *The Economics of Property Rights*, edited by E. Furubotn and S. Pejovich (Cambridge, Mass.: Ballinger Pub. Co., 1974).

44. See Anderson and Hill, "The Evolution of Property Rights: A Study of the American West," in *Journal of Law and Economics* 18 (1975): 163: "Establishing and protecting property rights is very much a productive activity toward which resources can be devoted. But, like any other activity, the amount of this investment will depend upon the marginal benefits and costs to investors of allocating resources to these endeavors."

45. Demsetz, "Toward a Theory of Property Rights," 34.

46. Some economists distinguish between jointness of consumption and jointness of supply. This distinction is not relevant to our case, however.

47. Samuelson, "The Pure Theory of Public Expenditure," *Review Of Economics and Statistics* 36 (1954): 387, 389. Collective consumption goods are those "which all enjoy in common in the sense that each individual's consumption of such a good leads to no subtraction of any other individual's consumption of that good, so that $X_{n+j} = X^i_{n+j}$, simultaneously for each and every nth individual and each collective good."

48. M. Olson, *The Logic of Collective Action* (Cambridge, Mass.: Harvard University Press, 1965), 14: "A common, collective, or public good is here defined as any good such that, if any person X_i in a group $X_1, \ldots, X_i, \ldots, X_n$ consumes it, it cannot feasibly be withheld from the others in that group."

49. See T. Brennan, *"Harper & Row v. The Nation:* Copyrightability and Fair Use," *U.S. Department of Justice, Economic Policy Office Discussion Paper* (11 May 1984): "Intellectual property is a 'public good,' in that once the intellectual property is produced it can in principle be consumed by an additional user at virtually zero marginal cost."

50. At this point it may be useful to introduce a distinction between two kinds of scarcity: static scarcity and dynamic scarcity. The focus of most literature on intellectual property rights has been on the latter; if intellectual property rights are not recognized and legally enforced, then incentives for innovation and cre-

ativity will be diminished, if not eliminated outright. As we shall see later, the function of creating and maintaining exclusivity that characterizes property rights in tangible objects can be attained for ideal objects in other ways. Both tangible and ideal objects are scarce in the dynamic sense; only the former are scarce in the static sense. Further, scarcity does apply to the tangible instantiation or embodiment of ideal objects, for example, the tangible and material "book," which serves as the substrate for the author's immaterial product, for his "book." For this distinction, see I. Kant, *Was Ist Ein Buch,* in his *Die Metaphysik Der Sitten* (Bloomington: Indiana University Press, 1970); and in his essay, "Von der Unrechtsmässigkeit des Büchernachdrucks," in *Copyrights and Patents for Inventions,* trans. by R. Macfie (1883), 581–86.

51. Landes and Posner, "Economic Analysis."

52. Dr. Frank Conrad, assistant chief engineer of Westinghouse Electric in Pittsburgh, a leader among early amateur radio enthusiasts, was the founder of what later became station KDKA. On 17 October 1919, bored by discussing radio equipment, Conrad "placed his microphone before a phonograph and substituted music for voice. The song was 'Old Black Joe.' The music saved Dr. Conrad's voice, but more—it delighted and amazed 'hams' all over the country. Mail, heavy previously, now became a deluge with requests that music be played at special times so that the writer might convince some skeptic that music really could be transmitted through space. . . . These broadcasts soon exhausted Dr. Conrad's supply of records, and the Hamilton Music Store in Wilkinsburg, Pa. offered a continuing supply of records if he would announce that the records could be purchased at the Hamilton store. Dr. Conrad agreed and thus gave the world its first radio advertiser—who promptly found that records played on the air sold better than others." *Fiftieth Anniversary Golden Yearbook* (1959), 6. It was the teenage members of the Junior Wireless Club of America who succeeded in blocking state monopolization of the airwaves through their testimony and lobbying in 1910. See *Congressional Record,* 1910, Hearings of April 28, 1910, before the Committee on Commerce of the Senate of the United States. Thanks to them and to the owner of the Hamilton Music Store, Americans were spared complete state monopolization of broadcasting. I am indebted to Milton Mueller for alerting me to this history.

53. Thomas Jefferson, "Letter to Isaac McPherson, Monticello, August 13, 1813," in *XIII The Writings of Thomas Jefferson,* edited by A. Lipscomb (1904), 326–38. Jefferson does admit purely statutory—as opposed to natural—intellectual property rights "as an encouragement to men to pursue ideas which may produce utility," although he is ambivalent on this issue:

it is a fact, as far as I am informed, that England was, until we copied her, the only country on earth which ever, by a general law, gave a legal right to the exclusive use of an idea. In some other countries it is sometimes done, in a great case, and by a special and personal act, but, generally speaking, other nations have thought that these monopolies produce more embarrassment than advantage to society: and it may be observed that the nations which refuse monopolies of invention, are as fruitful as England in new and useful devices.

When this letter was written, Jefferson had already spent some years as a member of the patent board. Notably, he had earlier proposed an amendment as a part of the Bill of Rights, which would have nullified the patents and copyrights clause of Article 1, section 8 of the Constitution:

> I sincerely rejoice at the acceptance of our new constitution by nine States. It is a good canvass, on which some strokes only want retouching. What these are, I think are sufficiently manifested by the general voice from north to south, which calls for a bill of right. It seems pretty generally understood, that this should go to juries, habeas corpus, standing armies, printing, religion and monopolies. . . . The few cases wherein these things may do evil, cannot be weighed against the multitude wherein the want of them will do evil. . . . The saying there shall be no monopolies, lessens the incitements to ingenuity, which is spurred on by the hope of a monopoly for a limited time, as of fourteen years; but the benefit of even limited monopolies is too doubtful, to be opposed to that of their general suppression.

Jefferson, at "Letter to James Madison, Paris, July 31, 1788," vol. 7, 93–99. One year later he proposed strictly limiting the power of Congress to grant monopolies in literature and inventions, and forbidding all other monopolies altogether:

> I must now say a word on the declaration of rights, you have been so good as to send to me. I like it, as far as it goes; but I should have been for going further. For instance, the following alterations and additions would have pleased me: Article 9. Monopolies may be allowed to persons for their own productions in literature, and their own inventions in the arts, for a term not exceeding——years, but for no longer term, and no other purpose.

Jefferson, at "Letter to James Madison, Paris, August 28, 1789," vol. 7, 444–53. Note also the remarks of James Madison in *Federalist No. 43* (in defense of the patents and copyright clause of the new constitution):

> The utility of this power will scarcely be questioned. The copyright of authors has been solemnly adjudged, in Great Britain, to be a right of common law. The right to useful inventions seems with equal reason to belong to the inventor. The public good fully coincides in both cases with the claims of individuals.

54. A. Plant, *The Economic Theory Concerning Patents for Inventions* (1934), 36.

55. F. A. Hayek, *The Fatal Conceit: The Errors of Socialism* (1988), 6.

56. Demsetz himself questions whether his model is applicable to intellectual property rights ("Toward a Theory of Property Rights," 42, and "Commentary on Market and Meta-Market," Mont Pelerin Society General Meeting [1–5 September 1986]). Demsetz says that his essay on property rights was "stimulated

by, but different than, Coase's perspective" and that it "sought to explain the evolution of private rights as a social response to emerging scarcity problems. Land once superabundant becomes scarce and in need of more careful conserving. This leads to the development of rights in land that provide the incentives necessary for a proper response to this new scarcity problem."

57. B. Leoni, Lectures given December 2–6, 1963 (Freedom School Phrontistery, Colorado Springs, Colorado). See also Leoni, *Freedom and the Law* (1972).

58. For a game-theoretic treatment of the spontaneous emergence of property rights, see R. Sugden, *The Economics of Rights, Co-Operation and Welfare* (Oxford: B. Blackwell, 1986). Sugden criticizes the "U.S. Cavalry model of government," according to which "the government stands ready to rush to the rescue whenever the market 'fails', and the economist's job is to advise it on when and how to do so" (Sugden, 3). See also Sugden, "Labor, Property, and the Morality of Markets," in *The Market in History*, edited by B. Anderson and A. Latham (London: Croom Helm, 1986)(the morality of market arrangements). On the hubris of "designing" property rights systems and then imposing them on the market, see V. Smith, "Comment," *Progress in Natural Resource Economics*, edited by A. Scott (Oxford: Clarendon Press, 1985), 414:

> 'Can We Consciously Design New and Better Property Rights Systems?' Based on my interpretation of the origin and proem of property right formation, I am skeptical about whether, as professionals, any of us as yet knows and understands enough about our subject matter to allow an affirmative answer to this question. . . . What we lack is the knowledge that comes from practice, from trying, failing, and learning from the results. It is one thing to articulate an ex post property right interpretation of the mining district, the oil lease, or the fact that the individual members of OPEC combined the right to unrecovered oil with the right to recovered oil in the 1970s; it is quite another to design ex ante property right institutions that will operate in the way that we claim that these 'natural experiments' have operated. For one thing, our claims and interpretations may be wrong; for another, we may not permit our designs to be reshaped by the opportunity cost challenges that operate in less structured environments.

59. For a derivation of rights to tangible objects based on self-ownership, see J. Locke, *Second Treatise of Government in Two Treatises of Government*, edited by P. Laslett (New York: Cambridge Press, 1963); for a derivation of property rights from body rights, see S. Wheeler, *Natural Property Rights As Body Rights* (1980); for a theory of contract based on transfer of rights to alienable property, see Barnett, "A Consent Theory of Contract," *Columbia Law Review* 86 (1986): 269.

60. W. Leggett, *Democratick Editorials: Essays in Jacksonian Political Economy* (1984), 399.

61. See, for example, Thomas, "Record Makers May Ban Digital Audio Tape to Protect Copyright," *Financial Times*, 8 May 1987; Sanger, "Vexed by Tape Technology," *New York Times*, 13 May 1987.

62. Adelstein and Peretz, "The Competition of Technologies in Markets for Ideas: Copyright and Fair Use in Evolutionary Perspective," in *International Review of Law and Economics* 5 (1985): 209.

63. Adelstein and Peretz, "Competition of Technologies," 213.

64. Adelstein and Peretz, "Competition of Technologies," 215.

65. Adelstein and Peretz, "Competition of Technologies," 217.

66. Adelstein and Peretz, "Competition of Technologies," 222.

67. Cowen, "Public Goods and Their Institutional Context: A Critique of Public Goods Theory," in *Review of Social Economics* 43 (1985): 53. See also Cowen, *The Theory of Market Failure: A Critical Examination* (1988) (collects together numerous useful essays on the theory of public goods).

68. Goldin, "Equal Access vs. Selective Access: A Critique of Public Goods Theory," in *Public Choice* 29 (1977): 53 (emphasis in original).

69. See Boudewijn Bouckaert, "The Historical Evolution of Public Goods and State Monopolies" (unpublished manuscript on file with the author).

70. For the discussion of public goods and public goods production from a "dynamic," rather than a "static," perspective see A. Alchian and W. Allen, *University Economics* 3d ed. (Belmont, Calif.: Wadsworth Pub. Co., 1972), 147–48, 245–47.

71. Anderson and Hill, "Evolution of Property Rights," 169–72.

72. See, for example, Besen, "New Technologies and Intellectual Property: An Economic Analysis," The Rand Corp. (May 1987): "efficient distribution of a public good requires that it be made available to all consumers for whom its value at least equals the marginal cost of distribution." See also Brennan, "Taxing Home Audio Taping," Economic Analysis Group Division Paper (EAG 86–6), U.S. Department of Justice, Antitrust Division (15 April 1986): "Looking solely at the efficiency of the copyright markets, however, the pertinent standard is to bring the marginal social return to investments in producing copyrighted works and improving their quality closer to the marginal costs of those investments."

73. For a criticism of this implicitly "teleological" approach to market processes, see Buchanan, "Order Defined in the Process of Its Emergence," *Literature of Liberty* (1982), reprinted in *Liberty, Market, And State: Political Economy in the 1980's* (New York: New York University Press, 1985), 73–74.

74. Coase, "The Lighthouse in Economics," *Journal of Law and Economics* 17 (1974): 357.

75. Goldin, "Equal Access vs. Selective Access," 62. For a discussion of provision of public goods through free markets, see Palmer, "Infrastructure: Public or Private," *Poly Rep.*, (May 1983), 5.

76. Note that this exception is being weakened, as patents are being awarded to the creators of useful algorithms. See "Equations Patented: Some See a Danger," *New York Times*, 15 February 1989.

77. Most of these are discussed in E. Kintner and J. Lahr, *An Intellectual Property Law Primer* (New York: Macmillan, 1982), 18–22, 364–68.

78. Evidence of T. H. Huxley, Question 5610, quoted in Plant, *Economic Theory*, 84.

79. Alchian, Comment on Robert M. Hurt and Robert M. Schuchman, "The Economic Rationale of Copyright," *American Economic Review* 56 (1966): 421, 439.

80. Recent legislation (17 U.S.C. sec. 111) requiring compulsory royalty payments for cable transmissions of television signals does not significantly alter the analysis presented here. In their absence revenues might be greater due to the increased audience available for advertising.

81. "Word from the Front in War Against Unauthorized Copying," *Wall Street Journal,* 20 February 1987.

82. "Word from the Front in War Against Unauthorized Copying."

83. For an extensive discussion of bundled noncomplementary goods, see M. Olson, *Logic of Collective Action,* 132–67.

84. Klein, "Tie-Ins and the Market of Collective Goods," *Harvard Journal of Law and Public Policy* 10 (1987): 452.

85. See Besen, "New Technologies and Intellectual Property," 15–18:

Early radio stations did not possess the technical means to exclude nonpaying listeners. An enterprising station owner decided to experiment with advertising to see whether revenues might be generated in this manner. The result was far more successful than anyone had anticipated and advertising remains today the principal basis on which commercial radio and television stations are supported. Where exclusion of nonpayers is a problem, advertising may be an effective alternative means of support.

As noted above, the experiment was even more of an accident than Besen indicates.

86. Ithiel de Sola Pool, "Whither Electronic Copyright," in Martin Greenberger, *Electronic Publishing Plus* (White Plains, N.Y.: Knowledge Industry Publications, 1985), 226.

87. For a discussion of entrepreneurship and of competition as a "discovery procedure," see F. A. Hayek, "Competition as a Discovery Procedure," in Hayek, *New Studies In Philosophy, Politics, Economics, and the History of Ideas* (Chicago: University of Chicago Press, 1978), 179; G. O'Driscoll and Mario Rizzo, *The Economics of Time and Ignorance* (Oxford: B. Blackwell, 1985), 95–129.

88. Instead, we must suffer from the somewhat less monotonous and boring tyranny of a system of state management of the broadcast spectrum, licensing, and regulation. Freely transferable property rights to use of the electromagnetic spectrum, however, offer an alternative to state control. For an illuminating discussion of property rights in this field, see M. Mueller, "Reforming Telecommunications Regulation," in E. Diamond, N. Sandler, and M. Mueller, *Telecommunications in Crisis: The First Amendment, Technology, and Deregulation* (Washington, D.C.: Cato Institute, 1983), 95–100. Such transferable rights are based on rights to unhampered use of tangible broadcasting and receiving equipment, as Mueller explains.

89. See "Patently Outdated: Changes in the Way Drugs Are Invented Are Making Patents Unworkable," *The Economist,* 18 July 1987:

The product cycle of new drugs is becoming significantly shorter than the period covered by a patent (8–12 years of shelf life). Manufacturers know that biotechnology makes it likely that another firm will shortly find a better or cheaper product that will make theirs as outdated as the leech. The shorter the life cycle, the less the point in getting patents. In the microelectronics industry, where product cycles have also shortened dramatically, patents have become less and less used. The rewards for invention for drug firms will increasingly come from being first to market.

90. W. Blackstone, *Commentaries on the Laws Of England,* (Boston: Beacon Press, 1962), 395.

91. "Bailments May Be the Answer to a High-Tech Problem," *Washington Post,* 23 March 1987.

92. Restatement of the Law of Torts, quoted in E. Kintner and J. Lahr, *Intellectual Property Law Primer,* 134.

93. See the discussion in Holcombe and Meiners, "Market Arrangements Versus Government Protection of Innovative Activity," *Social Science Review* 5 (1983): 1, 3–6.

94. F. Machlup, *The Political Economy of Monopoly* (Baltimore: Johns Hopkins University Press, 1952), 281.

95. See Holcombe and Meiners, "Market Arrangements Versus Government Protection," 8: "The protection was not as great as the monopoly power that the holder of a patent has over his innovation, but the social benefits from the lower monopoly power of the innovator may outweigh the social costs (if any) of the lower protection of the innovator's invention."
The arrangement was ruled a violation of the Sherman Antitrust Act by the Supreme Court in *Fashion Originator's Guild of America v. Federal Trade Commission,* 312 U.S. 451 (1941); but, as Holcombe and Meiners argue, "without patent law and without antitrust law, the market would be better able to serve consumers" (Holcombe and Meiners, 6). While such arrangements have been ruled in violation of antitrust law, the new climate of judicial opinion on antitrust, especially if combined with diminution or elimination of monopoly patent or copyright privileges, could lead to a new stance toward such contractual arrangements on the part of the judiciary.

96. Quoted in Plant, *Economic Theory,* 63. See also Breyer, "The Uneasy Case for Copyright: A Study of Copyright in Books, Photocopies, and Computer Programs," *Harvard Law Review* 84 (1970): 281, 299–302.
For a helpful explanation of such retaliatory behavior and its role in generating and sustaining cooperation, see Witt, "Evolution and Stability of Cooperation Without Enforceable Contracts," *Kyklos* 39 (1986): 245–66. Witt uses a game-theoretic approach, adding to the standard prisoner's dilemma game an additional move, "which allows agents to respond to the opponent's choice post testum. [This captures] an important feature of reality: that in most cases people have the option of making trouble for someone who has upset them. This option, the basis of threat, can be utilized to affect the opponent's decision strategically ex ante."

But see, McGee, "Predatory Price Cutting: The Standard Oil Case," *International Journal of Law and Economics* 1 (1958): 137 (the model of "predatory pricing" is incoherent). This issue deserves more careful historical and economic examination.

97. Plant, *Economic Theory*, 63.

98. "Patently Outdated," *The Economist*, 18 July 1987, "The rewards for drug firms will increasingly come from being first to market."

99. See Breyer, "Uneasy Case for Copyright," 299–302; Plant, *Economic Theory*, 62–63; "Separate Report by Sir Louis Mallet, C.B.," in *Report Of The Royal Commission On Copyright*, 1878.

100. Plant, *Economic Theory*, 81.

101. For an illuminating discussion of the evolution of the videocassette sales and rental markets, see J. Lardner, *Fast Forward: Hollywood, the Japanese and the VCR Wars* (New York: Norton, 1987).

102. Martin, "Boffo Box Office from Videocassettes," *Insight*, 23 November 1987.

103. See Breyer, "Uneasy Case for Copyright," 294–99. For criticism of this view, see Tyerman, "The Economic Rationale for Copyright Protection for Published Books: A Reply to Professor Breyer," *UCLA Law Review* 18 (1971): 1100, 1108–12. Breyer responds in "Copyright: A Rejoinder," *UCLA Law Review* 20 (1972): 75.

104. See S. C. Littlechild, *The Fallacy of the Mixed Economy*, 2d ed. (London: Institute of Economic Affairs, 1986), 36:

Some firms may be producing products or varieties thereof which other firms have not seen profitable, or whose potential profitability they have recognized only belatedly. Providing competitors can enter, the monopoly position is then only temporary, and 'monopoly profits' are more accurately described as 'entrepreneurial profits,' for they result from the successful exploitation of an opportunity which others have not yet seen.

Littlechild also suggests abolition of patents, arguing that research and innovation would continue in the absence of such protection, for "there is still a gain (a temporary monopoly profit) to be made from being first in the field. Moreover, abolishing patent protection would encourage the early exploitation and improvement by competitors of those innovations made by others" (Littlechild, 49).

105. Besen, "Private Copying, Reproduction Costs, and the Supply of Intellectual Property," The Rand Corporation, 18–19 (December 1984).

106. See the discussion of the relationship between the demand for originals and the demand for copies in Noves and Waldman, "The Emergence of Copying Technology: What Have We Learned?" *Contemporary Policy Issues* 5 (1987): 34.

107. See Hirschleifer, "The Private and Social Value of Information and the Reward to Inventive Activity," *American Economics Review* 61 (1971): 561, 573:

[The standard literature] overlooks the consideration that there will be, aside from the technological benefits, pecuniary effects (wealth redistributions due to price revaluation) from the release of the new information. The innovator, first in the field with information, is able through speculation or resale of the information to capture a portion of these pecuniary effects. This fact is socially useful in motivating release of the information. Even though practical considerations limit the effective sale and/or resale the gains thus achievable eliminate any a priori anticipation of underinvestment in the generation of new technological knowledge.

108. Brubaker, "Free Ride, Free Revelation, or Golden Rule?" *Journal of Law and Economics* 18 (1975): 147, reprinted in Cowen, *The Theory of Market Failure: A Critical Examination.*

109. See Breyer, "Uneasy Case for Copyright," 302–06.

110. For an extremely illuminating discussion of the dynamics of pre-contract excludability, see Schmidtz, "Contracts and Public Goods," *Harvard Journal of Law and Public Policy* 10 (1987): 475. Schmidtz uses a game-theoretic approach to show how conditionally binding assurance contracts reduce the payoffs of both cooperation and detection to zero in all cells of the payoff matrix save the lower right cell, in which both parties cooperate.

111. "Custom Audio Tape-Recording System to Be Introduced in Retail Record Stores," *Wall Street Journal,* 5 May 1987.

112. F. Machlup, "An Economic Review of the Patent System," *Patent Studies,* no. 115, Sub-Committee on Patents, Trademarks, and Copyrights of the Committee on the Judiciary, United States Senate, 85th Congress, Second Session.

113. Levin, "A New Look at the Patent System," *American Economic Review* 76 (1986): 199–202. In answer to the question "Why do firms use patents?" Levin suggests that "patents are useful for purposes other than establishing property rights. Patents may be useful to measure the performance of R&D employees, to gain strategic advantage in interfirm negotiations or litigation, or to obtain access to foreign markets where licensing to a host-country firm is a condition of entry." All of these functions could be performed by other, non-patent, mechanisms. See also "Will Software Patents Cramp Creativity? Growing Threat of Litigation Worries Firms," *Wall Street Journal,* 14 March 1989: " 'We use patents principally as trading material for our own freedom of action in the marketplace,' says Roger S. Smith, IBM's director of intellectual property law. He says IBM will license all its patents for up to 5% of the sales price of a patent."

114. Mansfield, "The R&D Tax Credit and Other Technology Policy Issues," *American Economic Review* 76 (1986): 190–94.

115. See Bittlingmayer, "Property Rights, Progress, and the Aircraft Patent Agreement," *Journal of Law and Economics* 30 (1988): 227. The solution to the conflict (engineered by the U.S. government in order to facilitate aircraft production for the war) was a patent pooling system, in which members of the pool licensed patents to other members in exchange for similar access to their patents. This system lasted from 1917 until it was challenged by the Justice Department on antitrust grounds in 1972 and dismantled in a consent decree in 1975. One wonders whether such a system would prove so stable unless the members reaped

greater benefits from access to the innovations of others than they lost from making their own patents freely available to their competitors thereby losing their exclusive rights. (As Bittlingmayer shows, the pool did not allow members to curb competition or reap monopoly rents by slowing down innovation.)

116. "Will Software Patents Cramp Creativity? Growing Threat of Litigation Worries Firms," *Wall Street Journal*, 14 March 1989.

117. See Bresnaham, "Post-entry Competition in the Plain Paper Copier Market," *American Economic Review* 75 (1985): 15: "When IBM and Litton entered the PPC market in 1972, Xerox sued to block entry under literally hundreds of patents. IBM had spent millions to 'invent around' Xerox's major patents—with 25 percent of the budget going for patent counsel, not R&D." Patents may also lead to distortion of research and development incentives. See Beck, "Patents, Property Rights, and Social Welfare: Search for a Restricted Optimum," *S. Economics Journal* 43 (1976): 1045.

118. See Barnett, "A Consent Theory of Contract"; see also Barnett, "Contract Remedies and Inalienable Rights," *Social Philosophy and Policy* 4 (1986): 179; Barnett, "Pursuing Justice in a Free Society: Power v. Liberty," *Criminal Justice Ethics* 4 (1985).

119. B. Leoni, *Freedom and the Law*, 22 (emphasis in original).

120. See the comparison between the law and economics of Leoni and that of Judge Posner in Peter Aranson, "Bruno Leoni in Retrospect," 692–701.

121. As Hayek points out:

> The preservation of a free system is so difficult precisely because it requires a constant rejection of measures which appear to be required to secure particular results, on no stronger grounds than that they conflict with a general rule, and frequently without knowing what will be the costs of not observing the rule in a particular instance. . . . [The judge] is not concerned with any ulterior purpose which somebody may have intended the rules to serve and of which he may be largely ignorant; and he will have to apply the rules even if in the particular instance the known consequences will appear to him wholly undesirable. . . . What must guide his decision is not any knowledge of what the whole of society requires at the particular moment, but solely what is demanded by general principles on which the going order of society is based. (*Law, Legislation, and Liberty* [1973], 57, 87).

8

Property, Monopoly, and Intellectual Rights[*]

Michael I. Krauss

Tom G. Palmer has, in "Intellectual Property: A Non-Posnerian Law and Economics Approach," advanced multifold arguments opposing two kinds of intellectual property rights, namely copyright and patent.[1] In this chapter I will review Palmer's principal contentions in the rough order of their presentation. I will then analyze them and demonstrate why I believe Palmer is wrong about intellectual property law. In doing this I hope also to parenthetically illustrate problems that "Austrian" approaches to (economic analysis of) law encounter if not informed by a sophisticated understanding of the legal process.[2]

A. Summary of Palmer's Arguments

1. Palmer perceives much contemporary justification of patent and copyright law as rooted in "Posnerian wealth-maximization," which, he feels, remains Benthamite in its consequentialism.[3] Palmer qualifies Posner's jurisprudence as "constructivist and interventionistic, an attempt to reorder economic institutions to attain a particular end."[4] He contrasts this with what he calls a "non-Posnerian law and economics approach" where the

*This essay was originally published as "Property, Monopoly, and Intellectual Rights," by Michael I. Krauss, in the *Hamline Law Review* 12 (1989): 305–20. Copyright © 1989 by Hamline University School of Law. Reprinted with permission of publisher.

role of the lawmaker is limited to initial definitions of rights and that of the judge to determining who holds the relevant right in uncertain situations, notwithstanding the consequences of each decision.[5] This tradition is, says Palmer, "influenced by the more mainstream [i.e., "Austrian"] law and economics of . . . Bruno Leoni."[6]

2. Palmer distinguishes (corrupt) patent and copyright law, on the one hand, from (proper) trade secret and trademark law on the other. He announces early on that the reason for this distinction "should become clearer as the chapter proceeds."[7] This reason seems to be that trade secrets are the result of contracts, that is, transfers of previously recognized rights, which are enforced by the judiciary.[8] These contracts are not the result of "constructivist" legislative acts, and are therefore worthy of judicial enforcement. Trademarks also appear to Palmer to be the result of contracts ("between buyer and seller") that "emerge from actions taken at the common law," not from statute. Copyright and patent, on the other hand, are rights defined by legislation.[9] They are thus suspect. In a surprisingly legalistic portion of his chapter, Palmer is at pains to demonstrate that copyright and patent have a legislative (and not a common law) origin, despite contrary U.S. practice and despite a key decision by England's Court of King's Bench in *Millar v. Taylor*.[10]

3. A distinct argument by Palmer is that copyright law is dysfunctional today. Technology has in one very particular sense taken us back to pretypesetting days; that is, a "text" is no longer reliably fixed in time by its original author, and can therefore be easily modified. In scribal days, enforcement of copyright law would have been prohibitively expensive. Enforcement of copyright was not attempted then, and should not be now.[11]

4. Palmer denies that "market failure" or "public goods" problems warrant state formulation of patent or copyright rules. He asserts that contractual means of protecting (fencing) ideas from non-owners exist, and that this availability of market alternatives unmasks the brazen rent-seeking function of patent and copyright. In a parable felt by him to be apposite to patent and copyright, Palmer points out that a person who shows movies can either bear the cost of building a walled theater (the technological means of fencing out those who have not paid the admission price), or can parasitically attempt to avoid these costs by lobbying the legislature for a bill preventing passersby from watching the open-air spectacle. This part of Palmer's argument reflects his ambitious anarcho-capitalistic claim that virtually no public goods (classical liberals' justification for state action) really exist.[12]

5. Palmer applauds protection of property rights. He contends, how-

ever, that patent and copyright are not *bona fide* property rights, since the latter *result from* scarcity while patent and copyright in fact *create* scarcity. This is essentially a restatement of Arnold Plant's opinion, according to which

> it is a peculiarity of property rights in patents (and copyrights) that they do not arise out of the scarcity of the objects which become appropriated. They are not a consequence of scarcity. They are the deliberate creation of statute law; and, whereas in general the institution of private property makes for the preservation of scarce goods, tending . . . to lead us 'to make the most of them,' property rights in patents and copyright make possible the creation of a scarcity of the products appropriated which could not otherwise be maintained.[13]

Related to this argument are Palmer's doubts about the wealth maximizing effects of patent/copyright law. Although he states that evidence of their efficiency is "ambiguous," Palmer details costs of patent and copyright protection and sees no countervailing benefits.[14] The implication is that patent and copyright law are wealth-*reducing*.

B. Analysis and Critique of Palmer's Arguments

1. There are, economically, two ways to envisage intellectual property rights. On the one hand, their "grant" by the government may be perceived in the light of a state's "grant" of land or other property rights. Better the state "grant" the land to an individual (preferably one who has some moral, Lockean title to it) than that it proclaim itself sole owner! One can of course object to state land grants as illegitimate, and assert that "natural" rights to land derive solely from "working it" in a Lockean fashion. Note, however, that many land grants were and are conditional on labor expenditures by the grantee. In any case, if the legitimacy of state land grants is denied, then the root of virtually all existing land titles is also.

Land grants do create problems of bilateral monopoly, of course, in that any non-owner who proposes a more valued use for a given plot of land must perforce negotiate a Pareto-superior contract of sale with the owner. Hold-out problems and strategic behavior may prevent, at the margin, some such deals from ever occurring, to the detriment of both parties and (barring negative, non-pecuniary, third-party externalities) of society. An omniscient utility-measurer could therefore constantly re-arrange "property" rights in order to reach new "potential" Pareto optima, also called Kaldor-Hicks optima.[15] But it is precisely the case that if one values the notion of individual rights, one is precluded from invoking bilateral monopoly as a justification for taking property from its existing owner. Indeed, non-consensual takings deny the fundamental characteristic of property.[16] Coercive transfers or deprivations of property should therefore be condemned by Lockeans like Palmer. Does it not follow that legislative protection of property rights would surely be good, and judicial dissipation of property bad, however odious (or benevolent, respectively) the institutions from which they emanate?[17]

On the other hand, and in contrast to the "grant" thesis, patent can be seen as a *monopoly*, i.e., a state-sponsored *deprivation* of property. If X has an antecedent right to grow strawberries on his land, and Y then obtains from an organ of the state the exclusive right to grow strawberries, then of course X's property has surely been "taken": it affords less freedom to X, and (another way of saying the same thing) its economic value is now less than it once was.[18] Again, whether the deprivation of this property is legislative in origin or whether a judge originally "declared" Y's exclusive privilege to grow strawberries is irrelevant to the moral (not to mention economic) wickedness of the thing.

Query then whether patent, monopoly, trade secrets, and trademarks more closely resemble land grants or exclusive strawberry charters. This is an interesting and important question, to which I will return below. It is useful to note immediately, however, how little of Palmer's chapter really deals with this crucial issue. Much of his chapter is devoted to extraneous and ideologically prompted questions that blur any focus on patent and copyright and greatly attenuate his thesis.

2. It is in this light, for example, that Palmer's harping on "Posnerian" law and economics must be interpreted. Posner's ambitious and prolifically described model of wealth maximization is both a positive (purporting to explain much of the present configuration of legal rules) and normative (outlining measures that lawmakers, legislative and judicial, should adhere to in deciding whether or not to modify existing legal rules) theory of law.[19] Applied to copyrights, this theory modestly outlines advantages and disadvantages of allowing property rights over ideas, and attempts to elucidate the current, limited property rights scheme as a reasonable effort to maximize benefits while minimizing costs.[20] Quite logically, Posner asserts that the normative companion to this positive overview is that judges should interpret copyright disputes (interstitially, when there is ambiguity) so as to maximize these same net gains.

To this effort Palmer has a curious, and I think confused reaction. He maligns Posnerian methodology with the now-common complaint that judges must determine rights, *not* maximize wealth (or utility).[21] This critique is indeed quite powerful in the abstract, but I think it ignores the juridical realities to which Posner implicitly alludes. As jurists know, litigation tends to arise precisely when rights are *unclear* and in those cases both parties typically offer powerful syllogisms based on current cases, which sustain their claims of right.[22] Surely it is not illegitimate, or even radical, for a lawyer to claim that in these cases the role of a judge is to choose the *best* answer, by ascertaining the dominant theme of current law and then determining which of the competing syllogisms best matches this theme (i.e., best realizes the value-maximizing result entailed by the policy choice of the legislator).[23] Some critiques of Posnerian jurisprudence seem to testify to a one-L-type perception of adjudication as necessarily involving clear cases opposing the (good) party with the Right and the (evil) party trying to convince the court to achieve some maximand by depriving the good guy of his right.

Palmer's reaction to Posner is more than just curious, though: it is incongruous. For Palmer himself seems to play Posner's game when he devotes the last part of his chapter to a discussion of the wealth-reducing effects of patent and copyright.[24] If the role of judges is not to interpret a law in accordance with its purpose, why then need Palmer devote space to *refuting* the theme Landes and Posner see in the law? Is Palmer an unknowing adherent to Posnerian methodology who simply disagrees about its correct application to issues of copyright? If so, he is out of order to indulge in the popular sport of Posner-bashing. That this is more than a rhetorical question is illustrated by the fact (discussed immediately below) that Palmer shares Posner's fetish with the common law (as opposed to statutory legislation). Indeed, Palmer's squabble with Posner about the wealth-maximizing effects of copyright legislation might not affect their shared vision of law generally.

The second superfluous question Palmer feels the need to address in his discussion of patent and copyright is the advantage of "spontaneous," that is, decentralized (judge-made) rule-making, as contrasted with its constructivist, that is, centralized (legislative) alternative. Palmer appears to be preoccupied by the claim that the historic 1769 judgment in *Millar v. Taylor* confirms the existence of a common law copyright.[25] What concerns me here is, emphatically, *not* whether Palmer is correct to state that this case was in every respect overruled by a subsequent Privy Council (a committee of a feudal, constructivist, legislative body, by the way) decision.[26] My query is why this arcane question should matter to Palmer, assuming that his real concern is to condemn patent and copyright law.[27] If the latter are examples of monopoly as opposed to property, it is of no concern that the judicial arm of a legislative body recognized or denied its common law existence! Why does it matter so much to Palmer that the historical debate come down one particular way, since the moral and economic natures of patent and copyright in no way depend on this? My suggestion is, of course, that it *does* matter to Palmer, and that the moral value of patent and copyright may, to him, be necessarily, or axiomatically, determined by their pedigree.

Palmer devotes considerable space to the claim that trade secret and trademark law are not evil monopolies, precisely because they were supposedly the product of contracts (enforced by common law) before being recognized by statute.[28] This is strange reasoning.

a) First, and as Palmer freely admits, trade secrets may be negotiated contractually precisely because they deal with ideas that can be hidden from public view.[29] To use economic jargon, the contract of trade secrecy is possible precisely because the secret is a "private good"; that is, exclusion is feasible under current technology. Many inventions are not protectable *via* the trade secret route, as they are ascertainable through commercial exploitation of their product. Such is the case for any simple gadget that can be readily "reverse engineered": because its "secret" is uncovered as soon as the invention is exploited, and because trade secrecy contracts cannot bind non-signatories, legal protection for it *as a trade secret* is lost upon sale. The tone of Palmer's reasoning seems to be that since some inventions may be adequately protected by trade secrets, *all* inventions deserve only that protection. Economically put, since private goods may be efficiently produced and allocated contractually, we may not allow non-private goods to be afforded non-contractual protection . . . Both these statements are, obviously, *non sequiturs*.

b) Second, Palmer's defense of trademarks as contractual in origin is intriguing.[30] Although the first owner of a trademark may indeed license it to a user, this contract does not bind a third party who sees the trademark, likes it, and decides to imitate it. Present federal trademark legislation has in fact resulted in a close patent-trademark interface, trademark law performing the same function for the product's "package" that patent law performs for the content of the package.[31] Indeed, dual protection from design patent and trademark often exists.[32] Again, why should it matter to Palmer that trademark was first recognized by a court (although much legislation exists today to implement it), while patent and copyright were (he claims) first enshrined by legislatures, although their common law origins are taken for granted by most attorneys in the United Kingdom and the United States?

Palmer's emphasis on essentially extraneous components of patent and copyright highlight what I feel to be a central position for him. I have, perhaps outlandishly, called it Palmer's fetish for the common law. Following some of the later Austrian writings, Palmer seems to see *judicial* lawmaking as intrinsic to freedom, while *legislative* lawmaking tends to be tyrannical.[33] Significantly, a prime non-Austrian defender of this position is none other than Judge Richard Posner. The most contested aspect of Posner's jurisprudence has surely been his claim that the common law courts, whose judges are not directly responsible to any electorate, will tend toward wealth maximization, while legislation has absolutely no tendency in this direction. The validity of Posner's claim that common law rules are efficient has been doubted by many scholars in and out of law and economics. Without entering this debate here, the least that can be said is that virtually all agree the Chicago school has not made its case conclusively.[34]

It is true, of course, that judges have immediate jurisdiction over small numbers of people, while a legislature may enforce its *fiat* over multitudes. A judge may deliberate alone, while councils debate publicly. To conclude from this that judicial rule-making is "spontaneous" and good, while legislatures are "constructivist" and bad, is to borrow from what must surely be the least persuasive part of the Austrian *corpus*. What of the fact that it costs less to "purchase" (by explicit or implied offers) a judgment from one judge than to buy a law from a collectivity of checked-and-balanced legislators?[35] What of the gross uncertainty rightsholders feel when confronted by retroactive, arbitrary, and conflicting judgments, which Max Weber has demonstrated to be epistemologically inferior to prospective, meditated, coherent, and rationally formal Civil Codes?[36] The classically liberal Codes of the 19th century are eloquent demonstrations that wise codifiers, convinced both of their lack of omniscience and of the need to provide a rational backdrop for individually ordered society, can do much better than common law. This "legislation" is not rights-denying. On the other hand, Comparative law scholars are aware of many common law ("spontaneous") rules that limit or even deny property rights.[37]

Rather than invoke as "mainstream law and economics" the works of an Italian who remains virtually unknown in North American legal circles, "Austrians" would do well to acquire a sophisticated understanding of Anglo-Saxon legal process. They would then be able to improve Chicagoan jurisprudence, instead of paradoxically sharing its most prominent vice.[38]

3. Radically abandoning his anti-Posnerian standpoint, Palmer claims that copyright (and patent?) are dysfunctional in an electronic universe.[39]

He implicitly concludes that copyright enforcement has become too expensive to be worth the candle.

This part of Palmer's thesis seems clearly inadmissible. To illustrate this, consider how Palmer can even consider the cost-of-enforcement argument, which is explicitly consequentialist and therefore rights-denying, open to him. If murderers suddenly found new methods of homicide that rendered detection and capture quite costly, would Palmer then argue for the legalization of murder? Presumably not: Palmer above others would insist that murder violates rights, and that these violations must be prohibited regardless of consequences.[40]

Of course, the point is that Palmer feels differently about patents and copyrights, which (to him) do not represent legitimate rights. Thus, discussion of enforcement costs by Palmer is question-begging and methodologically incoherent. Again, the real problem consists of determining whether patent and copyright confer legitimate rights or illegitimate monopolies. If the former, Palmer may not invoke costs; if the latter, costs are equally irrelevant, as the institution should be abolished even if its operation is inexpensive.

4. Palmer argues that alternate contractual "fencing" arrangements exist to allow authors and inventors to protect their rights without invoking patent or copyright monopolies. I have alluded to weaknesses in this argument above; a more general comment is appropriate here.[41]

My point can be introduced rhetorically, by wondering if Palmer would advocate the abolition of, for example, tort law and its replacement by contract law. If private property rights were totally specified (to make the same point another way, if "transaction costs" were minimal), people would allocate all goods and bads contractually.[42] What passes now as tort law would become suits for violations of contract. Unfortunately, and totally aside from the common law's present aversion to contract, contract law is not all-encompassing.[43] Contract implies property, and in the absence of legislative intervention to define property rights, it is simply the case that not all goods (e.g., some air, water, ideas) can be economically fenced. Palmer is correct to see that where fencing is feasible (walls around a theater, or tie-in arrangements for help dealing with software), it does indeed tend to be used as a substitute for state enforcement.[44] This does not dispose of those cases where fencing is not feasible.

Remember that Palmer goes so far as to assert that individual fencing has become *more* difficult with respect to some ideas in the computer age, but he appears blind as to the implications of this claim for *state* action.[45] Thus, to assert (as Coase correctly does) that a private market will provide *some* lighthouses (with fencing accomplished by the lighthouse builder's vertical integration as a harbor master who charges entry tolls sufficient to pay for the light) does not imply that no state-operated lighthouses should be built.[46] Passing ships could benefit from the private light without being made to pay (and therefore, there would be an undersupply of lights) if they were not docking nearby: unless, that is, vertical integration extended to ownership of *all relevant harbors and all relevant lights*. But then, of course, this owner would begin to resemble the (minimal) state, which has persuasively been defined as the naturally dominant provider of collective goods.[47] And if new technology (increasing the sailing range of ships, for example) made individual supply of lighthouses more problematic (because "fencing" was more costly), would not the concomitant state duty increase?

Palmer's unwillingness to see the need for state action (even state action to define property rights) leads him to make three awkward mistakes.

a) At one point he asserts that even grossly inadequate private measures of fencing are enough, as a matter of policy, if they enable a producer "to sell the good *profitably* on the market."[48] How does this address the underproduction problem alluded to immediately above? The implicit notion of "adequate profit" or "just price" in that claim smacks of a medieval objectivism to which "Austrians" cannot subscribe.

b) At another point Palmer claims that the demand for noted authors (like Milton Friedman) on the lecture circuit is "natural fencing," that is, proof that copyright is not necessary, in that audiences demand "the real thing" as opposed to some pirate copy.[49] But people do not pay hundreds of dollars to hear Friedman *read from* his works: some people simply want to hear Friedman amplify on them, apply them, and defend them against critics.[50] This is no substitute for insufficient "fencing" for his book.

c) Lastly, Palmer argues that without any copyright law an effective competitive technique by the "legitimate" book publisher (who has paid the author for his work), against "pirate" publishers (who have not, and who therefore can make a profit by selling at a lower price, *ceteris paribus*) is predatory pricing. Not only is it not clear why the owner (as opposed to the pirate) is the superior predator, it is also economically unambiguous that predatory pricing cannot succeed as a competitive strategy. Palmer is informed of this; he lamely admits that the predatory pricing option is "incoherent," and concludes that the question "deserves more careful historical and economic examination."[51]

Again, Palmer's diversion (this time into the contractual means to fence off property) appears to be mildly question-begging. Are patent and copyright the legal backdrops required to *allow for* subsequent fencing (in which case they are like the land grants, and alternate fencing arrangements in other fields are irrelevant), or are they analogous to the *destruction of competitor's fences* (in which case, they are classic monopolies, and subsequent fencing by the monopolist is irrelevant)? No amount of sidestepping can avoid this one crucial issue.

5. The only aspect of Palmer's chapter that addresses this question is his adoption of Arnold Plant's monopoly thesis of patent law.[52] To Plant, even without intellectual property rights there would be no market failure for inventions or publications (i.e., there is no scarcity of them, or [implicitly] of the intellectual resources needed to produce them).[53] On the contrary, the existence of patent diverts resources into ideas deemed patentable: the ensuing "rush to invent," or to be the first at the Patent Office, leads to a waste of resources analogous to that provoked by common pool problems.[54]

Plant's contentions are possibly true. They are also possibly false. They are true if and only if inventions (or publications) would generally be produced in the absence of the property rights protection afforded by patent or copyright. They are not true if the ideas, or the resources required to produce the ideas, are sufficiently scarce so as to preclude production without this protection.

Nor are they true if patent rents are too small to justify the expensive investments needed to be registered as the first inventor. So, for example, Professor Edmund Kitch has compiled evidence that a broad range of substitutes exists for most every product that might be patentable (and, of course, as for the copyright the choice of books or software programs is endless): building a better mousetrap will not generate much deadweight monopoly loss so long as the mousetrap is only marginally superior to its competitors.[55] Scant monopoly rent means minimal common pool problems: this would contradict Plant's hypothesis. But Kitch's empirical data is scant, and begs for confirmation or refutation.

Concluding that this empirical route must be traveled would lead Palmer down a slippery Posnerian slope, I think. It means that one cannot decide whether and to what extent patent (and copyright) law is good or bad without delving into legal details, just as Landes and Posner have done.[56] When exactly is an idea eligible for patent/copyright protection? Are common (easy to invent, effortless) ideas patentable? (If so, then patent is clearly like a "strawberry charter.")[57] Can Las Vegas sue Atlantic City for patent infringement? How long do patent and copyright protections last? Long enough to encourage invention, but not so long as to unduly discourage third-party improvements?[58] To none of these questions does Palmer attempt an answer; his "clean" ideological opposition to copyright and patent seems to preclude "messy" discussion of legal complexities.

C. Conclusion

When the brush is cleared away, it appears trivially true that to the degree patent and copyright laws are effective, they will limit free use of the protected idea or form.[59] Inevitably, the positive transaction costs of licensing will preclude, at the margin, some *potentially* wealth-enhancing improvements.[60] It has been a major argument of this chapter that the valid Austrian contribution to economic thought leads one to reject this rights-denying and objectivist argument against patent and copyright.

The moral, Lockean concept of property as the product of honest labor is missing from Kaldor-Hicks wealth maximization. Is it possible that, unbeknownst to Tom Palmer, copyright and patent discern this moral quality? Empirical data may not be available, but it is surely true that framers of the document recognized to be one of the most eloquent declarations of the natural rights of man saw fit to proclaim the "right" of authors and inventors to the product of their writings and discoveries (the only mention in the Constitution proper of the word "right").[61]

As has been recently noted, this vision of natural right confirms the uniqueness of the human capacity for invention and discovery.[62] This capacity is non-corporeal, and for that reason may have to be subject to special property rules that cannot be identical to those covering corporeal things.[63] It is arguable that a considerable part of the moral attraction of capitalism derives from its being organized around products of the mind.[64] Patent and copyright, incorporation and corporate finance statutes can be seen in this light as legal tributes to the human capacity to invent and create.

It is also, trivially, true that if effort is expended on a "non-fencible" idea, lack of an enforceable property right in that idea is conducive to competitive production of artifacts at a price equal to marginal production costs, which exclude the inventive effort. Could this not stifle effort, all the while leaving the inventor feeling cheated? Is it possible that copyright and patent law are not only rights protecting (thus good), but wealth enhancing (thus good) as well?

Notes

1. T. Palmer, "Intellectual Property: A Non-Posnerian Law and Economics Approach," reprinted in this volume as chapter 7 (hereinafter "Intellectual Property"). Previously published in the *Hamline Law Review* 12 (1989): 261–304.

2. "Austrian," or (more accurately) subjectivist, economic theory constitutes the most original and powerful challenge to mainstream neo-classical economics. In particular, theorists of the stature of F. A. Hayek (see "Competition as a Discovery Procedure," in *New Studies In Philosophy, Politics, Economics and the History of Ideas* [Chicago: University of Chicago Press, 1978]); Ludwig Von Mises (see, e.g., *Human Action: A Treatise on Economics,* 3d. ed. [New Haven: Yale University Press, 1966]); and I. Kirzner (see, e.g., *Competition and Entrepreneurship* [Chicago: University of Chicago Press, 1973]), have correctly criticized the determinism of the neo-classical "clockwork" models, and questioned the pretense of knowledge in economic methodology. For an excellent primer on Austrian economic thought written for non-cognoscenti, see G. O'Driscoll and M. Rizzo, *The Economics of Time and Ignorance* (Oxford: B. Blackwell, 1985).

3. Posner has repeatedly denied this. See Posner, "Utilitarianism, Economics, and Social Theory," and "The Ethical and Political Basis of Wealth Maximization," *The Economics of Justice* (Cambridge, Mass.: Harvard University Press, 1981), 48, 88; see also Palmer, "Intellectual Property."

4. Palmer says "constructivists" feel they can identify problems, imagine solutions to them, and apply these solutions with a good chance of solving the problem. Anarcho-capitalistic strains of "Austrian" thought assert that inevitable human ignorance is so likely to misidentify the problem and/or the solution, or to misapply the solution even where it is correctly identified, that virtually all legal "planning" will likely fail. Only spontaneously and individually derived solutions have a good chance to succeed.

5. As I shall illustrate, Palmer really sees no role for the legislator. This is seemingly paradoxical, as Palmer insists on the declaratory function of the judiciary: it must find pre-existing rights as opposed to transforming these rights to attain some maximand. This declaratory function is of course impossible if these rights have not been antecedently created by a [constructivist?] legislature, unless, of course, the court's role consists of declaring rights that exist "in nature."

6. Palmer, "Intellectual Property," 181.

7. Palmer, "Intellectual Property," 181.

8. See, for example, Palmer, "Intellectual Property," 211.

9. Palmer, "Intellectual Property," 182.

10. Palmer, "Intellectual Property," 186; see also 4 Burr. 2303 (1769).

11. Palmer, "Intellectual Property," 188. See also, the Federal Copyright Law of 1976 (17 U.S.C. sec. 101, *et seq.*) governs from the date a work is "fixed" in a "tangible medium of expression."

12. Palmer, "Intellectual Property," 197. For good overviews of anarcho-capitalist theory, see P. Lemieux, *L'Anarcho-Capitalisme* (1988); and N. Barry, *On Classical Liberalism and Libertarianism* (Basingstoke: Macmillan, 1987), chap. 9.

13. See Demsetz, "Toward a Theory of Property Rights," *American Economic Review: Papers and Proceedings* 57 (1967): 347 (the evolution of property rights); see also, Palmer, "Intellectual Property," 192–93; Plant, "The Economic Aspects of Copyright in Books," in *Selected Economic Essays and Addresses* (1934). See

also Plant, "The Economic Theory Concerning Patents for Invention," *Economica* 1 (1934), 40 n.s; and Plant, "Economic Theory," 31.

14. Palmer, "Intellectual Property," 209.

15. One point is Pareto-superior to another if no one is (by her own subjective standards) worse off in the ex post position, while at least one person is better off. One point is "Kaldor-Hicks-superior" to another if those made better off in the ex post position could compensate those made worse off, while still leaving some surplus. See Kaldor, "Welfare Propositions and Interpersonal Comparisons of Utility," *Econ. Journal* 49 (1939): 549; Hicks, "The Foundations of Welfare Economics," *Econ. Journal* 49 (1939): 696. Note that only Kaldor-Hicks-superiority is rights-denying (losers, i.e., coercive takings, are tolerated), and that only Kaldor-Hicks-superiority requires an ordinal measurement of a maximand. The dollar, of course, is one such measuring stick. Thus, wealth maximization is a natural variant of Kaldor-Hicks consequentialism. See, on this question, M. Krauss, "Good as Gold? The Foundations of Posnerian Jurisprudence" (unpublished ms. obtainable from the author).

16. See Calabresi and Melamed, "Property Rules, Liability Rules, and Inalienability: One View of the Cathedral," *Harvard Law Review* 85 (1972): 1089. This is the whole difference between a "property rule" and a "liability rule."

17. For example, U.S. Constitution Amendment V ("takings" clause). Civil law jurisdictions typically enshrine a similar limitation on state power in the Property book of their Civil Codes. See, for example, art. 407 of Quebec's *Code Civil.* See also, *Ploof v. Putnam*, 81 Vt. 471, 71 A. 188 (1908)(held that in common law a dock owner could not prevent his dock's use by unauthorized persons during an emergency).

18. Note that the land presumably belongs to X by virtue of some title ultimately derived from a state land grant. This assumes, of course, that strawberry-growing is a valuable thing for X. This is not an unreasonable assumption to make, for if Y has invested in the lobbying necessary to obtain her monopoly, it is likely that Y considers the activity valuable to potential competitors like X. If not, of course, Y could simply grow strawberries (without incurring the lobbying investment) in the assurance that no one would imitate her.

19. See R. Posner, *Economic Analysis of Law*, 3d ed. (Boston: Little, Brown, 1986); see also R. Posner, *The Economics of Justice* (Cambridge, Mass.: Harvard University Press, 1981).

20. Landes and Posner, "An Economic Analysis of Copyright Law," *Journal of Legal Studies* 18 (1989). Of course, copyright covers the form, as opposed to the content, of ideas; the latter are the domain of patent and trade secret law.

21. Palmer, "Intellectual Property," 181.

22. See, for example, W. Twinning and R. Myers, *How to Do Things with Rules*, 2d ed. (London: Weidenfeld and Nicolson, 1977); Krauss, "Nihilisme et Interprétation des lois," *Revue Juridique Themis* 20 (1986): 527.

23. This "best-fit," or aesthetic, method of juridical interpretation is defended as a bulwark against the nihilism of Critical Legal Studies by decidedly non-Pos-

nerians. See, for example, Dworkin, "Law as Interpretation," *Texas Law Review* 60 (1982): 527.

24. Cf. Palmer, "Intellectual Property," 209.

25. 4 Burr. 2303, 98 Eng. Rep. 201 (1769). For the record, it is surely the case that in *Donaldson v. Beckett*, I Eng. Rep. 837 (1774), eight of eleven judges polled by the House of Lords, including Blackstone, felt that author's copyright existed as a matter of common law. Seven (again, including Blackstone) of eleven felt that initial publication did not exhaust an author's common law copyright.

26. *Donaldson v. Beckett*, I Eng. Rep. 837 (1774).

27. Palmer is driven to insist that although full-time judges opined that copyright existed as a matter of common law, members of a committee of the House of Lords disagreed, and that therefore copyright cannot acquire the (to Palmer) morally positive imprimatur of the common law. See Palmer, "Intellectual Property," 186.

28. Palmer, "Intellectual Property," 211.

29. Palmer, "Intellectual Property," 203–4.

30. According to 15 U.S.C. sec. 1127, the term "trademark" "includes any word, name, symbol, or device or any combination thereof adopted and used by a manufacturer or merchant to identify his goods and distinguish them from those manufactured or sold by others." This is also a good shorthand summary of what state common law recognized as constituting a trademark.

31. With the interesting difference that common law [i.e., state] trademark rights are potentially infinite in duration. Some well-known European trademarks are centuries old. Federal registrations of trademarks, on the contrary, are initially good only for twenty years. Thus, legislation has granted *less* extensive rights than has the common law.

32. See, for example, I. Kayton, *Patent Practice* (Washington, D.C.: Patent Resources Institute, 1985), 1–43.

33. The early Hayek was an admirer of European codifications, but the later Hayek, a war refugee from the Continent to two Anglo-Saxon countries, became enamored of English Common law.

34. *Inter alia*, Posner's analysis is virtually never informed by Comparative law insights that would have offered clues as to the existence of more efficient rules existing in non-Common law jurisdictions.

35. This explains why people like James Buchanan are avowedly constructivist, and see no advantage in judge-made rules. See J. Buchanan, "The Economy as a Constitutional Order," (15 February 1989)(unpublished ms. on file with the author).

36. See, for example, M. Weber, *Max Weber on Law and Society*, edited and intro. by M. Rheinstein, (New York: Simon and Schuster, 1954); Krauss, "Max Weber," *Canadian B. Rev.* 62 (1984): 451.

37. For example, *Ploof v. Putnam*, 81 Vt. 471, 71 A. 188 (1908)(imposition of duty to rescue). Other examples include the common law denial of contracted-for specific performance and freely negotiated penalty clauses.

38. There have been recent attempts to publicize him. See Aranson, "Bruno Leoni in Retrospect," *Harvard Journal of Law and Public Policy* 11 (1988): 661 (stating that Leoni's work "lay dormant"); Liggo and Palmer, "Freedom and the Law: A Comment on Professor Aranson's Article," *Harvard Journal of Law and Public Policy* 11 (1988): 713.

Improvements would occur by placing emphasis on subjective value (and implications for many Kaldor-Hicks-oriented aspects of the common law), on the mythical nature of equilibrium, on dynamics versus statics, etc.

39. Palmer, "Intellectual Property," 186–89.

40. I am defining "rights" here, of course, in an individualist sense that denies the effect that pernicious consequences of enforcement may have on the existence of the right itself. To borrow Dworkin's bridge metaphor, rights trump utility and other consequences.

Note that conventional economic analysis might argue for a different mix of enforcement and penalties as the crime became more difficult to detect. Thus, one could investigate murders less intensively, but guarantee a death penalty for all convicted murderers, such that the ex ante expected punishment remains the same. Arguably, this does not have the rights-denying effect that legalizing murder would have.

41. See Federal Copyright Law, 17 U.S.C. sec. 101, *et seq.* (1976). See also, Palmer, "Intellectual Property," 203.

42. The two conditions are really synonyms. As Demsetz has pointed out, private property rights will become specified precisely when the ambient technology makes "fencing," and transactions, economically feasible (see Demsetz, "Toward a Theory of Property Rights").

43. See for example, G. Gilmore, *The Death Of Contract* (Columbus: Ohio State University Press, 1974); P. Huber, *Liability*, chap. 2 (New York: Basic Books, 1988).

44. It is, however, the case that aberrant strains of antitrust law tend to discourage tie-ins and integration, and thus increase reliance on copyright and patent enforcement.

Ronald Coase made precisely this point in his famous article, "The Problem of Social Cost," *Journal of Law and Economics* 3 (1960): 1.

45. Palmer, "Intellectual Property," 186–89.

46. See Coase, "The Lighthouse in Economics," *Journal of Law and Economics* 17 (1974): 101.

47. This is of course a paraphrasing of the thesis of R. Nozick, *Anarchy, State, and Utopia* (New York: Basic Books, 1975).

48. Palmer, "Intellectual Property," 200 (emphasis added).

49. Palmer, "Intellectual Property," 206.

50. Unless, of course. the work is deemed to be poetry or literature, in which case the reading is in and of itself a different good than the printed work.

51. Palmer, "Intellectual Property," 204. Predatory pricing is selling of a good at a low price (below cost) until competitors drop out of the market, after which

the predator may raise the price to a supra-competitive level, which here would include a provision for author's royalties.

Note that since Palmer must (despite his *caveat* in note 96) believe that predatory pricing can succeed, he would be forced to establish a very constructivist antitrust police to prevent "bad" predatory pricing by the pirate, just as it permits "good" predatory pricing by the original publisher. What is this, if not the indirect enforcement of a form of copyright?

See also McGee, "Predatory Price Cutting: The Standard Oil (NJ) Case," *International Journal of Law and Economics* 1 (1958): 137; R. Bork, *The Antitrust Paradox* (New York: Basic Books, 1977), 148; and Palmer, "Intellectual Property," 204, note 96.

52. See Palmer, "Intellectual Property," 192—93.

53. Plant did see patents as being valuable in one case: where costly and prolonged research was necessary to produce a useful good that, for some reason, the market would not reward in the short run (i.e., while the discoverer had the benefit of being the first to produce the good or book). Of course, if the marketplace knew that low-cost copies would soon hit the market, it is not obvious that it would heap rents on the inventor in the short run. In any case, Plant saw this scenario as being exceptional, and therefore incapable of justifying a patent or copyright system applicable to inventions or publications in general. See, for example, Plant, "The Economic Theory Concerning Patents for Invention," *Economica* 1 (1934): 40, 43.

54. See Gordon, "The Economic Theory of a Common-Property Resource: the Fishery," *Journal of Political Economy* 62 (1954): 124.

55. Kitch, "The Nature and Function of the Patent System," *Journal of Law and Economics* 20 (1977): 265.

56. See Landes and Posner, "Economic Analysis of Copyright," note 20 and accompanying text.

57. See note 18 above.

58. Note that third parties can obtain a license from the patent holder, at Pareto-superior terms, if they believe that they will be able to add value. Of course, bilateral monopoly problems exist, and the patent holder may hold out and prevent this wealth-enhancing deal from occurring. But, as I have indicated above (note 15 and corresponding text), Palmer may not invoke bilateral monopoly problems, because they are a necessary result of property rights. The "cure" to them is to outlaw property rules and replace them with utility (or wealth)-maximizing liability rules.

59. See Palmer, "Intellectual Property," 180–81.

60. See note 58 above.

61. Note that the first federal trademark legislation was passed under the same constitutional authority as that allowing patents, eloquent proof that framers of the legislation recognized the analytical identity involved. Only when the judiciary invalidated the legislation (*The Trademark Cases*, 100 U.S. 81 [1879]) was a second effort made, this time under the rubric of interstate commerce. See also note 25.

62. Novak, "The Mind-Centered System," *Forbes*, 6 February 1989, 44.

63. Absent from Palmer's chapter is a sensitivity to the difference between corporeal and noncorporeal things in Law. Is it to misread his chapter to wonder whether he thinks that property may only lay over corporeal things? Does Palmer know that, in both Common and Civil law systems, the object of the property right is not the thing itself, but the (incorporeal) set of man-made legal relations and rules defining the rights and courses of permissible conduct? A simple test for determining whether a property right is present asks the reader to consider the following label attached to a tangible or intangible *res* "X":

To the world:
Keep off X unless you have my permission, which I may grant or withhold
Signed: Private Citizen
Endorsed: The State

See Cohen, "Dialogue on Private Property," *Rutgers Law Review* 9 (1954): 357.

64. *Caput* = head (possible etymological origin of "capitalism").

9

The TRIPS Agreement: Imperialistic, Outdated, and Overprotective[*]

Marci A. Hamilton

I. Introduction

The WTO/GATT Agreement involving Trade-Related Aspects of Intellectual Property Rights (Agreement or TRIPS) is a lot more than its moniker reveals.[1] Far from being limited to trade relations, correcting the international balance of trade, or lowering customs trade barriers, TRIPS attempts to remake international copyright law in the image of Western copyright law. If TRIPS is successful across the breathtaking sweep of signatory countries, it will be one of the most effective vehicles of Western imperialism in history. Moreover, the Agreement will have achieved this goal under the heading "trade-related," which makes it appear as though it is simply business. To understand TRIPS, it is important to embrace an interdisciplinary approach, to widen the copyright lens to include culture, politics, and human rights.

Despite its broad sweep and its unstated aspirations, TRIPS arrives on the scene already outdated. TRIPS reached fruition at the same time that the on-line era became irrevocable. Yet it makes no concession, not even a nod, to the fact that a significant portion of the international intellectual property market will soon be conducted on-line. This silence could trans-

*This essay was originally published as "The TRIPS Agreement: Imperialistic, Outdated, and Overprotective, by Marci A. Hamilton, in the *Vanderbilt Journal of Transnational Law* 29 (1996): 613–34. Copyright © 1996 by Vanderbilt University. Reprinted with permission of publisher.

form a troubling treaty into a weapon of extortion by the publishing industry, which has already succeeded in crafting TRIPS as a blunt instrument for copyright protection. While the corporeal universe has permitted Western societies to receive and copy large numbers of copyrighted works for free—through libraries, commercial browsing, personal lending, and copyright doctrines such as the first sale doctrine, fair use, and the idea/expression dichotomy—the on-line era raises the possibility that the publishing industry can track every minuscule use of a work and thereby turn the free use zone into a new opportunity for profit. TRIPS' silence threatens to make it both outdated and overprotective.

II. Copyright Norms and Freedom Imperialism

The cultural underpinnings of existing copyright law require a reevaluation to assess their appropriateness and usefulness in building a universal copyright scheme. The subject of the AALS Symposium—the TRIPS Agreement—is the first giant step toward globalization of intellectual property rights.[2] Globalization introduces a new level of complexity into copyright law and creates a need for more creative ways of understanding and justifying rights protected by copyright. The United States is no longer negotiating primarily with European countries which share a similar moral and religious heritage and economic understandings. Now, the United States is also dealing with the Eastern countries as well as with the world's developing countries. Therefore, focus on copyright must extend beyond markets and trade issues to interdisciplinary understandings. Cultural views on human effort and reward are particularly important.

With 117 signatory countries from around the world, TRIPS is ambitious, to say the least.[3] It is also old-fashioned, Western-style imperialism. One commentator describes the TRIPS Agreement as "impolite."[4] This description is too polite. Despite its innocuous name, TRIPS does not merely further trade relations between these many countries. Rather, TRIPS imposes a Western intellectual property system across the board[5]—which is to say that it imposes presuppositions about human value, effort, and reward. And it has appeared without serious public debate over its latent political mission.

It is not surprising that there might be uneven compliance across the world even after so many countries signed the TRIPS Agreement.[6] Intellectual property is nothing more than a socially recognized, but imaginary, set of fences and gates. People must believe in it for it to be effective.

To believe in the Western version of copyright rights, one must first accept some version of the following canon:

1. *Individualism:* Individual human creative effort is valuable.[7]
2. *Reward:* Society should single out original products of expression by granting their owners proprietary rights over them. Reward is determined according to the qualities of the product; mere effort is not sufficient to deserve such reward.
3. *Commodification:* Products should be capable of being disassociated from their producers and sent through the stream of commerce. In other words, product creators need not be the product's owners or distributors. Indeed, in the interest of achieving the greatest distribution of copyrighted goods worldwide, creators probably should not be the primary distributors.[8]

By strongly supporting the TRIPS Agreement, the United States—which is to say U.S. publishers—is exporting and imposing Protestant-based capitalism.[9] The United States is also endorsing the imposition of a revolution-tending construct of the person. Individualism, as captured in the Western intellectual property system, is the sine qua non for a society to recognize and honor personal liberty. TRIPS is nothing less than freedom imperialism.

Whether such imperialism is a good idea involves difficult questions of political, sociological, and legal import that are better served by later contemplation. This chapter is limited to describing the presumptuous sweep of the TRIPS Agreement and to suggesting that this is an important aspect of TRIPS that deserves open discussion and debate.

It is no accident that intellectual property norms are spreading worldwide at the same time that totalitarian regimes are falling. A people must value individual achievement and believe in the appropriateness of change and originality if it is going to concede to and adopt a Western-style intellectual property regime. Indeed, there is an intimate link between respect for individual human rights and respect for a copyright system that values and promotes individual human creative achievement.[10]

China—tellingly outside the TRIPS negotiations—is a vivid example of the hand-in-glove relationship between the suppression of individual rights and the complete disregard for copyright norms.[11] The institution of meaningful copyright reform in China is not likely to happen solely at the level of trade relations. Rather, it can be augmented and expedited by simultaneously penalizing violations of Western conceptions of human liberty. China has undergone one era after another in which new forms of liberty suppression have been practiced. The concepts that unite these political epochs and explain China's disregard for copyright norms are a vision of the family as the lowest social denominator, not the individual, and a marked disdain for change and originality.[12]

The Chinese culture does not elevate "the new" in the same way that the West does. Tradition is not a past to overcome but rather reversed. Indeed, copying is looked upon as a noble art. Copyright law appears impenetrable, artificial, and crass from such a perspective.

Given the link between intellectual property rights and human rights, TRIPS could spur further developments in human rights. TRIPS does not merely transplant Western-style industries to the rest of the world, it also foments anti-authoritarian revolution.[13] After the Berlin Wall fell, some said that East Germany fell because the East Germans were enthralled with the ethos and consumer goods viewed every Friday night on the U.S. television show *Dallas*. Apparently, like so many U.S. viewers, they imbibed the "good life" ethos of the show. The theory goes that *Dallas* led them to be unsatisfied, and to ask why they were not driving expensive cars or wearing finely tailored couture clothing. By foregrounding the ethos of individual freedom and power, albeit in a vulgar form, *Dallas* questioned the East German authoritarian structure of power.[14] It is doubtful that the United States fully understood that the signing of TRIPS would lead significant segments of the world to question political and social organizations of power. Yet, this is TRIPS' potential.

The TRIPS Agreement, in addition to transplanting an anti-authoritarian intellectual property ethos, has sought to establish a worldwide and lively free market in intellectual property goods. Publishers and the entertainment industry worked hard to protect global intellectual property rights in order to take advantage of this market. If and when a country adopts and enforces the Western-built fences and gates of capitalist intellectual property values, those international mega-oligopolies stand poised with ships full of products. Where the acceptance of Western-style intellectual property rules is only halfhearted, the deluge of artistic and entertainment products will hasten the saturation of Western perspectives and their concomitant inclination to challenge authoritarian institutions and their minions.[15]

The U.S. Constitution recognizes correctly that the substance of copyright is somehow different and more momentous than ordinary trade or commerce. Copyright protection is a strong indication of foundational political values. To date, TRIPS discussions have been overly focused on trade.[16] TRIPS is neither innocuous nor simple. It is a striking move to standardize the world's politics.

III. TRIPS in the On-line Era: Outdated and Overprotective

The TRIPS Agreement appears in the midst of the on-line era, but it is oblivious of this era's fundamental change in intellectual product transmission and generation. The on-line era, with its worldwide communication bridge, massive access capacity, and private home receipt of mountains of information, questions the existing fences and gates of intellectual property ownership and invites a reassessment of their proper placement in virtual space. Determining the optimal balance between ensuring a steady and ample supply of information to recipients and remunerating the authors of original contributions to the cultural store is a vexing problem. Drawing lines is particularly daunting in the emerging global information infrastructure (GII). There is no easy, automatic answer. TRIPS' treatment of copyright law does not introduce new law per se but rather refers to a limited number of issues, such as the copyrightability of computer programs, and incorporates by reference the outdated Berne Convention. By failing to adjust the Berne Convention to the GII, the TRIPS Agreement unwittingly bestows a windfall on copyright holders.[17]

A. Universal Access Norms vs. Copyright Norms on the GII

The emerging ethos of the GII revolves around two issues: information and access. Compelling policy concerns line up on both sides of the debate over copyright protection on the GII. On the one side, there is the value of universal access to information. Information and access are important to free speech values recognized by the U.S. Constitution's First Amendment and the International Bill of Human Rights.[18] In both spheres, more information is better than less information and access is better than exclusion. Indeed, a failure of information access, on both accounts, leads to ignorance and the consequent decay of the democratic propensities of the state.

In the evolving GII universe, universal access is a goal. For example, the G-7 countries, in consultation with various interested industries, have sketched an ambitious plan to include the developing and Third World countries, as well as the developed countries, within the reach of the GII.[19] A frequent analogy is drawn to the distribution of telephone service. The hope is to permit all sectors of the planet to provide, receive, and exchange information. Not coincidentally, as publishers have been lobbying for TRIPS' global protection of intellectual property, the G-7 has been working to expand the means of providing intellectual property to a worldwide market of potential consumers.

On the other side of the debate stands copyright law. In the U.S. system, copyright law protects original works of authorship while providing incentives to disseminate those works to the general public. Economic copyright permits authors to obtain monetary remedies or injunctive relief from those who substantially copy their works (in whole or in part). Under the European model of intellectual property, copyright is a moral right protecting personality, which justifies remuneration to authors and some control over the work even after it has been sold to the public.

The goal of information access challenges copyright norms. First, "information" is a vague and therefore potentially misleading term. Copyright does not protect the information content of expression. Rather, it only protects the particular "expression." If the works on the GII are characterized only as "information," it is deceptively easy to come to the erroneous conclusion that copyright is irrelevant in the "information era."

Copyright law also conflicts with the access norm in another way. Copyright law permits individuals through private rights of action to block access to works unless permission has been obtained and remuneration paid for access. At best, copyright seems ungenerous in the heady drive toward worldwide networking and information provision; at worst, it falsely appears downright antidemocratic. The GII surfaces a conflict between universal access norms and copyright values that has always been latent. This new era demands either a reconciliation of the two sides or the sacrifice of copyright to universal, free information access. Democracy suffers if either side is sacrificed.

Copyright should not be abandoned in the drive to realize a worldwide system of communication and cultural exchange. While often thought to be at odds, freedom of expression, provision of information, and copyright law serve similar goals. They operate together to increase the individual's capacity to challenge government's temptation to tyranny. They also maximize the capacity of the people to maintain their independence by constructing certain private power structures though religion, art, philosophy, politics, and family.[20] Copyright provides a reward to those who contribute original works of authorship to the cultural store. Such original works are worthy of reward because they generate and challenge discussion, perspectives, and world views.[21] In a world of diminished original works, the people's freedom is dramatically restricted.

Although some believe that copyright is a relic of the print era, sacrificing copyright protection would be antithetical in an era where the possibilities of cultural exchange are being dramatically increased. Rather than abandon copyright, the GII should reflect the most effective balance between universal access norms and copyright protection. Copyright holders should not be permitted to exploit this formative phase solely in their favor.

The question remains how to balance information access norms with copyright norms within TRIPS' current lopsided balance. The key to crafting the appropriate rules for copyrighted works on the GII is to find a balance between these two extremes.[22]

B. The Free Use Zone and Its Construction in the On-line Era

The threshold question for those attempting to craft copyright law for the GII is how to adapt existing copyright treaties and statutes to the new on-line era. In the pre-on-line universe, copyright law permitted authors to exercise a measure of monopoly power over the use of their creations by others. However, this right to exercise control over the copyrighted work has been subject to significant restrictions. There has been a cushion of "free use" surrounding the author's capacity to prohibit unauthorized or unpaid uses. Examples of free use include browsing among copyrighted books and magazines for sale in a bookstore, loaning a book to a friend, borrowing copyrighted works from public libraries, and visiting an art gallery or museum.[23] Copyright authors in the hard-copy universe have not been in a position to extract remuneration for any of these uses, hence my term "free use." Under U.S. law, these activities have been permitted under the "first sale" doctrine,[24] which draws a distinction between the corporeal version of the work and the intangible copyrightable expression. Under the first sale doctrine, one can do whatever one wants with the book one purchases, from loaning it to burning it. One cannot, however, copy the book and distribute it for profit.[25]

The first sale doctrine does not translate easily to the on-line environment, where most versions of the work are in an intangible format, whether stored, transmitted, or viewed on-screen. Until the work is printed onto paper (or perhaps saved to a floppy disk), there is no corporeal version of the work under traditional copyright notions. The on-line environment makes it tempting to view copyright law as a relic of the past or the first sale doctrine as a simple inconvenience that can be discarded in favor of copyright protection for every conceivable use of a work.

The free use zone has a second element. The U.S. copyright statute permits the copying of portions of copyrighted works under its fair use provisions, while most European countries recognize a personal use exemption. If one succeeds in proving that one's use of a copyrighted work is "fair" or for "personal use," then the work can be used for free, without fear of injunction.

Finally, the free use zone is also a product of the idea-expression dichotomy. In the hard copy world, copyright holders can claim monopoly privileges over the particular expression of a work, but they cannot prevent others from "stealing" the idea and crafting a different expression around it. This has always been an abstract concept, the application of which has caused consternation on the part of courts and commentators. In the virtual universe, however, the demarcation between idea and expression becomes even more abstract. Computerized creation and delivery of works makes it possible to transform any one work many times over, making this already elusive distinction even less certain.[26] With the distinction taking on such metaphysical proportions and TRIPS' clear directive to protect intellectual property products, there is likely to be a temptation to overprotect.

In the pre-on-line era, the browsing and borrowing privileges, fair use or personal use doctrines, and idea-expression dichotomy of the free use zone were quite considerable. In the virtual universe, however, it contracts considerably without some virtual tinkering. Fair use, personal exemptions, and the idea-expression dichotomy are grandfathered in by TRIPS' incorporation by reference of existing Western copyright law. Borrowing and browsing privileges have been the practical result of the first sale doctrine, which loses its force when works enter the on-line environment.

Because it only requires protection of intellectual property through simple incorporation of the pre-on-line era's Berne Convention, the TRIPS Agreement does not prohibit publishers in an on-line universe from extending their copyright monopolies well into the free use zone. TRIPS single-mindedly protects copyright owners' rights without providing the necessary limitations on copyright protection that make it an engine for change and originality rather than a one-sided anticompetitive mechanism. To the detriment of all, TRIPS transforms a copyright monopoly from one that serves the public interest into one that benefits only the copyright industries.[27]

The task for national and international policymakers lies in constructing an appropriate free use zone in an on-line world. Before offering a proposal to ensure the protection of creative works and the existence of the free use zone, it is worthwhile to examine the two poles in the spectrum over copyright on the GII. These two extremes can be described as the "hackers' " view and the "publishers' " view.

1. The Hackers

The GII follows a period in computer history when on-line communication was limited to a small set of computer experts, who valued computer literacy, especially the capacity to access encoded or secretly held information.[28] These experts have labeled themselves "hackers."[29] The motto of the hacker world is "Information wants to be free."[30] Some go so far as to argue that barriers to information, including copyright, are outdated impediments to truth and exploration.[31] They opine that copyright is an arcane phenomenon linked to the printing press that will be swept under the tide of the emerging on-line environment.

While copyright law appeared on the heels of publishing technology, its philosophical underpinnings are not intimately tied to the printing press. Whatever the means of copying, copyright law erects property boundaries around intangible expression so that it can be commodified, disseminated, and shared. Those statutorily constructed barriers are more necessary than ever in an on-line universe with its copying facility. A properly functioning copyright system rewards original expression and provides sufficient protection against unauthorized use to encourage authors to release their works into the stream of commerce. Abandoning copyright protection in the face of the prevalent universal access norms ironically would remove incentives to disseminate works.[32]

Even if copyright law is not outdated, the hackers do have a point, at least to some degree. Technology makes copying an evil that is difficult to police. The photocopying and tape industries have posed serious and persistent problems to the traditional copyright regime.[33] However, neither photocopying nor taping has ever produced a sufficiently high-quality product in sufficient volume completely to replace the market for most works. In contrast, high-quality copying and distribution of a work are very economical in the on-line environment.[34] One can download a work and send it simultaneously to millions of readers in the time it takes to photocopy a few pages of text. As the ease of copying increases so does the temptation to infringe.

In a system where infringement is so easy, copyright protection will only be as strong as its enforcement mechanisms. The existing on-line universe has yet to land upon an enforcement scheme that will safeguard the value of authors' works distributed on the network. The fear that they will be copied en masse is so real in the current environment that some publishers and artists may not release their works on-line.[35] These artists are proving what standard copyright analysis has assumed for decades:

adequate copyright protection encourages the distribution of creative works, while inadequate copyright protection lowers the birthrate of such works. The on-line environment will be a second-class medium lacking high-quality creative works, so long as copyright enforcement is not assured.[36] Without copyright enforcement and protection on-line, aesthetic holdings will be limited to those authored by part-time artists or artists with significant personal assets. In a virtual universe without copyright protection, the full-time artist loses twice: first, because only rich or part-time artists can afford to put their works on-line and still eat; and second, because consumers that would have supported them in the hard copy universe are now shopping in the on-line universe. Although there still may be a plethora of works on-line, they will not be the highest quality works possible.

The hackers have concluded that copyright law is likely to perish because of the GII's enforcement problems. This is a premature entombment. As discussed below, if the world community works together, the on-line community can be sufficiently policed to ensure fair remuneration to authors and artists.

2. The Publishers

For the publishing industry and authors, the international on-line environment raises the tantalizing possibility that all uses of a work can be tracked and subjected to a charge. With on-line bookstores, browsing can be monitored and a fee levied even if the work is not purchased. In addition, lending can be interpreted as copying. For example, once one has read a novel, one can easily send a new copy to one's mother via the network while retaining the original copy. In the pre-on-line era, one would have mailed one's mother the book, and, due to the first sale doctrine, no copyright rights would have been violated. To accomplish the same result in the on-line environment, one can simply punch a few buttons, sending a copy on its way. If the publishing industry can label this scenario an infringing activity, the free use zone will be eliminated.

Once the publishing industry enters the free use zone, it not only pushes the boundaries of copyright but also violates a significant sphere of privacy. Already, product marketers buy and sell address lists of individuals who have registered their preferences by purchasing particular products and services. By tracking and storing information about borrowing, lending, and browsing activity, the publisher obtains a profile of not only one's economic preferences but also one's predilections, whims, and desires. Building a free use zone in the virtual universe assists in the protection of that sphere of privacy.

Also worrisome is the possibility that the publishing industry may attempt to extract use royalties from works that are lodged with public lending libraries. The first sale doctrine, as well as pragmatic considerations, has historically prevented copyright authors from charging borrowers or libraries for lending activity. In an on-line environment, publishers are likely to view such lending as easily tracked and as a possible source of income.[37] Thus, the limited monopoly currently afforded copyright owners has the potential to become an "absolute monopoly over the distribution of and access to copyrighted information."[38] Publishers might think that they are well served by such a system, but the public would not benefit.[39]

By permitting the publishing industry to eliminate borrowing and browsing privileges on-line, a greater risk arises of increasing the disparity between the technology "haves" and "have-nots." Microsoft recently announced a plan to create a magazine that will appear on-line only. This is only the first of many on-line-exclusive works. If browsers and borrowers are liable to the publishers under copyright law, only the relatively wealthy will be able to gain access to these on-line-exclusive works. Unlike the current era in which anyone can be exposed to a vast panoply of works through free browsing and borrowing practices, the poor would be excluded.

There are those who predict the demise of copyright on the GII. They, however, have discounted the importance of copyright protection in order to ensure the widest possible dissemination of creative works. On the other side of the debate, there are those who believe that the GII offers an opportunity to tighten the monopoly over copyrighted works. Neither inclination should be indulged by the policymaker. Rather, policymakers should focus upon two goals: (1) ensuring that authors can obtain fair remuneration for their works through enforcement mechanisms that work and (2) protecting the public from an overreaching publishing industry by crafting a free use zone for borrowing and browsing.

3. Enforcement of Copyright on the GII

The GII poses, on a grand scale, the problem that the music industry has addressed through collective societies for years. Once a musical work has been recorded and distributed, it is easily copied and performed without permission. Use of such works in public places (e.g., night clubs or hotels) or on the air (e.g., radio or television broadcasts) has been monitored through collective efforts.

For any individual composer, monitoring every use of one's work is daunting. The same song might be heard simultaneously in a night club in Texas, as the background for a nationally televised show, and in a hotel lobby in New York. To solve the practical monitoring difficulties, BMI, ASCAP, and SESAC have formed collective licensing agencies that monitor and enforce the use of copyrighted music in public places.[40]

The GII suggests the need for the same sort of monitoring and enforcement scheme for all copyrighted works. Policing works on-line with its vast number of data ports poses a difficulty similar to the monitoring of public performance of copyrighted songs. Authors might have to devote so much time to tracking their works and then enforcing their rights that creative productivity would lag, or many infringements would be unanswered. Private societies devoted to copyright enforcement on-line, and charging modest percentages, would allow authors and artists to concentrate on creative rather than legal endeavors. Moreover, enforcement could become less expensive and more effective through economies of scale. Collective societies might also create a copyright culture on-line more quickly and more efficiently than the independent litigation of a variety of individual claims of infringement. In sum, collective agencies with international jurisdiction are a tool worth investigating for ensuring authors' fair returns for their works.[41]

The question remains how far such societies should be permitted to go in enforcing copyrights. A properly crafted free use zone should prevent publishers and authors from extending their existing monopolies into the spheres of borrowing and browsing.

4. The Free Use Zone on the GII

For works retaining a corporeal form, the first sale doctrine goes far to protect the free use zone. The question remains how to draw the lines that will create a free use zone on-line. The following are suggestions for achieving such a goal. They may either be used to amend existing national copyright laws or as a means of judicial translation of copyright coverage from the pre-on-line era to the on-line era. Constructing a free use zone in the on-line era will require some government intervention, largely by making explicit what is already accepted practice in a hard copy universe—that copyright owners do not have rights to prohibit individuals from browsing and borrowing their works.

a. Personal Lending

Individuals should be permitted to transmit copies of works on-line to friends or family for personal and private use. Personal lending should be an affirmative defense to charges of infringement.[42] This defense is a crucial means of preserving a zone of privacy in the face of the on-line era.

b. Library Lending and Copying

Traditionally, public libraries have permitted individuals to obtain access to copyrighted works without purchasing them. Patrons can read books and magazines, listen to music, and view artwork for free so long as they return the item to the library. Authors (and their copyright assignees) are not remunerated for each of these uses. Patrons, however, cannot make copies of the books, disks, or videos, or keep the library's holdings beyond a specified date. In other words, their use is limited in time and may not be augmented by making a permanent copy of the particular work. If a patron wants to keep a particular work, he or she must purchase the work outside the library system or pay a fine to the library (which is generally equivalent to the purchase price).

Authors and publishers should be prohibited from interfering with this system. A library free use zone would need to be instituted via statute(s) and treaties by cutting back on copyright protection in these circumstances. Similar to the photocopying context, libraries would need to work in conjunction with publishers to ensure that they manage their holdings to prevent copyright infringement. Libraries would be responsible for ensuring that their borrowers do not download the work or do not retain the work beyond a limited time frame. Public free libraries play an important role in an egalitarian society, making this aspect of the free use zone worthy of serious attention on constitutional and political grounds.

c. Commercial Browsing

Publishers should not be permitted to charge customers for browsing through their various products. Browsing would include brief perusal of the work and exclude permanent downloading of the work. Devices currently exist that would permit publishers to make the distinction between the two uses.[43] Conceivably, the market may take care of this problem by encouraging the use of free "teaser" previews to entice purchasers. Thus, it would be most prudent to observe how this market develops over the next several years before taking domestic or international action regarding commercial browsing.

5. Summary

To ensure the widest possible dissemination of creative works and fair remuneration to authors, GII policymakers face two tasks: (1) to foster means of ensuring that copyright owners can enforce their copyrights, such as private collective agencies and technological means of tracing use, and (2) to protect a free use zone that prevents copyright owners from transforming their limited monopolies into absolute monopolies. The free market is the most desirable means of accomplishing the first objective.

The second objective will require domestic government and international action. The free use zone's borrowing and browsing phenomena are a direct result of the hard copy paradigm: browsers can be stopped from carrying books out of bookstores; the volume of private lending is limited because photocopying is tedious and the product is not as desirable as the original; and libraries can police lending practices, including photocopying. As a practical matter, there has been effective means of enforcing copyright against borrowers and browsers in a hard copy universe.

In an on-line environment, the fences and gates that permit borrowing and browsing will have to be engineered by statute and treaty. To construct a free use zone, the scope of copyright protection needs to be reduced to exclude liability for borrowing or browsing copyrighted works, even though that borrowing and browsing may involve downloading. In addition, policymakers would do well to reinforce their support for personal use exemptions and fair use principles in the on-line era.

A cursory glance might suggest that universal access norms and copyright law are in irreconcilable conflict, that universal access is superficially more important than copyright protection, and therefore copyright protection should be abandoned. A more careful analysis, however, reveals that copyright law is one of the tools to ensure that there is a steady supply of original works of authorship released into the on-line stream of commerce. Existing copyright law, transported to the on-line environment, raises the possibility that on-line authors and publishers will be able to expand upon their existing monopolies by charging for browsing and borrowing privileges. The United States must ensure that a free use zone becomes a part of the on-line environment and prevent the overreaching permitted by the TRIPS Agreement's silence.

IV. Conclusion

There were times before the TRIPS Agreement was ratified when some predicted it would never come to pass. Yet, it materialized out of the stratified discourse of 117 countries, largely as a result of the intense lobbying efforts of the huge, international publishing entities. As so often happens with large, collaborative projects, "soul-searching" was left for later. TRIPS, in its present incarnation, requires us to search the soul of the Western copyright system. Enforcement disputes between countries sharing incongruent presuppositions about human creative effort and reward will test TRIPS' imperialistic mettle.

Even if TRIPS withstands the inevitable public and private challenges to its Western-style imperialism, it will find itself in the unfamiliar territory of the on-line universe, an environment for which it has not been well crafted in the interests of a global society. The hard copy universe's free use zone must be constructed out of virtual fences and gates to prevent TRIPS from becoming the "copyright grab" for all history.

The encoded message within TRIPS is that change, creativity, and originality are positive goods. In short, revolution and freedom are central to the highest standards of human existence. As this message finds its way into unfamiliar hearts, the copyright industries hope to take more than they have ever been able to take in the past. This will be a clash worth watching. If only we were nothing more than spectators.

Notes

1. Final Act Embodying the Results of the Uruguay Round of Multilateral Trade Negotiations, April 15, 1994, Annex IC: Agreement on Trade-Related Aspects of Intellectual Property Rights [hereinafter TRIPS], reprinted in *The Results of the Uruguay Round of Multilateral Trade Negotiations—The Legal Texts*, edited by GATT Secretariat (Geneva, 1994), 1–19, 365–403.

2. "[TRIPS] is the highest expression to date of binding intellectual property in the international arena" (David Nimmer, "The End of Copyright," *Vanderbilt Law Review* 48 [1995]: 1385).

3. John Worthy, "Intellectual Property Protection after GATT," *European International Property Review* 16 (1994): 195.

4. J. H. Reichman, "Intellectual Property in International Trade: Opportunities and Risks of a GATT Connection," *Vanderbilt Journal of Transnational Law* 22 (1989): 747, 813. Professor Reichman attributes this thought to Steven P. Ladas, stating, "Imposition of foreign legal standards on unwilling states in the name of 'harmonization' remains today what Ladas deemed it in 1975, namely, a polite form of economic imperialism" (Reichman, citing Steven P. Ladas, *Patents, Trademarks, and Related Rights: National and International Protection* [Cambridge, Mass.: Harvard University Press, 1975], 14–15). Paul Geller's work has been important in shaping my view of TRIPS as a "legal transplant." See Paul Geller,

"Legal Transplants in International Copyright: Some Problems of Method," *UCLA Pacific Basin Law Journal* 13 (1994): 199.

5. By the "West," the author means both Europe and the United States. See Whitmore Gray, "The Challenge of Asian Law," *Fordham International Law Journal* 19 (1995): 5–6.

> During the Nineteenth and the first half of the Twentieth Centuries, the principal migration of legal ideas was from Europe to countries attempting to create or modernize their legal systems. . . . After the Second World War, however, a new era of global interaction of legal systems developed. U.S. economic dominance reinforced the idea that U.S. legal institutions and, particularly, recent U.S. substantive law, should be considered as normal models for modernization.

Gray, "The Challenge of Asian Law." See also J. H. Reichman, "Charting the Collapse of the Patent-Copyright Dichotomy: Premises for a Restructured International Intellectual Property System," *Cardozo Arts and Entertainment Law Journal* 13 (1995): 475; J. H. Reichman, "Beyond the Historical Lines of Demarcation: Competition Law, Intellectual Property Rights, and International Trade after the GATT's Uruguay Round," *Brook. Journal of International Law* 20 (1993): 75, 113 (declaring that "the United States negotiators, blinded by a particular view of the cathedral, confined their efforts to securing copyright protection" to existing Western paradigms). As a historical matter, TRIPS' imperialistic character is not sewn out of whole cloth. TRIPS furthers, and incorporates by reference, the Berne Convention, which was the product of the nineteenth century's European empires. Berne's Western bias has been the subject of some discussion in the past. See Ladas, note 4; see also Sam Ricketson, *The Berne Convention for the Protection of Literary and Artistic Works* (London: Centre for Commercial LCW Studies, Queen Mary College, 1987), 1886–1996.

6. Cf. Tara K. Giunta and Lily H. Shang, "Ownership of Information in a Global Economy," *George Washington Journal of International Law and Economics* 27 (1933): 327, 333 (arguing that one reason it has been so difficult to draft a multilateral intellectual property agreement is that a favorable agreement for one country could be unfavorable for another country).

7. In the context of debate over international intellectual property protection, the German branch of the International Law Association makes this point clearly: "Protection of intellectual property . . . constitutes . . . a basic right of the individual" (Reflection Group Intellectual Economic Law of the International Law Association-German Branch, *Draft Proposal of the German ILA Branch—Existing and Evolving Principles and Rules on Freedom of Knowledge, International Protection of Intellectual Property and Transfers of Achievements of Science and Technology*, introduction by Meinard Hilf and Thomas Oppermann [1992], [hereinafter Munich Draft]).

8. This third criterion appears in its strongest form in the U.S. version of copyright law. As it may be the most important in the on-line era, global copyright law may not only look Western in the end, but decidedly American. See note 5.

9. This venue prevents me from fully explicating in detail the historical sources that support these claims. For the time being, it should be sufficient to indicate that my views have been influenced by the "Weberian hypothesis" that capitalism has its roots in Puritanism and the accompanying critical literature. See generally Max Weber, *The Protestant Ethic and the Spirit of Capitalism,* trans. by Talcott Parson (New York: Scribner, 1958); *Protestantism, Capitalism, and Social Science: The Weber Thesis Controversy,* edited by Robert W. Green (Boston: Heath, 1959).

10. Barbara Ringer, "Two Hundred Years of American Copyright Law," in *ABA, 200 Years of English and American Patent, Trademark and Copyright Law* (1977), 117, 118 (asserting that "we know, empirically, that strong copyright systems are characteristic of relatively free societies").

11. Although China is not a signatory to TRIPS, it is certainly a clear target for those industries that pushed TRIPS, and is probably one of the more difficult countries to bring into line with Western-based intellectual property values. In a fascinating article on the history of intellectual property protection in China, Professor William Alford explores the "political culture" that has not led China to a Western-style intellectual property system. See William P. Alford, "Don't Stop Thinking About . . . Yesterday: Why There Was No Indigenous Counterpart to Intellectual Property Law in Imperial China," *Journal of Chinese Law* 7 (1993): 3, 20; see also A. M. Rosenthal, "Washington Confronts China," *New York Times,* 6 February 1996. In addition to being unreceptive to a Western intellectual property law system, the Chinese have believed in the goodness of literary and idea censorship (Alford, "Don't Stop Thinking About . . . Yesterday," 27). Thus, in an era when more copyrighted works are becoming available worldwide, China is resisting that trend (Seth Faison, "Chinese Tiptoe into Internet, Wary of Watchdogs," *New York Times,* 5 February 1996).

12. Howard Gardner, *Art Education and Human Development* (Los Angeles: Getty Center for Education in the Arts, 1990), 51 (discussing Chinese attitudes toward art and artistic production and education); see also Marci A. Hamilton, "Art Speech," *Vanderbilt Law Review* 48 (1996): 73 (citing sources with relevant information). China's recent threats against Taiwan have arisen from its anti-democratic politics, which also create a hostile environment for Western copyright law. See Christopher J. Sigor, "Why Taiwan Scares China," *New York Times,* 19 March 1996; William Safire, "New Mandate of Heaven," *New York Times,* 25 March 1996.

13. Anti-authoritarianism lies at the heart of Calvin's response to Luther and the Catholic Church. See Weber, *Protestant Ethic.*

14. See Hamilton, "Art Speech," for a description of art's capacity to challenge status quo power relations.

15. See generally Hamilton, "Art Speech." See also Safire, "New Mandate" (referring to "telecommunications spreading democracy's contagion").

16. The right to scientific information did enter into discussions held in Germany. See generally Munich Draft. This appears to be the exception rather than the rule. It is not clear whether the International Law Association (I.L.A.) will

further address this topic. The author acknowledges a debt of gratitude to Professor Frederick Abbott for this information. See also Paul Geller, "Intellectual Property in the Global Marketplace: Impact of TRIPS Dispute Settlement," *International Lawyer* 29 (1995): 99, 115 (stating that TRIPS settlement dispute panels "may not be competent to resolve [privacy, free speech, and information access] issues").

17. Professor Pamela Samuelson has made the same argument regarding President Clinton's Information Infrastructure Task Force's recent proposals for amendment of domestic copyright law. See Bruce A. Lehman, *Information Infrastructure Task Force, Intellectual Property and the National Information Infrastructure—The Report of the Working Group on Intellectual Property Rights* (Washington, D.C.: Information Infrastructure Task Force, 1995) [hereinafter *White Paper*]. See Pamela Samuelson, "The Copyright Grab," *Wired*, January 1996, 135; see also Jessica Litman, "Revising Copyright Law for the Information Age," *Oregon Law Review*, 75 (forthcoming 1996) (stating that the *White Paper's* proposals for copyright law amendment in the information age are a boon to copyright owners).

18. See Philip H. Miller, "New Technology, Old Problem: Determining the First Amendment Status of Electronic Information Services," *Fordham Law Review* 61 (1993): 1147, 1158 ("One assumption that underlies the First Amendment is that the widest possible dissemination of information from diverse and antagonistic sources is essential to the welfare of the public"); see also Lisa J. Damon, Note, "Freedom of Information Versus National Sovereignty: The Need for a New Global Forum for the Resolution of Tradeborder Data Flow Problems," *Fordham International Law Journal* 10 (1986): 262; Giunta and Shang, "Ownership," at 330 ("Some developing countries maintain that knowledge and information are the common heritage of [humanity] and therefore should be made available at low costs"). The G-7 industrialized countries are Britain, Canada, France, Germany, Italy, Japan, and the United States (Keiko Tatsuta, "G-10 Echoes Concern over Recent Forex Moves," *Japan Economic Newswire*, 27 April 1995, available in LEXIS, News Library, Current News File).

19. Raf Casert, "Telecommunications Open Markets Urged," *Philadelphia Inquirer*, 25 February 1995.

20. Hamilton, "Art Speech."

21. See Hamilton, "Art Speech."

22. See Munich Draft, at B.III.9 (urging "fair and balanced system of licensing of intellectual property rights").

23. Although the products involved are not free to consumers, copyright authors have also been constrained from exercising their copyright against "free uses," such as secondhand bookstores that have been permitted to purchase works and resell them, and video rental stores that have been permitted to purchase videos and rent them for profit.

24. The European Community recognizes a similar principle. Once a hard copy of a copyrighted work is sold, the author's right to receive remuneration for

that particular copy is extinguished (Herman C. Jehoran et al., "The Law of the E.E.C. and Copyright," *International Copyright Law and Practice*, edited by Melville B. Nimmer and Paul E. Geller (1993).

25. Copyright Act of 1976, 17 U.S.C. sec. 109 [1988]).

26. I owe this idea to Neil Netanel.

27. Cf. Samuelson, "The Copyright Grab."

28. See Clifford Stoll, *Silicon Snake Oil* (New York: Doubleday, 1995).

29. See Stewart Brand and Matt Herron, " 'Keep Designing': How the Information Economy Is Being Created and Shaped by the Hacker Ethic," *Whole Earth Review*, May 1985 (describing hackers as "dedicated, innovative, irreverent computer programmers [who] are the most interesting and effective body of intellectuals since the framers of the U.S. Constitution"). For an entertaining discussion of the "true" meaning of "hacker," see Brand and Herron.

30. Stewart Brand, described as a "1960s activist turned digital savant," is credited with coining the phrase "Information wants to be free" (Jim McClellan, "Cyberspace Angelic Startups," *The Observer*, 21 January 1996; David Stipp and Steward Brand, "The Electric Kool-Aid Management Consultant," *Fortune*, Oct. 16, 1995 (characterizing "information wants to be free" as the "cyberhacker rallying cry" coined by Brand). The phrase is one of the cornerstones of the hacker movement, which is described in the book by Steven Levy, *Hackers: Heroes of the Computer Revolution* (New York: Dell Publishing Co., 1984). See Brand and Herron, 'Keep Designing.' It is also one of the central themes of the editorial pages of *Wired* magazine. See "Where is Wired @?" *Wired*, 14 November 1994. Indeed, the phrase has become so widely accepted that in 1994 it was referred to as an "ancient hacker war cry" (Vic Sussman, "Pamphleteering in the Electronic Era," *U.S. News & World Report*, 17 January 1994).

31. The League for Programming Freedom urges this view in its baldest form. Those espousing this view have not limited their thesis regarding copyright to words but have also participated in the free distribution of their own copyrightable works. See Sussman, "Pamphleteering."

32. See Litman, "Revising Copyright Law" (discussing the importance of copyright law to dissemination of works of authorship).

33. See "CONTU's Final Report and Recommendations," *Copyright, Congress and Technology: The Public Record*, edited by Nicholas Henry (Phoenix, Ariz.: Oryx, 1980).

34. Trotter Hardy, "The Proper Legal Regime for 'Cyberspace,' " *University of Pittsburgh Law Review* 55 (1994): 993, 1005 (cyberspace turns "every individual into a mass publisher . . . in a way that photocopying never really did").

35. Doreen Carvajal, "Book Publishers Worry About Threat of Internet," *New York Times*, 18 March 1996.

36. See John S. Rosenberg, "Copyright of Way on the Information Highway: Copyright Issues for Online Information Services," *Searcher*, March 1994 ("To the often heard refrain of many Netsurfers that 'information wants to be free,' current online vendors, publishers, and more than a few authors reply that if it is

completely free, there may be no information for payment, and the information superhighway will become a very expensive road to nowhere. Instead of the interactive multimedia future we've been promised, we'd have the database equivalent of home movies").

37. The American Association of Research Libraries anticipated the publishing industry's likely response to the on-line environment and responded with a public's bill of copyright rights, which delineates the browsing and borrowing privileges described here.

Without infringing copyright, the public has a right to expect:

• to read, to listen, or view publicly marketed copyrighted material privately, on site or remotely;
• to browse through publicly marketed copyrighted material;
• to experiment with variations of copyrighted material for fair use purposes, while preserving the integrity of the original;
• to make or have made for them a first generation copy for personal use of an article or other small part of a publicly marketed copyrighted work or a work in a library's collection for such purpose as study, scholarship, or research; and
• to make transitory copies if ephemeral or incidental to a lawful use and if retained only temporarily.

Association of Research Libraries, "Fair Use in the Electronic Age: Serving the Public Internet" (Working Document of 18 January 1995).

38. Association of Research Libraries, "Intellectual Property: An Association of Research Libraries Statement of Prinicples," May 1994.

39. See Litman, "Revising Copyright Law" (emphasizing the importance of asking what the public's needs are when crafting copyright boundaries).

40. On the way to arguing against any intellectual property protection in the on-line era, John Perry Barlow has argued that ASCAP (American Society of Composers, Actors, and Publishers) and BMI (Broadcast Music, Inc.) are not acceptable models for the on-line era because their "monitoring methods are wildly approximate. There is no parallel system of accounting in the revenue stream. It doesn't really work. Honest" (John P. Barlow, chap. 15 of this volume.) Barlow has missed the mark. While he is right about the monitoring difficulties in a hard copy universe, he underestimates the monitoring capacities of a universally linked on-line universe. Works may become marginally more difficult for individuals to monitor in the virtual universe. See generally Marci A. Hamilton, "Appropriation Art and the Imminent Decline in Authorial Control over Copyrighted Works," *Journal of the Copyright Society* 42 (1994): 93. Monitoring technology, however, is just now beginning to flourish and already offers the opportunity—to those who can afford the technology—of tracking every use of a work, from browsing to downloading. With the publishing, entertainment, and high-technology industries vitally interested in pursuing intellectual property protection on-line, the monitoring technology investment stream is highly likely to become a river, and

a fast-running one at that. While monitoring may be expensive and inaccessible for the individual author, it will surely be affordable for collective societies (which will assist individual copyright owners who are willing to sacrifice a portion of their income stream if it can be accurately monitored and copyrights enforced) and for large media and technology companies.

41. The on-line tracking tools that would make a collective society effective already exist. See Robert L. Jacobson, "Interest Tools Designed to Block Unauthorized Uses of Copyrighted Works," *Chronicle of Higher Education,* 22 March 1996. The question of who will employ such tools remains open. Candidates include the publishing industry, collection societies, individual authors, and the government.

42. See Litman, "Revising Copyright Law" (advocating a distinction between commercial and noncommercial use in the assignment of copyright rights).

43. See *White Paper,* at 38 (describing "smartcards" among other devices).

10

International Copyright: An Unorthodox Analysis*

Hugh C. Hansen

I. Introduction

Until recently, copyright laws throughout the world were domestically oriented. Copyright law is "territorial." Each nation determines the scope of protection and rights subject only to bilateral and multilateral agreements, which, before the Uruguay Round of the GATT negotiations and the adoption of the agreement on Trade-Related Aspects of Intellectual Property (TRIPS), were essentially unenforceable.[1]

Overall, there were two systems: (1) the Anglo-American so-called "economic" system and (2) the French and Continental "author's rights" system with its concomitant fascination with "moral rights." Within each system, countries established regimes of protection that were economically and philosophically compatible with their cultures. The broader differences and even the differences within each system were of mostly academic interest, as there was little transnational interaction among those subject to the various laws.

This situation changed dramatically when copyright industries, such as motion pictures, music, and computer software and hardware, began to export their products around the world massively and successfully. The

*This essay was originally published as "International Copyright: An Unorthodox Analysis," by Hugh C. Hansen, in the *Vanderbilt Journal of Transnational Law* 29 (1996): 579–93. Copyright © 1996 by Vanderbilt University. Reprinted with permission of publisher.

change was given additional impetus by the growth of exports in patent industries, such as pharmaceuticals, and the accompanying need for trademark protection abroad. Intellectual property became very important to the balance of trade and jobs. Government leaders, CEOs, and corporate boards in the United States and abroad took notice of the importance of intellectual property laws.

Government initiatives took two forms: a push by the United States to include protection for intellectual property in the Uruguay Round of GATT negotiations (TRIPS), and initiatives in Europe to increase patent and copyright protection. One of the purposes of the directives was to improve European competitiveness.[2]

The nations of the world can be divided broadly into three groups based upon their relationship to the production and consumption of intellectual property products: (1) net sellers-exporters; (2) those with the resources and industries to become net sellers-exporters; and (3) net users-importers. The first group, whose main member was the United States, wanted broad protection worldwide. The second group, which included some members of the European Community, also wanted broad protection worldwide and, in addition, wanted to increase protection domestically to give more incentives to their industries to create and compete domestically and abroad.[3] The third group, mainly developing and newly industrialized nations, sought to limit protection at least within their borders.

While those in groups one and two may have had disputes and concerns among themselves, they were for the most part united on the position that they wanted much greater protection in the countries in group three.[4] Obtaining this protection would require the conversion of those who were not true believers in the value of copyright or other forms of intellectual property.

This commentary attempts to address some of the problems that the United States and others faced in bringing about that conversion. The first question was who would be on the front line of the proselytizing efforts.

II. The Copyright Players

The Secular Priesthood

Until approximately fifteen to twenty years ago, copyright law was the province of a small bar and an even smaller cadre of law professors. The numbers were small because of the complexity of the law, the limited amount of copyright work, and the relatively few schools that taught it on a continuous and serious basis. These lawyers and professors practiced and wrote about copyright law in the context of traditional copyright industries: publishing, theater, motion pictures, music, and art. The lawyers related emotionally to the creators. No doubt many at one time may have had aspirations to be writers or other types of creators themselves. Regardless of what the doctrine stated, and without necessarily articulating this view in terms of natural law, they nonetheless believed that creators were entitled to copyright in their works.[5]

These lawyers and professors, who were primarily based in New York (with the later addition of Los Angeles) formed what amounted to a secular priesthood protecting the esoteric secrets of idea/expression, conceptual separability, and originality.[6] Copyright work was attractive because it presented the opportunity to work in one of the most, if not the most, intellectually challenging and interesting areas of the law.[7] Copyright also provided the opportunity to work with interesting, sometimes very gifted, people and with creative and engaging works.

International law and international trade were not of interest to most of these lawyers or their clients. To a large extent, they have remained outside of the international battles.

The Agnostics and Atheists

Many newcomers to copyright in the last ten to fifteen years, especially those in academia, do not accept the basic assumptions about creation and ownership long shared by the copyright community. Many do not identify with creators but rather with users: Internet (Net) users, developing nations, consumers, small competitors, and creators of derivative works. These newcomers to copyright came of age in a time when protection was broadly applied to utilitarian works, such as computer programs, and international copyright became trade oriented. They sensed that something was wrong with the current system. Copyright owners were not the Oscar Hammersteins but the Time Warners, Sonys, and MCAs. Whereas the secular priests were and are technically challenged, this new breed not only feels at home on the Net but is creating Web sites, home pages, and teaching cyberspace law.

If this group ever had a high-protection faith in copyright, they lost it. Today they are imbued with the culture of the public domain—a "living and vibrant" public domain. This group believes that the public domain will protect those on the Net, increase competition, allow cultural self-determination, and make multinational corporations atone for their sins. This is an unlikely group to enlist in the foreign copyright crusades.

The Missionaries

The copyright crusade in large part has been driven by trade considerations. It is not surprising to find people with backgrounds in this area (both inside and outside of government) at the forefront of the conversion effort. Joining them are lawyers for multinational corporations and trade associations, some of whom were in the secular priesthood. In addition, those entrusted with the protection of intellectual property in the European Union (EU) and in the United States government have played key roles. The effort has attracted people with considerable skill and ability and, to date, has been remarkably successful. Still, much work remains to be done before it can be assured that all souls have been saved.

III. The Religion

Wholesale conversion needs the tools of religion, and fundamentalist religion at that. Certain truths are revealed and meant to be learned, not debated. The intellectually complex points of copyright law are for seminary discussion over wine. Here, high protection is the key. The public domain is not a place where you will find Robin Hood in Sherwood Forest righting economic wrongs. Rather, the public domain is a place where bandits replenish supplies so they may cross the border to loot and plunder copyrighted works. For long forays into copyrighted lands, these public domain bandits are hidden and fed by consumers who want something for nothing and who have an apparently insatiable appetite for unprotected works.

As with all fundamentalist religions, this one has fundamental truths. One truth is that computer programs must be protected as literary works. The words "sui generis protection" would produce gasps from the faithful. Another truth is that a high level of protection for intellectual property would lead to more investment and jobs. A third truth is that so-called "national treatment" is the way to increase protection for all and that "reciprocity" is the nationalistic work of the devil.[8]

The faith in national treatment, which required action as well as belief, was harder for the righteous to adhere to fully. The United States inserted a reciprocity provision in its sui generis legislation to protect semiconductor computer chips.[9] The EU inserted reciprocity provisions in the proposed Database Directive and the term directive.[10] Even the Berne Convention allows for reciprocity in some circumstances. However, the slips and falls of our leaders do not mean that religious truths are false, only that the flesh is weak. The TRIPS Agreement, recognizing this, requires national treatment.[11]

IV. The Conversion of the Uninitiated

Once you have a religion and missionaries, how do you convert the uninitiated? There are two broad approaches to conversion: voluntary and involuntary.

Voluntary Conversion

Voluntary conversion is obviously the ideal. How does one achieve this? One way is by example. People see how you live your life and are impressed. They want to have the inner glow that they see in you. This way is somewhat problematic for the United States. If there is an inner glow, it has not been strong enough to be seen from abroad.

The United States did not provide protection for foreign works for over one hundred years. When the United States finally did begin to provide protection, it imposed a requirement that books be manufactured in the United States in order to protect the domestic printing industry. The United States imposed a system of formalities, the main purpose of which seemed to be to throw works into the public domain, including many famous foreign works. It just recently joined the Berne Convention, and did so only because other nations told it repeatedly, "If you are going to preach the religion, you must join the Church."

The U.S. consumer views intellectual property as a hindrance to immediate gratification and home-taping as something guaranteed by the Bill of Rights. United States corporations believe the French view of moral rights is sentimental slop. The proposed legislation in the U.S. Congress for a copyright term of life plus seventy years stands a chance only in the event money flows from Europe to the United States, which is not a copyright concern but a balance of trade concern.[12] Thus, conversion by example is a tough row to hoe.

A second traditional conversion argument focuses on the existence of an afterlife and one's place in it. While the copyright faithful might believe that the "free-access" or "pro-user" people will have some explaining to do, even they will concede that one's chances for salvation are not at stake.

A third argument for conversion is to show how the person will benefit. The consuming public, however, benefits in the short run from free access to intellectual property much as it does when a truck is hijacked and the goods are sold below cost. Moreover, some livelihoods in developing countries may be based upon "pirate" industries. Jobs will be lost, and it may not be apparent or obvious how protection of intellectual property will produce new jobs in those countries, if in fact it will. It may well be that the globalization of intellectual property is going to produce economic winners and losers, with little hope in the short run for the losers to change their status.

The benefit argument is that the protection of intellectual property will produce investment in new or current industries that, in the long run, will produce income and jobs. It has been said that "in the long run, we are all dead," and it is usually short-run arguments that the "person in the street" cares about.[13]

A fourth argument is that although in the short run it will cost money to pay for intellectual property, this cost is as morally appropriate and necessary as paying for food, transportation, and consumer goods. In short, it is simply wrong to take someone else's intellectual property. While this principle is undoubtedly correct, there are obstacles to winning converts on these grounds. First, the consuming public wants goods at lower prices and shows little concern for how it gets them. If a consumer is told that the expensive product being sold at a low price was stolen from a truck, the consumer's main concern may be the validity of the warranty.

Second, even if consumers were concerned with the morality of theft, they generally do not treat or value intellectual property in the same way that they do tangible property. For example, if a videotape of a movie costs forty-nine dollars, only a few dollars of that amount represents the costs of manufacturing and delivering the tangible property—the cassette. At least forty dollars, and probably more, of the cost is for the intangible property—the movie. Everybody thinks it wrong to shoplift the videocassette from a store. On the other hand, almost everybody considers it appropriate to videotape that same forty-dollar movie from a television set. Thus, it appears that the inexpensive but tangible videocassette is valued more than the expensive but intangible intellectual property.[14]

If the short-run self-interest of the people is an obstacle to conversion, the next step is converting the intellectual and power elites who may appreciate long-run benefits. In time, the religion can be passed on, imposed on, or trickled-down to the people. The problem is that intellectual and power elites are used to imposing their views on others, not vice versa.

An idea, whatever its merits, may be resisted because of its origin, particularly if it originates abroad. Autonomy, while not appropriate for the masses, becomes a mantra for the elites.

This is true for developed as well as developing nations. There are two recent examples. The first example is in the United States. Both the secular priests and agnostics are upset with the changes in U.S. law mandated by TRIPS.[15] Repeatedly one hears concerns that changes in copyright law that derive from international obligations do not give due regard to the Copyright and Patent Clause in the U.S. Constitution.[16] Moreover, there is fear that limitations on copyright set forth by the Supreme Court (for instance, in *Feist*) will not be respected.[17]

Whatever the merits of these arguments, disregard of the Constitution or Supreme Court opinions is not a recent phenomenon. Despite the fact that Professor Melville Nimmer raised the constitutional problems with various aspects of copyright law in his original treatise on the 1909 Copyright Act, few litigants or academics have sought to develop those points even after many years.[18] Moreover, a number of Supreme Court opinions have been ignored or not followed by lower courts.[19] Similarly, the Court itself has sometimes ignored, manipulated, or distorted its own precedents.[20] Even the exalted *Feist* opinion has been given lip service by some lower courts, including one on which retired Justice Powell was a member of the panel.[21]

While the recent changes in copyright law raise legitimate concerns, the concerns are no greater than those that existed before without much complaint. What might be particularly upsetting to both the secular priests and the agnostics is that these changes have been imposed from abroad, with little or no consideration of their views. Copyright is their area, and they are territorial about it. The message to the international set is: Mess around with tariffs, anti-dumping provisions and the like, but leave copyright to us.

The second example is in the United Kingdom. In the United Kingdom high protection is gospel and there are no known agnostics. Both television listings and government statutes have been protected under copyright law, which the secular priests in the United States would consider grossly overprotective and in bad taste.[22] But even in the land of high protection, increased-protection changes can cause resentment if imposed from abroad. Pursuant to the EU term directive, Kenneth Grahame's *Wind in the Willows* had come back into copyright. Alan Bennett had adapted it while it was in the public domain and produced an annual Christmas pageant. The new U.K. law allowed derivative works created while the work was in the public domain to remain free from new restraints. Thus

Bennett would not have to seek permission from or pay the owner of the rights to Grahame's works, the Oxford University Library.

Oxford, however, had been looking forward to the revenue from licensing Bennett's production. One might think that, in a high protection country, university students' sharing with Bennett the revenue for a derivative work for which Bennett never paid copyright fees would be warmly received. But this is how *The Times* (London) reported the facts:

> Toad of Toad Hall and his friends from the riverbank have escaped the clutches of the lawmakers in Brussels and are able to continue delighting children of all ages for the rest of the pantomime season in London.[23]

Of course, children of all ages would have continued to enjoy Toad of Toad Hall even with a licensing requirement. The slant of the story appears to derive from the fact that the law resulted from an EU directive. The bias against such directives appears to overshadow the potential benefit to Oxford and the under-financed educational system of Britain.[24]

A final problem with any conversion effort is the fact that the owners of the intellectual property are, for the most part, from the United States. This seems to upset people throughout the world. Fair-minded Europeans are comfortable with levy laws that do not fairly compensate U.S. producers for home-copying and standardization policies apparently aimed at getting U.S. technology at low cost through compulsory licensing.[25] Newly industrialized Asian nations that normally place a premium on being law-abiding are comfortable with their pirate industries that feed on U.S. products. The "Ugly American" today is the one who expects to be paid.

Involuntary Conversion

The prospects for voluntary conversion are not great. That leaves conversion by the sword. Apparently recognizing this early on, the United States favored proceeding through GATT and TRIPS, which had mechanisms for sanctions, rather than in the WIPO, which did not.[26]

The WTO, or TRIPS, regime provides mechanisms for both the United States and the European Union to enforce provisions that increase protection in newly industrialized and developing nations.[27] If these mechanisms fail, there is little doubt that bilateral trade restraints will be used in these religious wars, whether they be "Section 301" or ad hoc efforts.[28] When the United States and the European Union wanted to achieve increased protection in narrow areas of intellectual property between themselves, they each used reciprocity provisions, the mortars of religious wars.[29] This should remove any doubt that coercion will continue to be used against newly industrialized and developing nations when broad levels of protection are at stake.

V. Conclusion

Some parties might enjoy theological debates about the nuances and complexities of copyright law and the culture of the public domain. For developed nations, however, the trade stakes between them and the newly industrialized and developing nations with regard to international copyright protection are too high for such debates to occur. That is a luxury left for academics, the refined domestic practice of the secular priests, and, possibly, the developed nations in disputes among themselves.

Religious wars can be just as deadly as nonreligious ones. Individuals of good conscience in the past have converted to avoid the sword or economic or other sanctions. Today, the copyright wars are still being fought. The soldiers are in the field and the developed nations have won most of the initial battles. The question remains whether the newly industrialized and developing nations will ever fully convert. Lip service can be a valuable defense, and political leaders sometimes lose the stomach for war.[30] Time will tell.

Notes

1. See Final Act Embodying the Results of the Uruguay Round of Multilateral Trade Negotiations, Apr. 15, 1994, Annex 1C: Agreement on Trade-Related Aspects of Intellectual Property Rights, *International Legal Materials* (I.L.M.), vol. 33 (1994): 1197 [hereinafter TRIPS].

2. TRIPS. Regarding patent see, for example, Common Position (EC) 4/94 adopted by the Council on 7 February 1994 with a view to adopting European Parliament and Council Directive on the legal protection of biotechnological inventions, *Official Journal of European Communities* (O.J.) 1994 (C101), 65 [hereinafter Biotech Directive]; Council Regulation 1768/92 of 18 June 1992 on the creation of a supplementary protection certificate of medicinal products, 1992 O.J. (L182), 1 [hereinafter Supplementary Patent Protection Regulation]. The proposed Biotech Directive was originally published in October 1988. A common position was reached in February 1994. After a second reading by Parliament and a reconciliation proceeding, it was unexpectedly defeated at the last moment by the European Parliament in March 1995. The process to adopt a biotech directive

was started again in December 1995, when a new proposal was adopted by the commission and sent to the council. The Supplementary Protection Regulation was first proposed by the commission in 1990 and became effective on 2 January 1993.

Regarding copyright see Council Directive 91/250 of 14 May 1991 on the legal protection of computer programs, 1991 O.J. (L122) 42 [hereinafter Software Directive]; Common Position (EC) No. 20/95 adopted by the council on 10 July 1995 with a view to adopting Directive 95/ /EC of the European Parliament and of the council on the legal protection of databases, 1995 O.J. (C288) 14, 21. The European Parliament completed its second reading on 14 December 1995, with nonsubstantive amendments recommended, A4–0290/95. The commission then passed the proposed database directive as amended on to the council, which adopted it on 26 February 1996. The European Parliament then gave final approval on 11 March 1996. European Parliament and Council Directive 96–9–EC of 11 March 1996 [hereinafter Database Directive]. These two directives were intended to provide protection for expanded industries and, thus, revenue for the EU countries (see below and note 8). The EU has also adopted other copyright directives on the rental and lending right, satellite broadcasting and retransmission, and term of protection. The motivation for the adoption of these directives had more to do with harmonization and internal market efficiency matters than with international copyright or the creation of jobs.

Regarding European competitiveness: "It is particularly important to ensure that appropriate legal protection is available to computer programs and software generally, which will contribute to an environment favourable to investment and innovation by Community firms, thus permitting the Community industry to catch up with its competitors" (Commission Green Paper on Copyright and the Challenge of Technology, "Copyright Issues Requiring Immediate Action," COM [88] 172 final, at 175). The EC Biotech Directive was meant to establish a level of protection that would induce investment in research and development to compete with that in the United States and Japan. See Anna Booy and Audrey Horton, *Sweet and Maxwell's, E.C. Intellectual Property Materials* (1994), 96 ("Different levels of patent protection available in Member states could make the E.C. a less attractive place to invest in biotechnological research when compared with the United States and Japan"); Biotech Directive at recital 3 ("Protection of biotechnological inventions will definitely be of fundamental importance for the Community's industrial development"). Similarly, "the impetus [for the Supplementary Patent Protection Regulation] came from the enactment of similar legislation in the United States and Japan, to ensure the competitive position of the E.C.'s pharmaceutical industry . . ." (Booy and Horton, 147).

3. See note 2, and note 8.

4. The EU Database Directive and the Duration of Term Directives have reciprocity provisions that limit the ability of United States companies and nationals to take advantage of increased protection given to EU companies and nationals. See Database Directive, art. 11 (sui generis unauthorized-extraction right re-

stricted to EU nationals, companies with habitual residence in the EU, or companies with a registered office in a member state with a continuous link with economy of a member state, 1–2; nationals of other states may get protection when similar protection is granted in their country, 3); Council Directive 93/98 of 29 October 1993, Harmonizing the Term of Protection of Copyright and Certain Related Rights, art. 7(2), 1993 O.J. (L290) 9 (the "rule of shorter term" provision precludes life-plus-seventy-year term to works of U.S. companies and nationals).

5. Copyright doctrine for the most part rejects the view that authors are entitled to protection from the very fact of creation. Rather, the doctrine states that copyright laws are designed to primarily benefit the public by providing incentives to creation. Under this view, the benefits authors receive from the copyright laws are a means to an end and not the end in itself. See, for example, *Sony Corp. v. Universal City Studios, Inc.*, 464 U.S. 417, 429 (1984) ("Monopoly privileges that Congress may authorize are neither unlimited nor primarily designed to provide a special private benefit. Rather, the limited grant is a means by which an important public purpose may be achieved"); *United States v. Paramount Pictures, Inc.*, 334 U.S. 131, 158 (1948) ("Copyright law . . . makes reward to the owner a secondary consideration"); *Fox Film Corp. v. Doyal*, 286 U.S. 123, 127 (1932) ("Sole interest of the United States and the primary object in conferring the monopoly lie in the general benefits derived by the public from the labors of authors").

In John Locke's view of natural law, a person's individual effort or labor created an individual property interest. Natural law did not require balancing the laborer's property right against anyone else's needs as long as there was enough raw material left for others: "The labor of his body and the work of his hands . . . are properly his. Whatsoever then he removes out of the state that nature has provided and left it in, he has mixed his labor with, and joined to it something that is his own, and thereby makes it his property. . . . For this labor being the unquestionable property of the laborer, no [person] but he can have a right to what that is once joined to, at least where there is enough and as good left in common for others" (John Locke, *The Second Treatise of Government*, edited by Thomas P. Peardon (Indianapolis: Bobbs-Merrill, 1952), sec. 26–27 [1690]). For analyses of John Locke's natural-law theory in the context of intellectual property see Wendy J. Gordon, "A Property Right in Self-Expression: Equality and Individualism in the Natural Law of Intellectual Property," *Yale Law Journal* 102 (1993): 1533; Alfred C. Yen, "Restoring the Natural Law: Copyright as Labor and Possession," *Ohio State Law Journal* 51 (1990): 517.

6. Concerning this analogy, the author refers to priesthoods in ancient Greek and Roman times and not ones as found today.

7. In addition to teaching copyright law, this author has taught constitutional law, constitutional criminal law, antitrust, federal courts, EU intellectual property law, and trademark law. The author finds copyright law to be the most intellectually challenging.

8. The reasons for protecting computer programs as literary works had much

to do with the fact that this was the regime in the United States, and all countries adhering to the Berne Convention already had protection for literary works in place. This tradition of protection worked well in the early judicial protection of computer programs. See *Whelan Assoc. v. Jaslow Dental Lab. Inc.*, 797 F.2d 1222 (3d Cir. 1986), *cert. denied*, 479 U.S. 1031 (1987). But see *Computer Assoc. Int'l v. Altai Inc.*, 928 F.2d 693 (2d Cir. 1992). A sui generis regime, on the other hand, would require adoption of a new law by every country in the world. This would follow endless debate on the multilateral level on what and how much to protect. The result would be an uncertain future as to what, if anything, would make it into the national laws, without much hope of uniformity. Even a world of relatively low protection such as that advanced in *Altai* would be preferable.

Regarding protection, investment, and jobs, see note 2, European competitiveness. The Database Directive is also intended to provide protection for expanded industries and, thus, revenue for the EU countries. Recently, a member of the European Parliament's Legal Affairs Committee, Ana Palacio Vallelersundi (Spain), stated that she hoped that "the level of protection afforded by the [directive] and its application throughout the [EU] internal market will help to strengthen investment in this key sector and to create jobs" ("Euro-Parliament Approves Legislation on Copyright Protection of Databases," *World Intellectual Property Rep.* 10 [BNA] [February 1996]: 43). The Group of Seven ministerial conference, organized by the European Commission last February, concluded that "high levels of legal and technical protection of creative content" will be essential to ensure the "necessary climate for the investment needed for the development of the information society." The [United States] has always had strong copyright laws, allowing producers to enjoy full control over the exploitation of films. The alliance [of European film producers] argues this has been a significant factor in the strength of the [United States] in the global entertainment market (Robert Rice, "Gunning for the Pirates: The Film Industry Faces New Concerns over Copyright," *Financial Times*, 6 February 1996).

"National treatment" is a phrase that means that in country X a work originating in a foreign country will be given the same protection as works created in country X. "Reciprocity" means that in country X a work of foreign origin will only be given the protection to which that work is entitled in its country of origin.

9. Semiconductor Chip Act, 17 U.S.C. sec. 901, 902(a) (1), 914 (1995).

10. See note 4.

11. Berne Convention for the Protection of Literary and Artistic Works, 9 September 1886, as last revised 24 July 1971, art. 7(8), 828 U.N.T.S. 221. See also TRIPS, note 1, art. 3, 33 I.L.M. at 1199.

12. S. 483, 104th Cong., 2d Sess. (1995); H.R. 989, 104th Cong., 2d Sess. (1995).

13. John M. Keynes, *A Tract on Monetary Policy* (New York: Harcourt, Brace and Co., 1924), 88.

14. It is no response to this illustration, as a speaker said at a recent conference at the New York University School of Law, that the Supreme Court held that home-taping is legal in *Sony Corp. of America v. Universal City Studios, Inc.*, 464

U.S. 417 (1984) (Engelberg Center on Innovation Law and Policy, "The Culture and Economics of Participation in an International Intellectual Property Regime," 12 March 1996 [unpublished roundtable discussion]). First, the Supreme Court in a five to four decision only held that "time-shifting" is a fair use; it did not reach the issue of whether "librarying" is a fair use, which is the home-taping practice analogous to buying or shoplifting a videocassette. Moreover, there were not five votes for holding that librarying was a fair use. See Jonathan Band and Andrew J. McLaughlin, "The Marshall Papers: A Peek behind the Scenes at the Making of *Sony v. Universal*," *Columbia-VLA Journal of Law and Arts* 7 (1993): 427 (key to Justices Brennan and O'Connor's concurrence was lack of harm in time-shifting). Second, consumers were home-taping long before *Sony* was decided in the Supreme Court and after the Ninth Circuit in *Sony* had held that home-taping was a violation of copyright law. Home-taping, therefore, was not the result of the Supreme Court's decision, however construed by the public. Third, even if the Court had ruled that home-taping for all purposes was a fair use, this would only have shown that a majority of the Court shared the same relative valuation of tangible and intellectual property as the consuming public. It would reinforce the point in the text, not refute it.

15. See Uruguay Round Agreements Act, Pub. L. No. 103–465, 108 Stat. 4809 (1994) [hereinafter URAA].

16. U.S. Constitution, art. I., 8, cl. 8.

17. *Feist Publications v. Rural Telephone Service Co.*, 499 U.S. 340 (1991).

18. Melville B. Nimmer, *Nimmer on Copyright* (New York: M. Bendor, 1975), chap. 1. "It appears from examining a 1975 version of the treatise that the constitutional problems in copyright law were discussed in the treatise at least as of 1972, and may have been discussed as early as when it was first published in 1963."

For instance, no litigant, amicus curiae, or commentator raised, or discussed with regard to *Community for Creative Non-Violence v. Reid*, 490 U.S. 730 (1989), the issue that the work-made-for-hire doctrine, which bypasses the creator and calls the employer or hiring party the "author," is a legal fiction that violates the "author" requirement of U.S. Constitution, art. I., 8, cl. 8. See Nimmer, *Nimmer on Copyright*, 6.3.

19. For example, in broadly worded opinions, the Supreme Court in *Sears, Roebuck & Co. v. Stiffel Co.*, 376 U.S. 225 (1964), and *Compco Corp. v. Day-Brite Lighting*, 376 U.S. 234 (1964), seemed to preempt much of the law of unfair competition and bar protection for three-dimensional trademarks. In *Compco* the Court stated: That an article copied from an unpatented article could be made in some other way, that the design is "nonfunctional" and not essential to the use of either article, that the configuration of the article copied may have a "secondary meaning," which identifies the maker to the trade, or that there may be "confusion" among purchasers as to which article is which or as to who is the maker, may be relevant evidence in applying a state's law requiring such precautions as labeling; however, and regardless of the copier's motives, neither these facts nor any others can furnish a basis for imposing liability for or prohibiting the actual

acts of copying and selling (376 U.S. at 238). Lower courts largely ignored these two cases and, twelve years later, the Eighth Circuit held, in effect, that both Supreme Court opinions consisted entirely of dicta. See *Truck Equip. Service Co. v. Fruehauf Corp.,* 536 F.2d 1210, 1214 (8th Cir. 1976). Of course, the Supreme Court also ignored the above language and the policies espoused in *Sears* and *Compco* when it held not only that three-dimensional trade dress could be protected with secondary meaning but that such trade dress could be protected without secondary meaning (*Two Pesos, Inc. v. Taco Cabana, Inc.,* 112 S.Ct. 2753, 2758 [1992]). While *Two Pesos* was decided under 43(a) of the Lanham Act, 15 U.S.C. sec. 1125(a) (1994), there was no indication by the Court that state unfair competition or trademark law, which first protected trade dress, could not continue to do so.

20. In *Mazer v. Stein,* 347 U.S. 201, 217 (1954), the Court interpreted (manipulated) the "explanation/use" holding of *Baker v. Selden,* 101 U.S. 99, 104 (1879), which would have prevented the protection for applied art, to merely state that the "protection is given only to the expression of the idea—not the idea itself." In *Campbell v. Acuff-Rose Music, Inc.,* 114 S. Ct. 1164 (1994), the Court took the statement in *Sony Corporation of America v. Universal City Studios, Inc.,* 464 U.S. 417, 449 (1984), that if the allegedly infringing device "were used to make copies for a commercial or profit-making purpose, such use would presumptively be unfair" to stand only for the proposition that commercial use "is a factor that tends to weigh against a finding of fair use." See also the discussion of *Sears* and *Compco* and *Two Pesos,* in note 19. Perhaps the Court applied a better policy in the later cases, but it is clear that deference was not given to its earlier pronouncements.

21. *U.S. Payphone, Inc. v. Executives Unltd. of Durham, Inc.,* 18 U.S.P.Q. 2d 2049, 2050 (4th Cir. 1991) (per curiam) (unpublished opinion not subject to citation in Fourth Circuit) (reference guidebook that provided information for coin-operated telephone market including fifty-one-page section on state tariffs infringed when defendants copied this section verbatim). The court stated, "The evidence suggests that the Tariff Section could have been organized in many different ways and that Payphone expended a great deal of time creating the single-page-per-view format. The Guide, according to Payphone, is the result of hundreds of hours of reviewing, analyzing, and interpreting state tariffs and regulations" (*U.S. Payphone*).

22. See Copyrights, Designs and Patents Act of 1988, chap. 48, 164 (U.K.) (copyright protection for acts of Parliament); *BBC v. Time Out,* 1984 F.S.R. 64 (copyright protection for television listings); Broadcasting Act of 1990, chap. 2, 176 and sched. 17 (U.K.) (compulsory licenses for television listings).

23. *The Times* (London) reported this along with the fact that the Bennett production was not subject to copyright restraints (Emma Wilkins, "Toad Escapes Clutches of Copyright Law," *The Times* [London], 26 December 1995).

24. See John Authers, "Paying for Education: Government and Opposition Party Agree to Postpone Highly Contentious Issue," *Financial Times,* 20 February 1996 ("acute crisis" in U.K. university funding).

25. See, for example, Law No. 85–660, 1985 J.O. 7495 (14 July 1985) (Fr.) (U.S. producers and performers excluded from claiming on the producers' and performances' share by application of "first fixation in France requirement"—claims must be on works or performances first fixed in a tangible form and edited in France).

In 1988, at the urging of the European Commission (the commission), the European Telecommunications Standards Institute (ETSI) was created to become the pan-European standard-setting body in the telecommunications field. In March 1993, ETSI determined that its members should agree, as a condition of membership, to license their intellectual property rights for all standards that ETSI approved. Such licensing would be governed by the terms of ETSI's Intellectual Property Rights (IPR) Policy and Undertaking scheme (the IPR Undertaking or the Undertaking). Many IP owners viewed the Undertaking as a device to require the owners of valuable intellectual property to license at low costs and without cross-licensing to those with less valuable intellectual property. Most of those who would be required to license were U.S. corporations and most of those who would have received were Europeans. ETSI had adopted the IPR Undertaking despite a formal communication from the European Commission, which disapproved of involuntary use of IP in standard-making proceedings. Communication from the Commission: Intellectual Property Rights and Standardization, COM (92) 445 final (Oct. 27, 1992). In response to ETSI's adoption of the Undertaking, the Computer and Business Equipment Manufacturers Association (CBEMA) filed an antitrust complaint against ETSI with the commission, supported by the Business Software Alliance (BSA) and others. The commission's initial review found problems with the ETSI Undertaking and, on reconsideration, ETSI scrapped the Undertaking in August 1994 and determined to develop a new IPR policy. For a full discussion of the ETSI standardization debate and the policies involved, see Alan N. Dixon, "The ETSI Complaint and the European Commission's Communication on Standardization," in *International Intellectual Property Law and Policy*, vol. 1, edited by Hugh C. Hansen (forthcoming 1996), chap. 39.

26. This is not to say that the United States considers proceedings in WIPO to be not worthwhile. It is actively seeking solutions for the interplay of intellectual property and the global information infrastructure through a protocol to the Berne Convention. See World Intellectual Property Organization, Committee of Experts on a Possible Protocol to the Berne Convention, Draft Report (1996).

27. See TRIPS, note 1; J. H. Reichman, "Universal Minimum Standards of Intellectual Property Protection under the TRIPS Component of the WTO Agreement," *International Lawyer* 29 (1995): 382–88.

28. See 19 U.S.C. sec. 2241–42, 2411 (1994). The willingness of the United States to use 301 is evidenced by the recent amendments under URAA (see note 15) 314(c) (1), which allow a 301 proceeding to be brought "notwithstanding the fact that the foreign country may be in compliance with the specific obligations of the [TRIPS] Agreement" (See Reichman, "Universal," at 384).

29. See note 4.

30. See, for example, Seth Faison, "Copyright Pirates Prosper in China Despite Promises," *New York Times,* 20 February 1996.

Part III

Information and Digital Technology

11

Why Software Should Be Free*

Richard Stallman

Introduction

In the time that I've worked as a programmer, I've watched the field change from one of cooperation and sharing, where people could reuse previous work to advance the state of the art, to one in which cooperation is largely forbidden by trade secrecy and sharing is illegal.

These events led me to ask myself, as a software designer, what I should do with the software I develop in order to benefit humanity the most. In particular, I asked the question of whether it was ethical to make software proprietary.

Most people in the field do not ask this question. Usually they consider only whether it is profitable to do this, and compare the legal or other methods for doing so. In other words, they ask what developing software can do for them. But this selfishness is an unworthy goal for an ethical person. Following John F. Kennedy, we must ask what we, as programmers together, can do for the freedom of mankind. We must ask what we ought to do, not just what is profitable.

This question cannot be answered in terms of current law. The law should conform to ethics, not the other way around. Nor does current

---

*This essay was originally published as "Why Software Should Be Free," by Richard Stallman, in *Computers, Ethics, and Social Values,* edited by Deborah Johnson and Helen Nissenbaum (Englewood Cliffs, N.J.: Prentice-Hall, 1995). Copyright © 1990 by the Free Software Foundation, Inc. Verbatim copying and redistribution is permitted without royalty.

practice answer this question, although it is sometimes the start of an answer.

The only way to judge this question is to see who is helped and who is hurt by recognizing owners of software, why, and how much. In other words, we should perform a cost-benefit analysis on behalf of society as a whole, taking account of individual freedom as well as production of material goods.

In this chapter, I will describe the effects of having owners, and show that this is bad for society. My conclusion is that I and other programmers have the duty to encourage others to share, redistribute, study, and improve the software we write: in other words, to write free software. (The word "free" here refers to freedom, not to price.)

How Owners Try to Justify Their Demands

Those who benefit from the current system where programs are property offer two arguments in support of their claims to own programs: the emotional argument and the economic argument.

The emotional argument goes like this: "I put my sweat, my heart, my soul into this program. It comes from me, it's mine!"

This argument does not require serious refutation. The feeling of attachment is one that people can cultivate when it suits them, but is not inevitable. Consider, for example, how willingly the same authors usually sign over all rights to a large corporation for a salary; the attachment mysteriously vanishes. By comparison consider the great artists and artisans of medieval times, who didn't even sign their names to their work. To them, the name of the artist was not important. What mattered was that the work was done—and the purpose it would serve. This view prevailed for hundreds of years.

The economic argument goes like this: "I want to get rich (usually described inaccurately as 'making a living'), and if you don't allow me to get rich by programming, then I won't program. Everyone else is like me, so nobody will ever program. And then you'll be stuck with no programs at all!" This threat is usually veiled as friendly advice from the wise.

I'll explain later why this threat is a bluff. First I want to address an implicit assumption that is more visible in another formulation of the argument.

This form of the argument starts by comparing the social utility of a proprietary program with that of no program, and then concludes that proprietary software development is, on the whole, beneficial, and should be encouraged. The fallacy here is in comparing only two outcomes: proprietary software versus no software. These are not the only alternatives.

In our current system, software development is usually linked with deliberate obstruction by an owner of its use. As long as this linkage exists we are often faced with the choice of proprietary software or none. However, this linkage is not inherent or inevitable; it is a consequence of the specific social/legal policy decision that we are questioning: the decision to have owners. To formulate the choice as between proprietary software versus no software is to presuppose this decision. That is begging the question.

The Argument against Having Owners

The question at hand is "Should development of software be linked with having owners to restrict the use of it?"

In order to decide this, we have to judge the effect on society of each of those two activities *independently*: the effect of developing the software (regardless of its terms of distribution), and the effect of restricting its use (assuming the software has been developed). If one of these activities is helpful and the other is harmful, we would be better off dropping the linkage and doing only the helpful one.

To put it another way, if restricting the use of a program already developed is harmful to society overall, then an ethical software developer will not do it except in extremity.

To determine the effect of restricting use, we need to compare the value to society of a restricted (i.e., proprietary) program with that of the same program, available to everyone.

To elucidate this argument, let's apply it in another area: road construction. It would be possible to fund the construction of all roads with tolls. This would entail having toll booths at most street corners. Such a system would provide a great incentive to improve roads. It would also have the virtue of causing the users of any given road to pay for that road. However, a toll booth is an artificial obstruction to smooth driving—gratuitous, because it is not a consequence of how roads or cars work.

Comparing free roads and toll roads by their usefulness, we find that (all else being equal) roads without toll booths are cheaper to construct, cheaper to run, safer, and more satisfying and efficient to use. The conclusion is that toll booths (i.e., obstructions to use which are relaxed for a fee) are a bad way to raise funds for road construction. Use of roads, once built, should be free.

The advocates of toll booths would consider them simply a matter of how to raise funds for the road, but this is incorrect. They also degrade the road. The toll road is not as good as the free road; giving us more or technically superior roads may not be an improvement if this means substituting toll roads for free roads.

The issues of pollution and traffic congestion do not alter this conclusion. If we wish to make driving more expensive to discourage driving in general, it is disadvantageous to do this using toll booths, which contribute to both pollution and congestion. Likewise, a desire to enhance safety by limiting maximum speed is not relevant; a free access road enhances the average speed by avoiding stops and delays, for any given speed limit.

Of course, the construction of a free road does cost money, which the public must somehow pay. However, this does not imply the inevitability of toll booths. We who must pay in either case should at least get full value for our money: a free road instead of a toll road.

Note that this argument does not involve a claim that a toll road is worse than no road at all. That would be true if the toll is so great that hardly anyone uses the road—but this is unlikely. However, as long as the toll booths cause significant waste and inconvenience, it is better to raise the funds in a less obstructive fashion.

To apply the same argument to software development, I will now show that having "toll booths" for useful software programs costs society dearly: it makes the programs more expensive to construct, more expensive to distribute, and less satisfying and efficient to use. It will follow that program construction should be encouraged in some other way. In the following sections I'll go on to explain other ways in which development can be encouraged and (to the extent actually necessary) funded.

The Harm Done by Obstructing Software

Consider for a moment that a program has been developed, and any necessary payments for its development have been made; now society must choose either to make it proprietary or allow free sharing and use.

Assuming that the program is one whose very existence is not harmful, and ignoring the consequences of linking this decision with software development, restrictions on the distribution and modification of the program cannot facilitate its use. They can only interfere. So the effect can only be negative. But how much? And what kind?

Three different levels of material harm come from such obstruction:

1. Fewer people use the program.
2. None of the users can adapt or fix the program.

3. Other developers cannot learn from the program, or base new work on it.

Each level of material harm has a concomitant form of psychosocial harm. This refers to the effect that people's decisions have on their subsequent feelings, attitudes, and predispositions. These changes in people's ways of thinking will then have a further effect on their relationships with their fellow citizens, and can have material consequences.

The first two levels of material harm waste part of the value that the program could contribute, but they cannot reduce it to zero. If they waste nearly all the value of the program, then writing the program harms society by at most the effort that went into writing the program. Arguably a program that is profitable to sell must provide some net direct material benefit.

However, taking account of the third level of material harm, and the various kinds of psychosocial harm, there is no limit to the harm that proprietary software development can do.

Obstruction of Use

The first level of harm impedes the simple use of a program. A copy of a program has nearly zero marginal cost (and you can pay this cost by doing the work yourself), so in a free market, it would have nearly zero price. A license fee is a significant disincentive to use the program. If a widely useful program is proprietary, far fewer people will use it.

But this does not reduce the amount of work it takes to develop the program. As a result, the efficiency of the whole process, in delivered user satisfaction per hour of work, is reduced.

Here is a crucial difference between copies of programs and cars, chairs, or sandwiches. There is no copying machine for material objects outside of science fiction. But programs are easy to copy; anyone can produce as many copies as are wanted, with very little effort. This isn't true for material objects because they are conserved: each new copy has to be built in the same way that the first copy was built.

With material objects, a disincentive to use them makes sense, because fewer objects bought means less raw materials and work needed to make them. It's true that there is usually also a start-up cost, a development cost, which is spread over the production run. But as long as the marginal cost of production is significant, adding a share of the development cost does not make a qualitative difference. It does not require additional restrictions on the freedom of ordinary users.

However, imposing a price on something that would otherwise be free makes a large change. A centrally imposed fee for software distribution becomes a powerful disincentive.

What's more, central copying of software is simply more work than user copying. Central copying involves putting copies on transport media such as floppy disks or tapes, enclosing them in packaging, shipping large numbers of them around the world, and storing them for sale. This cost is presented as an expense of development; in truth, it is part of the waste caused by having owners.

Damaging Social Cohesion

If you want to use a program and your neighbor wants to use the program, then in ethical concern for your neighbor, you should want both of you to have it. You shouldn't be satisfied with a solution where you get it and the neighbor does not.

Signing a typical software license agreement means betraying your neighbors: "I promise to be unfriendly, I promise to tell my neighbors to get stuffed. To hell with everyone else—just give me a copy! Me, me, me!" People who think this way have become bad neighbors: public spirit suffers. This is psychosocial harm associated with the material harm of discouraging use of the program.

Many users unconsciously recognize this, so they decide to ignore the licenses and laws, and share programs anyway. But they feel guilty about doing so, because they haven't considered the matter clearly. They know that they must break the rules in order to be good neighbors, but they still consider the rules authoritative, and they conclude that being a good neighbor is naughty or shameful. That is also a kind of psychosocial harm, which one can escape by deciding that these licenses and laws have no moral force.

Programmers also suffer psychosocial harm knowing that many users will not be allowed to use their work. This leads to a general attitude of cynicism or denial. I have often heard a programmer describe enthusiastically the work that he finds technically exciting; then when I ask him, "Will I be permitted to use it?" his face falls, and he says, "Probably not." But he despairs of changing this, so he makes a joke about how the world is a jungle and one shouldn't expect otherwise, then distracts himself with what he hopes to buy with the proceeds of obstructionism.

Since the age of Reagan, our greatest scarcity is not technical innovation, but rather the willingness to cooperate for the public good. It makes no sense to encourage the former at the expense of the latter.

Obstruction of Custom Adaptation

The second level of material harm is the inability to adapt programs. The ease of modification of software is one of its great advantages over older technology. But most commercially available software isn't available for modification, even if you pay for it. It's available for you to take it or leave it, as a black box—that is all.

A program that you can run consists of a series of numbers whose meaning is obscure. No one, not even a good programmer, can easily change the numbers to make the program do something different.

Programmers normally work with the "source code" for a program, which is text written in a programming language. It contains names for the data being used and for the parts of the program and it represents operations with symbols such as + for addition and − for subtraction. This is because programming languages are designed to help programmers read and change programs.

But you can't do this unless you have the source code. Usually the source code for a proprietary program is kept secret by the owner, lest anybody else learn something from it. This means that only the owner can change the program.

A friend once told me of working as a programmer in a bank for about six months, writing a program similar to something that was commercially available. She thought that if she could have gotten the source code for that commercially available program, it could easily have been adapted to their needs. The bank was willing to pay, but the source code was not available—it was a secret. So she had to do six months of make-work, work that inflates the GNP but was actually wasted.

I have had a similar experience. In the MIT Artificial Intelligence lab, our first graphics printer was the XGP, given to us by Xerox around 1977. It was run by free software to which we added many convenient features. For example, it would send you a message when your document had actually been printed; if there was a paper jam, it would send a message to everyone who had a job in the queue, asking someone to fix the jam.

Later Xerox gave us a newer, faster printer, one of the first laser printers. It was driven by proprietary software that ran in a separate dedicated computer, so we couldn't add any of our favorite features. We could arrange to send you a notification that "Your document has been sent," but that just meant it was sent to the dedicated computer. There was no way to find out when the job was actually printed: you could only guess. And no one was informed when there was a paper jam, so the printer might sit for an hour without being fixed. People would send jobs to the printer, receive the "has been sent" message, and then wait for an hour before looking for the output. So nobody would notice the jam.

The system programmers at the AI lab were capable of fixing such problems, probably as capable as the original authors of the program. But it was profitable for Xerox to prevent us, so we could do nothing but suffer. The problems were never fixed.

Most good programmers I have met have experienced the frustration of using a program whose deficiencies they were forbidden to correct. The bank could afford to cover the expense of circumventing this obstacle, but a typical user would simply have to give up.

Giving up causes psychosocial harm—to the spirit of self-reliance, which used to be prized in America. It is demoralizing to live in a house that you cannot rearrange to suit your needs. You come to say, "Yes, this system isn't what we want, but we'll never be able to change it. We'll just have to suffer." People who feel this way do not do good work and do not have happy lives.

Imagine what it would be like if recipes were hoarded in the same fashion as software. You'd say, "How do I change this recipe to take out the salt?" and the great chef would say, "How dare you insult my recipe, the child of my brain and my palate, by trying to tamper with it? You don't have the judgment to change my recipe and make it work right!"

"But my doctor says I'm not supposed to eat salt! What can I do? Will you take out the salt for me?"

"I would be glad to do that; my fee is only $50,000." Since the owner has a monopoly on changes, the fee tends to be large. "However, right now I don't have time. I am busy with a commission to design a new form of ship's biscuit for the Navy Department. I might get around to you in about two years."

Obstruction of Further Advances

The third level of material harm affects software development. Software development used to be an evolutionary process, where a person would take a program and rewrite parts of it for one new feature, and then another person would rewrite parts to add another feature; this could continue over a period of twenty years. Meanwhile, parts of the program would be "cannibalized" to form the beginnings of other programs.

The existence of owners prevents this kind of evolution, making it necessary to start from scratch when developing a program. It also prevents new practitioners from studying existing programs to learn useful techniques or even how large programs can be structured.

Owners also obstruct education. I have met bright students in computer science who have never seen the source code of a large program. They may be good at writing small programs, but they can't begin to learn the different skills of writing large ones if they can't see how others have successfully done it.

In any kind of intellectual field, progress is built by standing on the shoulders of others. That's no longer generally allowed in the software field—you can only stand on the shoulders of the other people *in your own company.*

The associated psychosocial harm affects the spirit of scientific cooperation, which used to be so strong that scientists would cooperate even when their countries were at war. In this spirit, Japanese oceanographers abandoning their lab on an island in the Pacific carefully preserved their work for the invading American army, and left a note explaining its purpose.

Conflict among individuals has destroyed what international conflict spared. Nowadays, I am told, scientists in many fields don't publish enough in their papers to enable you to replicate the experiment. They publish only enough to enable you to marvel at how much they were able to do. This is certainly true in computer science, where the source code for the programs reported on is usually secret.

It Does Not Matter How Sharing Is Restricted

I have been discussing the effects of preventing people from copying, changing, and building on a program. I have not specified how this restriction is carried out, because it doesn't affect the conclusion. Whether it is done by copy protection, or copyright, or licenses, or encryption, or ROM cards, or hardware serial numbers, if it succeeds in preventing use, it does harm.

Users do consider some of these methods more obnoxious than others. I suggest that the methods most hated are those that accomplish their objective.

Software Should Be Free

I have shown how ownership of a program—the power to restrict changing or copying it—is obstructive. Its negative effects are widespread and important. It follows that society shouldn't have owners for programs.

Why People Will Develop Software

If we eliminate this method of encouraging people to develop software, at first less software will be developed, but that software will be more widely available. It is not clear whether the overall delivered user satisfaction will be less; but if it is, or if we wish to increase it anyway, there are other ways to encourage development, just as there are ways besides toll booths to raise money for streets. Before I talk about how that can be done, first I want to question how much artificial encouragement is truly necessary.

Programming Is Fun

There are some lines of work that no one will enter except for money—road construction, for example. There are other fields of study and art in which there is little chance to become rich, which people enter for their fascination or their perceived value to society. Examples include mathematical logic, classical music, and archaeology, and political organizing among working people. People compete, more sadly than bitterly, for the few funded positions available, none of which is funded very well. They may even pay for the chance to work in the field, if they can afford to.

Such a field can transform itself overnight if it begins to offer the possibility of getting rich. This has happened in the field of software, and also that of genetics. When one worker gets rich, others demand the same opportunity. Soon you will find that no one is willing to work in the field without a clear shot at getting rich. Another couple of years go by, and people will deride the very idea. They will advise social planners to assume that work can never be done in this field unless workers have the chance to get rich; and they will prescribe special privileges, powers, and monopolies as necessary to ensure them this chance.

This change happened in the field of computer programming in the past decade. Fifteen years ago, there were articles on "computer addiction": users were "on-lining" and had hundred-dollar-a-week habits. It was generally understood that people loved programming enough to break up their marriages. Today, it is generally understood that no one would program without an exorbitant rate of pay. People have forgotten what they knew fifteen years ago.

It may be true at one moment that people will work in a field only for high pay, but it need not remain true. The dynamic of change can run backward as effectively as forward. If we were to take away the possibility of great wealth, then after a while, when the people had readjusted their attitudes, they would once again be eager to work in the field for the joy of discovery.

Funding Free Software

The question "How can we pay programmers?" becomes an easier question when we realize that it's not a matter of paying them a fortune. A mere living is easier to raise.

Institutions that pay programmers do not have to be software houses. Many other institutions already exist that can do this.

Hardware manufacturers must support software development even if they cannot restrict its use. In 1970, much of their software was free because they did not consider restricting it. Today, their increasing willingness to join consortiums shows that they are realizing that owning the software is not what is really important for them.

For example, universities conduct many programming projects. Today, they often sell the results, but in the 1970s, they did not. Is there any doubt that universities would develop free software if they were not allowed to sell software? These projects could be supported by the same government contracts and grants that now support proprietary software development.

It is common today for university researchers to get grants to develop a system, develop it nearly to the point of completion, and call that "finished," and then start companies where they really finish the project and make it usable. Sometimes they declare the unfinished version "free"; if they are thoroughly corrupt, they instead get an exclusive license from the university. This is not a secret; it is openly admitted by everyone concerned. Yet if the researchers were not exposed to the temptation to do these things, they would still do their work.

Programmers can also make their living as I have for six years: by making custom improvements to free software. I have been hired to port the GNU C compiler to new hardware, and to make user-interface extensions to Emacs. (I offer these improvements to the public once they are done.) There is now a successful corporation that operates in this manner.

New institutions such as the Free Software Foundation can also fund programmers. Most of our funds come from people buying tapes through the mail. The software on the tapes is all free, which means that every user has the freedom to copy it and change it, but many people will still pay to get a copy. (Recall that "free software refers to freedom, not to price.") Some people order tapes who already have a copy, as a way of making a contribution they feel we deserve. We are also getting increasing amounts of donations from computer manufacturers.

The Free Software Foundation is a charity, and its income is spent on hiring as many programmers as possible. If it had been set up as a business, offering the same products to the public, it would provide a very good living for its founder.

Because the Foundation is a charity, programmers often work for the Foundation for half of what they could make elsewhere. They do this because we are free of bureaucratic silliness, and because they feel better about themselves, knowing that their work will not be prevented from benefiting humanity to the fullest of its potential. Most of all, they do it because programming is fun. In addition, increasing numbers of volunteers write useful programs for us. (Recently even technical writers have begun to volunteer.)

This confirms that programming is among the most fascinating of all fields, along with music and art. We don't have to fear that no one will want to program.

What Do Users Owe to Developers?

There is a good reason for users of software to feel a moral obligation to contribute to its support. Developers of free software are contributing to the users' activities, and it is both fair and in the long-term interest of the users to give them funds to continue.

However, this does not apply to proprietary software, since obstructionism deserves a punishment rather than a reward.

We thus have a paradox: the developer of useful software is entitled to the support of the users, but any attempt to turn this moral obligation into a requirement destroys the basis for the obligation. A developer can either deserve a reward or demand it, but not both.

I believe that an ethical developer faced with this paradox must act so as to deserve the reward, but should also entreat the users for voluntary donations. Eventually the users will learn to support developers without coercion, just as they have learned to support public radio and television stations.

What Is "Software Productivity"?

If software were free, there would still be programmers, but perhaps fewer of them. Would this be bad for society?

Not necessarily. Today we have fewer farmers than in 1990, but we do not think this is bad for society, because the few deliver more food to the consumers than the many used to do. We call this improved productivity. Free software would require far fewer programmers to satisfy the demand, because of increased software productivity at all levels:

- Wider use of each program that is developed
- The ability to adapt existing programs for customization instead of starting from scratch
- Better education of programmers
- The elimination of duplicate development effort

When people object to cooperation because it would result in the employment of fewer programmers, they are actually objecting to increased productivity. Yet these people usually accept the widely held belief that the software industry needs increased productivity. How is this?

"Software productivity" can mean two different things: the overall productivity of all software development, or the productivity of individual projects. Overall productivity is what society would like to improve, and the most straightforward way to do this is to eliminate the artificial obstacles to cooperation that reduce it. But researchers who study the field of "software productivity" focus only on the second, limited, sense of the term, where improvement requires difficult technological advances.

Is Competition Inevitable?

Is it inevitable that people will try to compete, to surpass their rivals in society? Perhaps it is. But competition itself is not harmful; the harmful thing is combat.

There are many ways to compete. Competition can consist of trying to achieve ever more, to outdo what others have done. For example, in the old days, there was competition among hackers—competition for who could make the computer do the most amazing or pretty thing, or for who could make the shortest or fastest program for a given task. This kind of competition can benefit everyone, as long as the spirit of good sportsmanship is maintained.

Constructive competition is enough competition to motivate people to great efforts. For example, a number of people are competing to be the first to have visited all the countries on earth. They even spend fortunes trying to do this. But I have not heard that they bribe ship captains to strand their rivals on desert islands. They are content to let the best man win.

Competition becomes combat when the competitors begin trying to impede each other instead of advancing themselves—when "Let the best man win" gives way to "Let me win, best or not." Proprietary software is harmful, not because it is a form of competition, but because it is a form of combat among the citizens of our society.

Competition in business is not necessarily combat. For example, when two grocery stores compete, their entire effort is to improve their own operations, not to sabotage the rival. But this is not due to any ethical commitment; it simply happens that there is nothing much to be gained from combat in this line of business. Such is not true in all areas of business. Withholding information that could help everyone advance is a form of combat.

American business ideology does not prepare people to resist the temptation to combat the competition. Some forms of combat have been made illegal with antitrust laws, truth in advertising laws, and so on, but rather than generalizing this to reject combat in general, executives invent other forms of combat that are not specifically prohibited. Our society's resources are being squandered on economic civil war.

"Why Don't You Move to Russia?"

Any advocate of other than the most extreme form of laissez-faire selfishness has often heard this question. The idea that citizens should have aims other than purely selfish ones is identified in America with communism. But how similar are they?

Communism as practiced in the Soviet Union is (or at least was until recently) a system of central control where all activity is regimented, supposedly for the common good. And where copying equipment was closely guarded to prevent illegal copying.

The American system of intellectual property exercises central control over distribution of a program, and guards copying equipment with automatic copying protection schemes to prevent illegal copying.

By contrast, I advocate a system where people are free to decide their own actions; in particular, free to help their neighbors, and free to alter and improve the objects that they use in their daily lives. A system based on voluntary cooperation, and decentralization. Clearly it is the software owners, if anyone, who ought to move to Russia.

Conclusion

We like to think that helping your neighbor is as American as apple pie; but each time we reward someone for obstructionism, or admire them for the wealth they have gained in this way, we are sending the opposite message.

Software hoarding is one form of our general willingness to disregard the welfare of society for personal gain. We can trace this disregard through all of society, from Ronald Reagan to Ivan Boesky, from Jim Bakker to Exxon, from the Walker family to Neil Bush. This spirit feeds on itself, because the more we see that other people will not help us, the more it seems futile to help them. Thus society decays into a jungle.

If we don't want to live in a jungle, we must change our attitudes. We must start sending the message that a good citizen is one who cooperates when appropriate, not one that is successful at taking from others. I hope that the free software movement will contribute to this: at least in one area, we will replace the jungle with a more efficient system that encourages and runs on voluntary cooperation.

12

The Virtues of Software Ownership*

David H. Carey

Three broad approaches seem to dominate recent work in ethics: the consequentialist, the deontological, and the emphasis on character or virtue. The consequentialist approach evaluates an action (rule, policy, etc.) by its net consequences or effects. On this approach, for example, good policies are those that on balance do more good than harm for the people affected. The deontological approach, in contrast, appeals to universal principles on which a decision should be based rather than the actual outcome of that decision. On this approach, for example, a decision has moral worth if it respects a right, fulfills an obligation, or follows from a duty. Typically, such rights, obligations, or duties have a universal and necessary quality; that is, they would hold for anyone in a given situation, even if undesirable consequences would result from recognizing them. Finally, the third approach (that of so-called "virtue ethics") emphasizes long-term, habitual character traits (virtues and vices) rather than actions, policies, or principles.

On consequentialist grounds, for instance, one might argue that if allowing some algorithms to be patented benefits society in the long run more than it costs society temporarily to forgo unrestricted use of those algorithms, then such patents are morally defensible.[1] The consequentialist approach reflects the spirit and motivation of U.S. law more than the

---

*This essay was originally published as "The Virtues of Software Ownership," by David H. Carey, in *Software Ownership and Intellectual Property Rights,* edited by Walter Maner and John L. Fodor (New Haven: Research Center on Computing & Society, 1992). Copyright © 1992 by the Research Center on Computing & Society. Reprinted with permission of publisher.

other two approaches do. In contrast, elsewhere in the world (among other signatories to the Berne Convention), intellectual property laws smack more of deontology. The French, for instance, appeal to what they call *droits morals* such as *paternité*—the inherent right of a creator to control the treatment of his or her creation, analogous to the alleged right that parents have with respect to their own children. On this approach, to infringe on a copyright is to violate a personal right, not merely to fail to uphold a social bargain.

Here, however, I want to take the third approach, which emphasizes character traits, virtues. My reasons for taking this approach are twofold: First, of the three approaches just outlined, virtue ethics has the most venerable pedigree, tracing its development from the earliest days of philosophy among the ancient Greeks. (I suspect a similar pedigree may be found in non-Western thought, but I am here focusing my attention on Western traditions of ethics.) Second is the belief that moral discourse should indicate not merely what is permissible but also what is noble. While I uphold the permissibility, the justification, of intellectual property laws applied to computational resources, I also applaud the nobility of a character like Richard Stallman's.[2] So, for example, I am both willing to defend AT&T's rights to its Karmarkar algorithm and, at the same time, to challenge its executives, directors, and shareholders to be generous in permitting its liberal use. Since I am focusing on virtue ethics here, my concern is not so much for the goodness, fairness, and coherence of an intellectual property system as with the goodness, fairness, and integrity of individual persons. Systems, as analogues of persons, may have virtues, too, but my focus here will be on the characters of people.[3]

Specifically, my guiding question is this: How might a virtue-centered ethics in the Aristotelian-Thomistic tradition bolster Stallman's position philosophically? Several years ago (1987), Stallman gave a talk at the University of Texas, a transcript of which was widely circulated on e-mail lists and bulletin boards (see also chapter 11). In this talk he referred to "spiritual harm" that results from placing some intellectual property restrictions on software:

The spiritual harm comes from the nondisclosure agreements and licenses that people sign, because each buyer is asked to betray his neighbors. If you want to use a program and your neighbor wants to use the program, the Golden Rule says that you should want both of you to get that program. You shouldn't aim for a solution where you get it and the other people don't, if you want to be a good citizen, that is. And the nondisclosure agreement essentially says "I promise to be a bad citizen—I promise to say 'To hell with my neighbors!' To hell with everyone! Just give me a copy!" And you can see the spiritual effect that has on the community you live in.

I claim that what Stallman calls "spiritual harm" can be understood, and his thesis defended, in terms of the Aristotelian-Thomistic tradition's virtue-centered ethics.

Aristotle claims that it is better (*beltion*) for acquisitions (*tas kteseis*) to be one's own (*idias*), on the one hand, but on the other hand, to make them available to the public (*koinas*) with respect to their use (*tei chresei*—the cognate noun *chreia* and the root verb *chraomai* can connote poverty, need, or want; so we might expand the last phrase to read "with respect to their use by those in need"). He illustrates this claim with the example of Spartans who use one another's slaves, horses, and dogs as if they were their own (*hos eipein idiois*), "even if they have occasion to lack supplies for a journey (*ephodion*—cf. the Latin *viaticum*) in the countryside." Aristotle's concern here is not so much with rights or benefits but with character—that is, with virtue. For immediately he goes on to say that it is a proper function of the lawgiver how citizens become people of this sort (*ginontai toioutoi*—that is, disposed to share their possessions).[4] Later in the same passage he refers to the virtue of liberality (*eleutheriotes*) with respect to possessions (*to peri tas kteseis*): "To give favors and help to loved ones, guest-friends, or colleagues is the sweetest thing (*hediston*), and this is a consequence (*ginetai*) of the possession being one's own (*tes kteseos idias ouses*)." He also notes, in defense of property, that evils attributed to it (such as litigation over breach of contract) are due not so much to the political, economic, or legal system (i.e., the absence of communism—*akoinonesia*) as to human nature or character (wretchedness or wickedness—*mochtheria*).[5]

Echoing Aristotle's discussion, Aquinas asks whether someone may possess something as *propriam*—as one's own.[6] His answer to this question is a pair of theses, based on a distinction between (a) a power to manage and dispense (*potestas procurandi et dispensandi*) and (b) the use (*usus*) of external things (*res exteriores*). The first thesis is that with regard to the power to manage and dispense external things, a human being may possess *propria*. In fact, he says, humans not only may own things, in a certain sense they must (*est etiam necessarium ad humanam vitam*), for three reasons: (1) Everyone is more motivated, more anxious (*magis sollicitus*) to take care of something that concerns oneself alone than something shared by everybody or by a crowd. This reason has as its premise a belief about human laziness (*laborem fugiens*) to the effect that we are inclined to "let the other guy do it" when it comes to shared responsibilities. (2) Human affairs are conducted more ordinately (*ordinatius*) when an individual is saddled with responsibility for taking care of something than they are when anyone who wishes manages anything he wishes indiscriminately (*indistincte*). (3) Peace is better preserved when everybody is contented with his or her "own thing" (*re sua*), in contrast to a state of affairs in which people share something undivided. In the latter case, quarrels more frequently arise. It is interesting for our purposes here that the argument for property has a distinctly consequentialist flavor: If you want to get things done in a peaceful and orderly fashion, divide things up among individuals.

The second thesis, following Aristotle's thought, introduces a more virtue-centered emphasis, however: With regard to use, a human being ought not to hold (*habere*) external things as *propria* but as *communes* (things shared in common). This is so that someone (*aliquis*) may more readily (*de facile*) share them when others need them. The concern here is not merely with meeting needs (consequences) but also (and perhaps more directly) with a character trait, namely, the disposition to help others. This disposition seems to involve both a cognitive habit (holding, that is, considering, external things as *communes*) and a conative one (the readiness to share). While this disposition itself can be valued for a consequentialist reason, namely, the likelihood that in cases of need at least someone will be willing to help the needy by sharing resources, the disposition is also valuable in itself, as a readiness or facility, even when needs don't actually arise.

When the two theses are combined, Aquinas' position is roughly this: Responsibility for material resources should be an individual matter, but access to them should be communal. This does not seem to be far from the socialist slogan, "From each according to his ability, to each according to his need." Both views, the Thomistic and the socialist, seem to ascribe to individuals the burden but not the reward of property. Both views, to be plausible, need a theory of human motivation to undergird them. For the socialist, it may be Marxian doctrine that unalienated productive activity is desirable for its own sake, is its own reward, and indeed is the chief human need. For the Thomist or Aristotelian, it is the eudaimonistic value of virtue: That is, one must be virtuous in order to be happy. Insofar as we all want to be happy, we all have a motive for being virtuous. If virtue with regard to property involves both responsible management and willingness to share with others, then we have a motive for bearing these burdens of stewardship.

So what are the implications of the Aristotelian-Thomistic view for software ownership? A summary answer is that individual ownership can be a good thing insofar as it contributes to an incentive for software development (overcoming the tendency to "let the other guy do the work"), to an orderly division of labor, and to a settled understanding about what one can use and what is off limits. Stallman and others have pointed out many of the ways in which software ownership may in practice fail to optimize these desirable consequences, and these failures should be remedied. In principle, though, intellectual property in software is defensible.

At the same time, defense of property rights is only one side of the issue, and perhaps not the most important side. Another side of the issue, one that seems to call for more attention, is the challenge to owners (or rights-holders) to cultivate the virtues of ownership—what makes ownership excellent and noble, and not merely defensible. Noteworthy among these virtues is the disposition to regard software as destined for the public domain even while it enjoys the temporary protection of intellectual property law. This involves a disposition to put the needs of the public ahead of the desire for personal profit.

Many objections may be made to this view. I want to address one of them here. Adam Smith, in reference to the famous "invisible hand," wrote:

> By pursuing his own interest [the individual] frequently promotes that of the society more effectually than when he really intends to promote it. I have never known much good done by those who affected to trade for the public good. It is an affectation, indeed, not very common among merchants, and very few words need be employed in dissuading them from it.[7]

If one really wants to benefit the public, one might argue, forget about Aristotelian-Thomistic virtue and appeal to the profit motive.

In the light of the foregoing discussion, one may respond to this objection on many levels. First, benefiting the public may be a, or even the only, concern of consequentialist ethics, but it is not the only concern of ethics in general. Notions of rights, duties, obligations, character, virtue, motivation, and happiness must also be addressed. Second, Smith does not (nor does he intend to) give us a complete ethical theory here. He is not even offering (in this passage) a complete economic theory. He does not say that by pursuing his own interest the individual always, invariably, or even typically promotes that of the society more effectually than when he really intends to promote it. Rather, Smith says "frequently." His tone is anecdotal ("I have never known . . ."), not systematic. Indeed, his tone may even be construed as sardonic ("It is an affectation, indeed, not very common among merchants, and very few words need be employed in dissuading them from it"). In any case, mere affectation of concern for the public good is quite distinct from the actual virtue of stewardship, which is a thoroughgoing, stable, perduring disposition deeply involving the springs of motivation and therefore much more likely to be effective in contributing to the public good than mere affectation could ever be. So even if we confine our discussion to consequentialist ethics, the cultivation of Aristotelian-Thomistic virtue may be superior to the profit motive in maximizing social utility. Aquinas' position, of course, depends on many presuppositions the discussion of which would take us far afield here, but so does Smith's. The metaphysical reality of the "invisible hand" may be as elusive to empirical investigation as the *summum bonum* of Thomistic ethics. But to the extent that my response here is an invocation of the noble, Aquinas, I think, has the edge.

Notes

1. The League for Programming Freedom's paper "Against Software Patents" has persuaded me that many software patents ought not to have been granted and therefore should be invalidated, but I see no reason in principle why all algorithms should be excluded from patent protection; it may make sense to patent some algorithms or programs. The League for Programming Freedom partially agrees; they say, "We do not claim that every single software patent is necessarily harmful. Careful study might show that under certain specific and narrow conditions (necessarily excluding the vast majority of cases) it is beneficial to grant software patents." Yet they think that in general software patents have been so harmful that "the right thing to do now is to eliminate all software patents as soon as possible, before more damage is done. The careful study can come afterward."

2. Called "the last of the hackers" by Steven Levy (*Hackers: Heroes of the Computer Revolution* [New York: Dell Publishing Co., 1984], Epilogue), he opposes software ownership on principle and has been working for years to develop a complete, top-quality software library known as "GNU" (a recursive acronym for "GNU's Not UNIX") and make it available to the world free of charge. Recently, *The Wall Street Journal* (in a special report on technology, 20 May 1991, R23–24) described how his efforts were dealt a "major blow" earlier this year by AT&T—I take it, over patent number 4,555,775, "covering the use of 'backing store' in a window system that lets multiple programs have windows." (I'm referring here to the account in "Against Software Patents"—although the paper modestly declines to mention Stallman by name but refers instead to "computer companies distributing the free X Window System" and MIT.)

3. Perhaps the most successful attempt, and certainly the most famous, to parallel the virtues of a system with the virtues of individual persons is Plato's *Repub-*

lic. The concept of virtue that unfolds in that work significantly influences the Aristotelian-Thomistic tradition in which I situate my argument here.

4. *Politics*, 1263a, 35ff.

5. *Politics*, 1263a, 35ff.

6. *"Utrum liceat alicui rem aliquam quasi propriam possidere"* (*Summa Theologiae*, II-II, Q. 66, A.2).

7. A. Smith, *The Wealth of Nations* (New York: The Modern Library, 1937), 423.

13

Are Computer Hacker Break-ins Ethical?*

Eugene H. Spafford

Recent incidents of unauthorized computer intrusion have brought about discussion of the ethics of breaking into computers. Some individuals have argued that as long as no significant damage results, break-ins may serve a useful purpose. Others counter that the break-ins are almost always harmful and wrong. This chapter lists and refutes many of the reasons given to justify computer intrusions. It is the author's contention that break-ins are ethical only in extreme situations, such as a life-critical emergency. The chapter also discusses why no break-in is "harmless."

Introduction

On November 2, 1988, a program was run on the Internet that replicated itself on thousands of machines, often loading them to the point where they were unable to process normal requests.[1] This Internet Worm program was stopped in a matter of hours but the controversy engendered by its release has raged ever since. Other incidents, such as the "wily hackers" tracked by Cliff Stoll, the "Legion of Doom" members who are alleged to have stolen telephone company 911 software, and the growth of the computer virus problem have added to the discussion.[2] What con-

---

*This essay was originally published as "Are Computer Hacker Break-ins Ethical?" by Eugene H. Spafford, in the *Journal of Systems Software* 17 (1992): 41–47. Copyright © 1992 by Eugene Spafford. Reprinted with permission of Eugene Spafford.

stitutes improper access to computers? Are some break-ins ethical? Is there such a thing as a "moral hacker"?

It is important that we discuss these issues. The continuing evolution of our technological base and our increasing reliance on computers for critical tasks suggest that future incidents may well have more serious consequences than those we have seen to date. With human nature as varied and extreme as it is, and with the technology as available as it is, we must expect to experience more of these incidents.

In this chapter, I will introduce a few of the major issues that these incidents have raised, and present some arguments related to them. For clarification, I have separated several issues that often have been combined when debated; it is possible that most people agree on some of these points once they are viewed as individual issues.

What Is Ethical?

Merriam-Webster's Collegiate Dictionary defines ethics as "the discipline dealing with what is good and bad and with moral duty and obligation." More simply, it is the study of what is right to do in a given situation— what we ought to do. Alternatively, it is sometimes described as the study of what is good and how to achieve that good. To suggest whether an act is right or wrong we need to agree on an ethical system that is easy to understand and apply as we consider the ethics of computer break-ins.

Philosophers have been trying for thousands of years to define right and wrong, and I will not make yet another attempt at such a definition. Instead, I will suggest that we make the simplifying assumption that we can judge the ethical nature of an act by applying a deontological assessment: regardless of the effect, is the act itself ethical? Would we view that act as sensible and proper if everyone were to engage in it? Although this may be too simplistic a model (and it can certainly be argued that other ethical philosophies may also be applied), it is a good first approximation for purposes of discussion. If you are unfamiliar with any other formal ethical evaluation method, try applying this assessment to the points I raise later in this chapter. If the results are obviously unpleasant or dangerous in the large, then they should be considered unethical as individual acts.

Note that this philosophy assumes that right is determined by actions, not results. Some ethical philosophies assume that the ends justify the means; our society does not operate by such a philosophy, although many individuals do. As a society, we profess to believe that "it isn't whether you win or lose, it's how you play the game." This is why we are concerned with issues of due process and civil rights, even for those espousing repugnant views and committing heinous acts. The process is important no matter what the outcome, although the outcome may help to resolve a choice between two almost equal courses of action.

Philosophies that consider the results of an act as the ultimate measure of good are often impossible to apply because of the difficulty in understanding exactly what results from any arbitrary activity. Consider an extreme example: the government orders one hundred cigarette smokers, chosen at random, to be beheaded on live nationwide television. The result might well be that many hundreds of thousands of other smokers would quit cold turkey, thus prolonging their lives. It might also prevent hundreds of thousands of people from ever starting to smoke, thus improving the health and longevity of the general populace. The health of millions of other people would improve because they would no longer be subjected to secondary smoke, and the overall impact on the environment would be favorable as tons of air and ground pollutants would no longer be released by smokers or tobacco companies.

Yet, despite the great good this might hold for society, everyone, except for a few extremists, would condemn such an act as immoral. We would likely object even if only one person were executed. It would not matter what the law might be on such an issue; we would not feel that the act was morally correct, nor would we view the ends as justifying the means.

Note that we would be unable to judge the morality of such an action by evaluating the results, because we would not know the full scope of those results. Such an act might have effects, favorable or otherwise, on issues of law, public health, tobacco use, and daytime TV shows for decades or centuries to follow. A system of ethics that considered primarily only the results of our actions could not allow us to evaluate our current activities at the time when we would need such guidance; if we are unable to discern the appropriate course of action prior to its commission, then our system of ethics is of little or no value to us. To obtain ethical guidance, we must base our actions primarily on evaluations of the actions and not on the possible results.

More to the point here, if we attempt to judge the morality of a computer break-in based on the sum total of all future effects, we would be unable to make such a judgment, either for a specific incident or for the general class of acts. In part, this is because it is so difficult to determine the long-term effects of various actions and to discern their causes. We cannot know, for instance, if increased security awareness and restrictions are better for society in the long term, or whether these additional restrictions will result in greater costs and annoyance when using computer systems. We also do not know how many of these changes are directly traceable to incidents of computer break-ins.

One other point should be made here: it is undoubtedly possible to imagine scenarios where a computer break-in would be considered to be the preferable course of action. For instance, if vital medical data were on a computer and necessary to save someone's life in an emergency, but the authorized users of the system could not be located, breaking into the system might well be considered the right thing to do. However, that action does not make the break-in ethical. Rather, such situations occur when a greater wrong would undoubtedly occur if the unethical act were not committed. Similar reasoning applies to situations such as killing in self-defense. In the following discussion, I will assume that such conflicts are not the root cause of the break-ins; such situations should very rarely present themselves.

Motivations

Individuals who break into computer systems or who write vandalware usually use one of several rationalizations for their actions. Most of these individuals would never think to walk down a street, trying every door to find one unlocked, then search through the drawers of the furniture inside. Yet these same people seem to give no second thought to making repeated attempts at guessing passwords to accounts they do not own, and once into a system, browsing through the files on disk.

These computer burglars often give the same reasons for their actions in an attempt to rationalize their activities as morally justified. I present and refute some of the most commonly used ones; motives involving theft and revenge are not uncommon, and their moral nature is simple to discern, so I shall not include them here.

The Hacker Ethic

Many hackers argue that they follow an ethic that both guides their behavior and justifies their break-ins. This hacker ethic states, in part, that all information should be free. This view holds that information belongs to everyone and there should be no boundaries or restraints to prevent anyone from examining information. Richard Stallman states much the same thing in his GNU Manifesto.[3] He and others have stated in various forums that if information is free, it logically follows that there should be no such thing as intellectual property, and no need for security.

What are the implications and consequences of such a philosophy? First and foremost, it raises some disturbing questions of privacy. If all information is (or should be) free, then privacy is no longer a possibility. For information to be free to everyone and for individuals to no longer be able to claim it as property means that anyone may access the information if they please. Furthermore, as it is no longer property of any individual, anyone can alter the information. Items such as bank balances, medical records, credit histories, employment records, and defense information all cease to be controlled. If someone controls information and controls who may access it, the information is obviously not free. But without that control, we would no longer be able to trust the accuracy of the information.

In a perfect world, this lack of privacy and control might not be cause for concern. However, if all information were to be freely available and modifiable, imagine how much damage and chaos would be caused in our real world! Our whole society is based on information whose accuracy must be assured. This includes information held by banks and other financial institutions, credit bureaus, medical agencies and professionals, government agencies such as the IRS, law enforcement agencies, and educational institutions. Clearly, treating all their information as "free" would be unethical in any world where there might be careless and unethical individuals.

Economic arguments can be made against this philosophy, too, in addition to the overwhelming need for privacy and control of information accuracy. Information is not universally free. It is held as property because of privacy concerns, and because it is often collected and developed at great expense. Development of a new algorithm or program or collection of a specialized database may involve the expenditure of vast sums of time and effort. To claim that it is free or should be free is to express a naive and unrealistic view of the world. To use this to justify computer break-ins is clearly unethical. Although not all information currently treated as private or controlled as proprietary needs such protection, that does not justify unauthorized access to it or to any other data.

The Security Arguments

These arguments are the most common ones offered within the computer community. One argument is the same as that used most often to defend the author of the Internet Worm program in 1988: break-ins illustrate security problems to a community that will otherwise not note the problems.

In the Worm case, one of the first issues to be discussed widely in Internet mailing lists dealt with the intent of the perpetrator—exactly why the Worm program had been written and released. Explanations put forth by members of the community ranged from simple accident to the actions of a sociopath. Many said that the Worm was designed to reveal security defects to a community that would not otherwise pay attention. This was not supported by the testimony of the author during his trial, nor is it supported by past experience of system administrators.

The Worm author, Robert T. Morris, appears to have been well known at some universities and major companies, and his talents were generally respected. Had he merely explained the problems or offered a demonstration to these people, he would have been listened to with considerable attention. The month before he released the Worm program on the Internet, he discovered and disclosed a bug in the file transfer program ftp; news of the flaw spread rapidly, and an official fix was announced and available within a matter of weeks. The argument that no one would listen to his report of security weaknesses is clearly fallacious.

In the more general case, this security argument is also without merit. Although some system administrators might have been complacent about the security of their systems before the Worm incident, most computer vendors, managers of government computer installations, and system administrators at major colleges and universities have been attentive to reports of security problems. People wishing to report a problem with the security of a system need not exploit it to report it. By way of analogy, one does not set fire to the neighborhood shopping center to bring attention to a fire hazard in one of the stores, and then try to justify the act by claiming that firemen would otherwise never listen to reports of hazards.

The most general argument that some people make is that the individuals who break into systems are performing a service by exposing security flaws, and thus should be encouraged or even rewarded. This argument is severely flawed in several ways. First, it assumes that there is some compelling need to force users to install security fixes on their systems, and thus computer burglars are justified in "breaking and entering" activities. Taken to extremes, it suggests that it would be perfectly acceptable to engage in such activities on a continuing basis, so long as they might expose security flaws. This completely loses sight of the purpose of the computers in the first place—to serve as tools and resources, not as exercises in security. The same reasoning would imply that vigilantes have the right to attempt to break into the homes in my neighborhood on a continuing basis to demonstrate that they are susceptible to burglars.

Another flaw with this argument is that it completely ignores the technical and economic factors that prevent many sites from upgrading or correcting their software. Not every site has the resources to install new system software or to correct existing software. At many sites, the systems are run as turnkey systems—employed as tools and maintained by the vendor. The owners and users of these machines simply do not have the ability to correct or maintain their systems independently, and they are unable to afford custom software support from their vendors. To break into such systems, with or without damage, is effectively to trespass into places of business: to do so in a vigilante effort to force the owners to upgrade their security structure is presumptuous and reprehensible. A burglary is not justified, morally or legally, by an argument that the victim has poor locks and was therefore "asking for it."

A related argument has been made that vendors are responsible for the maintenance of their software, and that such security breaches should immediately require vendors to issue corrections to their customers, past and present. The claim is made that without highly visible break-ins, vendors will not produce or distribute necessary fixes to software. This attitude is naive, and is neither economically feasible nor technically workable. Certainly, vendors should bear some responsibility for the adequacy of their software, but they should not be responsible for fixing every possible flaw in every possible configuration.[4]

Many sites customize their software or otherwise run systems incompatible with the latest vendor releases. For a vendor to be able to provide quick response to security problems, it would be necessary for each customer to run completely standardized software and hardware mixes to ensure the correctness of vendor-supplied updates. Not only would this be considerably less attractive for many customers and contrary to their usual practice, but the increased cost of such "instant" fix distribution would add to the price of such a system and greatly increase the cost borne by the customer. It is unreasonable to expect the user community to sacrifice flexibility and pay a much higher cost per unit simply for faster corrections to the occasional security breach, assuming it is possible for the manufacturer to find those customers and supply them with fixes in a timely manner—something unlikely in a market where machines and software are often repackaged, traded, and resold.

The case of the Internet Worm is a good example of the security argument and its flaws. It further stands as a good example of the conflict between ends and means valuation of ethics. Various people have argued that the Worm's author did us a favor by exposing security flaws. At Mr. Morris's trial on federal charges stemming from the incident, the defense attorneys also argued that their client should not be punished because of the good the Worm did in exposing those flaws. Others, including the prosecuting attorneys, argued that the act itself was wrong no matter what the outcome. Their contention has been that the result does not justify the act itself, nor does the defense's argument encompass all the consequences of the incident.

This is certainly true; the complete results of the incident are still not known. There have been many other break-ins and network worms since November 1988, perhaps inspired by the media coverage of that incident. More attempts will possibly be made, in part inspired by Mr. Morris's act. Some sites on the Internet have restricted access to their machines, and others were removed from the network; other sites have decided not to pursue a connection, even though it will hinder research and operations. Combined with the many decades of person-hours devoted to cleaning up after the Worm, this seems a high price to pay for a claimed "favor."

The legal consequences of this act are also not yet known. For instance, many bills have been introduced into Congress and state legislatures over the last three years in part because of these incidents. One piece of legislation introduced into the House of Representatives, HR–5061, entitled "The Computer Virus Eradication Act of 1988," was the first in a series of legislative actions that have the potential to affect significantly the computer profession. In particular, HR–5061 was notable because its wording would prevent it from being applied to true computer viruses.[5] The passage of similar well-intentioned but poorly defined legislation could have a major negative effect on the computing profession as a whole.

The Idle System Argument

Another argument put forth by system hackers is that they are simply making use of idle machines. They argue that because some systems are not used at a level near their capacity, the hacker is somehow entitled to use them.

This argument is also flawed. First of all, these systems are usually not in service to provide a general-purpose user environment. Instead, they are in use in commerce, medicine, public safety, research, and government functions. Unused capacity is present for future needs and sudden surges of activity, not for the support of outside individuals. Imagine if large numbers of people without a computer were to take advantage of a system with idle processor capacity: the system would quickly be overloaded and severely degraded or unavailable for the rightful owners. Once on the system, it would be difficult (or impossible) to oust these individuals if sudden extra capacity were needed by the rightful owners. Even the largest machines available today would not provide sufficient capacity to accommodate such activity on any large scale.

I am unable to think of any other item that someone may buy and maintain, only to have others claim a right to use it when it is idle. For instance, the thought of someone walking up to my expensive car and driving off in it simply because it is not currently being used is ludicrous. Likewise, because I am away at work, it is not proper to hold a party at my house because it is otherwise not being used. The related positions that unused computing capacity is a shared resource, and that my privately developed software belongs to everyone, are equally silly (and unethical) positions.

The Student Hacker Argument

Some trespassers claim that they are doing no harm and changing nothing—they are simply learning about how computer systems operate. They argue that computers are expensive, and that they are merely furthering their education in a cost-effective manner. Some authors of computer viruses claim that their creations are intended to be harmless, and that they are simply learning how to write complex programs.

There are many problems with these arguments. First, as an educator, I claim that writing vandalware or breaking into a computer and looking at the files has almost nothing to do with computer education. Proper education in computer science and engineering involves intensive exposure to fundamental aspects of theory, abstraction, and design techniques. Browsing through a system does not expose someone to the broad scope of theory and practice in computing, nor does it provide the critical feedback so important to a good education; neither does writing a virus or worm program and releasing it into an unsupervised environment provide any proper educational experience. By analogy, stealing cars and joyriding does not provide one with an education in mechanical engineering, nor does pouring sugar in the gas tank.

Furthermore, individuals "learning" about a system cannot know how everything operates and what results from their activities. Many systems have been damaged accidentally by ignorant (or careless) intruders; most of the damage from computer viruses (and the Internet Worm) appears to be caused by unexpected interactions and program faults. Damage to medical systems, factory control, financial information, and other computer systems could have drastic and far-ranging effects that have nothing to do with education, and could certainly not be considered harmless.

A related refutation of the claim has to do with knowledge of the extent of the intrusion. If I am the person responsible for the security of a critical computer system, I cannot assume that any intrusion is motivated solely by curiosity and that nothing has been harmed. If I know that the system has been compromised, I must fear the worst and perform a complete system check for damages and changes. I cannot take the word of the intruder, for any intruder who actually caused damage would seek to hide it by claiming that he or she was "just looking." To regain confidence in the correct behavior of my system, I must expend considerable energy to examine and verify every aspect of it.

Apply our universal approach to this situation and imagine if this "educational" behavior was widespread and commonplace. The result would be that we would spend all our time verifying our systems and never be able to trust the results fully. Clearly, this is not good, and thus we must conclude that these "educational" motivations are also unethical.

The Social Protector Argument

One last argument, more often heard in Europe than the United States, is that hackers break into systems to watch for instances of data abuse and to help keep "Big Brother" at bay. In this sense, the hackers are protectors rather than criminals. Again, this assumes that the ends justify the means. It also assumes that the hackers are actually able to achieve some good end.

Undeniably, there is some misuse of personal data by corporations and by the government. The increasing use of computer-based record systems and networks may lead to further abuses. However, it is not clear that breaking into these systems will aid in righting the wrongs. If anything, it may cause those agencies to become even more secretive and use the break-ins as an excuse for more restricted access. Break-ins and vandalism have not resulted in new open-records laws, but they have resulted in the introduction and passage of new criminal statutes. Not only has such activity failed to deter "Big Brother," but it has also resulted in significant segments of the public urging more laws and more aggressive law enforcement—the direct opposite of the supposed goal.

It is also not clear that these hackers are the individuals we want "protecting" us. We need to have the designers and users of the systems—trained computer professionals concerned about our rights and aware of the dangers involved with the inappropriate use of computer monitoring and record keeping. The threat is a relatively new one, as computers and networks have become widely used only in the last few decades. It will take some time for awareness of the dangers to spread throughout the profession. Clandestine efforts to breach the security of computer systems do nothing to raise the consciousness of the appropriate individuals. Worse, they associate that commendable goal (heightened concern) with criminal activity (computer break-ins), thus discouraging proactive behavior by the individuals in the best positions to act in our favor. Perhaps it is in this sense that computer break-ins and vandalism are most unethical and damaging.

Conclusion

I have argued here that computer break-ins, even when no obvious damage results, are unethical. This must be the considered conclusion even if the result is an improvement in security, because the activity itself is disruptive and immoral. The results of the act should be considered separately from the act itself, especially when we consider how difficult it is to understand all the effects resulting from such an act.

Of course, I have not discussed every possible reason for a break-in. There might well be an instance where a break-in might be necessary to save a life or to preserve national security. In such cases, to perform one wrong act to prevent a greater wrong may be the right thing to do. It is beyond the scope or intent of this chapter to discuss such cases, especially as no known hacker break-ins have been motivated by such instances.

Historically, computer professionals as a group have not been overly concerned with questions of ethics and propriety as they relate to computers. Individuals and some organizations have tried to address these issues, but the whole computing community needs to be involved to address the problems in any comprehensive manner. Too often, we view computers simply as machines and algorithms, and we do not perceive the serious ethical questions inherent in their use.

However, when we consider that these machines influence the quality of life of millions of individuals, both directly and indirectly, we understand that there are broader issues. Computers are used to design, analyze, support, and control applications that protect and guide the lives and finances of people. Our use (and misuse) of computing systems may have effects beyond our wildest imagining. Thus, we must reconsider our attitudes about acts demonstrating a lack of respect for the rights and privacy of other people's computers and data.

We must also consider what our attitudes will be toward future security problems. In particular, we should consider the effect of widely publishing the source code for worms, viruses, and other threats to security. Although we need a process for rapidly disseminating corrections and security information as they become known, we should realize that widespread publication of details will imperil sites where users are unwilling or unable to install updates and fixes.[6] Publication should serve a useful purpose; endangering the security of other people's machines or attempting to force them into making changes they are unable to make or afford is not ethical.

Finally, we must decide these issues of ethics as a community of professionals and then present them to society as a whole. No matter what laws are passed, and no matter how good security measures might become, they will not be enough for us to have completely secure systems. We also need to develop and act according to some shared ethical values. The members of society need to be educated so that they understand the importance of respecting the privacy and ownership of data. If locks and laws were all that kept people from robbing houses, there would be many more burglars than there are now; the shared mores about the sanctity of personal property are an important influence in the prevention of burglary. It is our duty as informed professionals to help extend those mores into the realm of computers.

Notes

1. See D. Seeley, "A Tour of the Worm," in *Proceedings of the Winter 1989 Usenix Conference*, The Usenix Association, Berkeley, Calif., 1989; E. Spafford, "The Internet Worm: Crisis and Aftermath," *Communication ACM*, 32 (1989): 678–98; and E. Spafford, "An Analysis of the Internet Work," in *Proceedings of the 2d European Software Engineering Conference*, edited by C. Ghezzi and J. A. McDermid, (Berlin: Springer-Verlag, 1989), 446–68.

2. Many law-abiding individuals consider themselves hackers—a term formerly used as a compliment. The press and general public have co-opted the term, however, and it is now commonly viewed as pejorative. Here, I will use the word as the general public now uses it. See also, C. Stoll, *Cuckoo's Egg* (New York: Doubleday, 1989); J. Schwartz, "The Hacker Dragnet," *Newsweek*, 65, April, 1990; E. Spafford, K. Heaphy, and D. Ferbrache, *Computer Viruses: Dealing with Electronic Vandalism and Programmed Threats* (Arlington, Va.: ADAPSO, 1989); L. Hoffman, ed., *Rogue Programs: Viruses, Worms, and Trojan Horses* (Van Nostrand Reinhold, 1990); D. Stang, *Computer Viruses*, 2d ed. (Washington, D.C.: National Computer Security Association, 1990); and P. Denning, ed., *Computers Under*

Attack: Intruders, Worms, and Viruses (Reading, Mass.: ACM Books/Addison-Wesley, 1991).

3. R. Stallman, "The GNU Manifesto," in *GNU EMacs Manual* (Cambridge, Mass.: Free Software Foundation, 1986), 239–248.

4. M. McIlroy, "Unsafe at Any Price," *Information Technology Quarterly* 9 (1990): 21–23.

5. It provided penalties only in cases where programs were introduced into computer systems: a computer virus is a segment of code attached to an existing program that modifies other programs to include a copy of itself.

6. To anticipate the oft-used comment that the "bad guys" already have such information: not every computer burglar knows or will know *every* system weakness—unless we provide him or her with detailed analyses.

14

National and International Copyright Liability for Electronic System Operators[*]

Charles J. Meyer

I. Introduction

There is a revolution in progress that is creating unprecedented global access to information, literature, and software over electronic media collectively referred to as the "information superhighway." Today, individuals, corporations, and institutions have instant access to resources from around the world at the touch of a button. From electronic bulletin boards, to software archives and on-line libraries, a person with a minimal computer setup can see and use the creations of others around the world. Many of these creations are protected by copyright, but the laws in this area are imprecise and difficult to enforce.

The United States and other countries have domestic laws to govern copyright, but copyright infringement is a problem of international scope. In order to provide for and protect copyrights, there needs to be a uniform international system of rules and standards by which people around the world can operate. The need of users for access must be balanced against the need to protect creators' rights in order to maximize the benefits of creation and access for society.

---

[*]This essay was originally published as "National and International Copyright Liability for Electronic System Operators," by Charles J. Meyer, in the *Indiana Journal of Global and Legal Studies* 2 (spring 1995). Copyright © 1995 by Indiana University School of Law. Reprinted with permission of publisher. Parts of the text and notes of this article have been omitted.

321

II. The Problem

The information superhighway provides computer users with access to resources that range from small, privately run bulletin boards and computer systems to the sprawling worldwide network called the Internet. Sysop (system operator) is the name given to people who run these computer systems. These sysops are trying to strike a balance between the conflicting goals of creating access to information and providing for copyright protection.

When access is created by putting materials on-line, potential copyright problems abound. Before the invention of the computer and on-line access, it was difficult to use another's copyrighted work without spending time and money. Now it can be accomplished with a few keystrokes on a computer keyboard. One or two commands can copy an entire book, article, or piece of software. A few more commands can modify the material by erasing any references to previous creators, allowing use without proper creator credit or compensation.

These problems were aptly demonstrated in the case of *Playboy Enterprises v. Frena*.[1] An electronic bulletin board operator was held liable for copyright infringement of magazine pictures that had been put on-line. The operator did not know that the pictures were on-line and deleted them as soon as he became aware of the infringement. Other people had loaded the pictures onto the system, but the operator was held liable.[2]

If authors cannot get proper compensation, they only have a few alternatives. They may decide to restrict access, to refuse to allow electronic transcription, or to not create at all. This would defeat the entire purpose of copyright protection, which is to give authors an incentive to produce and publish for society. The government created the original copyright laws to provide this incentive. With changes in technology and increasing ease of infringement, the copyright laws must be reworked to continue to provide these incentives to authors while adjusting to the new, global methods of access.

III. Basics of Copyright

Ownership of a copyright gives an author control over the content and form of a work, and grants a monopoly for a period of time.[3] There are eight subjects to which copyright can be applied: (1) literary works (including scientific works and software); (2) musical works; (3) dramatic works; (4) pantomimes and choreographic works; (5) pictorial, graphic, and sculptural works; (6) motion pictures; (7) sound recordings; and (8) architectural works.[4] In order to be copyrightable, a work must be original[5] and in a tangible medium.[6]

Copyright protection provides a property interest in original intellectual creations. It gives the author control of the creation he has contributed to society. In return for this contribution, the author is given a monopoly for a set period of time. Copyright infringement occurs when someone violates that monopoly by copying the work or taking credit for the creation without giving the author credit or rewards.[7] Infringement arises from direct copying, a derivative work, substantial similarity, or non-independent creation.[8] Infringement is a violation of the author's right to recognition of authorship and/or the author's right to benefits.

Authors have various goals, which usually fall into the categories of reputational or financial gain. Authors who want reputational benefits are not concerned with multiple use and copies of their works, but want to be given credit. Authors who want financial benefits are much more concerned with reducing illegal use of their works and receiving appropriate payments.

The purpose of the copyright laws is to balance society's need for access to and use of these creations for growth against the author's rights to credit and payment. In the United States, copyright protection is codified in Title 17 of the United States Code. Internationally, copyright protection is recognized in the multilateral treaties of the Berne Convention, the Universal Copyright Convention (UCC), and in various bilateral treaties.[9]

IV. Resources on the Computer

A. Reasons to Place Material On-Line

The overriding reason material is put on-line is to improve access. A computer can search for, locate, and process information faster than can be done manually. When information is added to databases, storage centers, and archives, the improved access enhances the efficiency and productivity of researchers and other workers.

Scientific research was the original motivation behind the movement to put materials on-line.[10] Electronic communication has enabled scientists around the world to cooperate on research and share ideas in ways that were never feasible before, thus increasing their efficiency and reducing duplication. Electronic communication has since spread to other areas of academia, which have utilized this new speed and access to create public forums where a diversity of views can be heard and discussed. For example, philosophers discuss metaphysics and artists debate symbolism over the computer. More and more academic institutions are making resources available on-line so that they can be used by people elsewhere. Since many documents are now created in electronic form, and with the proliferation of paper scanners, it is now much easier and cheaper to put information on-line.

Other uses of on-line information are entertainment, communication with others, and profit. People can tailor their uses to reflect their tastes and to find the news and resources in which they are interested. On-line electronic bulletin boards allow people to discuss topics from shortcuts in the video game Mortal Kombat to the flaws in the most recent attempt to prove Fermat's Last Theorem.[11] "Libraries without walls" allow people to use materials such as magazines, journals, or newspapers; search card catalogs; or read books via their home computers. Corporations have taken advantage of the ability to offer materials electronically through popular services such as Prodigy and LEXIS.

B. Types of Access

The network of computers called the Internet connects information centers around the world. The amount of information on the Internet is astounding. Over 22,000 networks are connected to the Internet in 137 countries, and estimates of the number of people using the Internet are as high as thirty million.[12] The National Science Foundation logs eight terabytes of information transferred per month.[13] Access and use of the Internet is estimated to be growing at a rate of up to 15 percent per month.[14] It has grown from a project that was begun to promote research among scientists in the U.S. Department of Defense to a network of institutions, governments, corporations, and individuals around the world.[15]

Types of resources available on the Internet include bulletin board systems (BBS), software archives, library archives, and card catalogs, as well as musical compositions, literary and scientific works, and government documents. A person can use a personal computer with a connection such as a modem to access these resources, send electronic mail (e-mail), talk to others in real time, or upload and download materials.[16]

✻   ✻   ✻

C. System Operators: Who Runs the Computers?

Systems can range from a small bulletin board run by a private individual with a personal computer and one modem, to massive numbers of on-line connections to supercomputers run by corporations, universities, or governments. Sysops are responsible for monitoring activity on their systems and for controlling the types of information present. The smaller the system, the easier it is to monitor. Most systems are interactive so that once someone has "logged in" to the system, that person has the ability to read information, write information, and upload or download material.

Sysops can limit copyright infringement by not allowing users to log into a system, but this conflicts with the original goal of creating access. It is almost impossible for a sysop to allow a user to see information and, at the same time, keep that user from copying the information. Once material appears on a screen, it can be copied.

Sysops operate different types of computer systems for various reasons. Some sysops are devoted exclusively to providing a forum for discussions, while others concentrate exclusively on exchanging software. There are different types of software, such as public domain software, shareware, and commercial software.[17] Some systems give users access to government documents, literature, scientific documents, or news straight from the UPI newswire.[18] With the large amount of information, users, and access, it is impractical for sysops to monitor everything on their system at all times. Consequently, even if a sysop does not want to infringe, it is difficult to keep copyrighted material from being added to even the most carefully monitored on-line collections. The sysop may not know of the addition, or, if aware of the addition, the copyright notice may have been removed so that the sysop believes the material to be in the public domain.

D. Copyright Problems on the Information Superhighway

The amount of information available over electronic media is phenomenal and is growing at an incredible rate. Much of the information is in the public domain because the author does not claim a copyright or one has expired. However, for items where a copyright is valid, providing access to a greater amount of information has led to a proportional increase in the problem of copyright infringement.[19] Advances in personal computers and communications have simplified access, which has thus led to increased infringement through the uploading and downloading of information and software.

This new ease of copyright infringement is an extreme change from the historical difficulties involved in copyright infringement. Before the computer, in order to use another creator's work, an infringer had to invest time, money, and effort. The original idea of infringement came from a person copying by hand or modifying material and using it elsewhere while claiming it as original work. With the emergence of the photocopy machine, copyright infringement became easier; this technological advance required an adaptation of the copyright laws.[20] Now, the computer has further minimized what was before a disincentive: the investment in time and money needed to infringe.

In fact, the net gain from infringing on copyrighted works is higher than ever before. The ease of copying, combined with the speed and storage of computers, makes it easy for people to copy items at virtually no cost. Previously, the benefit a person received was balanced by the real cost of getting a copy of the work. Now, the benefit to the person greatly outweighs the minimal cost of making a copy. In addition, the lack of close supervision or a paper trail makes the risks of being punished, or even discovered, minimal. As with any free resource, use without cost leads to over-exploitation. This incentive to infringe is not controlled by the current availability and enforcement of copyright protection.

* * *

The next step in balancing the needs of access for users with the rights of the creators is to consider the effects and costs to society. A rational user will spend the least amount of money to obtain the most access, while the rational creator will maximize the reputational and financial rewards. If too much user access and frequent copyright infringement deprive the creators of their rewards, they will stop creating and publishing, which means society will lose. On the other hand, the information superhighway is a revolutionary new way for society to benefit by lowering the access and search costs in order to enable people to use resources more efficiently than ever before. An overly restrictive copyright law would deprive society of the benefits this revolution allows.

V. Copyright Law in the United States

A. Copyright Statute

The Constitution empowers Congress to establish laws to protect intellectual property.[21] In response to this empowerment, the first Congress established a copyright law.[22] That law has been revised over time to become the current Title 17 of the U.S. Code. Major revisions of the copyright law in 1976 and 1988 brought the U.S. laws closer to conformity with the laws of other countries.[23] Literary works, one of the eight classes of works that the United States protects, has been broadly interpreted to include scientific works and software.[24] To be protected, a work must be original and fixed in a tangible form.[25]

Once a creator has a copyright in a work, the owner has the exclusive rights to reproduce the work, to adapt the work, to distribute copies by sale or otherwise, or to perform or display the work.[26] In effect, the owner is granted a limited monopoly to control what is done with the work. Society is willing to grant this monopoly in consideration of the creator's contribution to society. These monopoly rights are granted to the owner for a limited period of time. The duration of a copyright in material created on or after January 1, 1978, is the life of the author plus fifty years.[27]

B. Infringement

An infringement of a copyright occurs when someone exercises the rights of the copyright owner without that owner's authorization. A copyright infringement is comprehensive when the entire work is copied, partial when only part of a work is used, or derivative when a later work is based on the copyrighted work. An infringement can be literal, using the author's exact words, or it can be non-literal, where the author's work is modified and claimed as a new creation.[28]

A copyright infringement does not have to be intentional. All that an owner has to prove to show infringement is ownership of the copyright and copying by the defendant. Since direct evidence of copying is rare, an inference of copying is established if the infringer had access to the work, and there is a substantial similarity between the copyrighted work and the alleged infringing work. Unless the infringer has a defense or authorization, the person is liable for infringement.[29]

Defenses to infringement of a copyright do exist. The first is fair use, discussed below. Certain institutions are also allowed to infringe copyrights for archival purposes. In other cases, the infringer can prove that the use was a normal use of the work, that he was an innocent infringer who did not know the work was copyrighted, or that he created the work independently.[30]

Sysops run the risks of various types of infringement by allowing access to their resources. The most important is direct infringement, where an unauthorized work is added to an on-line collection. Sysops could also be held liable for vicarious or contributory infringement by allowing other people to add copyrighted works to the collection without the sysop's knowledge of the copyright, or for allowing other people to violate the copyright by allowing use and copying without the owner's permission.[31]

The Supreme Court explained the concepts of contributory and vicarious liability in *Universal City Studios v. Sony Corporation of America.* Copyright owners sued to enjoin Sony from selling video recorders because the devices were being used to tape copyrighted material. The Court first held that a required element in a contributory infringement case was that the accused be in a position to control the use of copyrighted works by others. Sony was not in control of the recorders after purchase and therefore could not be held contributorily liable.[32]

The plaintiffs then argued that Sony had constructive knowledge that customers would make unauthorized copies of material and should therefore be vicariously liable. The Court held that since there were substantial non-infringing uses or authorized fair uses, Sony could also not be held vicariously liable.[33]

Computer systems are different from video recorders, but the same analysis applies. Problems of contributory and vicarious infringement are especially pervasive with bulletin boards, archive sites, and university computer systems. In contrast to the *Sony* case, sysops are in control of their systems and have much closer interactions with the users. Sysops can control access and copying to an extent. It could easily be argued that the institution is or should be in control of the infringer and should therefore be held liable. As previously stated, no intent to infringe is necessary for infringement.[34] Sysops allow users the opportunity to infringe easily and could therefore be held contributorily liable for encouraging, or at least knowing about, foreseeable infringement. The problem with this is that institutions cannot supervise everyone who has access all the time. There are no simple ways to prevent infringement; if material appears on a user's screen, it can be copied, and a sysop cannot prevent it. In this way, as in the *Sony* case, a sysop is not in control of the end users.

Normally, to be held vicariously liable, a person must, in addition to being in control of the infringer, receive a financial benefit from the infringement.[35] Any for-profit business that charges for access is receiving a direct financial benefit and must be especially careful to avoid vicarious liability. Though it would be hard to argue that a library or university receives a direct financial benefit from infringement, both measure their success by the use of their resources and receive an indirect benefit from increased traffic and reputation, thereby enhancing their status and financial income.

Sysops could also be charged with constructive knowledge that users will infringe copyrights. Following the *Sony* holding, the sysops can demonstrate that there is a substantial amount of non-infringing use for the material and therefore they should not be held vicariously liable. But, the

Sony Court also discussed the market effect in making its decision of what is a substantial non-infringing use.[36] If the infringement causes too great an effect on the market, it would mean that there is substantial infringing use. This would detract from the case for substantial non-infringing use, and the Court could decide that sysops should be held vicariously liable.

C. Exceptions to Infringement

When the 1976 Copyright Law was in Congress, the library and academic lobbies were intensely concerned about academic freedom and educational use. In response, the 1976 Copyright Law codified the doctrine of fair use. Fair use is an equity doctrine that allows use of a work "for purposes such as criticism, comment, news reporting, teaching (including multiple copies for classroom use), scholarship or research."[37] Four factors should be considered in determining fair use:

1. the purpose and character of the use, including whether such use is of a commercial nature or is for nonprofit education
2. the nature of the copyrighted work
3. the amount and substantiality of the portion used in relation to the copyrighted work as a whole
4. the effect of the use upon the potential market for or value of the copyrighted work[38]

In applying these factors, courts consider the intent and motive of the person in a context of "brevity, spontaneity and cumulative effect" to decide whether a use is a fair use or an infringement.[39] Fair use is the doctrine that educational and library sysops use to justify adding sources to on-line collections. The institutions claim that the resources are being used for educational purposes and that the on-line access has not affected the potential market or value of the work.

In addition to fair use, a library or archive has statutory authorization to reproduce one copy of a work for an archive if certain conditions are met. In order to satisfy archival requirements, the copy must (1) not be used for direct or indirect commercial advantage, (2) include a notice of copyright, and (3) the library or archive must be open to the public or outside researchers.[40]

*   *   *

Software is an especially easy target for electronic copyright infringement because it is designed to be run on a computer. Industry experts estimate that losses from software copyright infringement globally run from twelve to fifteen billion dollars a year.[41] A great deal of software is not copyrighted, and sysops can have a difficult time telling the difference between copyrighted and non-copyrighted software. However, Congress balanced the rights of users and creators by enacting a specific section of the copyright law to deal with software that is copyrighted.

Section 117 of the copyright law states that it is not an infringement for the owner of a copy of a computer program to make a separate copy, if needed to use the program, or for backup (archival) purposes.[42] In order to allow users to make these copies, manufacturers write the programs to be copyable. It is therefore quite simple to violate the copyright on a program by either uploading to or downloading from another system. Software archives and bulletin boards can violate the law when people upload copyrighted software without the sysop's knowledge of the copy and/or the copyright, or download software to their own systems.

D. Enforcement in the United States

The copyright law states, "Anyone who violates any of the exclusive rights of the copyright owner . . . or who imports copies . . . into the United States . . . is an infringer of the copyright." A copyrighted work must be registered with the Copyright Office in order for an owner to bring an infringement action. Once an infringement action is brought, there are several remedies that an owner can pursue.[43]

An owner can recover actual damages that have been suffered from infringement as well as any profits that the infringer has made as a result of infringement. Perhaps more important, the owner can obtain an injunction against the infringer to restrain further infringements, and can impound infringing copies of the copyright. In some instances, the owner can recover litigation costs and attorney's fees.[44]

Despite this array of seemingly impressive remedies available to copyright owners, enforcement against sysops in an electronic context is extremely difficult. With extensive computer networks such as the Internet or a database such as LEXIS, it is extremely simple for a person to violate a copyright and to go undetected. The owner may not be aware that the work is on-line, much less that there has been a violation.

VI. International Copyright Law

A. History

There is no general, sui generis copyright law between countries. The international law that exists is a result of multilateral and bilateral treaties.

When countries have a copyright agreement, there are two types of protection that can be given: national treatment or reciprocal treatment. A country can treat the other country's nationals and works the same way that the country treats its own nationals, or the country can give the other country's nationals the protection those nationals would receive in their home country. For ease of applicability and uniformity within a country, most treaties give national protection.[45]

There are two widely accepted multilateral treaties on copyright protection: the Berne Convention and the Universal Copyright Convention.[46] In addition to the multilateral treaties, there are numerous bilateral treaties between countries. Before these treaties, and still for non-member countries, there was no international copyright protection. The lack of protection made it quite simple for someone to buy one copy of a work, take it out of the country, and then reap huge profits by selling cheap copies. This was especially troubling to authors and software creators who were unable to recover their development costs because people bought the cheaper copies.

The Berne Convention was created in 1886, but the United States did not accede to the Berne Convention until a century later (1987), largely because U.S. law had requirements such as mandatory deposit with the Library of Congress, mandatory copyright notice, printing in the United States, and shorter terms of copyright duration. Congress decided that the United States should not join the Berne Convention, so the United States initiated the development of the Universal Copyright Convention, which was signed in 1952 and entered into force in 1956. The United States has also concluded bilateral treaties with a number of countries, and now has confirmed copyright protection relations with 110 countries.[47]

B. Application of Berne and Universal Copyright Conventions

The Berne Convention and the UCC protect works in the literary, scientific, and artistic domain. This definition is expansive enough to include scientific research and computer software. The treaties extend protection of works that are protected in the country of origin to all other member countries. The works must be first published by a national of a member country or be first published in a member country. The Berne Convention leaves the matter of when a work is considered published, such as a requirement of tangible form or of general distribution, to legislation for each member country, while the UCC defines publication.[48]

Once a work has been published in a member country, the owner of the copyright can enforce that copyright in other member countries without separate registrations or formalities. A member can enforce in another country the same rights that the nationals of that country would enjoy if the work was first published there. In addition to the rights of nationals, owners of copyrights are guaranteed certain specific, minimum rights under the conventions.[49]

Above the UCC minimums, the Berne Convention grants authors the rights of paternity and integrity, allowing the author to claim ownership and object to distortion of a work. As a general rule, the Berne Convention grants copyrights for the duration of the life of the author plus fifty years. In contrast, the UCC grants protection for the life of the author plus twenty-five years. These are minimum rights that countries are required to recognize; a country may grant more protection by legislation.[50]

By becoming member countries, nations recognize the exclusive rights of authors to receive the benefits and proceeds of their works. These basic rights ensure the authors' economic and reputation interests. In general, the conventions also grant copyright owners the rights to reproduce and translate their works.[51]

Like U.S. law, the conventions have exceptions that allow copyrighted works to be used in ways such as fair use and for archival purposes; these exceptions are governed by the separate countries.[52] The exceptions are limited and must still provide reasonable protection to the copyright owner.

There is no international court with jurisdiction for copyright claims. The remedies that are available for an infringement of a copyright are governed and enforced by the country where protection is claimed. This means that the owner must go to each country where infringement occurs and sue in the local judicial system to enforce a copyright. Separately, the Berne Convention grants owners the right to seize infringing copies in all member countries. Berne Union countries have the additional right to retaliate and deny protection to the nationals of any country that does not recognize the rights of the member's own nationals.[53]

C. Comparison of Conventions to U.S. Copyright Law

Before the 1976 and 1988 revisions of U.S. copyright law, protections existing under the Berne and UCC Conventions were not given to foreign works in the United States. Foreign authors had to conform to all of the requirements of U.S. law to gain copyright protection. U.S. nationals did not have protection in other countries (unless there was a bilateral treaty). Although the United States was a founding member and driving force behind the UCC, the protections granted under it were not as extensive as those of the Berne Convention. Similarly, the UCC is expressly written to not limit any rights granted by the Berne Convention.[54]

With the new U.S. copyright law, copyright requirements began to reflect the requirements of the Berne Convention. In the revisions of 1976 and 1988, Congress amended the copyright laws with respect to formalities and deposit requirements, duration of copyrights, mandatory notice, and available remedies. On March 1, 1989, the United States finally became a member of the Berne Convention and granted foreign nationals copyright protection in the United States.[55]

The Berne Convention is not a self-executing treaty in the United States and therefore will not create or trump U.S. law. The Berne Convention is also not a law in the United States. The Berne Convention grants foreign, treaty-member nationals standing in the United States in reciprocation for U.S. citizens having standing in member countries. If a copyright owner wants to sue an infringer in U.S. courts, the owner can only use U.S. laws that are codified or judicially created. Congress has not codified certain rights that the Convention grants, such as the "moral" rights of paternity and integrity. Instead, in considering whether to adopt the Convention, Congress concluded that these moral rights were adequately protected by existing laws.[56]

D. International Sysop Treatment

Sysops within the United States are governed by the copyright laws of the United States, but with the globalization of the information superhighway, it is simple to be a sysop outside of the United States. Unfortunately, the jurisdiction of U.S. courts does not extend to sysops who operate in other countries. If a copyright owner wishes to enforce copyright protection against sysops in other countries, the owner must rely upon international agreements such as the Berne Convention and the UCC.

No agreements deal specifically with copyright law in the electronic medium. In order to obtain protection, copyright owners must use the provisions of the existing conventions. It is widely recognized that software and other material on the computer is in a tangible form that can be protected by copyright.[57] Therefore, authors of electronic works can own copyrights; the problems arise when the owners want to enforce their rights internationally.

*   *   *

A different and more complex problem created by computers and international ease of access is that sysops may not know that they are infringing a copyright. With the incredible amount of information that exists on-line and off-line, it is impractical in terms of time and money for sysops to check the copyright status of all information. Even if a sysop has the best of intentions to protect the copyrights of others, a third person can simply remove a copyright notice or modify a work so that it seems not to have a copyright or to have a copyright that belongs to someone else. Thus, if a country requires knowledge for copyright infringement, a defense of innocent infringement may bar recovery against sysops in many foreign countries.

VII. The Future of Sysops and Copyright

The current extreme disparity between supply and demand guarantees that the amount of information available through on-line resources will continue to expand. The goal of gaining users will encourage sysops to continue adding resources. Sysops enter the field for the reputation growth or the financial benefits derived from access by users. When one sysop adds resources on-line, others are forced to add more resources to compete for the users' attention. If a particular sysop does not put information on-line, demand ensures that the competitive market will add the information elsewhere. The challenge that all sysops face is to balance protecting the interests of the creators with the demands for access.

Access to the so-called information superhighway is exploding, and it will not be stopped. The demand for access and the ease of using resources will continue to promote on-line growth in the public and private sectors. As this growth continues, a new level of copyright policy must be created to deal with new issues.

It will always be impossible to eliminate copyright infringement totally. Hackers, professionals, and other people willing to spend the time and money will always be able to bypass limitations and protections to access.[58] The goal for the future should be to stop amateurs from infringing and to make the costs of infringing for hackers and other professionals outweigh the benefits. Widespread conformance with the copyright laws will only happen if it is the cheapest and easiest choice for users.

An ideal future copyright system must promote the same goals that previous copyright laws have: to balance the needs of users against the protection of creators' rights. The benefits that society receives from granting copyrights require that some form of protection be given. However, the phenomenal growth in the availability of on-line resources also proves that society demands increased ease of access.

A. An Ideal Copyright System

A sysop's dream for the future is that the growth of the information-on-line superhighway will result in instantaneous, global, personal access to a majority of the information on the planet. In the ideal system, only one copy of a resource would need to be placed on-line, and then anyone could use it. This total dissemination would allow the maximum amount of gain to society from access. If this access were free, however, the authors would gain no benefit from publishing and allowing on-line access. As a result, authors would respond by going to the opposite extreme and not creating or publishing at all, depriving society of continuing benefits.

The ultimate extreme of users' interests would be a decision to put all resources in the public domain. Public domain software, news, and creations whose copyrights have expired comprise a vast area of resources that already do not have protection. Having no copyright protection would eliminate society's enforcement costs, and would thus be a benefit to society. The problems that currently exist in international copyright protection rebut this idea by showing that a limited amount of protection only raises costs by sending copyright owners to other methods of protecting and gaining from their creations.

Putting all resources in the public domain is not the way to continue society's growth. Creation of an idea is property in its most original form.[59] When an author creates a work, the author has combined personal experiences and training in a way that is impossible to duplicate. This unique combination is a gain to society that must be encouraged. It is in society's best interests to retain incentives for creation and disclosure.

A copyright scheme for the future must balance these fundamental principles of allowing access while retaining incentives to produce. The growth of the information superhighway will turn the world into a library without walls. On-line resources anywhere should be available to everyone. This global access will allow society the greatest possible growth from use of a creation. Simultaneously, the cost of this access must not reduce the benefits that the creator receives. This means that creators must receive their benefits either before on-line access, or on-line access must increase these benefits instead of detracting from them.

For those creators who produce for reputation benefits, global access will mean an increase in the market of users and will satisfy their desires by making them even more well known to others. Following the same shift in demand through global access, copyright owners who seek financial rewards will have access to the largest possible market. This larger market will enable those who want financial rewards to lower their prices and still reap the same or greater rewards; the cost of access will then parallel the true value of the resource.

The simplest way to stop infringement is to create a system where there is no net benefit to infringing. This will be achieved when there is legitimate global access at prices equal to or below what people are willing to pay. If everyone has low-cost access to all resources, there will be no gain from infringement and, therefore, protection and enforcement of copyrights will not be needed. To do this, all countries must have uniform protection of creators' rights. By consolidating the separate countries into one global market, each country will benefit by the access to all other countries and it will be simpler to grant creators their rewards.

Copyright owners currently have the right to control reproduction of their works. Once there is global access to a resource anywhere, there will not be any need or desire to reproduce a work. One copy will be enough. Therefore, creators will not need to retain control over reproduction. Creators' incentives must be retained by other methods.

Several methods could be used to ensure creators the financial benefits from on-line access to their works. One possibility would be a flat tax on everyone to allow total access. This would not discriminate on the basis of the person's demand for access and thus would be an unequal burden. People who use the resources a great deal would pay comparatively little per use, while the burden would be greater for people who rarely use the resources. People who do not use the resources would object to subsidizing the use by others. A proposal that would cure this problem would be to require a use tax that each person must pay for using a resource. This is the method that many for-profit information providers use now. A fee is paid that is calculated by the amount of time spent on-line and the specific resources accessed. Another proposal would be for governments to buy the rights to creations. This proposal is flawed because of the high costs in trying to value a creation. Some creators would be overpaid for relatively small contributions to society, while others would be underpaid for valuable contributions.

The benefits that a creator receives must be related to the significance of the contribution to society. An ideal plan should value the benefits that the user gains from access and then pass on part of that value to the creator. This would be similar to a licensing agreement. Software and technology exist, or can be developed, to monitor the users and use of resources. Assuming that the amount of use is proportional to an item's value, a creator could estimate what a reasonable fee for use would be. The sysop would then assess the user this fee and pay it to the creator. The user would know the fee in advance, and would decide (consciously or intuitively) whether his benefit is equal to or greater than the fee. Creators would have an incentive to keep the fees as low as possible to induce the greatest number of people to use the resource. Low prices would encourage people whose benefit was greater than or equal to the price to use the resources. This would not be an exact measure of the value contributed by the creator, but the creators would have a net gain by large amounts of inexpensive legitimate use instead of a few legitimate expensive users and many non-paying users.

The doctrines of fair use and archival reproduction are currently included in copyright protections to serve important societal policies. Fair use serves the policies of education and research, which in turn are investments for future creations and gains to society. Archival reproduction serves the equally important policy of retaining creations and preventing waste by allowing reproduction to prevent permanent loss of works. It is important to preserve these goals to keep society advancing and to keep track of society's history.

This does not mean that the doctrines must remain. Once global, personal access has been achieved, there will be no educational need to copy resources. The resources will already be available. Similarly, it is important to keep backup copies of resources in case of accidents, but, since everyone has access, archival storage will not result in use by others. Ideally, unlimited copying should be allowed; because everyone already has legitimate access, there will be no market upon which to infringe.

In economic terms, demand currently exceeds supply. Only this current shortage induces infringement. Once global, personal access is achieved at low cost, the supply will be increased so that the legitimate demand will be satisfied and the demand for infringement will disappear.

B. Current Steps toward an Ideal Global Copyright Law

Sysops will be on the cutting edge of creating and enforcing future copyright policies because they are the nexus between the authors and the users. Users are demanding more access, so sysops will provide it. Even so, the authors are essential to the sysops because without the creators of the material, the sysops would have nothing to put on-line. Rational sysops will maximize their own financial or reputational gain by maximizing the supply of resources for users, while assuring future opportunities from satisfied creators.

If creators do not receive the benefits of their creations, they will resort to known or later discovered forms of self-help, which include restricting access, making files difficult to duplicate, charging a premium, or requiring complex contracts before allowing access. If the cost to society from these measures exceeds the cost of societal protection, then the interest of society would demand that the protection be given.

The Berne Convention and the UCC are the first steps toward a global ability to balance the demands of users and creators. With the increasing globalization of information technology, copyright protection will only be meaningful if it is globally enforceable. The recognition of this need is one of the primary forces behind the Berne Convention and the UCC.

The Berne Convention and the UCC require and give minimum amounts of protection to foreign authors as well as to nationals. These standards are minimal because they vary widely from country to country. The conventions fail because they only apply in member countries. Citizens of member countries can currently sidestep the treaties through loopholes and gaps, while citizens of non-member countries need not follow the guidelines at all. The increasing global interconnectivity of resources means that authors will demand global copyright protection and will take steps to procure it.

The most obvious self-help step that copyright owners have taken to protect their rights is to require a contract with each person to whom they allow access. Especially in the case of software, this has led to complex and restrictive contracts and licensing agreements that are hard to read and are of questionable legal validity.[60] These contracts raise the price charged users desiring access to a resource; as a result, people decide not to buy the resource and instead choose to infringe. In addition to discouraging use and encouraging infringement, the enforcement costs, legal and otherwise, of the contracts consume resources that could be better used elsewhere. The costs to society of creating these complex contracts, the loss of access, and the costs of enforcement are a waste of resources that society could be using for growth.

Another self-help method that creators use is to keep physical control of their creations. For a limited time, software creators encrypted commands into the programs so that they could not be copied. This practice has been largely abandoned because of the complaints from legitimate users who needed to make copies according to the guidelines in 117.[61] The encoded commands were also not as effective at preventing copying as hoped. The difficulty actually created a new market for decryption programs.

A compromise system that exists in the United States is the Copyright Clearing Center (CCC).[62] The CCC solicits authors for permission to license their copyrights to users, and in return pays a fee to the copyright owner each time their creation is used.[63] This system works well because it lowers transaction costs, but it is not universally accepted. Many creators would rather incur the higher costs of negotiating their own contracts with users. The CCC does not currently work with electronic resources and is not adapted to administer or enforce copyright guidelines over on-line systems. A global equivalent of the CCC is needed for the future, but electronic systems pose problems, such as ease of copying without knowledge, that must be solved before an electronic clearinghouse system will work.

Currently, some services such as LEXIS and Prodigy have systems analogous to the CCC. These databases have large amounts of copyrighted information on-line and have negotiated use fees with the copyright owners. In addition to posting prominent warnings and notices of copyright, these corporations make contracts with the users that only certain uses are allowed. The users pay fees depending on what and how much they use. This system is a crude method of protecting copyrights and makes it harder and more expensive for a person to infringe, but the opportunities for abuse are extensive. The monitoring and enforcement costs of these agreements mean that violations will only be prosecuted in the most egregious circumstances.

Another compromise solution, used in some European countries, is to allow anyone access and to recognize that copyright infringement will result. Therefore, the government charges everyone a photocopy tax and distributes the proceeds to the copyright owners.[64] In effect, copyright owners are required to license their copyrights to the government. This licensing is an unfair burden on non-infringers, since it shifts the costs of infringement onto all of society, while the benefits are retained by a few infringers. This does not serve society's best interests because it causes a classic free-rider problem in that an infringer takes a personal benefit while society pays the majority of the costs.

A comparable solution to this approach would be to tax blank media such as paper, tapes, or diskettes. This would raise the cost of infringing, but it would still impose a penalty upon people who use the media for non-infringing purposes. Unless the costs were raised prohibitively, it would not work because of the proliferation and reusability of computer information and storage. This transfer of infringement costs to all buyers of blank media is unfair since it would maintain the benefits for copyright owners, while making those who do not infringe pay for the loss due to infringers.

Currently, the Berne Convention and the UCC represent the largest steps toward the future by recognizing and facilitating the global market. A growing number of countries recognize the need for a uniform system of copyright practices and have joined these conventions. These conventions benefit creators by avoiding the incentives for self-help and by increasing the legitimate market for creations. As sysops connect to ever-increasing numbers of foreign countries, the historical and practical barriers to copyright infringement disappear. These conventions move toward the ideal future solution by creating a system that can protect copyright owners in an environment of global access.

C. Future Steps toward an Ideal Copyright Law

Copyright infringement will be greatly reduced when compliance with the laws is the easiest choice for the user. Once global, low-cost access is available, the demand will be satisfied and there will be no incentives to infringe. Until that time, society must try to minimize current infringement while working toward the long-term global goal.

One way to minimize current infringement would be to create an ethical code to define the rights of copyright owners and what is considered infringement.[65] When photocopying equipment came into common usage, libraries and authors debated over the liability of having equipment that simplified infringement on library premises.[66] The compromise from this debate was that a library is not required to monitor all photocopying, but was to post signs that reproduction of copyrighted material was illegal.[67] The equivalent in the electronic environment is to post frequent and obvious notices where copyrights exist. An educational campaign to tell people of the costs of infringement and the possible penalties will help to decrease the incidence of infringement.

An honor system and a code of trust are necessary until a universal system is in place. Until enforcement is unnecessary, the practical limitations mean that such a code is necessary to protect authors. Education and an ethical code will make people realize the costs of infringement and will create an incentive to follow the law for the personal reward of being ethical. A prominent policy will deter people who are innocent infringers and will make other people consider the consequences of their actions. This code should make it harmful to a person's reputation if a person infringes or helps others to infringe. Until enforcement is unnecessary, sysops will have an incentive to ensure their own gain by educating users to know when they are copying and the results of doing so. As more people who use the resources know the consequences, they will use common sense and act in ways to protect their long-term interests by not depriving copyright holders.

Sysops can make a concerted effort to work for the future and to minimize current infringement by educating people and monitoring resources to make sure that all copyright notices remain in place. Sysops can also self-monitor the amount and number of users with access to materials by using current accounting software and internal auditing. These self-imposed controls will not eliminate copyright infringement, but they can be used to reduce the amount of uncontrolled copying so that reasonable benefits are conferred on copyright owners. This will retain the incentive for owners to continue to contribute original works.

Sysops currently have the power to reduce the amount of infringement on their systems by not allowing access to infringers. If a sysop is aware of infringement by a user, the sysop should eliminate that user's access rights. This is a minimal screen because infringement is so difficult to detect, but the possible punishment would deter some users.

The most important step toward a global copyright ideal will be for more countries to work together by joining conventions such as the Berne Convention and the UCC. Current member countries must solicit and welcome new members. As more countries work together, other countries will realize the benefits of membership and will also join. This circular effect will continue to increase the legitimate markets for resources and will lower the costs to creators. As the countries create more access and give rewards to the creators, the copyright owners will have incentives to allow access in order to take advantage of the expanded market. The owners will also be able to lower prices for use because protection costs will be less, and bulk sales will make up for the lower profit per user.

Sysops of the future must work to keep copyright owners from employing self-help methods. They can do this by assuring creators of the benefits of their work. The creation of an accurate method to reward creators according to the benefits of their contribution is key to the future of complete access. Companies are now experimenting with procedures of charging for access: these include charging purely for time, charging per resource accessed, or charging for the type of use such as copying versus merely reading. As new technology is created for monitoring and auditing, the ability to reward creators correctly will be enhanced.

Sysops must also take advantage of new technology to satisfy the demands of users. In conjunction with the growth of member countries will be the growth of potential users. Sysops must ensure that the demands of these new users are met. Sysops can demand and receive more resources as their ability to disseminate creations, while rewarding the creators, increases. By ensuring that access is widespread and inexpensive, sysops will be satisfying the demand for resources and will eliminate the shortage that is currently resulting in infringement.

A sysop lobby needs to be organized to press for reorganization of the copyright laws for the future. The new laws need to deal with the future reality of global, personal access to resources. The laws must support the organization and development of technology to deliver access and reward creators. The doctrines of fair use and archival copying can be eliminated, and the penalties for infringement can be reduced, because the gains from infringement will disappear as the supply of legitimate access satisfies the demand.

VIII. Conclusion

The use of copyrighted resources has undergone a revolution since the latest version of the copyright laws was enacted. Global growth in electronic media, resources, and available access is not going to stop or even slow in the near future. To keep pace with these changes, sysops of the future need to balance the interests of users for access against the demands of the copyright creators for a return on their contribution. This means that authors must get fair compensation while the users pay a fair price.

This balancing act will be complicated by the sheer proliferation of easy, global electronic communication. The problems of free-riders from countries that do not recognize copyrights and the problems of enforcement will make this a continuing problem until a global policy has been promulgated. The information superhighway is changing the world into a global village and a library without walls. Global, personal access is becoming a reality; this calls for a reassessment of the copyright laws and a new method of balancing interests to maximize the benefits of creation and access for everyone in society.

Notes

1. 839 F. Supp. 1552 (M.D. Fla. 1993).
2. 839 F. Supp. at 1554–55, 1559.
3. A copyright can be assigned from an author to a different owner, but for purposes of this chapter authors will be treated as owners.
4. 17 U.S.C. sec. 102(a) (1988 & Supp. V 1993).
5. 17 U.S.C. sec. 102(a). Original, as the term is used in copyright law, means only that the work was independently created by the author (as opposed to being copied from other works), and that it possesses at least some minimal creativity (*Feist Publications v. Rural Telephone Service Co.*, 499 U.S. 340, 358 [1991]). Originality merely requires independent creation and at least some expressive choice

in composing the work (Raymond T. Nimmer, *The Law of Computer Technology* [Boston: Warren, Gorham, and Lamont, 1985], 1.03[3][a], at S1–20 [1992 Cum. Supp. No. 2]).

6. Copyrightable works must be "fixed in any tangible medium of expression, now known or later developed, from which they can be perceived, reproduced, or otherwise communicated, either directly or with the aid of a machine or device" (17 U.S.C. sec. 102 [1988]).

7. "Anyone who violates any of the exclusive rights of the copyright owner . . . is an infringer of the copyright" (17 U.S.C. sec. 501[a] [1988]).

8. "A derivative work is a work based upon one or more preexisting works" (17 U.S.C. sec. 101 [1988]).

9. Berne Convention for the Protection of Literary and Artistic Works, 9 September 1886, as revised Paris, 24 July 1971, and amended in 1979, S. Treaty Doc. No. 99–27, 99th Cong., 2d Sess. (1986), 828 U.N.T.S. 221 [hereinafter Berne Convention]; Berne Convention Implementation Act of 1988, Pub. L. No. 100–568, 102 Stat. 2853 (1988) (entered into force for the United States Mar. 1, 1989) (codified at 17 U.S.C. sec. 101 [1988 & Supp. V 1993]) [hereinafter Berne Convention Implementation Act]. See also, Universal Copyright Convention, 6 September 1952, 6 U.S.T. 2731 (1952), revised July 24, 1971, 25 U.S.T. 1341, 943 U.N.T.S. 178 (1974) [hereinafter UCC]. For various bilateral treaties, see "Copyright: Agreement Between the United States of America and Indonesia," 22 March 1989, U.S.-Indon., T.I.A.S. No. 11,608.

10. See A. Lyman Chapin, "The Internet Architecture Board and the Future of the Internet," *Educom Review*, September/October 1992, 42.

11. Electronic bulletin boards have different "rooms" that are devoted to discussions of various subjects. Anyone with access to the bulletin board can read or write messages in the rooms. Almost any subject is discussed on a bulletin board somewhere.

12. Vinton Cerf, president of the Internet Society, Address at the Online '93 CD-ROM Conference Exposition (1 November 1993); Frank Vizard, "Building the Information Superhighway: Construction Begins on an Interstate Data Highway That Promises to Revolutionize Communication and the Way We All Live," *Popular Mechanics*, January 1994, 28, 32.

13. Cerf, Address at '93 CD-ROM Conference. Eight terabytes is 8,000,000,000,000 bytes.

14. Michael W. Miller, "Contact High," *Wall Street Journal*, 15 November 1993, at R4.

15. Chapin, "Internet Architecture."

16. A modem is the electronic hardware needed for a computer to communicate over a telephone line. A telecommunications software package is also needed to tell the computer how to use the modem. Talking in real time is similar to using a telephone; the person on the other end of the line sees the information as it is typed. This enables simultaneous conversations and differs from e-mail, where a message is sent, received, and then answered.

17. Public domain software is either software that is not original enough to obtain a copyright or software that a programmer releases to gain a reputation. Shareware is software that is freely distributed on an honor system where a user is supposed to test a program and then send a payment to the author if use is continued. Commercial software is written by a company that seeks a profit from all sales of the software. See also the discussion of public domain materials in John Lautsch, *American Standard Handbook of Software Law* (Reston, Va.: Reston Pub. Co., 1985), sec. 5.35.

18. The LEXIS service provides access to many court cases, government publications, journal articles, and magazine and newspaper stories for a fee. Similarly, but for free, people can read UPI bulletins as they are sent over the UPI system by using a system on the Internet called "Usenet." Many research and academic services also give free access to court decisions or government documents over the Internet.

19. "Information Highway Raises Copyright Questions," *Indianapolis News*, 7 July 1994, A–11.

20. See 17 U.S.C. sec. 108 (1988), discussed in H.R. Rep. No. 1476, 94th Cong., 2d Sess. (1976), reprinted in 1976 U.S.C.C.A.N. 5659, 5688–92. Before passage of this law in 1976, there was an extensive debate about the interaction of photocopying and copyright. See J. Lawrence and B. Timberg, *Fair Use and Free Inquiry* (Norwood, N.J.: Ablex Pub. Corp., 1980), 207–9; William Z. Nasri, *Crisis in Copyright* (New York: M. Dekker, 1976), 17, 65, 138; James M. Treece, "Library Photocopying", in *Technology and Copyright*, edited by Bush and Dreyfuss (Mt. Airy, Md.: Lomond Books, 1979), 415; *Reprography and Copyright Law*, edited by Hattery and Bush (Washington, D.C.: American Institute of Biological Sciences, 1964).

21. "Congress shall have Power . . . to promote the Progress of Science and useful Arts, by securing for limited Times to Authors and Inventors the exclusive Right to their respective Writings and Discoveries" (U.S. Constitution, art. I, 8, cl. 8).

22. "An Act for the encouragement of learning, by securing the copies of maps, charts, and books, to the authors and proprietors of such copies, during the times therein mentioned" (Act of 31 May 1790, chap. 15, 1 Stat. 124 [1790]).

23. The 1976 Act revised the scope of works protected to include creation instead of publication, abolished common law copyright, codified fair use, and added electronic copyrights. For a discussion of the 1976 revisions, see Patterson and Lindberg, *The Nature of Copyright* (Athens: University of Georgia Press, 1991), 90–106; *N.Y.L.J. and the Copyright Society of the U.S.A., The Copyright Act of 1976: Dealing with the New Realities* (1977); Copyright Revision Act of 1976 (CCH 1976). The Berne Convention Implementation Act further amended the copyright law to conform to the requirements of the treaty.

24. See 17 U.S.C. 102(a); see also text accompanying note 4. Software (computer programs) was specifically defined and allowed copyright protection in 17 U.S.C. sec. 101 (1988 & Supp. V 1993), by the Computer Software Copyright Act of 1980, Pub. L. No. 96–517 10(a), 94 Stat. 3015, 3028 (1980).

25. See notes 3 to 6 and accompanying text.

26. 17 U.S.C. sec. 106 (1988).

27. 17 U.S.C. sec. 302(a) (1988). Material before the 1976 act had to be published to have copyright protection, and the protection was only for twenty-eight years, with a possible renewal for another twenty-eight years (Act of 4 March 1909, ch. 320, 35 Stat. 1075, 1080 [1909]). If the author is a corporation, the duration is the shorter of seventy-five years from publication or one hundred years from creation (17 U.S.C. sec. 302[c] [1988]).

28. 17 U.S.C. sec. 501 (1988).

29. Stephen A. Kroft, "Copyright Litigation Overview," in *How to Handle Basic Copyright and Trademark Problems* (1992), 405, 430, 437.

30. 17 U.S.C. sec. 108 (1988). The total defense of innocent infringement was deleted by the Copyright Act of 1976 by not requiring intent. A defense of innocent infringement can still be valid for a court to reduce damages (17 U.S.C. sec. 504[c][2] [1988]).

31. See Latman et al., *Copyright for the Nineties: Cases and Materials*, 3d ed. (Charlottesville, Va.: Michie Co., 1989), 666–74.

32. *Universal City Studios v. Sony Corp. of America*, 464 U.S. 417, 437–38 (1984).

33. *Universal City Studios*, 439, 444.

34. *Playboy Enterprises v. Frena*, 839 F. Supp. 1552, 1559 (M.D. Fla. 1993).

35. Frank H. Andorka, "What Is Copyright?" *ABA Sec. Pat., Trademark and Copyright Law* (1992).

36. Sony Corp. of America, 464 U.S., 442–56.

37. See 122 Cong. Rec. H31,977, 31,980–81, Sept. 22, 1976 (debate of H. Res. 1550).

38. 17 U.S.C. sec. 107 (1988).

39. Copyright Act, Pub. L. No. 94–553, 1976 U.S.C.C.A.N. 5659, 5682–83.

40. 17 U.S.C. sec. 108 (1988).

41. The Software Publishers Association estimates 1990 software copying losses of $2.4 billion in the United States and $10–$12 billion overseas (Patrick G. Marshall, "Copying Computer Programs Puts Byte on Software Firms," *Star Tribune* [Minneapolis], 1 July 1993, 16E).

42. 17 U.S.C. sec. 117 (1988).

43. 17 U.S.C. sec. 411, 501(a) (1988).

44. 17 U.S.C. sec. 502–505 (1988).

45. See M. M. Boguslavsky, *Copyright in International Relations: International Protection of Literary and Scientific Works*, edited by David Catterns and trans. by N. Poulet (Sydney: Australian Copyright Council, 1979), 19, 20, 25–28.

46. See Berne Convention. There were eighty-four members of the Berne Convention as of 25 January 1990 (Beryl R. Jones, "Legal Framework for the International Protection of Copyrights," in *Global Intellectual Property Series*, Siegrun D. Kane et al. chair [1992]: 263). See UCC. There were eighty-one contracting states to the UCC as of 1 January 1990 (Jones, "Legal Framework," 264).

47. The Berne Convention was concluded 9 September 1886. The history of the Berne Convention is discussed in World Intellectual Property Organization, Guide to the Berne Convention for the Protection of Literary and Artistic Works (World Intellectual Property Organization Series No. 615(E), 1978). See also, Berne Convention Implementation Act; Copyright Act of 1909, ch. 320, 35 Stat. 1075 (1909). The UCC was signed in 1952. H.R. Rep. No. 2608, 83d Cong., 2d Sess. (1954), reprinted in 1954 U.S.S.C.A.N. 3629, 3630. It entered into force 16 September 1955. U.S. Copyright Off., Circular 38A, International Copyright Relations of the United States 2 (July 1992).

The majority of copyright relations with the United States are via multilateral treaties. Bilateral treaty provisions are normally similar to those of the multilateral conventions. See, for example, Copyright: Agreement between the United States of America and Indonesia, 22 March 1989, U.S.-Indon., T.I.A.S. No. 11,608. Most bilateral treaties are superseded by the multilateral treaties, but the United States is limited to solely bilateral treaties with China, Cuba, El Salvador, Indonesia, and Singapore. See U.S. Copyright Off., Circular 38A.

48. See Berne Convention, art. 2(1); UCC, art. I, 25 U.S.T. at 1344, 943 U.N.T.S. at 195; see also, Berne Convention, art. 2(6); UCC, art. II(2), 25 U.S.T. at 1345, 943 U.N.T.S. at 195. Article 1 of the Berne Convention defines the countries as a "Union," but the UCC calls members "Contracting States." See Berne Convention, art. 3(1)(a) and (b); UCC, art. II(1), 25 U.S.T. at 1345, 943 U.N.T.S. at 195. Publication by a non-national in a member country is the so-called back door, where many U.S. authors simultaneously published in the United States and a Berne Union country to gain international protection when the United States was not a Berne Union member. See Berne Convention, art. 2(2), 3(3). "Publication, as used in this [UCC] Convention, means the reproduction in tangible form and the general distribution to the public of copies of a work from which it can be read or otherwise visually perceived" (UCC, art. VI, 25 U.S.T. at 1362, 943 U.N.T.S. at 203).

49. See Berne Convention, art. 5(2); UCC, art. III, 25 U.S.T. at 1345–46, 943 U.N.T.S. at 195. The work must meet the UCC requirement that all copyrighted copies of the work bear the copyright symbol, along with the copyright owner's name and year of first publication, all placed so as to give reasonable notice of a claim of copyright. See also, Berne Convention, art. 5; UCC, art. II, 25 U.S.T. at 1345, 943 U.N.T.S. at 195.

50. See Berne Convention, art. 6 bis (1); Berne Convention, art. 7(1); UCC, art. IV(2)(a), 25 U.S.T. at 1347, 943 U.N.T.S. at 196; Berne Convention, art. 7(6).

51. See Berne Convention, art. 5(1); UCC, art. IV bis, 25 U.S.T. at 1349, 943 U.N.T.S. at 196–97; UCC, art. IV bis, 25 U.S.T. at 1349, 943 U.N.T.S. at 196–97; Berne Convention, art. 8, 9; UCC, art. IV bis, V, 25 U.S.T. at 1349–51, 943 U.N.T.S. at 196–98.

52. See Berne Convention, art. 2 bis, 9, 10; UCC, art. IV bis (2), 25 U.S.T. at 1349, 943 U.N.T.S. at 197.

53. The UCC allows that in order to afford judicial relief a country may re-

quire formalities such as local counsel or deposit of a work, such as are required for nationals (UCC, art. III[3], 25 U.S.T. at 1346, 943 U.N.T.S. at 195); Berne Convention, art. 16; Berne Convention, art. 6.

54. See UCC, art. XVII, 25 U.S.T. at 1367, 943 U.N.T.S. at 205.

55. See Copyright Act of 1976. See also, Berne Convention Implementation Act.

56. Congress decided that the Berne Convention was not self-executing. This means that it may not be directly applied and that it does not create any rights (U.S. Copyright Off., Circular 93A, The United States Joins the Berne Union 2 [February 1989]). See also Berne Convention, art. 6 bis; see U.S. Copyright Off., Circular 93A, at 3.

57. In fact, "computer program" is specifically defined in 17 U.S.C. sec. 101 (1988) and given copyright protection. The Berne Convention and the UCC do not define a "computer program," but software and electronic files fall in the category of "literary works" and thus qualify for treaty protection.

58. A hacker is a computer user who specializes in breaking into private areas of a computer. These people have computer skills much greater than those of the average user and can bypass many security programs. For a discussion of hackers and electronic bulletin boards, see Charles Cangialosi, "The Electronic Underground: Computer Piracy and Electronic Bulletin Boards," *Rutgers Computer and Technology Law Journal* 15 (1989): 265.

59. As Nathaniel Shaler has stated: "It will be clearly seen that intellectual property is, after all, the only absolute possession in the world. . . . The man who brings out of nothingness some child of his thought has rights therein which cannot belong to any other sort of property . . . the inventor of a book or other contrivance of thought holds his property, as a God holds it, by right of creation" (Thorvald Solberg, "Copyright Reform: Legislation and International Copyright," *Notre Dame Law* 14 [1939]: 343, 358–59 [quoting Nathaniel Shaler, *Literary Property* [1878]).

60. These contracts can have complex clauses that are not always enforceable in courts for reasons ranging from illegality or unconscionability to lack of mutual assent. For criticism of these contracts, see Edward J. Valauskas, "Copyright: Know Your Electronic Rights," *Library Journal* 117 (August 1992):40.

61. See 17 U.S.C. sec. 117 (1988); note 37 and accompanying text.

62. See R. S. Talab, *Commonsense Copyright: A Guide to the New Technologies* (Jefferson, N.C.: McFarland and Co., 1986), 29.

63. Talab, *Commonsense Copyright.*

64. "Various European countries have made the legislative decision to protect the interests of copyright owners by imposing a surcharge on photocopying. The fees for copying ultimately inure, directly or indirectly, to the benefit of authors or publishers" (Gert Kolle, "Reprography and Copyright Law: A Comparative Law Study Concerning the Role of Copyright Law in the Age of Information," *International Review Indus. Prop. and Copyright Law* 6 [1975]: 382, cited in Treece, "Library Photocopying," at 418).

65. This would be similar to the guidelines recommended by the National Commission on New Technological Uses of Copyrighted Works (CONTU) for library photocopying (CONTU, "Final Report of the National Commission on New Technology Uses of Copyrighted Works," 31 July 1978, 54).

66. See 17 U.S.C. sec. 108 (1988), discussed in H.R. Rep. No. 1476, 94th Cong., 2d Sess. (1976), reprinted in 1976 U.S.C.C.A.N. 5659, 5688–92. See also, Lawrence and Timberg, *Fair Use and Free Inquiry,* 207–9; Nasri, *Crisis in Copyright,* 17, 65, 138; and Treece, "Library Photocopying," 415.

67. See 17 U.S.C. sec. 108(f)(1) (1988).

15

The Economy of Ideas: Everything You Know about Intellectual Property Is Wrong*

John Perry Barlow

If nature has made any one thing less susceptible than all others of exclusive property, it is the action of the thinking power called an idea, which an individual may exclusively possess as long as he keeps it to himself; but the moment it is divulged, it forces itself into the possession of everyone, and the receiver cannot dispossess himself of it. Its peculiar character, too, is that no one possesses the less, because every other possesses the whole of it. He who receives an idea from me, receives instruction himself without lessening mine; as he who lights his taper at mine, receives light without darkening me. That ideas should freely spread from one to another over the globe, for the moral and mutual instruction of man, and improvement of his condition, seems to have been peculiarly and benevolently designed by nature, when she made them, like fire, expansible over all space, without lessening their density at any point, and like the air in which we breathe, move, and have our physical being, incapable of confinement or exclusive appropriation. Inventions then cannot, in nature, be a subject of property.

—Thomas Jefferson

*This essay was originally published as "The Economy of Ideas: Everything You Know about Intellectual Property Is Wrong," by John Perry Barlow, in *Wired* (March 1994). Copyright © 1994 by Wired Magazine Group, Inc. Reprinted with permission of publisher.

349

Throughout the time I've been groping around cyberspace, an immense, unsolved conundrum has remained at the root of nearly every legal, ethical, governmental, and social vexation to be found in the Virtual World. I refer to the problem of digitized property. The enigma is this: If our property can be infinitely reproduced and instantaneously distributed all over the planet without cost, without our knowledge, without its even leaving our possession, how can we protect it? How are we going to get paid for the work we do with our minds? And, if we can't get paid, what will assure the continued creation and distribution of such work?

Since we don't have a solution to what is a profoundly new kind of challenge, and are apparently unable to delay the galloping digitization of everything not obstinately physical, we are sailing into the future on a sinking ship.

This vessel, the accumulated canon of copyright and patent law, was developed to convey forms and methods of expression entirely different from the vaporous cargo it is now being asked to carry. It is leaking as much from within as from without.

Legal efforts to keep the old boat floating are taking three forms: a frenzy of deck chair rearrangement, stern warnings to the passengers that if she goes down, they will face harsh criminal penalties, and serene, glassy-eyed denial.

Intellectual property law cannot be patched, retrofitted, or expanded to contain digitized expression any more than real estate law might be revised to cover the allocation of the broadcasting spectrum (which, in fact, rather resembles what is being attempted here). We will need to develop an entirely new set of methods as befits this entirely new set of circumstances.

Most of the people who actually create soft property—the programmers, hackers, and Net surfers—already know this. Unfortunately, neither the companies they work for nor the lawyers these companies hire have enough direct experience with nonmaterial goods to understand why they are so problematic. They are proceeding as though the old laws can somehow be made to work, either by grotesque expansion or by force. They are wrong.

The source of this conundrum is as simple as its solution is complex. Digital technology is detaching information from the physical plane, where property law of all sorts has always found definition.

Throughout the history of copyrights and patents, the proprietary assertions of thinkers have been focused not on their ideas but on the expression of those ideas. The ideas themselves, as well as facts about the phenomena of the world, were considered to be the collective property of humanity. One could claim franchise, in the case of copyright, on the precise turn of phrase used to convey a particular idea or the order in which facts were presented.

The point at which this franchise was imposed was that moment when the "word became flesh" by departing the mind of its originator and entering some physical object, whether book or widget. The subsequent arrival of other commercial media besides books didn't alter the legal importance of this moment. Law protected expression and, with few (and recent) exceptions, to express was to make physical.

Protecting physical expression had the force of convenience on its side. Copyright worked well because, Gutenberg notwithstanding, it was hard to make a book. Furthermore, books froze their contents into a condition that was as challenging to alter as it was to reproduce. Counterfeiting and distributing counterfeit volumes were obvious and visible activities—it was easy enough to catch somebody in the act of doing. Finally, unlike unbounded words or images, books had material surfaces to which one could attach copyright notices, publisher's marques, and price tags.

Mental-to-physical conversion was even more central to patent. A patent, until recently, was either a description of the form into which materials were to be rendered in the service of some purpose, or a description of the process by which rendition occurred. In either case, the conceptual heart of patent was the material result. If no purposeful object could be rendered because of some material limitation, the patent was rejected. Neither a Klein bottle nor a shovel made of silk could be patented. It had to be a thing, and the thing had to work.

Thus, the rights of invention and authorship adhered to activities in the physical world. One didn't get paid for ideas, but for the ability to deliver them into reality. For all practical purposes, the value was in the conveyance and not in the thought conveyed. In other words, the bottle was protected, not the wine.

Now, as information enters cyberspace, the native home of Mind, these bottles are vanishing. With the advent of digitization, it is now possible to replace all previous information storage forms with one metabottle: complex and highly liquid patterns of ones and zeros.

Even the physical/digital bottles to which we've become accustomed—floppy disks, CD-ROMs, and other discrete, shrink-wrappable bit-packages—will disappear as all computers jack-in to the global Net. While the Internet may never include every CPU on the planet, it is more than doubling every year and can be expected to become the principal medium of information conveyance, and perhaps eventually the only one.

Once that has happened, all the goods of the information age—all of the expressions once contained in books or film strips or newsletters—

will exist either as pure thought or something very much like thought: voltage conditions darting around the Net at the speed of light, in conditions that one might behold in effect, as glowing pixels or transmitted sounds, but never touch or claim to "own" in the old sense of the word.

Some might argue that information will still require some physical manifestation, such as its magnetic existence on the titanic hard disks of distant servers, but these are bottles that have no macroscopically discrete or personally meaningful form.

Some will also argue that we have been dealing with unbottled expression since the advent of radio, and they would be right. But for most of the history of broadcast, there was no convenient way to capture soft goods from the electromagnetic ether and reproduce them with the quality available in commercial packages. Only recently has this changed, and little has been done legally or technically to address the change.

Generally, the issue of consumer payment for broadcast products was irrelevant. The consumers themselves were the product. Broadcast media were supported either by the sale of the attention of their audience to advertisers, by government assessing payment through taxes, or by the whining mendicancy of annual donor drives.

All of the broadcast-support models are flawed. Support either by advertisers or government has almost invariably tainted the purity of the goods delivered. Besides, direct marketing is gradually killing the advertiser-support model anyway.

Broadcast media gave us another payment method for a virtual product: the royalties that broadcasters pay songwriters through such organizations as ASCAP and BMI. But, as a member of ASCAP, I can assure you this is not a model that we should emulate. The monitoring methods are wildly approximate. There is no parallel system of accounting in the revenue stream. It doesn't really work. Honest.

In any case, without our old methods, based on physically defining the expression of ideas, and in the absence of successful new models for nonphysical transaction, we simply don't know how to assure reliable payment for mental works. To make matters worse, this comes at a time when the human mind is replacing sunlight and mineral deposits as the principal source of new wealth.

Furthermore, the increasing difficulty of enforcing existing copyright and patent laws is already placing in peril the ultimate source of intellectual property—the free exchange of ideas.

That is, when the primary articles of commerce in a society look so much like speech as to be indistinguishable from it, and when the traditional methods of protecting their ownership have become ineffectual, attempting to fix the problem with broader and more vigorous enforcement will inevitably threaten freedom of speech. The greatest constraint on your future liberties may come not from government but from corporate legal departments laboring to protect by force what can no longer be protected by practical efficiency or general social consent.

Furthermore, when Jefferson and his fellow creatures of the Enlightenment designed the system that became American copyright law, their primary objective was assuring the widespread distribution of thought, not profit. Profit was the fuel that would carry ideas into the libraries and minds of their new republic. Libraries would purchase books, thus rewarding the authors for their work in assembling ideas; these ideas, otherwise "incapable of confinement," would then become freely available to the public. But what is the role of libraries in the absence of books? How does society now pay for the distribution of ideas if not by charging for the ideas themselves?

Additionally complicating the matter is the fact that along with the disappearance of the physical bottles in which intellectual property protection has resided, digital technology is also erasing the legal jurisdictions of the physical world and replacing them with the unbounded and perhaps permanently lawless waves of cyberspace.

In cyberspace, no national or local boundaries contain the scene of a crime and determine the method of its prosecution; worse, no clear cultural agreements define what a crime might be. Unresolved and basic differences between Western and Asian cultural assumptions about intellectual property can only be exacerbated when many transactions are taking place in both hemispheres and yet, somehow, in neither.

Even in the most local of digital conditions, jurisdiction and responsibility are hard to assess. A group of music publishers filed suit against CompuServe this fall because it allowed its users to upload musical compositions into areas where other users might access them. But since CompuServe cannot practically exercise much control over the flood of bits that passes between its subscribers, it probably shouldn't be held responsible for unlawfully "publishing" these works.

Notions of property, value, ownership, and the nature of wealth itself are changing more fundamentally than at any time since the Sumerians first poked cuneiform into wet clay and called it stored grain. Only a very few people are aware of the enormity of this shift, and fewer of them are lawyers or public officials.

Those who do see these changes must prepare responses for the legal and social confusion that will erupt as efforts to protect new forms of property with old methods become more obviously futile, and, as a consequence, more adamant.

From Swords to Writs to Bits

Humanity now seems bent on creating a world economy primarily based on goods that take no material form. In doing so, we may be eliminating any predictable connection between creators and a fair reward for the utility or pleasure others may find in their works.

Without that connection, and without a fundamental change in consciousness to accommodate its loss, we are building our future on furor, litigation, and institutionalized evasion of payment except in response to raw force. We may return to the Bad Old Days of property.

Throughout the darker parts of human history, the possession and distribution of property was a largely military matter. "Ownership" was assured those with the nastiest tools, whether fists or armies, and the most resolute will to use them. Property was the divine right of thugs.

By the turn of the first millennium, A.D., the emergence of merchant classes and landed gentry forced the development of ethical understandings for the resolution of property disputes. In the Middle Ages, enlightened rulers like England's Henry II began to codify this unwritten "common law" into recorded canons. These laws were local, which didn't matter much as they were primarily directed at real estate, a form of property that is local by definition. And, as the name implied, was very real.

This continued to be the case as long as the origin of wealth was agricultural, but with that dawning of the Industrial Revolution, humanity began to focus as much on means as ends. Tools acquired a new social value and, thanks to their development, it became possible to duplicate and distribute them in quantity.

To encourage their invention, copyright and patent law were developed in most Western countries. These laws were devoted to the delicate task of getting mental creations into the world where they could be used—and could enter the minds of others—while assuring their inventors compensation for the value of their use. And, as previously stated, the systems of both law and practice which grew up around that task were based on physical expression.

Since it is now possible to convey ideas from one mind to another without ever making them physical, we are now claiming to own ideas themselves and not merely their expression. And since it is likewise now possible to create useful tools that never take physical form, we have taken to patenting abstractions, sequences of virtual events, and mathematical formulae—the most unreal estate imaginable.

In certain areas, this leaves rights of ownership in such an ambiguous condition that property again adheres to those who can muster the largest armies. The only difference is that this time the armies consist of lawyers.

Threatening their opponents with the endless purgatory of litigation, over which some might prefer death itself, they assert claim to any thought which might have entered another cranium within the collective body of the corporations they serve. They act as though these ideas appeared in splendid detachment from all previous human thought. And they pretend that thinking about a product is somehow as good as manufacturing, distributing, and selling it.

What was previously considered a common human resource, distributed among the minds and libraries of the world, as well as the phenomena of nature herself, is now being fenced and deeded. It is as though a new class of enterprise had arisen that claimed to own the air.

What is to be done? While there is a certain grim fun to be had in it, dancing on the grave of copyright and patent will solve little, especially when so few are willing to admit that the occupant of this grave is even deceased, and so many are trying to uphold by force what can no longer be upheld by popular consent.

The legalists, desperate over their slipping grip, are vigorously trying to extend their reach. Indeed, the United States and other proponents of GATT are making adherence to our moribund systems of intellectual property protection a condition of membership in the marketplace of nations. For example, China will be denied Most Favored Nation trading status unless it agrees to uphold a set of culturally alien principles that are no longer even sensibly applicable in their country of origin.

In a more perfect world, we'd be wise to declare a moratorium on litigation, legislation, and international treaties in this area until we had a clearer sense of the terms and conditions of enterprise in cyberspace. Ideally, laws ratify already developed social consensus. They are less the Social Contract itself than a series of memoranda expressing a collective intent that has emerged out of many millions of human interactions.

Humans have not inhabited cyberspace long enough or in sufficient diversity to have developed a Social Contract that conforms to the strange new conditions of that world. Laws developed prior to consensus usually favor the already established few who can get them passed and not society as a whole.

To the extent that law and established social practice exists in this area, they are already in dangerous disagreement. The laws regarding unlicensed reproduction of commercial software are clear and stern . . . and rarely observed. Software piracy laws are so practically unenforceable and breaking them has become so socially acceptable that only a thin minority appears compelled, either by fear or conscience, to obey them. When I give speeches on this subject, I always ask how many people in the audience can honestly claim to have no unauthorized software on their hard disks. I've never seen more than 10 percent of the hands go up.

Whenever there is such profound divergence between law and social practice, it is not society that adapts. Against the swift tide of custom, the software publishers' current practice of hanging a few visible scapegoats is so obviously capricious as to only further diminish respect for the law.

Part of the widespread disregard for commercial software copyrights stems from a legislative failure to understand the conditions into which it was inserted. To assume that systems of law based in the physical world will serve in an environment as fundamentally different as cyberspace is a folly for which everyone doing business in the future will pay.

As I will soon discuss in detail, unbounded intellectual property is very different from physical property and can no longer be protected as though these differences did not exist. For example, if we continue to assume that value is based on scarcity, as it is with regard to physical objects, we will create laws that are precisely contrary to the nature of information, which may, in many cases, increase in value with distribution.

The large, legally risk-averse institutions most likely to play by the old rules will suffer for their compliance. As more lawyers, guns, and money are invested in either protecting their rights or subverting those of their opponents, their ability to produce new technology will simply grind to a halt as every move they make drives them deeper into a tar pit of courtroom warfare.

Faith in law will not be an effective strategy for high-tech companies. Law adapts by continuous increments and at a pace second only to geology. Technology advances in lunging jerks, like the punctuation of biological evolution grotesquely accelerated. Real-world conditions will continue to change at a blinding pace, and the law will lag further behind, more profoundly confused. This mismatch may prove impossible to overcome.

Promising economies based on purely digital products will either be born in a state of paralysis, as appears to be the case with multimedia, or continue in a brave and willful refusal by their owners to play the ownership game at all.

In the United States one can already see a parallel economy developing, mostly among small, fast moving enterprises who protect their ideas by getting into the marketplace quicker than their larger competitors who base their protection on fear and litigation.

Perhaps those who are part of the problem will simply quarantine themselves in court, while those who are part of the solution will create a new society based, at first, on piracy and freebooting. It may well be that when the current system of intellectual property law has collapsed, as seems inevitable, no new legal structure will arise in its place.

But something will happen. After all, people do business. When a currency becomes meaningless, business is done in barter. When societies develop outside the law, they develop their own unwritten codes, practices, and ethical systems. While technology may undo law, technology offers methods for restoring creative rights.

A Taxonomy of Information

It seems to me that the most productive thing to do now is to look into the true nature of what we're trying to protect. How much do we really know about information and its natural behaviors?

What are the essential characteristics of unbounded creation? How does it differ from previous forms of property? How many of our assumptions about it have actually been about its containers rather than their mysterious contents? What are its different species and how does each of them lend itself to control? What technologies will be useful in creating new virtual bottles to replace the old physical ones?

Of course, information is, by nature, intangible and hard to define. Like other such deep phenomena as light or matter, it is a natural host to paradox. It is most helpful to understand light as being both a particle and a wave, an understanding of information may emerge in the abstract congruence of its several different properties which might be described by the following three statements:

Information is an activity.
Information is a life form.
Information is a relationship.
In the following sections, I will examine each of these.

Information Is an Activity

Information Is a Verb, Not a Noun

Freed of its containers, information is obviously not a thing. In fact, it is something that happens in the field of interaction between minds or objects or other pieces of information.

Gregory Bateson, expanding on the information theory of Claude Shannon, said, "Information is a difference which makes a difference." Thus, information only really exists in the Delta. The making of that difference is an activity within a relationship. Information is an action which occupies time rather than a state of being which occupies physical space, as is the case with hard goods. It is the pitch, not the baseball, the dance, not the dancer.

Information Is Experienced, Not Possessed

Even when it has been encapsulated in some static form like a book or a hard disk, information is still something that happens to you as you mentally decompress it from its storage code. But, whether it's running at gigabits per second or words per minute, the actual decoding is a process that must be performed by and upon a mind, a process that must take place in time.

There was a cartoon in the *Bulletin of Atomic Scientists* a few years ago that illustrated this point beautifully. In the drawing, a holdup man trains his gun on the sort of bespectacled fellow you'd figure might have a lot of information stored in his head. "Quick," orders the bandit, "give me all your ideas."

Information Has to Move

Sharks are said to die of suffocation if they stop swimming, and the same is nearly true of information. Information that isn't moving ceases to exist as anything but potential . . . at least until it is allowed to move again. For this reason, the practice of information hoarding, common in bureaucracies, is an especially wrong-headed artifact of physically based value systems.

Information Is Conveyed by Propagation, Not Distribution

The way in which information spreads is also very different from the distribution of physical goods. It moves more like something from nature than from a factory. It can concatenate like falling dominos or grow in the usual fractal lattice, like frost spreading on a window, but it cannot be shipped around like widgets, except to the extent that it can be contained in them. It doesn't simply move on; it leaves a trail everywhere it's been.

The central economic distinction between information and physical property is that information can be transferred without leaving the possession of the original owner. If I sell you my horse, I can't ride him after that. If I sell you what I know, we both know it.

Information Is a Life Form

Information Wants to Be Free

Stewart Brand is generally credited with this elegant statement of the obvious, which recognizes both the natural desire of secrets to be told and the fact that they might be capable of possessing something like a "desire" in the first place.

English biologist and philosopher Richard Dawkins proposed the idea of "memes," self-replicating patterns of information that propagate themselves across the ecologies of mind, a pattern of reproduction much like that of life forms.

I believe they are life forms in every respect but their freedom from the carbon atom. They self-reproduce, they interact with their surroundings and adapt to them, they mutate, they persist. They evolve to fill the empty niches of their local environments, which are, in this case, the surrounding belief systems and cultures of their hosts, namely, us.

Indeed, sociobiologists like Dawkins make a plausible case that carbon-based life forms are information as well, that, as the chicken is an egg's way of making another egg, the entire biological spectacle is just the DNA molecule's means of copying out more information strings exactly like itself.

Information Replicates into the Cracks of Possibility

Like DNA helices, ideas are relentless expansionists, always seeking new opportunities for Lebensraum. And, as in carbon-based nature, the more robust organisms are extremely adept at finding new places to live. Thus, just as the common housefly has insinuated itself into practically every ecosystem on the planet, so has the meme of "life after death" found a niche in most minds, or psycho-ecologies.

The more universally resonant an idea or image or song, the more minds it will enter and remain within. Trying to stop the spread of a really robust piece of information is about as easy as keeping killer bees south of the border.

Information Wants to Change

If ideas and other interactive patterns of information are indeed life forms, they can be expected to evolve constantly into forms that will be more perfectly adapted to their surroundings. And, as we see, they are doing this all the time.

But for a long time, our static media, whether carvings in stone, ink on paper, or dye on celluloid, have strongly resisted the evolutionary impulse, exalting as a consequence the author's ability to determine the finished product. But, as in an oral tradition, digitized information has no "final cut."

Digital information, unconstrained by packaging, is a continuing process more like the metamorphosing tales of prehistory than anything that will fit in shrink-wrap. From the Neolithic to Gutenberg (monks aside), information was passed on, mouth to ear, changing with every retelling (or resinging). The stories which once shaped our sense of the world didn't have authoritative versions. They adapted to each culture in which they found themselves being told.

Because there was never a moment when the story was frozen in print, the so-called "moral" right of storytellers to own the tale was neither protected nor recognized. The story simply passed through each of them on its way to the next, where it would assume a different form. As we return to continuous information, we can expect the importance of authorship to diminish. Creative people may have to renew their acquaintance with humility.

But our system of copyright makes no accommodation whatever for expressions that don't become fixed at some point nor for cultural expressions that lack a specific author or inventor.

Jazz improvisations, stand-up comedy routines, mime performances, developing monologues, and unrecorded broadcast transmissions all lack the Constitutional requirement of fixation as a "writing." Without being fixed by a point of publication the liquid works of the future will all look more like these continuously adapting and changing forms and will therefore exist beyond the reach of copyright.

Copyright expert Pamela Samuelson tells of having attended a conference last year convened around the fact that Western countries may legally appropriate the music, designs, and biomedical lore of Aboriginal people without compensation to their tribes of origin since those tribes are not an "author" or "inventor."

But soon most information will be generated collaboratively by the cyber-tribal hunter-gatherers of cyberspace. Our arrogant legal dismissal of the rights of "primitives" will soon return to haunt us.

Information Is Perishable

With the exception of the rare classic, most information is like farm produce. Its quality degrades rapidly both over time and in distance from the source of production. But even here, value is highly subjective and conditional. Yesterday's papers are quite valuable to the historian. In fact, the older they are, the more valuable they become. On the other hand, a commodities broker might consider news of an event that occurred more than an hour ago to have lost any relevance.

Information Is a Relationship

Meaning Has Value and Is Unique to Each Case

In most cases, we assign value to information based on its meaningfulness. The place where information dwells, the holy moment where transmission becomes reception, is a region which has many shifting characteristics and flavors depending on the relationship of sender and receiver, the depth of their interactivity.

Each such relationship is unique. Even in cases where the sender is a broadcast medium, and no response is returned, the receiver is hardly passive. Receiving information is often as creative an act as generating it.

The value of what is sent depends entirely on the extent to which each individual receiver has the receptors—shared terminology, attention, interest, language, paradigm—necessary to render what is received meaningful.

Understanding is a critical element increasingly overlooked in the effort to turn information into a commodity. Data may be any set of facts, useful or not, intelligible or inscrutable, germane or irrelevant. Computers can crank out new data all night long without human help, and the results may be offered for sale as information. They may or may not actually be so. Only a human being can recognize the meaning that separates information from data.

In fact, information, in the economic sense of the word, consists of data which have been passed through a particular human mind and found meaningful within that mental context. One fella's information is all just data to someone else. If you're an anthropologist, my detailed charts of Tasaday kinship patterns might be critical information to you. If you're a banker from Hong Kong, they might barely seem to be data.

Familiarity Has More Value Than Scarcity

With physical goods, there is a direct correlation between scarcity and value. Gold is more valuable than wheat, even though you can't eat it. While this is not always the case, the situation with information is often precisely the reverse. Most soft goods increase in value as they become more common. Familiarity is an important asset in the world of information. It may often be true that the best way to raise demand for your product is to give it away.

While this has not always worked with shareware, it could be argued that there is a connection between the extent to which commercial software is pirated and the amount that gets sold. Broadly pirated software, such as Lotus 1–2–3 or WordPerfect, becomes a standard and benefits from Law of Increasing Returns based on familiarity.

In regard to my own soft product, rock 'n' roll songs, there is no question that the band I write them for, the Grateful Dead, has increased its popularity enormously by giving them away. We have been letting people tape our concerts since the early seventies, but instead of reducing the demand for our product, we are now the largest concert draw in America, a fact that is at least in part attributable to the popularity generated by those tapes.

True, I don't get any royalties on the millions of copies of my songs that have been extracted from concerts, but I see no reason to complain. The fact is, no one but the Grateful Dead can perform a Grateful Dead song, so if you want the experience and not its thin projection, you have to buy a ticket from us. In other words, our intellectual property protection derives from our being the only real-time source of it.

Exclusivity Has Value

The problem with a model that turns the physical scarcity/value ratio on its head is that sometimes the value of information is very much based on its scarcity. Exclusive possession of certain facts makes them more useful. If everyone knows about conditions that might drive a stock price up, the information is valueless.

But again, the critical factor is usually time. It doesn't matter if this kind of information eventually becomes ubiquitous. What matters is being among the first who possess it and act on it. While potent secrets usually don't stay secret, they may remain so long enough to advance the cause of their original holders.

Point of View and Authority Have Value

In a world of floating realities and contradictory maps, rewards will accrue to those commentators whose maps seem to fit their territory snugly, based on their ability to yield predictable results for those who use them.

In aesthetic information, whether poetry or rock 'n' roll, people are willing to buy the new product of an artist, sight-unseen, based on their having been delivered a pleasurable experience by previous work.

Reality is an edit. People are willing to pay for the authority of those editors whose point of view seems to fit best. And again, point of view is an asset that cannot be stolen or duplicated. No one sees the world as Esther Dyson does, and the handsome fee she charges for her newsletter is actually payment for the privilege of looking at the world through her unique eyes.

Time Replaces Space

In the physical world, value depends heavily on possession or proximity in space. One owns the material that falls inside certain dimensional boundaries. The ability to act directly, exclusively, and as one wishes upon what falls inside those boundaries is the principal right of ownership. The relationship between value and scarcity is a limitation in space.

In the virtual world, proximity in time is a value determinant. An informational product is generally more valuable the closer purchasers can place themselves to the moment of its expression, a limitation in time. Many kinds of information degrade rapidly with either time or reproduction. Relevance fades as the territory they map changes. Noise is introduced and bandwidth lost with passage away from the point where the information is first produced.

Thus, listening to a Grateful Dead tape is hardly the same experience as attending a Grateful Dead concert. The closer one can get to the headwaters of an informational stream, the better one's chances of finding an accurate picture of reality in it. In an era of easy reproduction, the informational abstractions of popular experiences will propagate out from their source moments to reach anyone who's interested. But it's easy enough to restrict the real experience of the desirable event, whether knock-out punch or guitar lick, to those willing to pay for being there.

The Protection of Execution

In the hick town I come from, they don't give you much credit for just having ideas. You are judged by what you can make of them. As things continue to speed up, I think we see that execution is the best protection for those designs which become physical products. Or, as Steve Jobs once put it, "Real artists ship." The big winner is usually the one who gets to the market first (and with enough organizational force to keep the lead).

But, as we become fixated upon information commerce, many of us seem to think that originality alone is sufficient to convey value, deserving, with the right legal assurances, of a steady wage. In fact, the best way to protect intellectual property is to act on it. It's not enough to invent and patent; one has to innovate as well. Someone claims to have patented the microprocessor before Intel. Maybe so. If he'd actually started shipping microprocessors before Intel, his claim would seem far less spurious.

Information as Its Own Reward

It is now a commonplace to say that money is information. With the exception of Krugerrands, crumpled cab fare, and the contents of those suitcases that drug lords are reputed to carry, most of the money in the informatized world is in ones and zeros. The global money supply sloshes around the Net, as fluid as weather. It is also obvious that information has become as fundamental to the creation of modern wealth as land and sunlight once were.

What is less obvious is the extent to which information is acquiring intrinsic value, not as a means to acquisition but as the object to be acquired. I suppose this has always been less explicitly the case. In politics and academia, potency and information have always been closely related.

However, as we increasingly buy information with money, we begin to see that buying information with other information is simple economic exchange without the necessity of converting the product into and out of currency. This is somewhat challenging for those who like clean accounting, since, information theory aside, informational exchange rates are too squishy to quantify to the decimal point.

Nevertheless, most of what a middle-class American purchases has little to do with survival. We buy beauty, prestige, experience, education, and all the obscure pleasures of owning. Many of these things can not only be expressed in nonmaterial terms, they can be acquired by nonmaterial means.

And then there are the inexplicable pleasures of information itself, the joys of learning, knowing, and teaching; the strange good feeling of information coming into and out of oneself. Playing with ideas is a recreation that people are willing to pay a lot for, given the market for books and elective seminars. We'd likely spend even more money for such pleasures if we didn't have so many opportunities to pay for ideas with other ideas. This explains much of the collective "volunteer" work that fills the archives, newsgroups, and databases of the Internet. Its denizens are not working for "nothing," as is widely believed. Rather they are getting paid in something besides money. It is an economy that consists almost entirely of information.

This may become the dominant form of human trade, and if we persist in modeling economics on a strictly monetary basis, we may be gravely misled.

Getting Paid in Cyberspace

How all the foregoing relates to solutions to the crisis in intellectual property is something I've barely started to wrap my mind around. It's fairly paradigm warping to look at information through fresh eyes—to see how very little it is like pig iron or pork bellies, and to imagine the tottering travesties of case law we will stack up if we go on legally treating it as though it were.

As I've said, I believe these towers of outmoded boilerplate will be a smoking heap sometime in the next decade, and we mind miners will have no choice but to cast our lot with new systems that work.

I'm not really so gloomy about our prospects as readers of this jeremiad so far might conclude. Solutions will emerge. Nature abhors a vacuum and so does commerce.

Indeed, one of the aspects of the electronic frontier that I have always found most appealing—and the reason Mitch Kapor and I used that phrase in naming our foundation—is the degree to which it resembles the nineteenth-century American West in its natural preference for social devices that emerge from its conditions rather than those that are imposed from the outside.

Until the West was fully settled and "civilized" in this century, order was established according to an unwritten Code of the West, which had the fluidity of common law rather than the rigidity of statutes. Ethics were more important than rules. Understandings were preferred over laws, which were, in any event, largely unenforceable.

I believe that law, as we understand it, was developed to protect the interests that arose in the two economic "waves" which Alvin Toffler accurately identified in *The Third Wave*. The First Wave was agriculturally based and required law to order ownership of the principal source of production, land. In the Second Wave, manufacturing became the economic mainspring, and the structure of modern law grew around the centralized institutions that needed protection for their reserves of capital, labor, and hardware.

Both of these economic systems required stability. Their laws were designed to resist change and to assure some equability of distribution within a fairly static social framework. The empty niches had to be constrained to preserve the predictability necessary to either land stewardship or capital formation.

In the Third Wave we have now entered, information to a large extent replaces land, capital, and hardware, and information is most at home in a much more fluid and adaptable environment. The Third Wave is likely to bring a fundamental shift in the purposes and methods of law that will affect far more than simply those statutes that govern intellectual property.

The "terrain" itself—the architecture of the Net—may come to serve many of the purposes that could only be maintained in the past by legal imposition. For example, it may be unnecessary to constitutionally assure freedom of expression in an environment that, in the words of my fellow EFF co-founder John Gilmore, "treats censorship as a malfunction" and reroutes proscribed ideas around it.

Similar natural balancing mechanisms may arise to smooth over the social discontinuities that previously required legal intercession to set right. On the Net, these differences are more likely to be spanned by a continuous spectrum that connects as much as it separates.

And, despite their fierce grip on the old legal structure, companies that trade in information are likely to find that their increasing inability to deal sensibly with technological issues will not be remedied in the courts, which won't be capable of producing verdicts predictable enough to be supportive of long-term enterprise. Every litigation will become like a game of Russian roulette, depending on the depth of the presiding judge's clue-impairment.

Uncodified or adaptive "law," while as "fast, loose, and out of control" as other emergent forms, is probably more likely to yield something like justice at this point. In fact, one can already see in development new practices to suit the conditions of virtual commerce. The life forms of information are evolving methods to protect their continued reproduction.

For example, while all the tiny print on a commercial diskette envelope punctiliously requires a great deal of those who would open it, few who read those provisos follow them to the letter. And yet, the software business remains a very healthy sector of the American economy.

Why is this? Because people seem to eventually buy the software they really use. Once a program becomes central to your work, you want the latest version of it, the best support, the actual manuals, all privileges attached to ownership. Such practical considerations will, in the absence of working law, become more and more important in getting paid for what might easily be obtained for nothing.

I do think that some software is being purchased in the service of ethics or the abstract awareness that the failure to buy it will result in its not being produced any longer, but I'm going to leave those motivators aside. While I believe that the failure of law will almost certainly result in a compensating re-emergence of ethics as the ordering template of society, this is a belief I don't have room to support here.

Instead, I think that, as in the case cited above, compensation for soft products will be driven primarily by practical considerations, all of them consistent with the true properties of digital information, where the value lies in it, and how it can be both manipulated and protected by technology.

While the conundrum remains a conundrum, I can begin to see the directions from which solutions may emerge, based in part on broadening those practical solutions which are already in practice.

Relationship and Its Tools

I believe one idea is central to understanding liquid commerce: Information economics, in the absence of objects, will be based more on relationship than possession.

One existing model for the future conveyance of intellectual property is real-time performance, a medium currently used only in theater, music, lectures, stand-up comedy, and pedagogy. I believe the concept of performance will expand to include most of the information economy, from multicasted soap operas to stock analysis. In these instances, commercial exchange will be more like ticket sales to a continuous show than the purchase of discrete bundles of that which is being shown.

The other existing model, of course, is service. The entire professional class—doctors, lawyers, consultants, architects, and so on—are already being paid directly for their intellectual property. Who needs copyright when you're on a retainer?

In fact, until the late eighteenth century this model was applied to much of what is now copyrighted. Before the industrialization of creation, writers, composers, artists, and the like produced their products in the private service of patrons. Without objects to distribute in a mass market, creative people will return to a condition somewhat like this, except that they will serve many patrons, rather than one.

We can already see the emergence of companies that base their existence on supporting and enhancing the soft property they create rather than selling it by the shrink-wrapped piece or embedding it in widgets.

Trip Hawkins's new company for creating and licensing multimedia tools, 3DO, is an example of what I'm talking about. 3DO doesn't intend to produce any commercial software or consumer devices. Instead, it will act as a kind of private standards-setting body, mediating among software and device creators who will be their licensees. It will provide a point of commonality for relationships between a broad spectrum of entities.

In any case, whether you think of yourself as a service provider or a performer, the future protection of your intellectual property will depend on your ability to control your relationship to the market—a relationship that will most likely live and grow over a period of time.

The value of that relationship will reside in the quality of performance, the uniqueness of your point of view, the validity of your expertise, its relevance to your market, and, underlying everything, the ability of that market to access your creative services swiftly, conveniently, and interactively.

Interaction and Protection

Direct interaction will provide a lot of intellectual property protection in the future, and, indeed, already has. No one knows how many software pirates have bought legitimate copies of a program after calling its publisher for technical support and offering some proof of purchase, but I would guess the number is very high.

The same kind of controls will be applicable to "question and answer" relationships between authorities (or artists) and those who seek their expertise. Newsletters, magazines, and books will be supplemented by the ability of their subscribers to ask direct questions of authors.

Interactivity will be a billable commodity even in the absence of authorship. As people move into the Net and increasingly get their information directly from its point of production, unfiltered by centralized media, they will attempt to develop the same interactive ability to probe reality that only experience has provided them in the past. Live access to these distant "eyes and ears" will be much easier to cordon than access to static bundles of stored but easily reproducible information.

In most cases, control will be based on restricting access to the freshest, highest bandwidth information. It will be a matter of defining the ticket, the venue, the performer, and the identity of the ticket holder, definitions which I believe will take their forms from technology, not law. In most cases, the defining technology will be cryptography.

Crypto Bottling

Cryptography, as I've said perhaps too many times, is the "material" from which the walls, boundaries—and bottles—of cyberspace will be fashioned.

Of course there are problems with cryptography or any other purely technical method of property protection. It has always appeared to me that the more security you hide your goods behind, the more likely you are to turn your sanctuary into a target. Having come from a place where people leave their keys in their cars and don't even have keys to their houses, I remain convinced that the best obstacle to crime is a society with its ethics intact.

While I admit that this is not the kind of society most of us live in, I also believe that a social overreliance on protection by barricades rather than conscience will eventually wither the latter by turning intrusion and theft into a sport, rather than a crime. This is already occurring in the digital domain as is evident in the activities of computer crackers.

Furthermore, I would argue that initial efforts to protect digital copyright by copy protection contributed to the current condition in which most otherwise ethical computer users seem morally untroubled by their possession of pirated software.

Instead of cultivating among the newly computerized a sense of respect for the work of their fellows, early reliance on copy protection led to the subliminal notion that cracking into a software package somehow "earned" one the right to use it. Limited not by conscience but by technical skill, many soon felt free to do whatever they could get away with. This will continue to be a potential liability of the encryption of digitized commerce.

Furthermore, it's cautionary to remember that copy protection was rejected by the market in most areas. Many of the upcoming efforts to use cryptography-based protection schemes will probably suffer the same fate. People are not going to tolerate much that makes computers harder to use than they already are without any benefit to the user.

Nevertheless, encryption has already demonstrated a certain blunt utility. New subscriptions to various commercial satellite TV services skyrocketed recently after their deployment of more robust encryption of their feeds. This, despite a booming backwoods trade in black decoder chips, conducted by folks who'd look more at home running moonshine than cracking code.

Another obvious problem with encryption as a global solution is that once something has been unscrambled by a legitimate licensee, it may be available to massive reproduction.

In some instances, reproduction following decryption may not be a problem. Many soft products degrade sharply in value with time. It may be that the only real interest in such products will be among those who have purchased the keys to immediacy.

Furthermore, as software becomes more modular and distribution moves on-line, it will begin to metamorphose in direct interaction with its user base. Discontinuous upgrades will smooth into a constant process of incremental improvement and adaptation, some of it manmade and some of it arising through genetic algorithms. Pirated copies of software may become too static to have much value to anyone.

Even in cases such as images, where the information is expected to remain fixed, the unencrypted file could still be interwoven with code which could continue to protect it by a wide variety of means.

In most of the schemes I can project, the file would be "alive" with permanently embedded software that could "sense" the surrounding conditions and interact with them. For example, it might contain code that could detect the process of duplication and cause it to self-destruct.

Other methods might give the file the ability to "phone home" through the Net to its original owner. The continued integrity of some files might require periodic "feeding" with digital cash from their host, which they would then relay back to their authors.

Of course files that possess the independent ability to communicate upstream sound uncomfortably like the Morris Internet Worm. "Live" files do have a certain viral quality. And serious privacy issues would arise if everyone's computer were packed with digital spies.

The point is that cryptography will enable protection technologies that will develop rapidly in the obsessive competition that has always existed between lock-makers and lock-breakers.

But cryptography will not be used simply for making locks. It is also at the heart of both digital signatures and the aforementioned digital cash, both of which I believe will be central to the future protection of intellectual property.

I believe that the generally acknowledged failure of the shareware model in software had less to do with dishonesty than with the simple inconvenience of paying for shareware. If the payment process can be automated, as digital cash and signature will make possible, I believe that soft product creators will reap a much higher return from the bread they cast upon the waters of cyberspace.

Moreover, they will be spared much of the overhead presently attached to the marketing, manufacture, sales, and distribution of information products, whether those products are computer programs, books, CDs, or motion pictures. This will reduce prices and further increase the likelihood of noncompulsory payment.

But of course there is a fundamental problem with a system that requires, through technology, payment for every access to a particular expression. It defeats the original Jeffersonian purpose of seeing that ideas were available to everyone regardless of their economic station. I am not comfortable with a model that will restrict inquiry to the wealthy.

An Economy of Verbs

The future forms and protections of intellectual property are densely obscured at this entrance to the Virtual Age. Nevertheless, I can make (or reiterate) a few flat statements that I earnestly believe won't look too silly in fifty years.

In the absence of the old containers, almost everything we think we know about intellectual property is wrong. We're going to have to unlearn it. We're going to have to look at information as though we'd never seen the stuff before. The protections that we will develop will rely far more on ethics and technology than on law. Encryption will be the technical basis for most intellectual property protection. (And should, for many reasons, be made more widely available.) The economy of the future will be based on relationship rather than possession. It will be continuous rather than sequential. And finally, in the years to come, most human exchange will be virtual rather than physical, consisting not of stuff but the stuff of which dreams are made. Our future business will be conducted in a world made more of verbs than nouns.

Selected Bibliography

Adelstein, Richard P. and Steven I. Peretz. "The Competition of Technologies in Markets for Ideas: Copyright and Fair Use in Evolutionary Perspective." In *International Review of Law and Economics* 5 (1985).

Adler, R. G. "Biotechnology as an Intellectual Property." *Science* 224, (1984): 357–63.

Allan, Steven. "New Technology and the Law of Copyright." *U.C.L.A. Law Review* 15 (1968): 993–1028.

Anderson and Hill. "The Evolution of Property Rights: A Study of the American West." *Journal of Law & Economics* 18 (1975).

Ayres, R. "Technological Protection and Piracy: Some Implications for Policy." *Technological Forecasting and Social Change* 30 (1986).

Becker, Lawrence C. *Property Rights: Philosophic Foundations*. London: Routledge and Kegan Paul, 1977.

———. "Deserving To Own Intellectual Property." In *Chicago-Kent Law Review* 68 (1993): 609–629.

Benko, Robert P. *Protecting Intellectual Property Rights*. Washington, D.C.: American Enterprise Institute for Public Policy Research, 1987.

Boonin, Leonard G. "The University, Scientific Research, and the Ownership of Knowledge." In *Owning Scientific and Technical Information*, edited by V. Weil and J. Snapper. New Brunswick and London: Rutgers University Press, 1989.

Boyle, James. *Shamans, Software, and Spleens*. Cambridge, Mass.: Harvard University Press, 1996.

Bringsjord, Seinfer. "In Defense of Copying." *Public Affairs Quarterly* 3 (1989): 1–9.

Buchanan, Allen. *Ethics, Efficiency, and the Market*. Totowa, N.J.: Rowman & Littlefield Publishers, 1985.

Bugbee, Bruce. *Genesis of American Patent and Copyright Law*. Washington, D.C.: Public Affairs Press, 1967.

Carey, David. *The Ethics of Software Ownership*. Ph.D. Dissertation at University of Pittsburgh, 1988.

Clark, A. *The Movement for International Copyright in Nineteenth Century America.* Westport, Conn.: Greenwood Press, 1973.

Cleveland, H. "Can Intellectual Property Be Protected?" *Change*, May/June 1989, 10–11.

Cohen, G. A. "Self-Ownership, World-Ownership, and Equality." *Justice and Equality Here and Now*, edited by F. S. Lucash. Ithaca: Cornell University Press, 1983.

Croskery, Patrick. "The Intellectual Property Literature: A Structured Approach." In *Owning Scientific and Technical Information*, edited by V. Weil and J. Snapper. New Brunswick and London: Rutgers University Press, 1989.

———. "A Selected Annotated Bibliography of the Intellectual Property Literature." In *Owning Scientific and Technical Information*, edited by V. Weil and J. Snapper. New Brunswick and London: Rutgers University Press, 1989.

———. "Institutional Utilitarianism and Intellectual Property." *Chicago-Kent Law Review* 68 (1993): 631–657.

DaSilva, R. J. "Droit Moral and the Amoral Copyright: A Comparison of Artists' Rights in France and the U.S." *Bulletin of the Copyright Society of the USA* 28 (1980): 1–58.

Davidson, D. M. "Common Law, Uncommon Software." *University of Pittsburgh Law Review* 47 (1986): 1037–117.

Davis, Michael. "Patents, Natural Rights, and Property." In *Owning Scientific and Technical Information*, edited by V. Weil and J. Snapper. New Brunswick and London: Rutgers University Press, 1989.

Dworkin, R. *Taking Rights Seriously.* Cambridge: Cambridge University Press, 1980.

Feinberg, J. "The Nature and Value of Rights." *Journal of Value Inquiry* 4 (1970): 243–57.

Foster, Frank H. and Robert L. Shook. *Patents, Copyrights, & Trademarks.* 2d ed. New York: John Wiley & Sons, Inc., 1993.

Frey, R. G. "Act-Utilitarianism, Consequentialism, and Moral Rights." In *Utility and Rights*, edited by R. G. Frey. Minneapolis: University of Minnesota Press, 1984.

———. "Rights, Interests, Desires and Beliefs." In *Social and Political Philosophy*, edited by E. Smith and H. G. Blocker. Englewood Cliffs, N.J.: Prentice-Hall Inc., 1994.

Gadbaw, M. R. and T. J. Richards, eds. *Intellectual Property Rights: Global Consensus, Global Conflicts?* Boulder, Col.: Westview Press, 1988.

Gauthier, David. *Morals by Agreement.* Oxford: Clarendon Press, 1986.

Gibbard, Allan. "Natural Property Rights." *Nous* 10 (1976): 77–88.

Gilbert, S. W. and P. Lyman. "Intellectual Property in the Information Age: Issues Beyond Copyright Law." *Change*, May/June 1989, 23–28.

Goldberg, Morton and John Berleigh. "Copyright Protection for Computer Programs: Is the Sky Falling?" American Intellectual Property Law Association, New York: Computer Law Association, 1989.

Gurnsey, John. *Copyright Theft*. London: The Association for Information Management, 1995.

Hardin, Garrett. "The Tragedy of the Commons." *Science* 162 (1968): 1243–48.

Hayek, Frederick A. *The Constitution of Liberty*. Chicago: University of Chicago Press, 1960.

Hegel, G. *Philosophy of Right*, trans. T. M. Knox. Oxford: Clarendon Press, 1967.

Held, Virginia. "John Locke on Robert Nozick." *Social Research* 43, (spring 1976): 169–95.

Hohfeld, Wesley N. *Fundamental Legal Conceptions*. New Haven: Yale University Press, 1923.

Holcombe and Meiners, "Market Arrangements Versus Government Protection of Innovative Activity." *Social Science Review* 5 (1983).

Honoré, A. M. "Ownership." In *Oxford Essays In Jurisprudence*, edited by A. D. Guest. Oxford: Clarendon Press, 1961.

Johnson, Deborah. *Computer Ethics*. Englewood Cliffs, N.J.: Prentice-Hall, 1985.

Kahin, Brian. "Software Patents: Franchising the Information Structure." *Change*, May/June 1989, 24–25.

Katz M. "The Doctrine of Moral Rights and American Copyright Law—A Proposal." *South California Law Review* 24 (1951).

Kuflik, Arthur. "The Moral Foundations of Intellectual Property Rights." In *Owning Scientific and Technical Information*, edited by V. Weil and J. Snapper. New Brunswick and London: Rutgers University Press, 1989.

Kwall R. "Copyright and the Moral Right: Is an American Marriage Possible?" *Vanderbilt Law Review* 38 (1985): 1–100.

Levy, Steven. *Hackers: Heroes of the Computer Revolution*. New York: Dell Publishing Co., 1984.

Lieberstein, Stanley H. *Who Owns What Is in Your Head? Trade Secrets and the Mobile Employee*. New York: Hawthorne Books, 1979.

Lindy, Alexander. *Plagiarism and Originality*. New York: Harper, 1952.

Locke, John. *Two Treatises of Government*, edited by Peter Laslett. New York: New American Library, 1965.

Lomasky, Loren E. *Persons, Rights, and the Moral Community*. New York and Oxford: Oxford University Press, 1987.

Machlup, F. *Production and Distribution of Knowledge in the United States*. Princeton: Princeton University Press, 1962.

Machlup and Penrose. "The Patent Controversy in the Nineteenth Century." *Journal of Economic History* 10 (1950): 1–29.

McMullin, E. "Openness and Secrecy in Science: Some Notes on Early History." *Science, Technology, and Human Values* 10 (1985): 14–23.

Miller, Arthur R., and Michael H. Davis. *Intellectual Property—Patents, Trademarks, and Copyright*. St. Paul, Minn.: West Publishing Co., 1983.

National Assembly of France 1791. "Declaration of the Rights of Man and of Citizens." In *Social and Political Philosophy*, edited by E. Smith and H. G. Blocker. Englewood Cliffs, N.J.: Prentice-Hall, 1994.

Nelkin, D. *Science as Intellectual Property*. New York: Macmillan, 1984.

Nimmer, Melville. "Does Copyright Abridge the First Amendment Guarantees of Free Speech and Press?" *U.C.L.A. Law Review* 17 (1970).

Nozick, Robert. *Anarchy, State, and Utopia*. New York: Basic Books, 1974.

Patterson, L. R. "Free Speech, Copyright, and Fair Use." *Vanderbilt Law Review* 40 (1987): 1–66.

Pennock, J. R., and J. W. Chapman, eds. *Property: Nomos XXII*. New York: New York University Press, 1980.

Plant, A. *The Economic Theory Concerning Patents for Inventions*. 1934.

———, "The Economic Aspects of Copyright in Books." In *Selected Economic Essays and Addresses*, 1934.

Posner, Richard A. *Economic Analysis of Law*. Boston: Little, Brown and Co., 1972.

———. *The Economics of Justice*. Cambridge, Mass.: Harvard University Press, 1981.

Posner and Landes. "An Economic Analysis of Copyright Law." *Journal of Legal Studies* 17 (June 1989).

Prescott, P. "The Origins of Copyright: A Debunking View." *European Intellectual Property Review* 11 (1989): 453–55.

Proudhon, P. J. *What Is Property? An Inquiry into the Principles of Right and of Government*, trans. by D. Kelly and B. Smith. New York: Cambridge University Press, 1994.

Rawls, John. *A Theory of Justice*. Cambridge, Mass.: Harvard University Press, 1971.

Roeder, M. A. "The Doctrine of Moral Rights: A Study in the Law of Artists, Authors and Creators." *Harvard Law Review* 53 (1940): 554–578.

Samuelson, P. "Creating a New Kind of Intellectual Property: Applying the Lessons of the Chip Law to Computer Programs." *Minnesota Law Review* 70 (1985): 471–531.

———. "Why the Look and Feel of Software User Interfaces Should Not Be Protected by Copyright Law." *Communications of the ACM* 32, (1989) 563–572.

Schmidtz, David. "When Is Original Appropriation Required?" *The Monist* 73 (October 1990): 504–18.

Stallman, R. "The GNU Manifesto." *GNU EMacs Manual*. Cambridge, Mass.: Free Software Foundation, 1986.

Strong, William S. *The Copyright Book: A Practical Guide*. 3d ed., Cambridge, Mass.: MIT Press, 1990.

Tussie, D. *The Less Developed Countries and the World Trading System: A Challenge to the GATT*. New York: St. Martin's Press, 1987.

U.S. Patent and Trademark Office. "Patentable Subject Matter: Mathematical Algorithms and Computer Programs." *Official Gazette*, September 1989, 1106.

Waldron, Jeremy. "From Authors To Copiers: Individual Rights and Social Values In Intellectual Property." *Chicago-Kent Law Review* 68 (1993): 841–887.

Weil, V., and J. Snapper, eds. *Owning Scientific and Technical Information.* New Brunswick and London: Rutgers University Press, 1989.

Wolf, Clark. "Contemporary Property Rights, Lockean Provisos, and the Interests of Future Generations." *Ethics* 105 (July 1995): 791–818.

Worlock, D. "The Challenge of Network Publishing." In *Online Information* 92. 16th International Online Information Meeting proceedings, London, December 1992. Oxford: Learned Information, 1992.

Index

Adelstein, Richard, 194–96
anti-property arguments, 19–21, 192–98, 209–10, 248, 349
antitrust, 221n95, 279n25, 296
appropriation, 9, 27, 44, 46, 57–60, 64, 67–69, 72n2, 73n10, 81–85, 93, 97, 113, 121, 131, 137, 144, 147, 349
Aquinas, Thomas, 301–4
architectural works, 2, 13n3, 113, 133–34, 323
Aristotle, 74n25, 98, 214n38, 301–2
Austrian school of economics, 79n49, 225–26, 231, 233, 235, 236n2
autonomy, 9, 28–29, 42, 84, 117, 271

Baird, Douglas, 117
Barry, Vincent, 58, 61–72, 74n24, 75n33, 76n35, 77n45
baseline problem, 87, 90, 92, 94, 96–97
Becker, Lawrence, 25, 36n25, 61, 118, 169
Bentham, Jeremy, 180
Berki, R. N., 142–43
Berne Convention, 6, 7, 14n23, 167n19, 176n166, 247, 250, 258n5, 268, 269, 276n8, 299, 323, 331–33, 338–39, 341
biotechnology, 202, 205, 221n89, 273n2
Blackstone, W., 202–3, 238n25
Boorstin, Daniel, 188

Brand, Stewart, 359
Brubaker, Earl, 207–8
Bugbee, Bruce, 183, 187, 212n12
Burke, Edmund, 109–10, 166n8–11

capitalism, 30, 61, 66, 70, 76, 96–97, 235, 241n64, 245, 258n9
censorship, 110, 162, 182–84, 214n19, 259n11, 366
China, 245–46, 259n11–12, 346n47, 355
classical liberal. See libertarianism
Coase, Ronald, 189, 193, 198, 232
Coleman, Jules, 181
common law, 13, 180, 202, 211, 212n3, 214n31, 231–32, 237n17, 239n38, 354, 365; copyright, 53n10, 140, 160, 183, 185–87, 217n55, 229, 344n23; trade secret, 21, 46, 55n24, 66, 193, 230; trademark, 193, 226, 230
commons. See frontier of intellectual property
computer, 123, 188, 193, 289, 295, 307–18, 321–25, 330, 333, 339, 351, 361, 369–70; break-ins, 12, 307–12, 317, 369; hackers, 250–52, 261n29, 295, 304n2, 307, 310, 314, 316, 318n2, 334, 347n58, 350; scientists, 130, 152, 250, 290, 316–17; software, 1–3, 8, 11, 18, 20, 26, 34n8, 82–83, 92, 98,

379

123, 130, 151–52, 180, 200, 207, 212n1, 247, 251, 265, 267, 268, 276n8, 292, 330–31, 371; systems, 163, 310, 315–16, 321, 328, 330; virus, 305, 314–15, 319n6
confidentiality (confidential relationships), 40–50
consequentialism, 63, 121, 225, 232, 299, 302–4. *See also* deontology; utilitarianism; virtue ethics
copying, 2, 18, 26, 28, 33, 51, 53n8, 81, 98n1, 127, 135, 200, 202, 206–7, 214n38, 246, 249, 251–52, 255, 272, 287–88, 291, 296, 323, 325–42, 345n41, 355–56, 359
copyright: basics of, 2–4, 8, 18–19, 109–14, 181–187, 322–23, 326; computer software, 1–3, 8, 206, 265, 281–97, 299–303, 322, 325, 329–31, 333, 336, 338, 355–56, 362; fair use, 4, 8, 11, 19, 34n9, 112, 171n84, 244, 249, 250, 256, 262n37, 277n14, 327–29, 332, 337, 342; first sale, 4, 8, 11, 244, 249, 250, 252–54; fixation requirement for, 8, 279n25, 360; idea/expression distinction, 3, 125–28, 180, 244, 248, 250, 267, 350–52; infringement of, 2–3, 13n5, 113, 134, 161, 251, 254–55, 321–30, 327–29, 332–42, 345n30; international aspects of, 244–56, 265–73, 330–42; obsolescence of, 139, 241–47, 251–52, 350–52, 371; rights, 2–4, 8, 109–14
Copyright Act, 2, 13n3, 127, 140, 345n30
Cowen, Tyler, 196
creation *ex nihilo* (from nothing), 22, 68–70, 77n42
cryptography, 369–70
cyberspace, 267, 349, 351, 353, 355–56, 360, 365, 369, 371

Demsetz, Harold, 189–90, 193–94
deontology, 63, 99n5, 299–300, 308–9.

See also consequentialism; utilitarianism; virtue ethics
digital information, 1, 12, 98, 360, 367
disclosure of information, 5, 9, 19, 21, 32, 34, 35n14, 41–47, 50, 53n12, 54n16, 160–62, 203, 335
dissemination of ideas, 41, 48, 51n3–5, 52, 53n6–7, 55n34, 161, 180, 201, 253, 255, 260n18, 335
domain of intellectual property. *See* basics of copyright; patent; trade secret
droits morals. See moral rights

economic: analysis of intellectual property, 147, 180, 189, 191, 211, 225, 239n40; argument, 181, 284, 311; efficiency, 180, 211; rights, 6–7; value (*see* market value)
Eisenstein, Elizabeth, 188, 215n41
electronic: bulletin boards, 321, 322, 324, 343, 347; communication, 179, 323, 342; media, 325, 342; system operators, 12, 321–42
Electronic Frontier Foundation, 12, 366
eminent domain, 8
employee freedom, 24, 28–29, 31–34, 37n39, 40, 45, 48, 51, 223n113
encryption, 12, 197, 291, 369–71
Epstein, Richard, 115–16, 118, 168n33
espionage, 6, 46–49, 135
European intellectual property, 2, 6, 10, 13n8, 142, 173n112, 176n164, 238n31, 248, 260n24, 266, 272, 274n2, 339, 347n64
exclusion condition, 65
externalities, 103n48, 189–91, 193–94, 196, 199, 202, 208, 227

fair use, 4, 8, 11, 19, 34n9, 112, 171n84, 244, 249–50, 254–56, 262n37, 277n14, 278n20, 327–29, 332, 337, 342, 344n23

finitude condition, 65, 68
first sale, 4, 8, 11, 244, 249–50, 252–54
fixation requirement, 8, 127, 279n25, 360
flourishing. *See* well-being
free rider problem, 44, 86, 194–95, 197–8, 200, 208, 339, 342
Free Software Foundation, 293–94
freedom of expression, 20, 42, 111–12, 127–29, 161–62, 247–48, 353, 366
Fressola, Anthony, 101n22
frontier of intellectual property, 59–60, 83, 128–37

GATT, 243, 265–66, 272, 355
Gauthier, David, 85
Global Information Infrastructure (GII), 247–55, 279
Goldin, Kenneth, 196, 198
government control of intellectual property, 10, 19, 28, 31, 110, 182, 198, 200, 218n58, 223n115, 227, 248, 254, 256, 265, 268, 271, 293, 311–12, 316, 322, 336, 339

hackers, 250–52, 261n29, 295, 304n2, 307, 310, 314, 316, 318n2, 334, 347n58, 350
Hayek, F. A., 79, 181, 192, 212, 224, 238
Hegel, G. W. F., 10, 108–9, 141–65, 166n8, 173n117, 174n127
Held, Virginia, 58, 61–67, 69–72, 74n19, 75n33, 76n35, 77n45
Hohfeld, W., 8
Holmes, Oliver Wendell, 46, 150, 159, 160, 176n170
Honoré, A. M., 8, 61
Huxley, T. H., 199, 204

idea/expression distinction, 3, 125–28, 180, 244, 248, 250, 267, 350–52
incentives to produce intellectual works, 9, 11, 26, 29–32, 37n44, 39, 46, 53n10, 81–82, 97, 108, 124–25, 130, 169n49, 180, 185–86, 189, 192,

195, 200, 210–11, 215n50, 218n56, 224n117, 248, 251, 266, 275n5, 322, 335–36, 341
information access, 11, 49, 117, 127, 247–49, 253, 255, 270, 321–22, 325, 335
infringement. *See* copyright; patent; trade secret
internet, 1, 12, 267, 307, 312, 314, 322, 324, 330, 350–51, 365–66, 368, 370
internet worm, 307, 311, 313, 315, 370

Jefferson, Thomas, 98, 192, 216n53, 349, 353, 371
justification of intellectual property: Lockean, 9–10, 21–27, 57–72, 81–98, 114–41, 227; personality, 6–7, 10, 42, 141–64, 248; privacy/sovereignty, 28–30, 41–51, 160–62; utilitarian (incentives), 7, 9–10, 30–33, 39–40, 51, 82–83, 116, 119, 121, 125, 150–51, 180, 211, 227–30, 284–85, 304, 309. *See also* anti-property arguments

Kaplan, Benjamin, 134, 164, 185
Kirzner, Israel, 77n45, 79n49
Klein, Daniel, 201
Knowles, Dudley, 143–44
Kwall, Roberta, 163

labor theory, 10, 23, 108, 114–20, 125, 141, 145, 149–50, 165, 169n49
Landes, William, 180, 191, 229, 234
Leggett, William, 194
Leoni, Bruno, 181, 193, 211, 212n9–10, 226
Levmore, Saul, 133
libertarianism, 35n21, 74n19, 80n53, 142–43, 226
libraries, 18–19, 205, 244, 249, 253, 255–56, 262n37, 321, 324, 340, 353, 355
licensing agreements, 93, 110, 124,

175n159, 214n19, 235, 279n25, 336, 338, 339

Lincoln, Abraham, 110, 120, 166n12

literary products, 2, 188, 192, 193, 211n1, 214n37, 215n41, 268, 276n8, 322, 326

Locke, John, 9, 10, 21, 22, 27, 33, 57–72, 73n10, 74n15–19, 75n35, 81, 83–86, 98, 114–18, 129, 131–32, 136–41, 164, 168n30, 172n103–4, 275n5

Lockean theory of intellectual property, 9–10, 21–27, 57–72, 81–103, 128, 114–41, 227

Machlup, Fritz, 36n35, 183, 204, 209

market/economic value, 21–24, 26, 150, 156, 160, 228

Marx, Karl, 74n25, 110, 146, 166n7, 174n134, 302

merger doctrine, 3, 13n9, 170n76

Mill, J. S., 20

misappropriation. *See* trade secret infringement

monopolies, 4–5, 10, 23, 47, 51, 55n29, 78, 134, 181–85, 204, 206, 211, 212n12, 213n13, 217n53, 221n95, 222n104, 225, 227–34, 249–50, 253–54, 256, 290, 292, 322–23, 327

moral rights, 2, 6–7, 13n8, 14n23, 23, 61, 99, 159, 160, 173n112, 176n164, 248, 265, 269, 300, 332–33

musical works, 1–2, 8, 18, 82, 126, 150, 156, 161, 163, 199, 208, 212n1, 253, 255, 265, 267, 292, 294, 322, 324, 353, 367

Nimmer, Melville, 128, 271

non-exclusive nature of ideas, 8, 19, 20, 27, 33, 39, 65, 190, 197

non-waste condition, 27–28, 33, 72n2, 115, 116–17, 137, 139–41, 164, 172n104

Nozick, Robert, 21, 27, 57, 62–63, 72n2, 73n10, 100n20, 131–32, 136–39

objective value, 74n25, 88, 140, 233. *See also* market value; subjective value

on-line, 1, 11–12, 243, 247, 249, 250–56, 322, 324–25, 327, 334–36. *See also* internet

opportunity cost, 88–91, 94, 96, 97, 102n32, 190, 218n58

original acquisition, 57, 83, 86–87, 90, 93, 101n23, 168n30

ownership of business enterprises, 70–72, 76n40, 80n53. *See also* justification of intellectual property; tangible property rights

Pareto conditions: improvement, 72, 79n51, 85, 101n23; optimality, 137, 227; superiority, 85, 87, 100n14, 227, 237n15, 240n58

Pareto-based proviso, 60, 85–93

parody, 131–32, 171n84

patent: basics of, 4–5, 8, 18–19, 181–83; design, 4, 230; infringement, 5, 234; paradigm, 67–69; rights, 4–5, 8, 182–83; software, 34n8, 223n113, 304

Penrose, Edith, 183

Peretz, Steven, 194–96

personality theory, 7, 10, 42, 49, 108–9, 141–61, 164–65, 175n150, 248

photocopying, 18, 179, 200, 251, 255–56, 261n34, 340, 344n20, 347n64. *See also* copying

piracy, 18, 20, 35n12, 98n1, 151, 163, 183, 204, 355, 357, 362, 268

plagiarism, 3, 34n10, 53n6, 214n37

Plant, Arnold, 184, 186, 192, 205, 227, 234, 240n53

Plato, 68, 109, 126–27, 129–30, 166n11, 304n3

Posner, Richard, 10, 179–81, 191, 225, 228–29, 231, 234, 236n3, 238n34

privacy, 9, 28–29, 36n36, 42, 55n25, 108, 130, 160–61, 252, 255, 310–11, 318, 370 project pursuit, 88, 101n22, 101n27

Proudhon, P. J. 109, 166n6–7

proviso (Locke's sufficiency requirement), 9, 26–27, 33, 57–61, 64, 66–67, 70–71, 72n2, 73n10, 74n19, 78n49, 80n53, 82–87, 90–97, 100n11, 102n38, 132, 137

public goods, 41, 65, 76n39, 189–98, 207, 215n48, 219n67–70, 219n72, 226

Radin, Margaret, 141, 145–47, 154

radio broadcasting, 151, 191, 202, 216n52, 220n85, 253, 294, 352

Rawls, John, 26, 36n28, 137, 173n120

reverse engineering, 19, 47, 230

rights: to abstract ideas, 3, 8, 18, 20–21, 41–45, 48–50, 77n41, 112–13, 180, 244, 250, 267, 350–52; bundle of, 3–5, 40, 53n9, 112–13, 155; civil, 108, 160, 308; to control initial disclosure, 41–50; desert-based, 24–29, 114–15, 120–28, 354; to fruits of labor, 21–27, 35n21, 57–58, 83–84, 117–22, 163, 284; natural, 23–24, 33, 35n21, 186, 235. *See also* copyright; moral rights; patent; trade secret

Ringer, Barbara, 183, 259n10

rival/non-rival consumption, 65, 82–83, 86, 190, 207

Rosenberg, Peter, 120, 123

Ryan, Alan, 58

Samuelson, Pamela, 215n47, 360

scarcity, 57–58, 65, 85, 95–96, 183, 191–93, 215–18, 227, 234, 288, 356, 362–63

secrecy, 6, 8, 19, 21, 36n36, 40, 47–49, 96, 181, 209, 230. *See also* trade secret

self-actualization, 141, 144, 146–47, 153–54. *See also* personality theory

self-ownership, 96, 194, 218n59

Smith, Adam, 198, 303–4

social utility, 26, 121–25, 131, 140, 149, 354

software, 1–3, 8, 11, 18, 20, 26, 34n8, 52n5, 82–83, 92, 98, 123, 130, 151–52, 180, 200, 207, 211n1, 247, 251, 265, 267–68, 274n2, 276n8, 292, 330–31, 347n57, 371

source code, 3, 289–91, 317

state of nature, 57–58, 60–64, 66–67, 69, 73n10, 74n15, 75n25, 90, 101, 114, 138–39

Statute of Anne, 184–87, 53n10, 214n31

Statute of Monopolies, 182, 213n12

Steiner, Hillel, 78n49, 136

subjective value, 70–71, 87, 101n24, 361. *See also* market value; objective value

Taiwan, 111, 259n12

tangible property rights, 21–27, 57–67, 83–91, 114–16

technology and intellectual property, 66, 123–24, 139–40, 163, 184, 187–89, 195, 226, 230, 233, 239, 251, 322, 338, 350, 353, 356–57, 367, 369

tie-ins, 10, 200–202

Toffler, Alvin, 365

trade secret: basics of, 5, 18–19, 133–36, 181; domain of, 5, 8, 18–19, 133–36; infringement of, 5–6, 8, 45–46, 122; rights, 5, 8, 18–19, 40–41, 135

trademark, 8, 34n10, 53n6, 66, 69, 110–11, 135, 156, 181, 193, 226, 228, 230, 238n30–31, 240, 266, 278n19

Trade-Related Aspects of Intellectual Property Rights (TRIPS), 11, 243–57, 258n5, 259n11, 265–66, 269, 271–72, 273n1–2

tragedy of the commons, 94–98

unfair competition, 29, 121–22, 167n17, 278n19

Universal Copyright Convention
(UCC), 331–34, 339
utilitarianism/utilitarian justifications,
7, 9–10, 30–33, 37n39, 39–40, 51,
51n3, 52n4, 56n36,
82–83, 99n5–7, 116, 119, 121, 125, 150–
51, 180, 211, 227–30, 284–85, 304,
309

virtue ethics, 299–304. *See also* conse-

quentialism; deontology; utilitarianism

well-being, 40, 87–95, 101n28, 102n30,
157

zero-sum condition, 9, 61–69, 71,
75n33–34, 76n35, 78n49, 85, 86

Notes on the Contributors

John Perry Barlow is cofounder and executive chair of the Electronic Frontier Foundation and writes for *Wired* magazine. He has written a number of articles, including "Comming into the Country" and "Private Life in Cyberspace," both appearing in *Communications of the ACM*. He is also a retired cattle rancher and a lyricist for the Grateful Dead.

David H. Carey is associate professor of philosophy at Whitman College and received his Ph.D. from the University of Pittsburgh. His interests lie primarily in the history of ethics, with an emphasis on ancient Greek and medieval Latin sources. He has sought to apply that history to contemporary issues, particularly in medical, business, and computer ethics.

James W. Child is professor of philosophy and senior research fellow at Bowling Green State University. He has a J.D. degree from Harvard Law School. Professor Child is the author of *Nuclear War: The Moral Dimension* (Transaction, 1986) and the coauthor, with Donald Scherer, of *Two Paths Toward Peace* (Temple University Press, 1992). He is currently finishing a book tentatively entitled *The Ethics of Research in the Humanities*.

Marci A. Hamilton received an M.A. in philosophy and English from Pennsylvania State University (1982 and 1984 respectively), and a J.D. degree in 1988 from the University of Pennsylvania. She is currently professor of law at the Benjamin N. Cardozo School of Law and is interested in intellectual property and constitutional law.

Hugh C. Hansen is an associate professor of law at Fordham University School of Law.

Edwin C. Hettinger is assistant professor of philosophy at the College of Charleston. His articles have appeared in a number of academic journals, and his research interests include affirmative action, animal experimentation, and ecological sabotage.

Justin Hughes holds a J.D. degree from Harvard Law School (1986) and was a Luce Scholar/Mellon Fellow in the Humanities (1988).

Michael I. Krauss is professor of law at George Mason University and is currently a Salvatori Fellow at The Heritage Foundation.

Charles J. Meyer received a J.D. degree from the Indiana University School of Law in 1995 and is currently practicing law at Woodard, Emhardt, Naughton, Moriarty & McNett.

Adam D. Moore teaches philosophy at Ohio State University and specializes in the areas of ethical theory, applied ethics, social and political theory, and philosophy of law. He has written "Against Rule-Utilitarian Intellectual Property." He is currently finishing a manuscript entitled *Intellectual Property and Digital Information*.

Lynn Sharp Paine is associate professor at the Harvard Business School and was a fellow in Harvard's Program in Ethics and the Professions. She has published a number of articles in the area of business ethics and is currently working on the ethical and legal dimensions of controlling information and ideas.

Tom G. Palmer is currently a research fellow in political theory at the Institute for Humane Studies at George Mason University and a fellow of the Cato Institute in Washington, D.C. He has published on the theory of property in a number of academic and popular journals, including another treatment of intellectual property in "Are Patents and Copyrights Morally Justified? The Philosophy of Property Rights and Ideal Objects," *Harvard Journal of Law and Public Policy* 13 (Summer 1990). He is currently completing a book on cosmopolitanism and distributive justice.

Eugene H. Spafford is associate professor of computer science at Purdue University. He is the author of numerous books and articles and is the coauthor, with K. Heaphy and D. Ferbrache, of *Computer Viruses: Dealing with Electronic Vandalism and Programmed Threats* (Arlington, Va.:

ADAPSO, 1989). Professor Spafford's current research centers on the ethical and societal implications of computing.

Richard Stallman is a founding member of the Free Software Foundation and has lectured widely on the moral issues of software ownership. He is also the author of numerous articles, including "Are Computer Rights Absolute?" appearing in *Communications of the ACM 27* (1984).